DATE DUE

3/06/88			
MAY 2 1 1992			

Lemba, 1650–1930

A Drum of Affliction in Africa and the New World

Volume 11

Critical Studies on Black Life and Culture

John M. Janzen

Lemba, 1650–1930

A Drum of Affliction in Africa and the New World

Garland Publishing, Inc. New York and London
1982

Library of Congress Cataloging in Publication Data

Janzen, John M.
Lemba, 1650–1930.

(Critical studies on Black life and culture ; v. 11)
Bibliography: p.
Includes index.
1. Lemba (Cult) I. Title. II. Series.
BL2470.C6J36 967 80-9044
ISBN 0-8240-9306-2 AACR2

Printed on acid-free, 250-year-life paper
Manufactured in the United States of America

Contents

Plates

(Plates 1–4 follow p. xv; plates 5–20 follow p. 257.)

Figures

Preface

Friends and colleagues alike have encouraged me to declare openly that I have written a book about a seventeenth-century "cure for capitalism," created by insightful Congo coast people who perceived that the great trade was destroying their society. I have tried to avoid the faddish language of contemporary social analysis, both of the value-neutral school and of the critical Marxists, and have instead tried to marshal the evidence needed to show how one segment of coastal African society tried, in its own idiom—that of the *ngoma*, the "drum of affliction"—imaginatively to cope with a force that transformed African society, like many others, from what it must have been in earlier centuries into what it was when colonial flag-planters claimed the coastal Congo region in the late nineteenth century. We see, in accounts like those of Cabinda story teller Solomo Nitu, how the wealth to be earned at the coast is characterized in images of a siren woman who lures a young man to her, exacting from him the terrible price of forever giving up relations with his father. How the coastal culture came to terms with this force, over three centuries, is the story told in this book.

As I have worked on different manifestations of *Lemba*—the myth narratives, the initiation reports, the regional economic and political history—I have gradually perceived the scale of the system—truly a "world system"—to which *Lemba*'s adherents were responding, namely the expanding imperium of European trade and influence. In North Africa, more specifically in Egypt, there are examples of seventeenth-century Islamic brotherhoods which organized merchants and businessmen into tight, ethically-conservative groups to protect their interests in an enhanced economic status while, at the same time, preserving their Islamic social and religious identity. In North American Indian societies there are similar examples. The eastern Calumet system organized trading relationships prior to the French usurpation of this system, and on the Plains the Hako ceremonial trading society of the Pawnee brought trade relations under an umbrella of ritual kinship adoptions, again, seemingly for the protection of trade interests and also for the protection of the social fabric. This is the larger, world-wide, context of *Lemba*, beyond the "world system" of recent scholarship.

A work such as this, begun more than a decade ago when I pursued my own curiosity in a north-Kongo field study, also becomes a scholarly pilgrimage. It offers the opportunity—a danger to clarity, perhaps—of adding paradigm upon paradigm to a subject matter requiring explanation from several sides. The pilgrimage's steps will be evident in the orientations taken in the book's three sections: first, a political-economic study of a region; second, a symbolist-structuralist study of myths and rituals; third, a humanistic interpretation of Kongo's therapeutic effectiveness, especially that of *Lemba*.

I owe my scholarly journey in part to generous benefactors who have permitted travel and study resources. My original field studies in Equatorial Africa were sponsored by the Foreign Area Fellowship Program and the Social Science Research Council (United States). The Canada Council provided funds for a summer's exploration in 1971 in Sweden where I discovered (for myself) the Congo catechists' notebooks of the Laman collection which became the primary texts for the reconstruction of the *Lemba* inauguration rites. I am also indebted to the University of Kansas Graduate Research Fund for the means to microfilm these notebooks and to prepare them for further analysis and publication here and elsewhere.

I am deeply appreciative to the Alexander von Humboldt Stiftung of the Federal Republic of Germany for granting me a research fellowship in 1977 to pursue work in Central-European archival and museum sources pertaining to *Lemba*, especially those of the German Loango Expedition of the 1870's found in Berlin, and those of numerous Belgian collectors found in the Royal African Museum in Tervuren, Belgium.

I am also indebted to the National Endowment for the Humanities for a six-month research fellowship in spring 1978, which permitted further work on the *Lemba* manuscript and the exploration of *Lemba*'s New-World distribution.

I wish to thank staff members of museums and archives who have helped identify collections pertaining to *Lemba*, especially Drs. Maesen and Van der Gelwe of the Central Africa Museum of Tervuren, Belgium; Drs. Zwerneman and Lohse of the Hamburg Völkerkunde Museum; Dr. J.F. Thiel and others of the Anthropos Institute of St. Augustine, Germany; Dr. Krieger of the Berlin-Dahlem Museum für Völkerkunde; Dr. Koloss of the Linden Museum, Stuttgart; Dr. H. Witte of the Afrika Museum, Berg en Dal, The Netherlands; Mme. N'diaye of the Musée de l'Homme, Paris; staff members of the Göteborg and Stockholm Ethnographic Museums in Sweden; R. Widman of the Svenska Missionsforbundet,

Stockholm and Lidingö; and the personnel of the Jesuit Institute of Bonn. I am also grateful to Eugenia Herbert, who looked for *Lemba*-related articles at the British Museum, and Stanley Yoder, who examined collections of the National Museum of Zaire in this connection. This museum research has been extensive but not exhaustive, so I expect other *Lemba*-related objects to be identified once this book appears.

I am grateful to several talented persons for assisting me with the translation of enigmatic KiKongo songs found in the *Lemba* inaugurations. I mention especially Milembamani, Wamba dia Wamba, and Fukiau, all of whom cherish their language and know it far better than an outside student like myself ever will. Responsibility for lingering errors is mine.

I acknowledge those who read earlier versions of the manuscript and offered corrections and revisions, in particular Jan Vansina, Victor Turner, Wyatt MacGaffey, and Robert F. Thompson, as well as several anonymous readers.

I must acknowledge my wife Reinhild's continued encouragement and criticism and the gracious forbearance of my children, Bernd, Gesine, and Marike, during the years of my preoccupation with "*Lemba*-kinship-medical-systems" as they once succinctly parodied it.

Lastly, I acknowledge an intellectual indebtedness to my teacher, the late Professor Lloyd A. Fallers of the University of Chicago, who led me to see anthropology as a discipline broad enough to allow one to perceive the unexpected and to interpret it without destroying it.

J M J
Heubuden
January 1981

Plate 1. Loango, mid-seventeenth century, at the time *Lemba* is first recorded as a medicine of the king and the nobility. This print, taken from the 1670 French edition of O. Dapper, *Description de l'Afrique*, bears inscriptions of the original 1668 Dutch edition, indicating the following details: (a) king's palace; (b) wives' compound; (c) crier's tower;

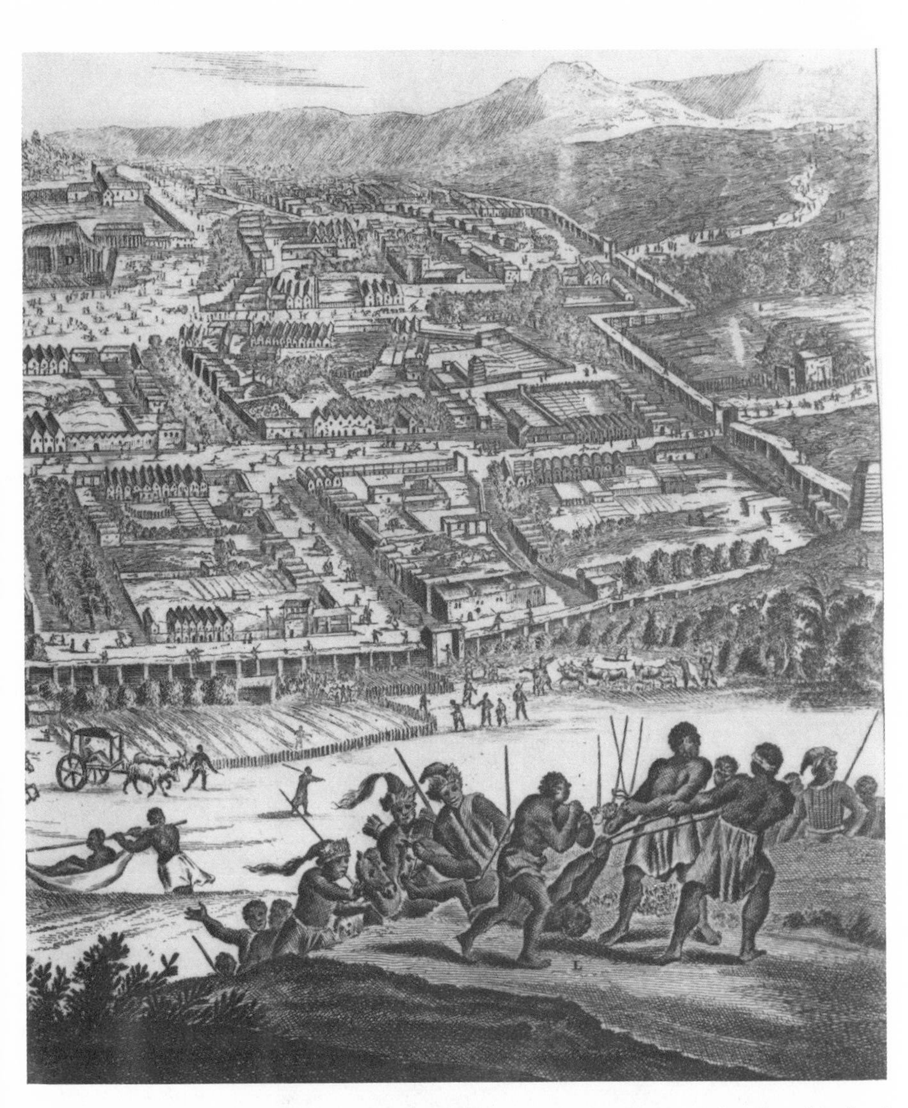

(d) royal wine house; (e) royal dining house; (f) public audience court; (g) royal garden; (h) wives' garden; (i,k) two fetishes; (l) road criminals are taken to capital punishment. (Courtesy of Department of Special Collections, Spencer Research Library, University of Kansas.)

Plate 2. Market scene in *Lemba* country, late nineteenth or early twentieth century, showing pigs and goats of the kind used in *Lemba* feasts. (Svenska Missionsforbundet Archives, Lidingö)

Plate 3. Market entrance (*fula dia zandu*), scene of drinking and social intercourse, often actual place of trading. In *Lemba* symbolism, it is the basis of the idea of "trading with ancestors at the entrance from whence comes wealth" (text 9, line 17; Chapter 7). (Svenska Missionsforbundet Archives, Lidingö)

Plate 4. Lemba medicine chest (*n'kobe* Lemba) from N'goyo bearing characteristic petal motif. Collected by L. Bittremieux prior to 1933. (Musée royale de l'Afrique centrale, Tervuren, 35191.) Contents depicted in Figure 20.

Lemba, 1650–1930

A Drum of Affliction in Africa and the New World

Figure 1

Distribution of *Lemba*, based on territorially-designated ethnographic, textual, and artifactual sources (see key to numbers)

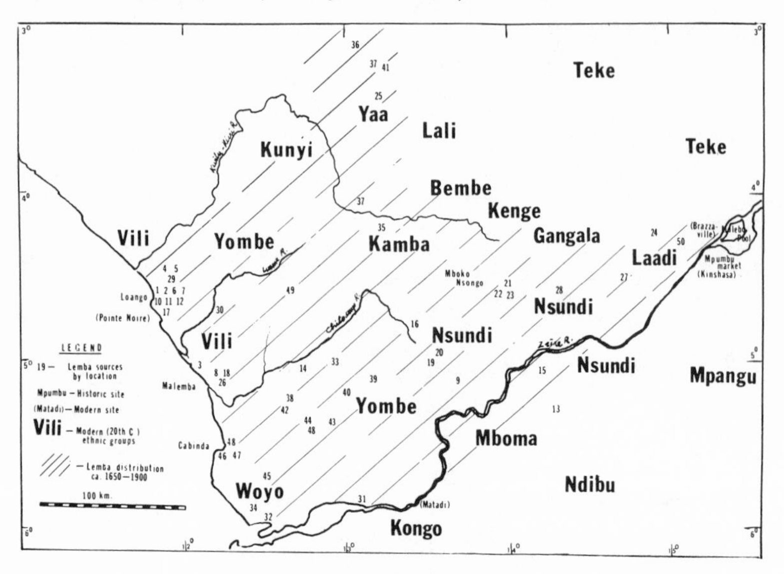

Key

E = Ethnography
T = Text
A = Artifact

B-D = Berlin-Dahlem Museum für Völkerkunde
GEM = Göteborg Ethnographic Museum
LMS = Linden Museum Stuttgart
LRM = Leiden Rijksmuseum
MAC = Musée d'Afrique Central (Tervuren)
SEM = Stockholm Ethnographic Museum

1. (E) Dapper, 1670, p. 536
2. (E) Bastian, 1874, pp. 170–3
3. (A) Loango Expedition, 1875, B-D III C 347, engraved copper bracelet
4. (A) Visser, n.d., B-D III C 8136, "BaVili," balsa wood bracelet model template
5. (A) Visser, n.d., B-D III C 13810a-f, "BaVili," clay mold for bracelets
6. (A) Bastian, 1874, B-D Catalogue § 372, Lemba pipe
7. (A) Bastian, 1875, B-D III C 423, engraved copper bracelet
8. (A) Visser, 1900, B-D III C 13871, Lemba sack charm
9. (A) Hammar, 1910, GEM 68.11.241, "Nganda," drum
10. (E) Dennett, 1907, pp. 11, 89, 91, 133
11. (E) Güssfeldt, Falkenstein, Pechuel-Loesche, 1879, p. 71
12. (E/A) Bastian, 1874, B-D
13. (E) Cuvelier, 1946, p. 326
14. (E) Deleval, 1912
15. (E/A) Laman, SEM 1919.1.583, "Mukimbungu" Lemba *n'kobe*
16. (A) Hammar, 1906, GEM 68.11.171, "Babwende-BaYombe," at "Manianga-Mayombe," drum
17. (A) Loango Expedition, 1875, B-D III C 710b, brass bracelet
18. (A) Visser, 1901, B-D III C 13743, "Kayo," Lemba sack charm
19. (E/T) Konda, "Mamundi" near Kinkenge, ca. 1918
20. (E/T) Babutidi, "Mamundi" near Kinkenge, ca. 1918
21. (E/T) Kwamba, "Mongo-Luala" near Kingoyi, ca. 1918
22. (A) Hammar, Kingoyi, GEM 68.11.241, drum, ca. 1910
23. (E/T) Kionga, Kingoyi, ca. 1916–18
24. (E/T) Kimbembe, "Madzia," ca. 1918
25. (E/T) Lunungu, "BaYaka," Indo, ca. 1918
26. (A) Visser, "Kayo," 1904, B-D III C 13744, Lemba sack charm
27. (E/T) Stenström, 1969, pp. 37–57; Andersson, 1953, fig. 22, Musana
28. (E/T) Fukiau, "Nseke-Mbanza," 1969, pp. 41–56, figs. 37–39
29. (A) Visser, "BaVili," 1904, B-D III C 18921, drum
30. (A) Visser, "Luema River," 1905, LMS 38363, Lemba necklace charm
31. (A) Anon., "Boma," LRM 1032/136, casting mold for bracelet
32. (A) Anon., "Banana," LRM 1032/53, 1032/59, 1032/60, Lemba bracelets
33. (A) Maesen, "Tshela," 1954, MAC 53.74.1333, Lemba bracelet
34. (A) Lagergren, "Kitona," n.d., GEM 1966.15.3, Lemba bracelet
35. (A) Andersson, "Kinzaba," "BaKamba," n.d., GEM 1938.28.16a, Lemba drum
36. (A) Hammar, "BaKuta-BaTeke," GEM 1968.11.208, rattle, and 1968.11.241, Lemba drum
37. (A) Andersson, "BaKuta-BaYaka," "Ntele," GEM 1938.31.11–12, Lemba bracelets
38. (A) Maesen, "Tsanga," 1954, MAC 53.74.1332, Lemba bracelet
39. (A) Laman, "Mayombe," SEM 1919.1.445, drum
40. (A) Laman, "Mayombe-Sundi," SEM 1919.1.437, drum
41. (A) Anon., "BaKuta-BaYaka," "Ntele," GEM 1938.31.11–12, Lemba bracelets
42. (A) Maesen, "Tsanga," 1954, MAC 54.74.1335, Lemba bracelet
43. (E/A) Bittremieux, "Mayombe," 1937, MAC 37972, Lemba *n'kobe*
44. (E/A) Bittremieux, "Kangu," 1937, MAC 43040, Lemba *n'kobe*
45. (A) Bittremieux, "BaWoyo," 1933, MAC 35191, 35192, 2 *n'kobe* Lemba
46. (T/E) Tastevin, Cabinda, 1935, pp. 105–111, 191–7, 257–73
47. (A/T/E) Vaz, 1969, pp.116f., 320f., 413f., 420f., pot lids
48. (E) Bittremieux, 1925, "Kangu"
49. (T) Nitu, "Masala, Luadi river, Zala area, Cabinda," 1961, MS.
50. (T/E) Malonga, "Lari," 1958, pp. 45–9, 51–61

Chapter 1

Introduction to *Lemba*

Lemba: *Historic Equatorial African Drum of Affliction*

Lemba, a major historic cult of healing, trade, and marriage relations, came into being in the seventeenth century in a triangular region extending from the Atlantic coast to Malebo Pool between today's cities of Kinshasa and Brazzaville, and from the Congo (Zaire) River northward to the Kwilu-Niari River valley (figure 1). Mpumbu market, situated on a hilltop overlooking Malebo Pool, was the western end point of the vast riverain trade network which covered the Congo Basin. From Mpumbu westward, rapids on the Congo River required trade to the coast to follow land routes. Until railroads were built from Malebo Pool to Pointe Noire and Matadi three centuries later, caravans of porters brought ivory, copper, slaves, and other products to the coast, and European wares such as cloth, guns, liquor, and beads back inland over the same routes. *Lemba* controlled this trade on the north bank, keeping the routes open, regulating local markets, and assuring that the massive international trade did not destroy local communities. In the mid-eighteenth century, for example, fifteen thousand slaves were being shipped annually from the ports of Loango, Cabinda, and Malemba. These slaves were drawn from inland societies which tended to see the trade, despite its economic advantages, as disruptive. Conflicts of interest between the trade and social order may explain why *Lemba*—a word meaning "to calm" (*lembikisa*)—took the form of a therapeutic association, a "drum of affliction" (*ngoma* or *nkonko*).

Lemba's illness is described in a variety of ways: as possession by *Lemba*'s ancestors, common in drums as a mode of affliction; as any illness affecting head, heart, abdomen, and sides, that is, the key organs of the person; as difficulty breathing, a typical witchcraft symptom; as miraculous recovery from a deadly disease, and more. However this erratic list of *Lemba* symptoms and causes tells less about it than does identification of the types of individuals afflicted and directed toward membership in *Lemba*. They normally were the region's elite, prominent healers, chiefs, and judges, especially those engaged in mercantile work. Their ability to succeed in commerce and their aspirations to wealth made them vulnerable to the envy of their kinsmen, thus in a sense marginal in the society and "sick" with the *Lemba* affliction.

In typical drum of affliction manner, *Lemba* doctor-priests took the "sufferer" in hand and administered the initial purification. If he could muster further sponsorship, he would undergo full therapeutic initiation before the priests and priestesses of the locality. A ceremonial *Lemba* marriage with his leading wife, a lavish feast for *Lemba* priests and priestesses as well as for the public, and extensive instructions made up part of the initiatory ritual, before the priestly couple were qualified to themselves perform *Lemba*'s therapy.

Given such characteristics among many more to be explained in this book, it is not surprising that *Lemba* is considered by those who saw it in full bloom as an extraordinary institution, the most important of the consecrated medicines (*min'kisi*) among those that achieved corporate status. It is described as having been "a medicine of the village"; "a medicine of the family and its perpetuation"; "fertility medicine"; "the sacred medicine of governing" (*Lemba i n'kisi wangyaadila*) according to one clan head; "the government of multiplication and reproduction" (*luyaalu lua niekisa*), by a former *Lemba* wife; and "sacred medicine integrating people, villages and markets" (*n'kisi wabundisa bantu, mavata ye mazandu*), by a contemporary merchant and clan head who wrote a local history. In effect, although couched in the mold of a drum of affliction, *Lemba* was the governing order in a region much of which had no centralized institutions.

The *Lemba* region was bordered by prominent historical states—centralized kingdoms—which predate the international trade that began from the Congo coast in the sixteenth century (figure 2). South of the Zaire/Congo River stretched the great Kongo kingdom with its capital at Mbanza Kongo. Its northern province, Nsundi, extended from the southern bank of the river across to the north, although probably not as far as some early maps indicate. Smaller kingdoms and chiefdoms such as Vungu, Mbanza Mwembe, and Mwembe Nsundi existed along the river and northward into what became the *Lemba* region. On the coast were situated the famous old states of Loango, Kakongo, and Ngoyo, well documented by five centuries of European explorers, traders, and missionaries. To the north and east of the *Lemba* region could be found the great Teke (or Tio) complex of federated lords around their king Makoko of Mbé.

Figure 2

Political and economic map of *Lemba* region, 1600–1930 (Based on maps in Vansina's *The Tio*)

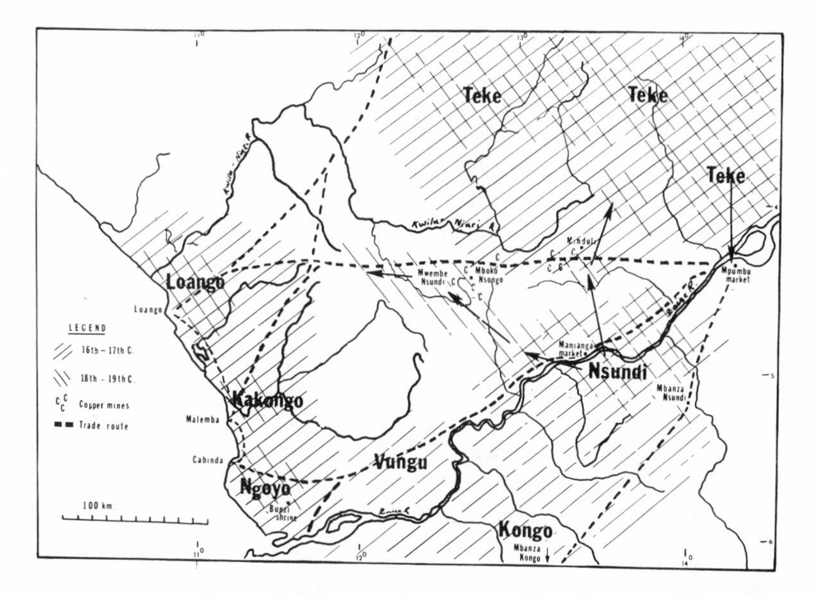

The distinctiveness of the *Lemba* system of government compared to that of the surrounding kingdoms can be illustrated by briefly noting different approaches to justice, the use of force, and the structure of economic resources. In the kingdoms, judicial order was maintained by courts of the principal chiefs or kings, which became courts of appeal in specific cases. The instrument for enforcing order at the disposal of some of the kingdoms included a hastily assembled army, most fully developed in the riverain polities, to defend the capital when it was under attack and to exert control over recalcitrant subordinate chiefs. A third expression of state order in the kingdoms was the levying of tribute by the center upon subordinate levels. At the zenith of each of these kingdoms tribute networks were widespread. Finally, the kingdoms were characterized by the symbolism of sacred and semidivine kingship, which was passed out along the tribute routes to extend the cloak of royal identity to outlying areas of the kingdom.

Under *Lemba*'s influence, justice, the exercise of force, and economics were institutionalized in "horizontal" mechanisms, most important of which was, beside *Lemba*'s ceremonial exchange system, the market and trade network. Local markets, sponsored and owned by adjacent villages, were organized into cycles, or weeks, of four days. A code of market laws prescribed the details of trade, justice, capital punishment, and peacemaking. Although markets existed in the kingdoms, these market laws took on greater prominence in the acephalous regions of the Lower Zaire. Feuds between local groups could not, as in the kingdoms, be arbitrated by a central regent or his army. Conflict had to be absorbed by communities adjoining those of the antagonists through mechanisms spelled out in the market laws. The vertical exchange of tribute for symbols of kingship found its acephalous equivalent in the way *Lemba*'s protection of the markets acted, in effect, as a consecrated commodity to be exchanged against significant goods. *Lemba*'s priests enhanced regional trade by maintaining peace in the marketplace. The effect of *Lemba*'s high initiation fees and its encouragement of redistribution and consumption of locally-produced and trade-produced goods in the séances, stimulated exchange. The regional network of kinship ties established in the special *Lemba* marriages strengthened alliances between prominent local clans. By making prominent judges, clan heads, and reputable healers, along with their principal wives, priests and priestesses of *Lemba*, a regional integration was achieved as well suited, perhaps even better suited, to the conditions of the international trade as that which existed in the localized chiefdoms and kingdoms.

Although *Lemba* disappeared from the scene as an active institution in the first decades of this century in the face of Belgian, French, and Portuguese colonial rule, mission activity, European commercial hegemony, and mechanized transport, its three-century presence across the north-bank Lower Congo/Zaire region, and its move with slave-emigrants to the New World where it still survives, make it not only one of the longest-enduring Bantu drums of affliction on record but one which has not heretofore received its due attention in scholarship. Its significance is comparable to that of major West-African cults such as *Poro* and *Sande* on the Guinea coast, *Ikenga*, the cult of the hand in Eastern Nigeria, *Bwiti* in Gabon, *Nzila* in Western Zambia, as well as *Beni-Ngoma* and the *Kalela* Dance in East Africa, and the Copper Belt, or the *Isangoma* diviners association in South Africa.

Going beyond the concerns of historical social research in Africa, a study of a major therapeutic society has a special modern appeal arising from our postindustrial concerns with the nature of organization in handling chronic afflictions not dealt with by biomedical professionals. At a time when noncentralized therapies of the "anonymous" variety are scoring successes in such areas as alcoholism, drug addiction, child abuse, cardiac rehabilitation, and a myriad of other cultural illnesses, research into alternative modes of conceptualizing and organizing health is in order. Planners in Africa itself may find the study of a highly developed example of a drum of affliction helpful in drafting present health care policies toward traditional therapies, or in the development of secular therapies based upon indigenous genres of care and organization. The present study will, we hope, illuminate the implications of a radically broadened definition of health, and of illness, going beyond the strictly personal, physical, realm of modern medicine.

Issues in the Study of Lemba *of Theoretical Significance*

The study of a major historical drum of affliction of Equatorial Africa abounds with issues of theoretical significance. Perhaps the most pressing need is to bring this discussion into closer congruence with sophisticated indigenous theories on the subject. Scholarly analyses have frequently made distinctions where none exist in indigenous thought, or have failed to take note of important cues in indigenous expressions. This problem is particularly acute in the interpretation of the corporate, therapeutic institutions which controlled major social and economic resources, thus combining functions normally kept discrete in Western thought. A more accurate understanding is required of the complex of cults, shrines, movements, and political structures in relation to therapeutics as a type of social process. The historical perspective of this study implies a concern for the rise, persistence, and decline of particular institutions, that is, the "waxing and waning" characteristic of cultic and therapeutic institutions in Bantu Africa. Scholars are divided over whether cults, drums, and shrines are to be seen as merely reactive barometers of social processes, or as creative efforts actually to construct social orders. The fundamental question behind both views, and the one which must be asked before embarking on this venture, is: what, in effect, are the independent and dependent variables of Central-African social and cultural change? And, necessarily, what theories are best suited for answering this question?

The present volume brings several analytic perspectives to the task of understanding *Lemba* and institutions like it. One perspective, developed in Part I, reconstructs the societies of the *Lemba* region in terms of political and economic structures over the past three centuries, roughly the period of *Lemba*'s rise, its domination, and its demise. This is essentially a history of corporate institutions and the control of public resources—people, food production, symbols of prestige, strategic locations, and key political roles. Although conventional history rarely views therapeutics together with corporate politics, this juxtaposition is necessary to an understanding of the role of consecrated medicines and their clientele in the public life of the seventeenth- to the early twentieth-century Western Congo.

Another perspective, developed in Part II, uses a more precise, closer-range, analytic language for the understanding of rituals and myths of *Lemba* initiatory and therapeutic séances. This perspective draws from structuralism, symbolic anthropology, and semiotics in an effort to order and draw maximum understanding from the diverse and uneven sources available for a project such as this: fieldwork notes, historic indigenous accounts, colonial archives, travelers accounts, and museum collections. (A fuller discussion of the particular theories used here may be found in the introduction to Part II.)

A further perspective, developed in Part III, uses the combined analytic tools of structuralism, symbolic anthropology, and semiotics to grasp self-conscious ideas of illness causation and classification in *Lemba* thought, the nature of therapies, and the rather explicit *Lemba* image of the healthy—or virtuous—society.

These approaches move sequentially from an historical analysis of the organization of public resources, to a closer-range study of symbols and meanings in ceremonial events, to an understanding of a self-conscious *Lemba* therapeutics found among a limited segment of the populace—the elite faced with problems of wealth and power in a redistributive, community-based society. All of these approaches are needed to account for the forces, consequences, and internal views of social change.

Understandably, there has not been general agreement among scholars regarding the character and purpose of African therapeutic cults. Indeed, the history of scholarship on them in the Lower Congo and in Africa as a whole reads much like a history of social science in the twentieth century, reflecting many trends and perspectives. Because many of these perspectives continue to maintain credence in one circle or another of scholarship, a detailed review of their applications to Lower-Congo and Equatorial-African societies seems warranted.

During the early colonial years African therapeutic cults aroused lively scholarly attention in Europe under the rubric of "secret societies," with the Lower Congo being in the forefront. *Lemba*, however, due perhaps to its practitioners' extreme skill in eluding investigation or to the relative absence of masks and exotic displays in its ritual, rarely figured in the discussions. A summary of the views of Belgian ethnologist Edward DeJonghe from the turn of the century until World War II offers an understanding of prevailing scholarly approaches to secret societies.[1]

Psychological interpretations of secret societies were led by Heinrich Schurtz whose *Altersklassen und Männerbünde* (1902)[2] postulated that secret societies constitute a synthesis between puberty rites and adult social groupings, in turn reflections of the two dominant instincts of human life: a natural sexual instinct governing puberty rites, and an artificial instinct (or need) for gregariousness leading to age grades and other ties across local communities. Accordingly, women, possessing an abundance of the sexual instinct, belonged in the home with children, whereas men, possessing an abundance of the social instinct, belonged in public life. Despite their patent Victorian ethnocentricity, these theories were influential, finding their way into the work of Meyer, Meinhof, Weule, Lasch, Freud (see his *Totem and Taboo*),[3] and Wundt, whose *Folk Psychology*[4] had a strong influence on Makinowski.[5] DeJonghe recognized the wide appeal of the psychological approach, but doubted the applicability of such a universal explanation to an institutional type whose forms varied so extremely from place to place.

Religious studies of secret societies were heavily influenced by the work of James Frazer, including his well-known *Golden Bough* (1890) and *Totemism and Exogamy* (1910ff.).[6] In these works Frazer linked rites of puberty and rituals of death and resurrection—whether simulated or real—to the social process of assimilating a youth to his clan or totemic group. Although Lower-Congo ritual symbolism used death and resurrection symbolism in initiations to secret societies, DeJonghe rejected the full application of Frazer's totemic theories on the basis that totemism was not worldwide, hence could not be applied naively everywhere, especially where it was barely represented as in the Lower Congo. Of more validity in the study of secret societies DeJonghe found the work of Durkheim's sociological school and the new field of European folklore, especially Van Gennep's *Les rites de passage* (1909).[7] Addressing the same issues as Frazer, Van Gennep postulated his now well-known stages of ritual not only in initiation to special associations but in most social transitions, groups, and activities. Separation from the old status or role, a threshold, "liminal" stage of transition, and reincorporation in a new position marked all status changes, however varied the form. Van Gennep's research model was praised for its insight, but judged too subtle for work with most sources available to scholars of the time. Although Van Gennep himself used examples from the Loango coast in his famous book, full-scale application of his analytic ideas to Central-African ritual would need to wait decades until Victor Turner would use them in studies of Ndembu drums of affliction, a subject taken up later in this chapter.

The culture-historical tradition of research under the inspiration of Leo Frobenius and Fritz Gräbener was DeJonghe's own theoretical preference for the study of secret societies. Great praise had been lavished on Frobenius' magnificently illustrated work *Masks and Secret Societies* (1898).[8] Masks from Loango and Cabinda figured prominently in the volume, and although *Lemba* was ignored—because it had developed few masks?—other Kongo societies such as the puberty initiation activities of *Khimba*, and a parallel society, *Ndembo*, were featured. Frobenius had given West-African secret societies his attention under the rubric of "culture areas" and "culture complexes." Masking in this part of the world had a Malaysian origin, he believed, with close associations to sun and nature worship and other elements of the African worldview. Central to this worldview was its "manism," whereby ancestors over the course of time underwent a gradual "spiritization" (*Vergeisterung*), in the process becoming deities, abstract ideas, masks, and cults. Although the ancestor cult of a particular social group might be central to this local world view, other levels of collective spirit symbolism could be interpreted as having grown from it. Masks represented the effort to consolidate disparate elements in spiritization, whence arose two-, three-, and four-faced masks throughout the secret-society culture area of Africa. This notion had a direct impact on many Africanists, including Karl Laman whose interpretation of Kongo consecrated medicines is that they are the representation of ancestors whose individual identities have been lost in time.[9]

According to DeJonghe, the foregoing theoretical approaches to Africa's and especially the Lower Congo's secret societies were all either too reductionist, prone to explain all in terms of individual needs and instincts, or too nominalist, forcing data into abstract categories. He advocated an inductive approach based on the ethnographic material itself. In this vein he recommended the use of Fritz Gräbener's special application of Frobenius' culture-area method, finding ideal Gräbener's study of Oceania's "patriarchial totemic cycle," a complex of elements including the puberty rite, death and resurrection symbolism, the boomerang, lunar mythology, the breaking out of teeth, and so on.[10] Just as analysis of these elements as parts of a complex had clarified Oceanic cultural history, so the institutional complex of Africa's secret societies would be clarified by a similar analysis.

Because African cultural complexes were, however, mixed together in a tangle of cross-cutting influences, noted DeJonghe, it would be necessary to begin with inductive studies, shorn of preconceived ideas, in the comparison of peoples and their characteristic complexes and in the geographic distributions of the latter. DeJonghe identified twelve elements which, taken as a complex, characterized Lower-Congo secret societies. These were: the extension in space and time of a name for the society; a normative age for adepts; criteria and procedures for admission of adepts; duration of ordeals; place of ordeals relative to other significant locations; the entrance ceremony; special names for the cult and its various features; deformations or special identifying decorations donned by participants such as tattoos and costumes; instructions given the adepts; prescriptions and prohibitions; exit ceremonies; and activities related to, but outside, the direct initiation.[11] *Khimba*, *Longo*, *Kimpasi*, and *Ndembo* were analyzed in terms of this grid; *Lemba* was again overlooked.

In the conclusion of a lecture given in 1923 to the Semaine d'Ethnologie Religieuse DeJonghe departed from his well-reasoned, academic survey to give a more visceral summation of African secret societies. They are a "threat to the colonial order," he began. Although they are "a very old type of organization, new versions arise under your eyes in opposition to the European." Although they are often "tribal in their boundaries, they can become intertribal," like the notorious Aniota leopard cult which utilized violence on its opponents. DeJonghe characterized the institution "from Senegal to Congo" as a "secret religious fraternity whose eponymous tutelary spirit, often a forest spirit, appears in the village 'speaking' with a bull roarer, not out of love of music but with an aim of tyrannizing and dominating. They are successful in convincing the populace, for everywhere there has been resistance to colonial government. They are, in short, a *significant political force*, regulating justice, policing markets, establishing the price of merchandise, issuing boycotts, even killing to get their wishes fulfilled. Their front is extremely varied; some resemble castes, others cults to certain spirits. Yet others are grafted onto initiations; others pursue social and political aims." Concluded DeJonghe, "it is no exaggeration to say that secret societies are one of the largest and most serious infections (*plaies*) on Africa!"[12]

DeJonghe's impassioned remarks on secret societies, despite their partisan procolonial sound, were better than received scientific theories in one important sense. They acknowledged the substantial political character of these institutions. Unlike kingdoms and chiefdoms of Africa which had been early acknowledged by colonialists to be political entities and had been incorporated where possible into the colonial structure, the horizontally-organized "drums" were not understood in political terms at all, and even when they were, they could not easily be accommodated. Therefore, in the years surrounding DeJonghe's 1923 lecture, which was itself two years after the massive disturbances accompanying the appearance of the Kongo prophet Kimbangu, secret societies of the Congo coast, including *Lemba*, were banned for resisting colonial "progress," and for diverting economic and labor resources away from colonial goals into lavish feasts and resistance. With this redefinition of the "secret society" from object of general scholarly curiosity to mechanism for resistance to colonialism, went the gradual decline of "secret society" as a research paradigm. And, although writers like DeJonghe,[13] Van Wing,[14] and Bittremieux[15] continued to find and describe new secret societies in the twenties and thirties, for all intents and purposes this paradigm had been exhausted in serious ethnological scholarship by World War II.

Social research in Africa since World War II has inserted institutions such as *Lemba* into a more diversified rubric of movements, social and political organizations, cults, and ritual idioms, especially the therapeutic. Among the most important of the postwar scholars in this field has been Victor Turner whose fieldwork in the fifties on the ritual process among the Ndembu of Zambia has set the pace for a generation of scholarship. In particular, Turner has defined precisely the nature of drums of affliction—based on the Bantu cognate term *ngoma*—or, as they are more widely known, "cults of affliction." Turner's portrayal of the cult of affliction begins with a cultural interpretation of misfortune (for example, bodily disorders, accidents) in terms of domination by a specific nonhuman agent, and proceeds with an attempt to remove the source of misfortune by bringing the sufferer into closer association with a cult group venerating that specific agent.[16] Turner's carefully conducted work among the Ndembu revealed a range of such drums devoted to specific problem idioms in areas such as hunting, reproduction, and sickness, as well as in growing dislocations resulting from colonialism and labor migration.

Turner's work on the ritual processes giving rise to drums of affliction stresses the presence of a system of thought about misfortune and its treatment which may well be as widespread as the Bantu-speaking societies of Central and Southern Africa. A number of excellent field studies have identified common elements of this system, from Equatorial Africa to East Africa, and from the rain forests to the mountains of the south.[17]

The causal premises behind health and disease in this "Bantu" cosmology trace all of life to a central source of power, often named God or some spirit immanent in nature. This power is mediated by middle-range spirits and consectrated human priests or visionary prophets who maintain contact with, or derive inspiration from, the source of power and life. Misfortune, including disease, is any condition whether social, personal, physical, or mystical which falls short of the ordered universe of life—in other words, chaos. Balance between the universe's elements is a subordinate theme, as is purity.

A crucial cosmological notion, therefore, is the distinction drawn in many Bantu societies between "naturally-caused" (God-caused) diseases or misfortunes and those attributed to "human cause." The former misfortunes "just happen" or are "in the order of things,"[18] as, for example, in the death of a very old person or in an affliction with readily recognized symptoms and signs which respond to treatment as expected. A widespread range of treatments such as plant preparations, massages, and manipulative techniques are appropriate for afflictions of this type, as are nowadays techniques of modern biomedicine practiced by Western-trained doctors and nurses in hospitals and dispensaries.

In contrast to natural misfortunes and diseases are those caused by chaos in the human world or in the relationship of humans to their environment. An individual may bring disease and suffering upon himself by disregarding social etiquette, ignoring good eating habits, or by turning his back on kinsmen, elders, ancestors, and spirits. An aura of ritual pollution frequently accompanies sickness by "human cause," requiring the sufferer and his fellows to seek ritual purification through sacrifices and confessions so as to achieve reintegration with the good graces of society. Most human-caused affliction in Bantu thought is attributed to the evil intentions of others, or situations of contradiction in which persons are at odds or cross-purposes with one another, as, for example, in the struggle to distribute land equitably from a limited estate at a time when the dependent population is increasing or in launching an enterprise for profit in the face of a strong ethic of the redistribution of goods. Such situations are believed to incur the ill will or envy of others and to lead directly to the breakdown of health in a person, to visible physical sickness, or even to the person's death. This belief in mystically channelled ill wishing operates to reinforce the morality of social redistribution and loyalty to family and kin.

Bantu therapeutic systems follow from these assumptions about the nature of the world and the causes of misfortune, articulating techniques—empirical, social, symbolical—and their specialized experts. Not all medicines are highly specialized. Many are household techniques practiced by parents on children, or by anyone on himself. Yet in areas of life where there is crisis, transition, danger, recurrent accident, high responsibility, or a focus on core social values, consecrated medicines appear, complete with origin charters, exact codes for their use, and the dangers of their misuse. These consecrated medicines may be techniques, chemotherapeutic treatments, behavioral procedures, or highly magical and esoteric affairs. The emergence of a consecrated medicine in an area of life probably derives from the perception that the technique so consecrated, or the ingredient, is powerful, effective, and in need of legitimate control. It is said that "a medicine that can kill, can also heal," and therefore must be carefully used and authorized, the same as in other therapeutic traditions.[19]

A Bantu therapeutic system is commonly, then, organized into a series of specialist types (for example, *nganga*, pl. *banganga*) each of which has knowledge in one or more specialized and consecrated medicines.[20] Among the Kongo, classically, the *nganga mbuki* (from *buka*, to heal) is the local doctor who uses herbs; the *nganga n'kisi* is a more advanced or powerful doctor competent in numerous consecrated mèdicines, especially those pertaining to anger and magically caused afflictions; the *nganga ngombo* (named for the basket he uses) is a diviner. The diviner's specialty is the sorting out of particular details of cases brought to him or her and the offering of an expert diagnosis of the affliction or misfortune's cause, whether it be of natural or human cause, or another, spirit-related, cause. Because of its integral place in the analysis and interpretation of human misfortune in Bantu society, divination has responded sensitively to social change. Particular perspectives in divination have come and gone; inspirational diviners and prophet-seers, even mission-trained pastors and priests, have taken on the role in the past century. And where the divination specialist has disappeared as a consecrated role specialty, kinsmen of sufferers do this work in the form of a "therapy managing group."[21] The institution of divination—analysis and diagnosis—has permitted Bantu therapeutics to generate new consecrated medicines, like surface transformations, without violating or changing basic premises.

In most local Bantu therapeutic systems a few of the consecrated medicines take on the public stature of corporate drums of affliction. As Turner has noted for the Ndembu, sickness is seen as a sacred calling, manifested in the form of a possession. In a consecrated medicine that becomes a drum, those afflicted and initiated to the cure or stabilized in their relationship to the sickness are the best suited to become doctors of the ailment. It is a form of religious immunization such that as the disease is conquered, the possessing spirit is placated; the ordeal purifies and energizes the sufferer, placing him in debt to society so that he is henceforth expected to devote his newly acquired gift of mediumship in a specialized idiom to the service of others.

Reference in the foregoing sentences to social change, the divinatory "reading" of current events, the interpretation of new kinds of misfortune, and the generation of new consecrated medicines with the creation of major drums of affliction that wax and then wane call to mind the fact that any standardized picture of Bantu therapeutics is only as good as its depiction of local variance and historical vicissitude. The perspective must be historical. The waxing and waning phenomenon of consecrated medicines and therapeutic movements, linked as they are to a close reading of misfortune in individuals' lives, can be used to understand the nature of social instability, the sources of stress and chronic affliction in a society. Read longitudinally, that is historically, these taxonomies, as they unfold, become barometers of the local human condition. (In Chapter 2 such an historical reading will be done of consecrated medicines in Loango over three centuries to detail the background against which *Lemba* emerged and endured, Loango being the only region of Equatorial Africa known to have this depth of documentation.[22]) Read latitudinally, that is synchronically at a given moment, medical taxonomies indicate the contours of the system of dealing with adversity and the lines of shifting orientation. Such a slice of medical taxonomy is offered here from the *Lemba* region to situate the theoretical discussion more fully in evidence pertinent to the subject of the book.

In about 1900 a Lower-Congo/Zaire writer sketched the then current array of consecrated medicines (*min'kisi*) in the north-bank region, noting those that were of major status, that is "those drummed up with *ngoma*." The inventory included such areas as "personal physical growth," "a child's upbringing," "spirit children and how to deal with them," "twinship and the parenting of twins," "headache," "purification with the cupping horn," numerous approaches to "divination," "origin, residence, identity," a variety of women's troubles, and at least five drums of affliction: *Kinkita,* devoted to "clan leadership," *Bunzi* and *Matinu* for "chiefship," *Mbola* for "water spirits," *N'kondi* for "judicial affairs," and *Lemba* for "order in markets and public sites."[23] A static taxonomy such as this may be studied in terms of analytical questions that indicate points of change. Thus, the inventory of consecrated medicines may indicate a change of particular items within consistent categories like divination, or it may indicate the emergence of new categories and new medicines. In line with this, the categories which contain major public medicines—drums, cults—may demonstrate either a waxing and waning of particular organizations within them, or the emergence of innovative categories and public organizations.

Considerable scholarship in recent years has gone into the discernment in Central- and Equatorial-African cult history of the rise of large-scale, regional units in conjunction with historical forces such as trade networks, colonial empires, labor migration, and the modern nation-state.[24] A crucial analytical distinction has been drawn, once more by Turner, between areas of ritual organization that represent local "ancestral" identities and those which represent "earth" identities.[25] The former are maintained by political rituals and divisive polarities such as lineage segmentation, whereas the latter are maintained by fertility rituals and nonsectarian religious specialists. Often political conquerers are aligned in opposition or in contrast to indigenous priests. Citing examples from the Shilluk of the Sudan, the Tallensi of Ghana, and the Shona of Zimbabwe, thus from three widely differing cultures across Africa, Turner suggests that this distinction between "exclusive" sectional ritual identities and "inclusive" ritual identities creates a system of shrines or medicines which is characterized by overlapping and interpenetrating fields of ritual relations: the first type of identity representing power divisions and classificatory distinctions, including factional conflict, and giving rise to homicide; the second type representing ritual bonds between groups, common ideals, and values, such as are needed in the purification of the land by earth priests in the event of fratricidal murder in some societies.[26] Although the former ritual levels are not displaced, they are overlaid, as it were, with universalistic ideas of ethics and morality such as brotherhood, purity, love, the "kinship of all people," and related notions found in world religions.

The important distinction drawn by Turner, and others, between "exclusive" and "inclusive" ritual orders may readily be discerned in the taxonomy of sacred medicines and drums from Lower Zaire given above. Those pertaining to chiefship (*Matinu, (Ma)Bunzi*) and to clan leadership (*Kinkita*) are exclusive, whereas those pertaining to water spirits (*Mbola*), judicial affairs (*N'kondi*) and order in markets and public places (*Lemba*) are inclusive. Particularly *N'kondi*, the well-known nail-and-blade charm used in the regulation of feuds between local groups, and *Lemba* were the most explicit articulations of regionalism.

More work has been done recently on "regional cults" as reported in a volume of this same title recording the 1976 Association of Social Anthropology (ASA) conference. Regional cults are defined as cults "in the middle" between the "parochial cult of the little community" and the world religion with its universal form. The central places of these regional cults are shrines in towns and villages, at crossroads or even in the wild, "where great populations from various communities or their representatives come to supplicate, sacrifice, or simply make pilgrimage."[27] Such cults have a topography of their own, conceptually defined by the people themselves and marked apart from other features of cultural landscapes and ritual activities. This group of scholars emphasizes the fixed central shrine as a key feature in regional cults. Contributions from the Islamic north to the Bantu southeast of Africa are used to illustrate this. Van Binsbergen, writing on regional drums of affliction in Western Zambia, emphasizes as criteria the specific healing idiom, representation in congregations over a vast area, overarching organizational ties binding local chapters into a region, further identified by controlled information and communication within the organizational structure. *Nzila* and *Bituma*, the major Western Zambian regional cults of affliction, have central shrines and headquarters for a centralized staff.[28] Schoffeleers' study of the *Mbona* cult of Malawi also emphasizes these points.[29].

The criteria of regional cults developed by the ASA group, which are largely built upon earlier work by Turner, suggest that Lower-Zaire historical developments in this area may be somewhat anomalous in one respect. The cults or ritual orders most readily expressing general values and identities, namely *Mbola*, *Nkondi*, and *Lemba*, lack centralized shrines. Of those expressing exclusive values, only *Bunzi* has (or had) a central shrine (in Ngoyo kingdom near the Congo River at the Atlantic Coast) and thus meets the criteria for a regional cult. As more detailed accounts in Chapter 2 will show, already by the sixteenth century *Bunzi*'s priests were consecrating the kings of Loango, Kakongo, and Ngoyo on the coast. In time, apparently, *Bunzi* spawned secondary "*MaBunzi*" throughout the Mayombe, with their subsidiary territorial shrines. This may have been the result of a regional consciousness. But what is even clearer about cultic changes in the sixteenth and seventeenth centuries is the emergence of movable shrines such as those kept by *Lemba* priests, their *tukobe*. Comparable developments characterize the rise of movable shrines in the hands of Tio lords, vis-à-vis the fixed earth shrine of the Tio king to earth spirit N'kwe Mbali.[30]

I mention these details only to suggest that the fixed shrine center, and a centralized organization with a recognizable leader, may not be as instrumental to the creation of a regional consciousness as the ASA group suggests.[31] In some cases, such cultic centers as *Bunzi* may actually lose out at the expense of other, moving, ritual varieties of the kind that *Lemba* characterizes. *Bunzi* will receive fuller comment in later chapters, for it is apparent that it consecrated not only the three coastal kingdoms but a number of horizontal cults such as *Lemba* in the eighteenth and nineteenth centuries.

The characterization of regional cults is no more important in scholarship, however, than the question of what forces bring them about. How are the transformations to be explained? As suggested earlier, analytic distinctions such as that drawn by Turner between inclusive and exclusive ritual orders and by the ASA group between cults with regional organization and those with localized small-scale organization are made so that the student may obtain a grasp of the phenomenon of social change. As Werbner, in his introduction to the ASA volume, points out, much of the work on African history in the therapeutic and religious arena is grounded in the correspondence theory of religion, propounded by Durkheim, and before him

Robertson-Smith.[32] The theory states that religious consciousness, cult forms, and the deities worshipped or evoked are a function of the social system, its contours, and its changes. The emergence of regional cults, and the waxing and waning of drums of affliction, religious movements, and shrines and therapeutic systems, are readily explained in terms of social change. Thus, Van Binsbergen, writing about the three major cults of affliction in Western Zambia—*Nzila*, *Bituma*, *Moya*—states that the political and economic changes of recent decades constitute the "motor" behind religious transformation. The cults and the way they draw differently from the populace express "the emergence of interlocal structures and movements of peoples, due to precolonial and colonial state formation, raiding, long distance trade, labour migration, all of which calls for new religious and social forms to legitimate new structures and meet existential and interpretive needs of people."[33]

In a comparable line of explanation, Van Velzen offers an explicitly materialist interpretation of the emergence of the *Gaan Tata*, high-God, cult among Bush Negro and Maroon tribes of Surinam and French Guiana, who from 1880 to 1920 and decreasingly thereafter controlled the river traffic in connection with the exploitation of gold in the interior.[34] The cult emerged in several locations along the transportation network and then coalesced into a regional cult with a central shrine and a hierarchic structure in its heyday in the 1890's, monopolizing river transport and maintaining high wages and freight prices for the Bush Negro and Maroon workers. The resemblances of *Gaan Tata* to *Lemba* are so striking that I shall develop in fuller detail Van Velzen's approach.

Van Velzen calls the independent variable in his analysis of regional cults the "alteration in the mode of production."[35] In the case of *Gaan Tata* this was the introduction into Bush Negro and Maroon society of a massive new resource from the outside—the discovery of gold, and the consequent need of transport by outside prospecting and mining interests—resulting in a sudden influx of wealth and setting off a polarization of the society. The centrifugal effects of this polarization created a powerful need to allay anxiety about witchcraft on the part of those benefitting from the wealth. Simultaneously, there emerged an increased vigilance for a stonger morality, a more generalized, even universal, ethic, supported by a new and centralized high-God cosmology at odds with the traditional one. Van Velzen argues that the universalizing ethic in *Gaan Tata* was an outcome of the cult's oracle to protect the entrepreneurs from kin envy, to uphold their reputation, and to establish antiwitchcraft standards of social life. Thirty to forty percent of goods received were channeled to kinsmen; another substantial portion was dumped at *Gaan Tata*'s shrines. Only a minimal portion was "used" by an elite. In effect, the cult managed to thwart the more exaggerated forms of elitism. How *Lemba* resolved this problem will be a major discussion in the present work.

In some writing on cults, drums, and therapeutics, there is an undertone of criticism toward the correspondence theory, which tends, it is argued, to represent these ritual orders as tails that are wagged by the dog of the socioeconomic order. Such explanation, it is asserted, often neglects the generic qualities of heightened concern with ethics and morality; the development of sophisticated concepts of redemption such as grace, purity, and balance; the methods of sacrifice, prayer, and devotion before deities worshipped; or, above all, the manner in which individuals seek redemption in the midst of chaos, suffering, and evil. This criticism echoes a point made by Burridge about the explanation of millenarian movements in the social sciences,[36] or by Geertz on the general study of religion.[37] Turner cleverly addresses these issues without abandoning the socioeconomic correspondence theory altogether by locating most religious activity in the "liminal" mode of human life, that apparently universal aspiration to escape, periodically, the structures of social life with their deadening formalism and routine.

But surely, the challenge in theory-building is to offer a sound basis for interpretation of intrinsic characteristics of regional cults, cults or drums of affliction, consecrated medicines, independent churches, and related rituals; and not to pass them off as mere dependent variables—mirrors—of socioeconomic forces, or unpredictable, inverse occurrences in the cracks of society's structures. Put another way, the theoretical question most acutely in need of attention is: do these institutions creatively shape society? Or are they a reaction to it? What is the most sophisticated way of measuring the mixture of the two possibilities?

Lemba offers new and important information about the subject under discussion. It provides evidence from the study of a more substantial therapeutic order than has been documented heretofore of the way cults can act as a creative impulse to shape a region's society. Certainly it reacted in some senses to the external pressures of the international trade. But several alternative responses would have been possible, among them doing nothing. Ranger argues that choosing the institutional form of the drum of affliction made the response a creative, positive effort in the formation of a "new society." Just as kinship has been seen in some social theories as a metaphor for the construction of the social order, so here, and in other drums of affliction, sickness and healing provided a metaphor for the construction of a new social order.[38] The concept of a new society ordered in terms of cults of affliction is frequently idiomatic and partial, dealing with such areas as twinship, hunting, purity, witchcraft eradication, or fecundity. But potentially, therapeutics may be the metaphor serving to facilitate consolidation of substantial resources, material and human, and to aid long-term re-ordering of institutions of redress, economic redistribution, and ideological change.

Theoretical discussion of the conditions giving rise to new cults should, therefore, compare ritual and institutional phenomena across a broad spectrum, including the formation of states. Once this is done it is immediately apparent that the various theories of cult emergence are the same ones used in accounting for the rise of traditional states, at least in Africa. Most are "correspondence" theories, such as that which makes economic surpluses a precondition of state emergence, or that which links the rise of the centralized state to an expanding regional sphere of activity in trade, warfare, or the movement of peoples. I cannot here survey in any detail the voluminous literature on state formation skillfully handled or reviewed by such scholars as Vansina,[39] Goody,[40] Miller,[41] de Heusch,[42] and others. My concern is rather with the apparent lack of discussion between those who study state formation and those who study cult cycles, and the failure of these persons to address the question of why such similar preconditions as both groups often consider give rise in the one case to a "state," and in the other to a "cult."

A theoretical framework is called for which bridges organizational gradations from centralized to decentralized; from an institution with multiple idioms to one with a specific idiom; from collegial forms of authority to serially-occupied offices of solitary authority, and so on. Much writing on "states" is couched in assumptions of nineteenth-century teleology by which less centralized social forms become transformed, through economic, social, or ideational impetus, into centralized forms. The present work will interpret the divergent institutions such as centralized shrines (*Bunzi, N'kwe Mbali*), kingdoms (Loango, Kakongo, Ngoyo, Tio), movable shrines or major drums (*Lemba*, the Tio *n'kobi*), local horizontal specialists' medicines (*N'kondi* feud resolution techniques), and other institutions in terms of corporation theory as developed by Maine,[43] Smith,[44] and for Central Africa by MacGaffey.[45] Corporate theory acknowledges authority and power of both centralized and decentralized polities in terms of corporateness: that is, a presumptive perpetual aggregate with a unique identity; having determinate social boundaries and membership; possessing the autonomy, organization, and agreed upon procedures to regulate exclusive collective affairs. In other words, a corporate group forms a social structure around a set of diverse issues. In *Lemba*, this would include the maintenance of order in market places, regulating trade over long distances, establishing marriage alliances between local lineages, and healing the personality disorders of the "marginal" mercantile elite.

Corporate theory goes on to elaborate the measure of a group's corporate strength by the manner in which it develops leadership roles (or commissions, consecrated leadership roles); how this authority is delegated, and administratively coordinated; how a constitution making explicit the premises and understandings of the corporation is articulated. In *Lemba*, this would include the adaptation of regional cosmologies to unique *Lemba* values, and the development of codes of behavior, purity laws, and levels of morality for the *Lemba* membership and for public society under its influence.

Corporate theory makes a further distinction between the *corporation sole* and the *corporation aggregate*, the former a leadership role or commission standing for the group in which a series of individual officeholders move through an office in succession; the latter an office occupied by multiple officeholders simultaneously. The distinction, in theory, readily clarifies the nuances of difference between a centralized kingdom, chiefdom, or shrine, and a network-like aggregate of figures in a major drum of affliction such as *Lemba*. That this is a distinction of degree and not of kind might be suggested from the fact that drum symbolism, denoting consecrated leadership, exists across the set of political types.

Corporate theory, furthermore, offers a theoretical avenue for an understanding of the phenomenon of "waxing and waning" of kingdoms, drums of affliction, and shrines, as well as the transformation of the one into the other. Corporations sole may be based upon the consolidation of corporations aggregate. One suspects that this is the way kings emerged in some African states. It is clear however that transformations can go the other way. The proliferation of *Bunzi*'s "daughters" in the cults *Lemba*, *Pfemba*, and *Lunga* (see figure 26 below) and into chiefdoms inland represents a case in point.

Corporate theory, finally, distinguishes between corporate groups, discussed in the foregoing lines, and corporate categories. These latter lack the power and authority of the corporate group, because they lack the organization, internal hierarchy, and command of resources. However, a corporate category meets criteria of presumptive perpetuity, determinate social boundaries, identity, and membership. In the Lower Congo, for example, a matrilineal clan is a corporate category because of the putative descent of its members from a common ancestor. It is distinguished from the local clan, or set of related lineages, in that these have internal organization, leadership, common affairs, property relations, and a command of resources. The distinction between corporate category and corporate group would also, at the level of theory, explain the difference between adepts of a simple consecrated medicine whose only common experience would be their individual interaction with a given medicine and its priests, and adepts of a powerful corporate medicine, a public "drum of affliction," whose common affairs, command of resources, and coordination would give them greater power and authority in public affairs.

Once spelled out in this wise, it is apparent that the waxing and waning of kingdoms, centralized shrines, diffuse cults, drums of affliction, ephemeral movements, and consecrated medicines can best be accounted for in terms of a unified theory of differential corporateness. This I attempt in the next two chapters for the *Lemba* region: the Malebo Pool (Mpumbu)-Cabinda-Loango triangle north of the Congo River, from the seventeenth to the early twentieth centuries.

Part I

The Public Setting of *Lemba*: Management of Society and Its Resources

"Les auteurs ont . . . des notions très vagues sur les populations de la rive droite du Congo infèrieur." —J. VAN WING, *Études BaKongo*, (1959)

Chapter 2

Economic, Social, and Political History of the *Lemba* Region

Environment, Resource Use, Adaptation, Trade and Currency

The *Lemba* region is defined by natural boundaries, the Zaire and Kuilu-Nyari River systems on the south and north, respectively, and by the ocean on the west. These river valleys are, however, quite different one from the other. The Kwilu-Nyari, which begins in the area and flows through a fertile alluvial plain, offers excellent possibility for cultivation. The Zaire valley, by contrast, is the end-point of the great and mighty river system of Central Africa. It is marked by its deeply eroded canyon and dangerous cataracts, making it hostile in places to boat travel and useless for cultivation. Fishing is the only resource common to both rivers. The Atlantic coast, by comparison, offers some possibility for fishing, and was in the past an important site for the gleaning of salt. Tributaries of the Zaire and the Kwilu-Nyari, and rivers such as the Loango flowing directly into the ocean, offer these same possibilities for fishing, and are in part navigable.

Between these major rivers mountains rise to a level of 750 meters in the region of Mboko Nsongo, containing deposits of iron, copper, and lead in some quantity. These minerals have been instrumental in the wider region for centuries as material for the tools of cultivation, hunting, warfare, and trade.

The terrain eastward of the mountains levels off into the vast, sandy Teke Plateau. Westward toward the ocean, a deep rain forest covers the Mayombe. The central area is covered with a mixed vegetation, and rain forests are present where slash and burn agriculture has not been followed by secondary scrub woods and savanna grassland. The soil of the region is characteristically tropical. Where forest exists, the lush tree growth protects the delicate balance of the elements. Where clearings have been cut out of the forest, mixed cropping produces an initial rich harvest, but soon the devastation of soil leaching because of high rainfall reduces the terrain to less productive and barren grassland or even rock-like laterite.

Until recently hunting was an important subsistence activity in the entire region. Its important status is attested to by the knowledge of the net, trap, and stalking techniques found in adjoining regions such as the Cameroons where hunting still survives as a primary activity.[1] Of edible animals, elephants, buffalo, a variety of antelope, and smaller animals as well as birds of many kinds constituted the source of food. This status is still reflected in the symbols of *Lemba*. Archaeological research in the region has documented the existence of a variety of prehistoric lithic industries and of ancient hunting traditions dating back for millennia.[2] Knowledge of metalworking had been introduced by the middle of the first millennium A.D. Metalworking, according to north-bank oral traditions, was known by the "Teke" peoples who gradually gave it to the "Kongo" peoples. Iron arrow tips and knives, as well as spears, were used widely in intensified hunting. By the eighteenth century, however, guns were introduced in massive quantities on the coast, replacing the bow and arrow and lance as main hunting instruments. These guns were rapidly incorporated into the regional smithing industry, whose artisans soon reworked old barrels, made bullets of lead, and manufactured gunpowder locally.

Trade had a devastating effect on some types of wildlife. Several decades after the beginning of ivory trade in the seventeenth century—before the gun—delivery of ivory to the Loango coast declined as a result of an annual elephant kill of between 3000 and 4000 animals, a rate which nearly depleted the herds.[3] Not until the late nineteenth century, following the end of the international slave trade, were ivory tusks to become important again. At that time elephants were again hunted—this time with a gun—nearly to extinction in the region.[4] By the mid-twentieth century only a few small elephant herds still remained in the Mayombe forest and in swampy lands along the Zaire River. The gun had a similar effect on other wildlife, so that less and less did the highly romanticized life of the hunter, important for the male image, correspond to the actual role of hunting in the economy.

The tradition of cultivation remained that of the hoe, ax, adze, and bush knife from the time ironworking was introduced in the region. Malaysian crops—yams, bananas—entered the region and with African crops—possibly millet, the palm (*Elaeis guineenis*), various cucurbits, and fruit trees (*Canarium schweinfurthii*, for example)—

constituted the staple foods until the seventeenth century. Portuguese trade with Brazil beginning even earlier than the seventeenth century brought manioc, maize, and beans into the diet, exerting a significant change in cultivation patterns. Manioc, in particular, introduced a heavier use of fields with the resulting tendency to clear wide areas of forest. By the late nineteenth century, that is after several centuries of manioc cultivation, the central and northern region of the Lower Congo/Zaire had been largely deforested, and what was left was falling year by year before the ax and hoe. Dupont, who made these observations as a foot traveler in 1887, also suggested that the firewood need of the metalworking industry of the region from Mboko Nsongo to Mindouli had contributed its share to the extensive depletion of the forest.[5] Later, around 1885–1900, colonial governments began to levy agricultural taxes to support caravans, porters, and soldiers, a practice that placed further pressure upon the land. Export possibilities in the late nineteenth century for palm oil, palm nuts, ground nuts, and rubber gum (from 1869) introduced cash cropping, which became the major burden upon the population and the environment. We will return to the nature of trade at the end of this section.

The foregoing paragraphs have reviewed natural resources available in the *Lemba* region, and the technology used to exploit rivers, soil, metal, wildlife, domestic crops, and trees. In a region as diversified as this, trade is a logical human activity for the redistribution of localized resources. For example, salt, gathered at the ocean, was traded for metal from the highlands. Active trade of this kind existed long before European merchants arrived in the sixteenth century with their goods. But as coastal trade intensified, it not only stimulated this internal trade, it created a unique coastal trade. The resulting mixed internal and external commercial system had the effect of thrusting into sharper juxtaposition the value equivalency of nearly all cultural objects, from food, drink, animals, clothing, metals, to the human being.

Local markets, tied to the four-day week, fed into the long-distance trade routes and their markets, key among which were Mpumbu at the pool, controlled by Tio lords; Manianga on the Zaire; the copper markets from Mboko Nsongo to Mindouli; San Salvador, the capital of the Kongo kingdom; and the ports of Loango Bay, Cabinda, and Malemba and Ambriz on the coast (see figure 2 above). Long-distance caravans of up to 500 persons carried thousands of tons hundreds of kilometers in this trade.

The extremely complex question of resource value in the *Lemba* area has to be limited in this study to the period from approximately 1850 to 1920, which commercially means the transition from full slavetrading to so-called legitimate trade, followed by the early colonial era. Within this scope I am primarily concerned with illuminating the value of the units used in *Lemba* inaugurals and traded by *Lemba* adherents in markets of the region.

An 1885 market list from the mining area of Mboko-Nsongo, in the heart of *Lemba* area, offers a glimpse of the "internal" trade of the region.[6] On sale were:

a large antelope, cut into pieces	gun powder
	copper wire
tripe	lead ingots
rats on sticks	goat skins
smoked fish	raphia cloth
chicken	mats
yams	baskets
sweet potatoes	egg plant
manioc roots	corn
manioc bread	pepper
peas or beans	bananas
cabbage	ground nuts
green legumes	palm nuts
mushrooms	sugar cane
red earth	tobacco leaves
salt	calabashes of palm wine

In another market at Ngoyo, upstream from Manianga, in 1877, local items (left column) were exchanged for foreign goods (right column).[7]

bananas	cloth
pineapples	beads
guavas	wire (brass?) (*mitako*)
limes	guns
onions	powder
fish	crockery
casava bread (*chikwanga*)	
groundnuts	
palm butter	
earthenware pots	
baskets	
nets	

These items fill the major categories of resources in the *Lemba* region. Much of the list consists of locally-grown food, Malaysian and American. These items, perishable and thus not suited for long-distance trade, nevertheless constitute the mainstay of prestations used in local social transactions. Palm wine is the smallest unit of this exchange system, being measured either in terms of the "cup"—what one man can drink—or in terms of the calabash or the demijohn. The "cup" is an etiquette measure, used to open a transaction or ritual, to lodge a request, or to close a deal. It is an important sign in prayers and purification rites. The "chicken" is a larger unit in this system of exchange, used for interpersonal gifts as rewards or tokens of appreciation, as well as for sacrifices. Naturally, these uses imply the consumption of chicken, making it both a nutritional and a transactional resource. The "pig" is the largest unit in this social currency. It is not mentioned in the Mboko Nsongo market list, but from all evidence including the *Lemba* inauguration reported from the area, pigs were common and greatly appreciated. Pigs were reserved for major rituals in which their exchange constituted a sign of reconciliation or obligation met between clans. The pig was considered (and still is) the appropriate unit of recompense for human blood shed in a quarrel.

These three units—the "cup" (*mbungu*), the "chicken" (*n'susu*), and the "pig" (*n'gulu*)—should be considered abstract values in regional society, because they are frequently substituted for in concrete exchanges by other items or by currency of another sort. Palm wine is preferred in the "cup," but other natural wines, or European-type liqueurs in bottles, will do, as will cash. In a 1915 *Lemba* initiation in the Mboko Nsongo region, for example, mention is made of "pig of five baskets of raphia cloth."[8] In local parlance, the authentic items are identified as "wet" cups, and "blood" chickens or pigs, while substitution in cloth or money constitutes a "dry" cup, chicken, or pig. Goats and sheep may sometimes be substituted for pigs; however, wild game is not entered into this exchange system.

In the Mboko Nsongo market list several categories of items may be singled out as important in the legitimate trade following the slave trade, most of which continue to have a local use value. Foodstuffs include especially groundnuts and palmnuts and oil. Other items are long-standing trade items, and can be understood in terms of their historic uses. "Red earth for body paint" was a highly popular cosmetic but already a major export item in the seventeenth century for use in European textile dyes. Salt, which probably came from the coast, was cherished in seasoning and preservation. Remaining items relate to metalworking (copper wire, lead, gunpowder), and cloth "money" (raphia, baskets).

Mboko Nsongo constituted a strategic point in the mining region that extended to Mindouli. Copper, iron, and lead were the main ores mined, smelted, and sold to blacksmiths, jewelers, and traders. The copper trade around Mboko Nsongo alone constituted a major heavy industry. Dupont describes the largest of three mines in 1885, Songho, as a cut 250 meters long into a hillside, more than 10 meters deep in places. Such mines were owned by surrounding village communities and worked by local inhabitants. A special copper market once a week attracted buyers from all directions.[9] Mboko Nsongo's special "red" copper may have reached as far into the interior as the Alima River upstream on the Congo/Zaire,[10] and certainly in trade to Loango and Kongo coasts, where shipments as early as the seventeenth century are reported. For example, two ships sailed from Loango for Brazil in 1641 carrying 39,613 pounds of copper.[11] A trading agent on the coast estimated that the Loango coast—that is, its interior—could supply up to forty tons annually of the metal.[12] The most stable use over the centuries of copper from these mines, however, was in currency and jewelry. The *ngiele* copper rod is described variously as being as thick as a little finger and one inch long, or half an inch in diameter and three inches long, bent at the ends.[13] The rod constituted one of the region's main currencies until the 1880's when the European brass wire, the *mitako*, took its place in connection with colonial trade. The *ngiele* resembles the copper bracelet used for jewelry and for ritual in several orders of authority, especially *Lemba*. *Lemba*'s bracelets, poured into sand or clay molds in the ateliers of Vili and Yombe smith-jewelers, represented the artistic climax of this copperwork. Beyond *Lemba*'s borders, some lords of Tio wore such Vili-made copper bracelets with reliefs on them.[14] Even after imported European *mitako* brass money had replaced the copper *ngiele* as regional currency, the bracelets continued to be manufactured for *Lemba* initiation. Production of copper still continued in 1885 when Dupont visited Mboko Nsongo. Metals such as iron and lead were used for other specific purposes: iron for hoes, axes and adzes, knives and gun mechanisms; lead, sometimes for bracelets, but usually for gunshot.

The value of these metals, in trade or commercial power, varied over the centuries. I have found no exchange equivalents for the Manianga copper *ngiele*, although Vansina reports an exchange of one hundred *ngiele* (no doubt the smaller type) for one *ibuunu* of cloth among the Tio, and one hundred *nzi* shells for one *ngiele*.[15]

The *mitako* introduced by European traders had by 1880 become the colonial currency in the Mpumbu region at the east of the *Lemba* area. However, this unit, like the *ngiele*, soon experienced an inflationary spiral, reducing its value. On July 1, 1910, the Belgian colony introduced the Congo franc (5 francs = 1 *mpata*) as the currency of obligatory taxes; it also appeared in *Lemba*.

Cloth currencies seem over the centuries of coastal trade to have held a more stable valuation than metals. Raphia cloth, made from two types of palms, was a major exchange item in the sixteenth and seventeenth centuries when coastal trade began. Its smallest unit was the *libongo* (*mbongo*) or the *makute*, about the size of a large handkerchief, made on local looms. These raphia pieces were sewn together into a short loincloth, constituting what some coastal traders viewed as the "fathom"—one and one-half to two yards.[16] Raphia cloth continued to be woven in the twentieth century, and as *Lemba* initiation texts demonstrate, it continued to be used longest as ceremonial currency. However, very early on in the coastal trade European and Indian cloth came to be highly appreciated, both for its practical and stylish purposes in apparel and as a medium of exchange; in effect a major exchange item which, like raphia, tended not to lose its value as quickly as metal currencies. One type of cloth might replace another, but throughout the centuries units of cloth appeared in exchange for ivory, metal, slaves, guns, camwood, and within African society, for ritual purposes. Coastal trade established cloth as a common denominator of raphia, woven in the interior and used in internal transactions, and of the European unit known, depending on the language as the *pièce*, *péçà*, *long*, and *cortado*: a cloth approximately six yards in length—the same as the piece of cloth sold in the Kinshasa market in 1977!

Before correlating the various resources, currencies, and cloth units so as to glean an estimate of *Lemba*'s worth in these terms during the period from 1850 to 1920, we must consider the impact of slavery on the local society and economy. Internal slavery no doubt existed in the seventeenth century, but in terms of our twentieth-century understanding of the phenomenon, the internal slave status was both more humane, and more varied, than the international slave status. Bond slaves, debt slaves, war prisoners, hereditary but well-placed slaves, all had their place in society. Jural slave status did not always necessarily mean *de facto* low status. In *Lemba* we see how slaves often belonged to the ruling elite. None of this, however, makes the coastal slave trade less despicable.

International trade was by 1600 exporting copper, ivory, red camwood, and raphia cloth. With the diminution of ivory, and the increase in demand for slaves on American plantations, Loango coast rulers and trading officers—the *mafouk*—began by 1650 to supply slaves to their Dutch, Portuguese and English trading partners. Traffic that began as a trickle had by 1680 reached 4000 persons per year from Ngoyo, Cabinda, and Loango.[17] By 1750 in Cabinda alone, 5000 to 6000 slaves were being exported annually; by the 1780's the three ports of Malemba, Cabinda, and Loango Bay were processing 15,000 slaves annually.[18] At the beginning of the eighteenth century a slave was worth from ten to fifteen pieces of cloth or 350 *makoute* in raphia.[19] An increasingly favored item traded for slaves was the gun, obsolete castoffs from European arsenals. During the increase of the Congo coast slave trade in the early eighteenth century, a slave could be had for about eleven to twelve guns, each worth around thirty *makoute*, or half a *pièce* of cloth.[20] At its peak in the mid-to-late eighteenth century, the slave trade on the north-bank ports annually imported up to 50,000 guns and an assortment of other items against roughly 15,000 slaves.[21]

The volume of all trade declined during the late eighteenth century because of growing opposition to the slave trade, increasing police action on the high seas against it, and internally because of a growing scarcity of slaves and an attendant rise in the price. This increase has been calculated in terms of the *pièce* of cloth per slave for Cabinda and Malemba.[22]

1702–13	10 to 15 *pièces*
1750–60	20 to 30 *pièces*
1770	30 *pièces*
1770's	40+ *pièces*
1780's	54 *pièces* + 10 *pièces* brokerage fee

The volume of the slave trade continued to decline in the nineteenth century and had ended completely by 1870. "Legitimate" trade now took its place, with the internal suppliers providing ivory once more, gum copal, palm oil, nuts, groundnuts, pepper, malachite, and baobab bark, in exchange for tobacco, rum and other liquors, cloth, gunpowder, guns, and assorted manufactured goods.

Lemba's role in the trade will be discussed more fully in the next section of this chapter. Here the commercial value of certain aspects of *Lemba* may be situated in respect to the foregoing review of trade and exchange of resources. An argument has sometimes been made for the specificity of domains of exchange in traditional African economies; a given commodity or resource is said to be specific to certain types of social and commercial transactions.[23] Such a characteristic is minimal if not altogether missing in the *Lemba* economy; wherever exchange is recorded, equivalents between items are also given. We have seen that in the late-nineteenth-century marketplaces of Mboko Nsongo and Ngoyo near Manianga, both subsistence and trade items were on hand. The same holds true for the exchanges within *Lemba*, ostensively for "ritual" purposes. The mechanism of equivalence in all cases is the "wet wine/dry wine," "blood chicken/dry chicken" comparison, permitting a specific domain of transaction defined functionally by a given item—chicken or wine—to substitute for another item—cash.

The question has also been raised as to why, given this equivalency mechanism, no single currency emerged. The answer may be that any single currency is vulnerable to inflation, as demonstrated by the copper *ngiele* in long-distance trade, and in the brass wire *mitako* in the early colonial period. Furthermore, a given abstract and general currency tends to be only as stable as the political order of which it is ultimately a value symbol. There is greater security in the simultaneous use of several currencies or value symbols deriving from objects which meet widespread human needs, as do cloth, wine, chickens, and pigs. Thus, *Lemba* transactions, like those in the history of much of the trade, tend to occur in combinations (bundles) of items.

For example, a *Lemba* inaugural in the Mboko-Nsongo/Kingoyi/"Bakamba" region around 1910 (analyzed at length in Chapter 4) cost the neophyte priest and his clan twenty-five pigs, numerous chickens, palm wine, and manioc loaves. Since pigs are hardly mentioned in the international trade literature—for reasons having to do with the transportation of pigs—it is necessary to convert this cost to items already mentioned. The author of the report has given "equivalencies" of the payment of dues: "a pig of 5 *ntete* baskets, raphia cloth"; elsewhere in payment of his defilement, the priest collects "10 pigs or 1 person." The *Lemba* inauguration thus cost approximately twenty-five pigs, plus wine and chickens, and so forth; or 125 *ntete* baskets raphia at one pig/five baskets; or two and one-half persons, at ten pigs/one person. One person (slave) thus equalled fifty *ntete* baskets raphia in the Mboko Nsongo region at the turn of the century.

A report on *Lemba* from Yaa to the north gives as two persons the fee for the profanation of the *Lemba* priest (Text 2.23 below), a figure comparable to that in Mboko Nsongo. *Lemba*'s worth may be compared to yet other types of transactions at the turn of the century. At the Pool, where Vansina has extensively reported on equivalencies, a person varied in value from 200 *mitako* to upward of 1200, averaging around 500 to 600 *mitako*.[24] The only items which exceeded slaves in price were boats, at around 1000 *mitako*, and huge quantities of ivory (say 2,500 pounds for 12,500 *mitako*, thus five *mitako*/pound). In terms of these equivalencies, the *Lemba* inaugural would have cost anywhere from 1000 to 2000 *mitako*, at 1885 rates of exchange; that would be the price of a big boat, or 200 to 300 pounds of ivory.

Of course by 1910 the *mitako* had totally disappeared having been replaced by Belgian and French currency. Thereafter *Lemba* inaugurals begin to be paid in this currency. One *Lemba* inaugural in eastern Mayombe from the first decade of this century cost the neophyte and his supporters wine, chickens, manioc, and other banquet items, as well as two *mpidi* baskets raphia, two *nkwala* mats, and 565 francs, the equivalent of several years trading or wage labor. The bulk of the payment had here been converted to the new currency, although the inaugurated office was a continuation of the old.

However measured, *Lemba* may be seen as a significant institution in the region from the Pool to the ocean. I have tried to relate this significance quantitatively to *Lemba*'s inaugural fees, where such data are given. This measure of value may shift from subsistence resources such as chickens, wine, pigs, goats, etc., to labor power in slaves, to clothing and currency in raphia cloth and colonial "money." These quantitative measures do not however indicate just how *Lemba*'s qualitatively defined rights worked. I hope to show in subsequent parts of this book that *Lemba* arose with the copper and ivory "boom" of the seventeenth century, and remained a structuring institution for the era of heavy coastal trade that was to continue for several centuries. To the east this seventeenth-century development gave rise to the Tio order of lords, symbolized by the *nkobi* shrine basket, and in most places heavy copper bracelets worn by the lords and priests. *Lemba* priests and Tio lords converted their prowess in trade into social influence, becoming a mercantile elite which controlled—"calmed"—markets and trade and organized caravans.

Social Structure

Three centuries of trade with the coast established caravan routes across the north-bank territory; pulled out of their home communities hundreds of thousands of slaves and drove them over these routes to waiting ships; created floating "broker" colonies, tariff walls, invasions, and wars. Yet most ethnologies of the twentieth century describe the region's people and their organization in terms of territorially discrete tribes bounded by firm borders and identified with single names.[25]

To gain an historically accurate picture of the movements of people in the past 300 years in this region, it must be assumed that at various times the relatively quick wealth that was to be found in trade and resource exploitation unleashed great forces for change; the seventeenth-century "boom" in Manianga copper and inland ivory brought its "rushers" and "brokers," left its victims, and generally turned things topsy-turvy, and the eighteenth-century slave trade and the nineteenth-century legitimate trade on the coast had similar effects. The ethnic maps mentioned above tell us very little about wandering bands who came northward across the Zaire possibly toward the copper region, occupied the mines for a time, and settled there. Nor do such maps tell the story of Vili traders who came eastward from the coast, also seeking to capitalize on mining and trading and eventually settling in commercial enclaves up and down the coast and throughout the Lower Zaire where trade was the foremost public activity. Not only the Vili were thus involved in trade. Traders and caravans moved regularly across the entire area. At Manianga market, persons were noted in the 1880's from Ngoyo and Kakongo on the coast, Ntombo Mataka, Ngombi, Ilembi, Kingoma, Kilanga, Kinzore, Suki, Nguru; Mebelo, Zinga, and Nzabi up river, all coming into contact with those from Ndunga, Mbu, Bakongo, and Bassesse (a Tio group specialized in making raphia cloth).[26] These part-time traders could easily become full-time traders, as had the Pombieros at the Pool, or they could control trade as did the Yombe chiefs. All are to be compared to the Hausa, Lebanese, and Portuguese colonies of West and Equatorial Africa, the Indians of East Africa, or the Chinese of Indonesia. In all cases these ethnically identified groups acquired an identity linked with their trading profession.

An inverse process occurred too, in which populations of diverse origin "melted" into a single new identity defined by a locale or territory. By the nineteenth century the coastal "Vili," for example, included slave remnants from Teke, Yombe, Kongo, Songe, Mondongo, Bayangela, Babongo, Bayansi, Mboma, Sundi, Mbamba, and Mbete.[27] Also, many south-bank populations fled en masse north-ward from 1885 on, to escape colonial labor caravan recruitment.[28]

The Sundi invasion of the north bank of the Zaire from the seventeenth century on, and the way it has been recorded, is the most annoying example of confusion in the literature. Ethnographers such as Laman (edited by Lagercrantz), Soret, and Murdock have identified the central-north-bank "Sundi" and have shown spearheads of Sundi occupation extending northeastward into Teke country, northwest into Kamba and Kunyi country, and westward into Yombe country.[29] Ethnographers, like some Sundi informants, suggest that the regions were "uninhabited" in the seventeenth century and that the Sundi moved in without resistance to create their homogeneous culture. Closer probing and circumstantial evidence indicate the contrary. "Sundi" or "Kongo" communities often subjugated "Teke" mining camps, obliging the smiths and craftsmen to work under their hegemony. At Nsundi-Masiki (Lutete, BaKongo) south of Mindouli, these Nsundi immigrants moved alongside other groups such as the Kimbanga with extremely deep local genealogies and old cemeteries, and an affinity to Teke clans (Kimbanga = Imbaaw). The Sundi thus situated themselves among pre-existing populations, intermarried with them, and declared their Kongo-oriented hegemony over them.

The most serious difficulty in the studies positing a homogeneous ethnic group in Lower Zaire is their distortion of the organizational principles of the north-bank societies. Scholars who identify an indigenous equivalent for "tribe" or "*ethnie*" usually use the term *mvila* (also *luvila*, pl. *tuvila*). Deleval, for example, does this, but then wonders why so many people in the north "Yombe" are ignorant of their "tribe."[30] This query suggests that he may have been dealing with slaves who have no legal genealogical identity, and that like many other scholars he misunderstood the character of the *mvila*. The *mvila*—given such names as Nsundi, Manianga, Bwende, Kuimba, Yombe, etc.—should be defined as an exogamous, matrilineal descent category traced back to a putative common ancestor, with emphasis on its categorial nature. The *mvila* is not primarily an organized group; it is rather an element in a social worldview within which nine or twelve exogamous and therefore intermarrying *tuvila* are posited to have existed "in the beginning," and from which various bifurcations and branches may be traced. The list of particular names included in this set varies from version to version and from region to region; along the Zaire it tends to link with a royal, Kongo origin legend (*tuuka Kongo dia Ntootila*). In one area in the Mayombe it has to do with the westward movement of Manianga refugees in a great famine.[31] The persistence of these origin legends which integrate numerous *tuvila* into one scheme, and the *de jure* exogamic principle defining a single *mvila*, suggest quite clearly that this unit cannot be a homogeneous territorial "tribe" as the culture-area ethnographers would have it. It is a matrilineal descent category, a clan.

The *dikanda* (pl. *makanda*) by contrast is the local organization which carries the same name. For example, one may be a member of the Nsundi clan because one's mother was Nsundi; one lives in or is a member of a Nsundi *dikanda*. These "local" clan sections may ordinarily be found in three closely proximate settlements, each inhabited also with other clan sections of other extended clans. While the extended clan is the category of origin, and is exogamic only in principle, the *dikanda* bearing the same name is the organized exogamic group. The internal communities of exogamic and corporate local clan sections (*dikanda*), led by either a single head (*mfumu nsi*) or a type of committee executive, help each other in defense of their common land, in assembling alliance prestations, and in warfare where they are prohibited from killing one another "because they are of the same blood." These local clan sections are thus genealogically defined through memorized records used in time of need such as land defense, identification of a person's rights, and a variety of other situations.

Because these local clan sections are genealogically chartered, incorporated, and land-based, in time they experience natural segmentary growth. Junior, senior, and middle "houses" (*nzo*) emerge, each expecting its parcel of land in the local clan estate and its place "around the fire" in the men's house, that is, expecting to participate in collective clan affairs. Under certain circumstances the "house" may become the effective exogamous unit.[32]

Within the "house" are found lineages (*mwelo-nzo*, "door of the house"). These are residential clusters in settlements. They are also the effective familial units within which decisions regarding personal life and production are made. Rey has emphasized the former strategic importance of this unit among the Kunyi in organizing slavery and has devised the term "lineage mode of production" to characterize it.[33] It is the effective unit through which the "natural" matrilineal unit augments its productive and reproductive potential. As MacGaffey has pointed out, a woman's reproductive capacity cannot be transferred by rules of matrilineality alone;[34] there must be some form of nonmatrilineal recruitment such as slavery or clientage to augment the unit, to form a new estate out of the old one over time, to use Gluckman's phrase.[35]

The major alternative principle of recruitment is, of course, patrifiliality (*kise*, from *se*, father), which in native thought contrasts to matrilineality (*kingudi*, from mother), the normative principle for the formation of the clan, local section, house, and lineage. Most persons can identify their matrilineage and clan, knowing who their mothers are. However, patrifilial identity is the distinct mark of a freeman (*mfumu dikanda*), one whose relations to his "four corners of character" (*ndambu ziiya za muntu*) are legitimated by his own, his father's (his *kise*), his mother's father's, and his father's father's lines.

Patrifiliality and matrilineality are rooted in the ideology of descent which, while varying some across the territory being surveyed, generally regards matrilineality (*kingudi*) as a type of container for the individual, conveying membership in a group; whereas patrifiliality is thought of as the spiritual nurturance or identity, strengthened in the fetal stage by the semen of the father, which turns into blood creating the personality. Among the Vili and Yombe this paternal substance has been called *xina*, a name and a prohibition; inland it does not bear this name, but its contents are identical. Normative naming practices hyphenate a man's name to his father's. Filiation is thus, strictly speaking, bilateral in that a person traces his links if possible to all ascending groups, both patrifilial and matrilineal. However, descent is best characterized as double unilineal according to which principle complementary rights and links come togther into the individual. Local and general clan membership are always gained consanguineally, from the mother. Spiritual identity, personality, and perhaps the name are gained agnatically from the father.

The leading premise which flows from the foregoing beliefs is that an individual, indeed human society itself, must contain both principles, complementarily, to be complete. This theme is repeated at many levels of organization such as kinship terminology; it is the basis of judicial decisions on incest and marriage; it is present in much ritual, such as the *Lemba* inaugural; and it is articulated in legends.

Kinship terminology distinguishes the two ideas in the first ascending generation of one's immediate parentage by calling one's father and his classificatory brothers "*se*" (pl. *mase*), or "*tata*," and calling the father's uterine and classificatory sisters "female fathers" (*se dia nkento*). Conversely, mother and her classificatory sisters are termed "mother" (*ngudi*), and her brothers, uterine and classificatory, "male mothers" (*ngudi nkazi*). Thus the male/female, patrifilial/matrilineal dichotomy is incorporated into the immediate organization of kin. The alternative ascending generation is, however, again labelled uniformly as "*nkaka*," uterine and classificatory grandparent on both sides. One's own generation terms are also lumped together with reference to siblings, both uterine and classificatory brothers ("*mpangi*") and sisters ("*nkazi*" or "*busi*").

The first generation descending, is, like the first ascending, distinguished according to one's own embodiment of the matrilineal and patrifilial principles. A male ego speaks of the children within his own local clan or lineage as "*bana bankazi*," reckoned by the female principle; a female ego calls her own children "*bana*," but generalizes within her own clan to speak of "*bana bankazi*." By contrast, a person speaking of the first descending generation of children born to a local clan's or lineage's male members would call them "patrifilial children" (*bana bambuta*), children born to the clan or lineage, applying the complementary patrifilial principle (*kise* or *kimbuta*).

The role of the patrifilial children (*bana bambuta*) needs to be emphasized in connection with the principle of complementarity and of primary-group formation. In a given community, they are natural allies in that, having grown up in the midst of their fathers, they share common spiritual paternal substance (*kise*). They act as priests and arbiters on behalf of their fathers, conducting burials and mediating all contacts between the living and the ancestors of their fathers' matrilineage, as well as intervening in time of crisis—for example, segmentation rituals to guarantee peace. Finally, they act as political supporters and priests in creating and inaugurating consecrated offices of authority. Their role is crucial in the *Lemba* rites.

The ability of the local clan thus to retain its children, either as allies scattered throughout adjacent communities, or as continuing residents in their birthplace, depends on prowess in providing them with a livelihood in land, trade, or other form of support and opportunity. Normally, a free male child (*mwana*) goes to live with his mother's brothers at puberty; a girl (also *mwana*) when she marries moves to reside with her husband. Should the husband die, or they divorce, she would be free, with her children, to move to her clan home with her brothers and maternal uncles. Hereditary slaves or others lacking a means of livelihood in their home clan could prevail on their fathers to offer them a temporary opportunity; the fathers, in turn, could attract their children with such generosity in the hope of creating a following. Such people were often called "people wealth" (*bantu mbongo*) or "children of the village" (*bana bavata*). In the precolonial period a large clientele could be assembled in short order by the establishment of a landed estate, proper marriage policies, and the retention of both one's clan children (*bankazi*) and one's patrifilial children (*bambuta*), thereby making the village or town the dominant political unit (*mbanza*). There is some evidence that *Lemba* concentrated on strategic alliances between clans and their patrifilial children.

Marriage within the local clan is regarded as incestuous, both for spiritual and practical political reasons. However, marriage could be used effectively to build up the clan's following and to keep its own people together by retaining slaves and dependent clans, and by marrying and reproducing extensively with these local groups. Power was proportional to the number of people that could be organized into such a local unit—the unit of production—or into a cluster of several under one head. But the major drawback of such an approach to organization and influence was that it isolated the community of intermarrying clans and lineages, rendering it vulnerable to encroachments from its neighbors, and cutting it off from trade and exchange partners. In other words, although this was and is an attractive possibility for the short-run acquisition of influence and power, it is beset with dangers.

The solution to this dilemma was marriage with influential clans and lineages in neighboring settlements, thereby creating alliances which could be used to maintain peace and commerce. A survey of the north-bank region reveals two basic approaches to political organization through marriage: the *endogenous* approach, in which one marries within the local polity and settlement; and the *exogenous* approach, in which one marries between polities and settlements. The former tended to be used as a strategy to centralize power, wealth, and offices of authority; the latter, as a strategy to create regionally interlocking networks. In the former matrilateral cross-cousin marriage or a classificatory equivalent prevailed, in the latter, patrilateral cross-cousin marriage or its classificatory equivalent. Both could be found together in specific communities, with the one or the other receiving conscious preference.

The significance of this differential structuring of marriage types has been worked out at great length in the social-anthropological literature.[36] The salient points for our purposes are the following. If the matrilateral cross-cousin marriage form is not carried out as a so-called "circulating connubium," it becomes an asymmetrical relationship between unequal groups in which the offspring's position may be controlled. In the region with which we are concerned, a lineage or clan that can exercise influence over its female children and get them to marry its women's sons succeeds in short-circuiting the bride payment normally made to fathers and benefits politically as "fathers" or patrons of the offspring. This is above all true if such daughters are members of client groups, residing with and bound to their fathers' group.

In the patrilateral cross-cousin marriage, by contrast, women-giving over several generations becomes a reciprocal act between two exogamous groups which, because the bride's father is not also the mother's brother of the groom, tends to be a significant exchange of wealth each time an alliance is extended. Furthermore, this exchange, because reciprocal, enhances the status of the wife-giver at each juncture in the relationship, since goods are received in compensation for or as a gauge against the services and well-being of the bride. In practice this type of marriage relationship is maintained between landed free clan sections, or between lords and their dependents who, although in a status of jural subservience, in fact command sufficient people and wealth that they receive the recognition of status equals.

Alliance ideology recognized the integral contributions of the patrilateral cross-cousin marriage to the high ideal of "blood reciprocity" (*mvutudulu a menga*), the return of descent substance to its point of origin in a marriage transaction. The son who married his father's sister's daughter—or a classificatory equivalent—did this. In the central *Lemba* region such a person was pointedly named Masamba, one who crosses over, returns, or clears the way (*sambila*, *samba*) between two groups.

Kinship terminology in the central *Lemba* region reflects the preferred status of such a return-blood marriage. Same-generational patrilateral kinsmen are frequently called "grandparents" (*nkaka*), whereas their matrilateral counterparts are termed "grandchildren" (*ntekolo*). One's "fathers" (*mase*) are of a higher status: to marry into their group or to receive a wife from them is to marry "up." Furthermore, one is thereby balancing the credit sheet of the alliance relationship or even establishing a mutually enhancing exchange relationship which will stand well in the subsequent generation.

This discussion of the structural principles of north-bank social organization—probably of all local societies of the *Lemba* region—has established a basis for demonstrating how explicit policies and historical forces created alternative patterns of public order.

Throughout the north-bank region there were localized estates or domains known as *nsi*, or *tzi* (pl. *zitsi*) whose chief, *mfumu nsi*, was a lineal descendent (or proxy) of the dominant clan section of the locality. The *nsi* was land based, and right to its estate was claimed by asserting prior arrival and attachment to the lineal group possessing the area's main cemetery grove (*makulu*). Chiefship of the domain was consecrated to ancestor spirits buried in the grove, or to BiKinda, Simbi, earth, water, or other fixed spirits at that location. The domain frequently bore the same name as the chief. Where such domain chiefs consolidated their power, their identity could take the place of inhabitants' clan identities.[37] Under such circumstances the clan (*luvila*) of the chief of the domain (*nsi*) could, drawing on the power of the cult to the local spirit, gain prominence throughout an area and take on the appearance of a homogeneous cultural zone which ethnographers have mistakenly called "tribes"—Sundi, Mbenza, Mpudi a Zinga, for example.

The emergence of such a dominant clan domain created another problem, with its own unique solution. If a ruling clan became all pervasive in an area, absorbing lineages and children to itself, with whom did its members marry, given the clan endogamy prohibition? One solution (the endogenous approach) has already been illustrated, namely the mating of nobles or aristocrats with their clients, dependents, and slaves, that is their patrifilial children. The difficulty in this approach is that it isolates the endogamous group in an instable asymmetric marriage system. Another solution often chosen was for the dominant clan to segment into two separate entities through sacrifice of a pig, a ritual act intended to "sever" the unified blood. The ease with which a symbolic solution to a structural problem was found indicates the ideological nature of descent blood as an expression of corporate strength. Nsundi enclaves on the north bank are known to have taken this solution to the above dilemma.

In addition to these solutions of relatively greater centralization and relatively lesser centralization, there is a third alternative which became the *Lemba* organizational model. Where *Lemba* achieved its greatest structural consistency, on the periphery of and between kingdoms and aristocratic domains (*zinsi*), symmetrical marriage relationships were maintained between members of modest clan estates, *as well as with* their influential dependents, clients, and slaves. The marriage form sanctioned by *Lemba* was the symmetrical exchange between relatively powerful local clans. Only a "reciprocal blood" marriage of the type that would most readily have been the patrifilial cross-cousin marriage would have fit this expectation. Such a marriage stimulated exchange of moveable goods—an expected goal in a mercantile society; it wove a fabric of peaceful ties between communities, thus overcoming isolationistic tendencies; and it created a *nonterritorial estate* which emphasized movement, trade, influence, knowledge, and the maintenance of horizontal relationships across the dividing lines of local societies. It is fitting that the name of such an estate should have been "peace," *Lemba*, and the self-image of its rituals, therapy.

Political Systems of the Lemba *Region*

Thus far in this chapter I have sketched the natural resources of the *Lemba* region and the way subsistence exploitation as well as trade in these resources tied the various sectors of production into a complex economy. The great influx of trade in the seventeenth century brought this regional economy into integral involvement with the international economy of the maritime nations. I then sketched the social organization of the region, noting that this trade—especially the slave trade—introduced major upheavals, migrations, and power shifts into the populace, so that to speak of organization one must note movements of people. The common social structure of the region provided the terms of localized variations, particularly in marriage practices and offices of authority.

In this section I shall elaborate more fully on the distinct institutional forms that emerged within the common social structure: first, the coastal kingdoms of Loango, KaKongo, Ngoyo, Vungu, and the Yombe chiefdoms; second, the Teke federation in the east; third, the Nsundi enclaves which play a prominent role in this region's history; finally, I shall give fullest attention to "life between the kingdoms," where *Lemba* took on its most sophisticated form as "government medicine."

THE COASTAL KINGDOMS

The literature offers several alternative origins of the coastal kingdoms of Loango, KaKongo, Ngoyo, and Vungu: either origin from a common northern parent kingdom, Ngunu, or secession from the Kongo kingdom, or separation from one another. Despite this ambiguity over origins, the literature is clear that these kingdoms predate the coastal European trade and that they have similar historical structure.[38]

The internal structure of these kingdoms rested on the local chief of a given area and the resources and spirits of the earth. The chiefs paid tribute to the intermediary level of authority, usually the provincial governors, who paid it to the ruler himself, the MaLoango, the MaKongo, and the MaNgoyo. Each king maintained control over coastal trade within his kingdom, organized through a minister of trade (*mafouk*), for each of the three major ports, Loango Bay in Loango, Malemba in KaKongo, and Cabinda in Ngoyo. The international trade system was therefore controlled through the same centralizing structure as the internal tribute system. In Loango, where the provincial centralizing structure is best described and most likely to have been significant because of the local seat of Loango as a kingdom, the provincial governorship was an integral part of the maintenance of the overall structure. In the seventeenth century, Loango was ruled by a matrilineally related series of brothers or cousins, princes of the Kondi clan, who acceded to the throne after having successively held the provincial governorships. These provinces, Cane (Caye), Bukkameale, Dingy, and Kesok, were ruled by the governors called respectively Manicaye, Manibock, Manisalag, and Manicabango. On the death of the MaLoango, office holders of the provinces would shift to another province, Manicaye becoming the new MaLoango, Manibock becoming Manicaye, Manisalag becoming Manibock, Manicabango becoming Manisalag, and a new Manicabango being appointed from the ruling dynasty's princes.[39] Whether KaKongo and Ngoyo developed this system to the same extent as Loango is not clear.[40] In Kongo, where the candidate to the throne was also known as ManiKai, the leading dynasty had broken into two factions by the seventeenth century, suggesting that succession was as often from father to son as from brother to brother.[41] By the eighteenth century—thus by the time of accelerated coastal trade—this condition, which Europeans found detracted from royal power, had appeared also in Loango. Patrilateral succession suggested that power was shared by two intermarrying dynastic lines within an enduring state structure.

In Loango, as in the other coastal kingdoms, the king was spoken of as the "supreme lawgiver and protector of the people, the ultimate sanction of all administrative activities on a local and national level" who held a semi-divine status—a unique relationship with Nzambi the Creator—holding the title of *Ntotela*, supreme ruler, *Ntinu*, supreme judge.[42] Rituals of first fruits, rainmaking, and eating and drinking in isolation were attributed to him. The lighting of a central state flame maintained throughout his rule was part of the MaLoango's inauguration; it was distributed to the provinces, offering a source of fire to the people's hearths. Despite its prominence over Ngoyo and KaKongo and the divine trappings of its king, Loango was dependent on its southern neighbor for the ritual observance of the oracle to Bunzi, earth deity, whose main shrine was located in Ngoyo territory. In the late nineteenth century the relationship between the three rulers was seen in Loango as that of husband Loango (*nunni*) to wife KaKongo (*mokassi*), with Ngoyo as priest (*itomma*), terms that crop up to describe many ceremonial relationships including *Lemba*.[43] In Ngoyo, on the other hand, the three kingdoms of the coast were seen as having equal status in Bunzi's pantheon, with the first rulers being brothers born to the union of Bunzi, a female deity, with MeMbinda, the first human.[44] In all instances there existed a complementarity between cult and capital, priest and king, similar to that which existed in chiefdoms of the region (the *nsi*) and kingdoms, all of whom either participated in the shrine of Bunzi or some equivalent earth or water or place deity. The king's power, as reflected by these several cultic arrangements of Nansi and the earth shrine Bunzi, was shared with a female and priestly element. In the structure of the kingdoms the queen mother and princesses of the royal clan held prominent, legislative authority, helping represent the interests of the royal clan and themselves being the ground in which were born future leaders. In Loango this female figure was called the *Makunda*, either queen mother or sister to the MaLoango who protected interests of women throughout the kingdom and sometimes took over ruling clan interests during the interregnum.[45]

In addition to the female dimension of power embodied in the Makunda role and the Bunzi shrine, alternative power was held by the cadaver priest (*Nganga Mvumbi*), an interregnum figure who took over the kingdom and ruled until the new king could be inaugurated. In Loango, where this system is best described, the Nganga Mvumbi became relatively permanent in the eighteenth and nineteenth centuries because of the inability of the royal clan to consolidate its power and to stage the very costly inauguration of a king, part of which was the lavish burial of the incumbent. By the end of the nineteenth century in Loango, cadaver priests were already succeeding each other, and the interregnum of MaLoango had gone on for decades! Corresponding to this disintegration of kingship, trade control along the coast became dispersed among many brokers (*mafouk*) whose brokerage role had spread quite thin, each controlling only a small section of the total trade.

While the kingdoms on the coast are described as having progressively lost their power, falling to forces of disorganization from the eighteenth century on, the opposite can be said for the chiefdoms of the Yombe interior. Although these chiefdoms continued to pay token tribute to coastal kings, their own fortunes had risen through trade along the caravan routes into the interior. What few accounts exist of caravans suggest that great wealth was to be made from taxes levied on caravan organizers. Although eighteenth-century and earlier sources may not have been aware of the political structure of trade in the interior, late nineteenth-century accounts describe the existence of a tariff wall, made of poles and bamboo, between the Guena (Loeme?) and Kwilu Rivers at the boundary between the coastal Vili in the kingdom and the forest of Mayombe, allowing passage at only three points where brokers gathered taxes on all merchandise imported or exported.[46] Veistroffer observed in 1880 that the "king of mayombe" had reduced this to a single passage.[47] Others described further tariff walls and gates to the east of the Mayombe in the direction of Kunyi territory.[48] German merchant Robert Visser relates that the Mayombe trade barriers on the Loango were broken through by force as late as 1885 by the steamer *Pollux*.[49]

These Yombe who ruled as either hereditary clans or nineteenth-century "nouveau riches" created by control of the trade were legitimated by the same general religious concepts and symbols as the coastal kingdoms. In addition to the genealogical legends of the division of society into eight,[50] nine,[51] or twelve original and many more *de facto nsi*,[52] earth deity Bunzi was central to these symbols. Further charms were collected by Yombe chiefs as they were created and became available, such as the *nkisi tsi* cult.[53] The chief of Tseke Banza in Mayombe, for example, who had amassed a fortune on the slave trade, retained the right of investiture over subchiefs in his mini-kingdom for the price of two slaves, in exchange for all sorts of "fetish powers."[54]

Historians of coastal political entities become very uncertain about the late eighteenth century; they are prone to complain, as does Martin, that losses of political coherence occur for reasons that the literature does not document well: "By 1770, the Mayombe hinterland was a collection of small independent chieftancies. When and why this happened is not clear from the sources."[55] Closer attention to the social history of the region in terms of control of this trade and the structuring of society into a network of interconnected marriage and trading partners gives a fuller picture of the situation. It also allows us to indicate the role of *Lemba* as a legitimating symbol and social institution.

Already by the seventeenth and eighteenth centuries, observers were suggesting that the coastal kingdoms, with their matrilineal dynasties, often broke up into contesting factions and, permitting patrifilial succession, constituted rather fragile state systems by comparison to European states of the time. The kings married polygynously, usually with commoner and client women. Through sheer numbers these women and their children (*bana*) provided the rulers with political support and prestige. Noblemen married similarly, although on a smaller scale, only sparingly marrying noblewomen. These latter, by contrast, married monogamously, usually with a client or slave male, and sometimes they did not marry at all, retaining a series of male concubines. Noblewomen were closely guarded, since they were the mothers of potential rulers, and the noble male progeny had to be restricted as narrowly as possible to avoid succession feuds in the royal clan. The queen mother herself, who could choose her spouse or lover(s), was closely guarded by her brothers and uncles.[56]

This account, referring mainly to Loango, falls well within the picture of social structure drawn up earlier. But it is a variation well on the "endogenous" end, in which noble or aristocratic matrilineages protectively restrict their consanguineal offspring (from their women), while prodigiously producing "people power" (*mbongo-bantu*) from their males.

Hyacinthe de Bologne, a very observant early-eighteenth-century Capucin, describes in vivid detail the behavior of the princes of Sonyo, among the Solongo, farther to the south but still within the region that was becoming *Lemba* area. Father Hyacinthe noted that it was respectable for the groom to pay a bride price to the bride's family after she had borne a child. This payment obligated him to her for his lifetime, with the sanction of both their families. However, the princes were in the habit of doing something additional which Hyacinthe regarded as "coutume vraiment païenne!" They would contract a bride payment with one woman, and then go off and have children by another, leaving the first union unconsummated. He had difficulty understanding this bizarre form of marriage—"ce mariage disordonné"—which occurred primarily among the prominent people of the land, rarely among the commoners, and never among slaves.[57] What was also bad, in Hyacinthe's view, was that the fifteen or so "seigneurs" of Sonyo who paraded around as legitimate heirs to the throne—when there should have been only one—preferred to marry in this manner with their close relatives, even their "sisters." Hyacinthe advised priests to beware of the lords of Sonyo who would try to trick the church into sanctioning such a marriage not allowed by ecclesiastical law. For example, Don Compte Barreta de Sylva wanted to marry Dame Lucie Barrett (*sic*), his sister-in-law. He told the priests that he had paid the bride price for one Marie Nquemque. But when the time came for the ceremony in church, Dame Lucie was brought in disguised as Marie Nquemque, whereupon the priest announced he would excommunicate anyone who tried "marriage fraud," and had the charade stopped.[58] Most of the 400 marriages that Hyacinthe had performed were among commoners. The nobility and royalty desired to marry their close kin in the church, but would rarely consummate these relationships.

The picture that emerges of alliance patterns on the coast in the early eighteenth century is one in which the landowning freemen, nobility and royalty, marry close relatives who happen to fall within the Roman church's restricted list, presumably between cousins. Hyacinthe is not clear as to the degree of cousin, but the church forbids first cousins, parallel and cross. These cousin marriages are those in which the bride payment is used, *per contractum*, but they are the marriages which often are not consummated. On the other hand, these princes frequently have several "concubines" and other wives, with whom they have many children. Among commoners and slaves contractual marriages are consummated.

Hyacinthe reserved his most severe judgement, however, for an ancillary "pagan" rite performed in connection with the noble or royal marriages, contracted but frequently left unconsummated. The wife is obliged to "marry with the devil," and then she enjoys superintendence over the other wives of her husband. Only her sons succeed to paternal inheritance.[59] This combination of a marriage between lineages of high status, for apparently political alliance reasons, with ritual as well as economic sanctioning, and in which sons of the woman accede to their father's positions, would describe exactly the set of practices known as *Lemba*.[60]

In due course the princes of Sonyo, Ngoyo, KaKongo, and Loango succumbed to the threats and promises of the European missionaries and began to have children within monogamous unions between noble and royal clans. The direct consequence of this action was to increase significantly the number of legitimate heirs to the thrones, thereby virtually guaranteeing the disintegration of the matrilineal royal succession process. If Hyacinthe's "marriage with the devil" on the part of noble and royal women was indeed *Lemba*, it would have offered an alternative alliance structure to the narrow royal household, with one queen mother, a king, her brother, and only one or two contending princes. It would have constituted a sanctioned alliance between several prominent exogamous clans.

Evidence that we are dealing with *Lemba* here comes from further sources. A nearly identical marriage structure is reported among the late-nineteenth-century and early-twentieth-century Kavati (*nsi*) domain of Madula, in the north Yombe, inland from Loango. Noblewomen rarely marry. It is their custom to keep a series of male concubines until they tire of such an arrangement. Having borne only a few children, they live out their later years in their "home" lineage settlements with their brothers. They take on chiefly roles, and if especially winsome, make diplomatic calls to vassal chiefs to collect tribute. Those few noblewomen who marry formally are exchanged in marriage with their counterparts in neighboring domains and villages to stabilize the two groups' relationships. Noblemen marry polygynously, mostly with slave women. Commoners and slaves marry, as they can, with an exchange of the bride price. But the formal noble marriages between domains and villages are usually made in *Lemba*.[61] These accounts all suggest that *Lemba* emerged within the broadening power base of coastal populations in the seventeenth and eighteenth centuries when the coastal kingdoms were experiencing their initial trade upsurge with European merchants.

In this setting, *Lemba* was one of the large corporate sacred medicine cults (*min'kisi*) of the region. It is helpful to describe this ritual context briefly. In Loango an excellent historical record of medicines provides a "barometer" of change from the seventeenth to the twentieth centuries. The earliest direct reference to *Lemba* is Dapper's in the 1660's, where it was seen in the royal court.

> *Malemba* is a *moquissie* of great significance, worthy to be seen as sacred by the king, for whose bodily health it serves: for, as long as he does not become ill, he is surely kept well by it. It consists of a small four-cornered mat one-and-a-half feet large, with a string at the top, on which are hung several small calabashes, cuttlebones, feathers, dry shells, iron bits, bones,

> and such things, all colored with *tukula*-red which represents in this connection something special. To celebrate it a boy takes a small drum and strikes it in a distinctive way, accompanied by the resonance of rattling shell whistles. To this is added spitting of consecrated kola, and annointment with *tukula* and consecrated water out of a small pot with an asperge onto the *moquissie*, then onto the body of the *nganga*, then that of the king, to the accompaniment of singing or chanting appropriate to the occasion. Even the nobility who are in attendance receive for their efforts annointment of their bodies of a few red stripes (of *tukula*), receiving thereby the honor of *Lemba*, which they then carry away and hang in its place, its small pot, its asperge and satchel.[62]

Other major public medicines noted by Dapper in seventeenth-century Loango included *Tiriko*, a shrine located in nearby Boarie, with four anthropomorphic pillars to hold up the roof. The priest of *Tiriko*, accompanied by a boy, daily prayed for the health of the king and the well-being of the land, as well as the growth of crops, the luck of merchants and fishermen.

Boessi-Batta was another *n'kisi* of major importance focused on bringing into one's homestead objects acquired in long-distance trade, thus especially pertinent to merchants. It consisted of several parts: a large lion-skin sack filled with all sorts of shells, iron bits, herbs, tree bark, feathers, ore, resin, roots, seeds, rags, fishbones, claws, horns, teeth, hair and nails of albinos and other "unnatural" creatures (*ndondos*); to this satchel were added two calabashes covered with shells (*Schnackenhörnern*, *simbos*) and topped with a bush of feathers, decorated with iron hooks, and colored with *tukula* wood (red). Atop this calabash a mouth-like orifice had been carved, into which was poured wine to activate the *n'kisi*. The whole set of objects, satchel and calabashes, was placed atop a table-like construction outside the door of the house. When they would go out to fetch merchandise, even at a distance, adherents to *Boessi-Batta* would take the moveable part along with them, even though it weighed ten to twelve pounds. The *n'kisi* appears to have paralleled the movement of articles of trade. On returning with new wares, the priest would draw lines on his body and incant in a rising tone of voice as he unpacked the *n'kisi* ingredients. Presently his eyes would exorbit, and he would become possessed by the spirit of *Tiriko*. Drinking a liquid to calm himself, he would declare the wish of *Boessi-Batta*, the fee, and measure to be taken or other *min'kisi* to be used.[63]

Another *n'kisi* of seventeenth-century Loango was *Kikokoo*, an anthropomorphic wooden shrine standing in the seaside village of Kinga, at the side of a large cemetery common to the region, perhaps to Loango Bay itself. *Kikokoo* protected the dead against witches (*doojes* [*ndoki*?]) who in their nocturnal craft would drag off the souls of the dead to slavery and forced labor. *Kikokoo* also was to assure the arrival of ships with fish and merchandise.

N'kisi Bomba was celebrated, noted Dapper, in a special feast associated with the coming out of the *Khimba* initiates dressed in a head garb of feathers and skirts of palm raphia, and carrying a red and white hand rattle. He noted their frenzied drumming, their mock-mad behavior. This is the final public phase of the *Khimba* initiation which according to later observers included adoration of Mbumba Luangu, the rainbow serpent.

Other *min'kisi* reported by Dapper included *Makongo*, consisting of rattles, drums, small sacks, and red fish hooks; *Mimi*, a small house shrine in a banana grove with a throne holding a basket of objects including a "paternoster" of seashells and a wooden statue of Father Masako (?); *Kossi*, a sack of white snail shells, filled with white clay, used in rites of crawling between one anothers' legs, eating, washing, donning bracelets and bands of protection against lightning, thunder, and sickness; *Kimaje*, a pile of potsherds on which priests deposit old ragged caps and other worn out ritual paraphernalia and dedicate their new replacements, so as to assure the new moon and new year's coming, as well as protection on the seas; *Injami*, a shrine found in a village near Loango, represented in a huge statue in a house; *Kitauba*, a huge wooden gong used in swearing the oath or sending sickness to another; *Bansa*, another statue covered with red powder; *Pongo*, a "wooden" calabash or container covered with shells (*simbos*) and filled with many carved symbols, used in "black magic"; and *Moanzi*, a pot partially buried in the ground between dedicated trees, holding an arrow and a string on which hung green leaves, and whose adherents wore copper armrings and avoided eating kola.[64]

This seventeenth-century inventory of *min'kisi* sharpens the impression we already have of Loango. The kingdom is still intact, as repeated reference to the well-being of the king suggests. Many shrines and medicines combine the well-being of the king with plentiful harvests, good fishing expeditions, abundant trade goods, and control of rain, a common attribute of centralized African power. *Lemba* is referred to as a "big" *n'kisi*, and in many respects Dapper's account resembles later accounts, including the ritual elements and the emphasis on a gentry. This is however the only account of *Lemba* that includes a king in the rite.

There is some indication, in the symbolism of the *min'kisi Kikokoo* and *Boesi-Batta* that the kingdom is beset by serious problems resulting from trade, including the slave trade. *Kikokoo*'s characteristics are laced with slave-trade attributes, the theft of souls, their forced work, and the coming in of trade goods. *Boessi-Batta* appears even more sharply to express the concern for protecting the inner world of the household and homestead from the danger of things brought from afar. However this sense of protection at the house door is ambiguously charged with attractiveness of these same goods. The importance of *Boessi-Batta* in seventeenth-century Loango is indicated by the fact that it was exported with African slaves to Haiti, where, as shall be seen in Chapter 8, significant symbols of the contrast of the household with the beyond remain in the Bosu shrine of voodoo ceremonialism. Objectively, the seventeenth century saw the control of trade by the kings of coastal kingdoms, through their brokers, slipping from them into the hands of a mercantile elite. This elite, on the coast as well as inland, was mostly synonymous with the *Lemba* priesthood. The shifting base of power growing from control of the trade was also reflected in the structure of shrines. Generally, fixed territorial shrines such as *Tiriko*, *Kikokoo*, *Mimi*, *Kimaje*, and *Bunzi* did not get transported across the ocean in the rites and lives of slaves, as did some of the "portable" shrines or medicines. However, the fixed shrines such as *Bunzi* moved beyond the orbit of royal families and their priests, and came to be found in various chiefdoms (*zinsi*) of the coast and Mayombe, even inland as far as Kibunzi, in the form of what later observers called "pseudo-*Bunzi*" shrines and cults.

By the mid-nineteenth century, for which better sources are available on Loango's *min'kisi* system, a picture emerges that is quite different from Dapper's seventeenth-century account. The fate of the centralized, earth-cult inspired kingdoms on the coast is such that little mention is made of the king, let alone his well-being. Trade, adjudication, thief- and witch-finding medicine is widespread, and there is a serious concern for the fertility of women. The German Loango expedition of the 1870's describes this setting.[65]

Bunzi is considered an important palaver oracle, as well as a rainmaker, relating to the wind that brings rain. Pechuel-Loesche however considers this male version a pseudo-*Bunzi*, an unorthodox variant of the traditional earth shrine in Ngoyo.[66]

Gombiri, a female *n'kisi*, which protects Loango Bay and locates witches and murders, has replaced the now extinct *Kikokoo*, which it is noted served the Loango king as his major shrine. *Mansi*, mentioned by Dapper, is a protective shrine on the ocean coast which rose to great popularity as an oracle in the 1840's and 50's but disappeared in the 1860's after its main altar was demolished by an unknown person, animal, or storm. *Ngombo*, the widespread divination oracle, is used in Loango in the mid-nineteenth century.[67]

These sources list a long series of *min'kisi* concerned with adjudicatory and retaliatory functions, no doubt necessitated by the collapse of formal appeal courts in the kingdom. *Tschimpuku*, a woven bag, *Mpusu*, a four-cornered basket with tightly-fitting lid, is companion-piece with *Malasi*, a two-headed hippo-shaped sculpture; *Mboyo-zu-Mambi*, a pot lid resting on three legs, and *Mpangu*, a wooden block wrapped tightly with a chain—these are all juridical *min'kisi* found in Loango during the mid-nineteenth century, concentrating their songs, techniques, and symbolism upon measures that were thought to bring clarity and justice to the increasingly tangled social relations present in the port city. *Mboyo* was said to have been a direct successor of the now extinct *n'ḳisi Maramba*, mentioned in the sixteenth century by English sailor Battel.[68] Openly aggressive techniques of private self-defense and assertion are concentrated in *min'kisi* described by Bastian.[69] *Simbuka* can "kill with a quick strike"; *Kunja* lames, *Kanga ikanga* creates a headache in its victim, causing him to run off wildly into the wilderness; *Mabiala Mandembe (Mapanje)*, sometimes given human form, drives its victim, especially thieves, mad.[70]

Against these methods of active aggression, there were many protective *min'kisi*. *Mandombe*, embodied in an iron chain, protected its devotee in war and fighting; *Imba*, a bracelet with a shell affixed to it, protected its wearer from drawing blood in a fight or palaver. These latter, as well as the foregoing, are individualized *min'kisi*. But they suggest that collective institutions were unable to satisfy, or render security. Related to the theme of seeking security is *Njambe* (*Injami* of Dapper's seventeenth-century account). Using the medicine to drive away sleep and achieve ecstasy, an individual could take white seeds from *nganga Njambe* and to the accompaniment of musicians reach possession (*sulo umbuiti*).

Possibly because of the pervasive insecurity and the history of slavery on the Congo coast, medicine in this period turned toward the security of children, that is, fertility. Whereas in the seventeenth century generalized medicine had included fertility of crops and women, along with happy trading, now there is a proliferation of medicines for pregnancy and childbirth. *Mpemba* (also *pfemba, umpembe*) became very popular and consisted of one or several treatment centers drawing scores of women seeking advice and entrance to the rituals of *Mpemba*. Pechuel-Loesche thinks these shrines were derived from a famous midwife in Loango who had special techniques or power.[71] The movement gave rise to the celebrated *Mpemba* statues of women holding their breasts, and sometimes a child on their laps.[72] This *n'kisi* was off-limits to men, and its activities were carried out only in a moon-lit night. *Mbinda* supported marriages and healed women's problems; it too was strictly a woman's affair, carried out in the moonlight, with the women shaven and naked. Men, hair, tobacco smoke, liquor, and water were taboo to its adepts. *Sasi*, a drink administered by a female *nganga*, was created for pregnant women in childbirth, and for newly born children. *Kulo-Malonga* stopped excessive menstrual bleeding; *Bitungu* cured sterility in women; *Dembacani* and *Cuango-Malimbi* cured impotence in men.[73]

A variety of particular "secular" treatments could be added to these to suggest that Loango medicine in the middle of the nineteenth century resembled the Occidental concept of medicine more closely than the foregoing public medicine in certain respects. There were treatments for stomach ache, both simple and serious. *Mpodi* the cupping horn accompanied by skin incisions was used for all kinds of complaints. Bone setting was done in the case of fractures by the *Lunga* doctor and splints of bamboo or some other stiff bandage-like material were applied to support the break. Infections and swelling were handled by skin punctures with a knife, upon which was applied powder of the kola nut and other seeds. There were snake-bite remedies and many more herbal and manipulative treatments.

The largest category of public medicine evidencing growth, along with adjudication, aggression and fertility medicine, is that relating to trade and entrepreneurial undertaking. *Mangossu* is the lord of trade, travel, marriage, or any enterprise. The priests of this famous oracle were well recognized, but had a hard time finding a permanent home for the shrine since its spirit was a restless wanderer. *Tschivuku*, a man's *n'kisi*, was embodied in a woven ball kept in a rack-like shrine hut in a village, to assure successful trading. Its observation consisted, among other things, of the men returned from their trading journeys playing a sort of kickball with the *n'kisi*, laughing and carrying on, while the women remained out of sight.[74] *Mpinda* was a large bust, three-fourths human size, an *n'kisi* of the land, who protected river trade. Pechuel-Loesche mentions an unnamed trading *n'kisi* consisting of a red trunk kept in a "factory"—trading warehouse—containing all sorts of medicinal objects (see plates 19, 20).[75]

Lemba fits well into this taxonomy of nineteenth-century medicinal "growth" and development. Güssfeldt and Bastain of the German Loango expedition illustrate *Lemba* as combining fertility, marriage, adjudication, and trade control in a unique synthesis that became the wide regional system to which this book is devoted.

> Farther back from the village, surrounded by a papyrus fence, there is a hut called the *Lemba* house. It is accessible only by a couple which is associated with the *Lemba* fetish. All others are forbidden entrance. This consecrated house is used to store precious things, much as the Parthenon in Athens was a state treasurehouse.[76]
>
> The closest marriage relationship a man may have with a woman is in *Lemba*. She becomes his *nkazi Lemba*. She wears the *Lemba* charm. The bracelet (*malungu*) is an expensive affair, and the charm requires a decorated house, thus only the wealthy can afford it. Between the doors of the well-locked *Lemba* house, which constitutes the treasure-house of its possessor, are planted two trees, a baobab for the man, and a cottonwood (*mafuma*) for the woman. . . . the key of the house is given the wife with the *Lemba* ring, and her alone. This ring, worn on the right arm, is consecrated together with a roundbox (*ludu Lemba*). The second wife has a house too, and wears a small medicine satchel on her arm. . . .
>
> When husband and wife meet for marriage in the *Lemba* house, the man dons a large copper ring, and the woman a smaller one, the charm being consecrated with a spittle of wine. Whoever is intitiated into the secrets of *Lemba* can as "*Tata Lemba*" pass on the order to a "*mwana Lemba*", and when the latter, the *Lemba* child, becomes ill, he must come to his spiritual Father *Lemba* to be healed through his medicine. In a *Lemba* marriage husband and wife are obligated to mutually trust one another and confess all shortcomings to one another, lest they become sick when eating together.[77]

Not a trace of royalty is evident. The widespread existence of *Lemba* copper bracelets and drums in museum collections from the coast and from Mayombe dating from this time, as well as the accounts of broadening wealth in coastal societies following the complete collapse of royalty, give this account credence.

In the coastal societies, then, *Lemba* emerged in the seventeenth century in connection with copper trade and consolidated its strength in the eighteenth century. As royal clans found themselves overwhelmed by various political and economic problems, a wealthy mercantile class emerged to control the interior trade and the various posts that were needed to administer it. Traditional rules of exogamy and exchange ordered relationships between these clans, partially related to domainal *nsi* estates, partially linked to trade. *Lemba*, as both rite and organization, legitimated this new structure. Later chapters will show how it adapted conventional religious symbols to its own purpose, and developed a pervasive and unique ideology of healing relating to its concept of a stateless political order.

THE TEKE FEDERATION

The Tio king, Makoko, like those of Loango, Kakongo, Ngoyo, and Vungu, was ordained by a powerful, permanent spirit linked to a territorial domain. This was the spirit Nkwe Mbali, thought to be as old as Tio kingship itself. There are no good historical indicators of the date of origin of the Tio kingdom, although legends in the wider region—from Kongo to the coast of Loango—suggest its origin well before the fifteenth century. The ideology of the local authority rooted to an estate and ordained in a territorial or place-specific spirit is widespread in the Equatorial African region, as it was on the coast. Vansina believes that Tio kingship arose out of the acknowledgement of mystical superiority of one of the local authorities—"squires"—followed by a modest tribute payment in exchange for insignia of legitimation. The king thus became a *primus inter pares* among the regional domainal squires. This mystical—ideological—origin theory of the state among the Tio is defended by Vansina because of the low population densities of the region, which would rule out conquest as an explanation, and because of the structural similarity of the role of local squire to that of the king.[78]

The Tio kingdom was already an ancient and important presence by the sixteenth century. Variously named Anzicans, the Tege or Teke, or the kingdom of Macoco, this political entity is one of the best documented of Central Africa in the literature of travelers and chroniclers. Its territory covered extensive river trade routes north of the Congo/Zaire, and along its northern tributaries. Its miners and smiths developed advanced techniques of metalworking. Although

Vansina doubts any integral association of the kingdom's formation to the introduction of metal-working technology, royal symbolism closely associates the kingship with smithing. Royal anvils, a sacred fire, the royal smith, and the second title of the kingdom, *ngandzuunu*, "owner of anvils," gave the king an aura of mastery over this important technology. Teke miners and smiths worked the metals of the Mboko Nsongo and Mindouli region before the Kongo and Sundi invaders took over. Indeed, Teke forgers were often captured to teach smithing to the new Kongo masters.

In the mid-seventeenth century a major reform was introduced in Tio political structure related to emergence and spread of autonomous lords. The implications for the present study are considerable, since these lords possessed many characteristics in common with the *Lemba* priests, including their major insignium the *nkobi* charm box. The *nkobi* lords ruled over the squires, collected tribute from them, and were recognized by them as *nkani*, mediators of tribute to higher-up lords, and ultimately the king. About twenty lower-level *nkobi* lords became the *nkani* of the local squires. A few of these lords, and several major lords, constituted the first-rank *nkobi* lords of greatest prominence.[79]

A *nkobi* lord's autonomy was indicated firstly by his freedom of movement although he collected tribute and drew his spiritual strength from local squires. Each *nkobi* was rooted in a local *nkira* spirit and its local shrine. But the *nkobi* lords could travel; they had their own histories. Each *nkobi* had its own name, its master title. For example, Impaw *nkobi* was held by the lord Ngempaw, whose *nkira* was Ngaalito which resided in the forest of Kongo. Such lore constituted the foundation charter of the *nkobi*. The *nkobi* were graded according to their importance, and a lord's rank varied accordingly. This expressed the competition between major lords and made the system vulnerable to personal political ambition and historical opportunities. The major *nkobi* were in theory twelve in number, although actual lists varied. One reason for this was that the famous *nkobi* had "mothered" children which contained some of their ingredients. This mechanism of regeneration of the *nkobi* had the effect of extending the reward and the tribute system.[80]

The ambivalence of the lords' relationship to the king was expressed in two, clearly diverging, sets of myths of *nkobi* origin. The one set hold that one day a huge *nkobe* appeared at the king's capital, Mbe, after people from all over had waited for a long time for it. The king then distributed the twelve major *nkobi* to his deserving dependents praising his *nkira* earth spirit Nza, the creator himself.[81] This may be called the royal, centralizing, myth of *nkobi* authority. A second set of myths represents a more autonomous legitimation for the nobility. Accordingly, the *nkobi* came from Lord Ngia in Imbwe near Abala region, or even farther away from a great chief at Mpiina Ntsa on the Ntsaa plain. After he had brought the twelve *nkobi*, a war broke out near Mbe, the Tio capital, and in the peace settlement that followed it was agreed that the twelve *tukobe* should be divided between the lords of Ntsaa and Mbe. In this version the *nkobi* give a legitimate authority which does not derive from the king but which can be acquired by persons of wealth. Its antagonistic character to kingship is well expressed; it is a mythical way of saying that power flows from one's following and the number of guns one owns.[82]

Vansina suggests that the *nkobi* was a mystical force behind the lords' authority, a glorification of competition and power struggles, and an assertion of authority with regard to the kingdom and its ideologies. The *nkobi* lords were major judges, they controlled the trade, they were polygynists with many wives. Their courts were well built, even palisaded; their paths were cleared; their fields were big. Despite this clear autonomy, a new lord had to be confirmed in his title by the king, from whom he received a brass collar. The *nkobi* was somewhat independent of the king's approval. The king's inaugural incorporated formal recognition of the lords, in that at this occasion the rank and the role of the lords would be spelled out. But the real administration of the kingdom was carried out by the lords, who acted as judges, controlling trade and tribute, while the king granted ritual authority.[83] It is, says Vansina, as if the Tio kingdom had really two constitutions: one a very old one based on kingship and the domains; the other somewhat more recent (seventeenth century) based on the ranking of the nkobi and their lords.[84]

Two developments related to the *nkobi* reform of the seventeenth century bear special attention in a study of *Lemba*. The first is the role of trade in the rise of the Teke lords; the second is the similarity of the *nkobi* of the Teke lords with *nkobe Lemba*. No doubt the great river trade that linked Central Africa to the Atlantic coast provided the basis of the lord's growing autonomy. In his review of the Teke role in controlling the ivory, raphia, and slave trade, Vansina notes that "Teke" came to be known as a category of slave in Colombia as early as 1560, and later in the seventeenth century as a special class of slave in Brazil, the "Ansiku." Of particular importance is the Teke control of trade at the giant market of Mpumbu at Malebo Pool. Historical texts show strong centralized kingship up to the middle of the seventeenth century; the king is in charge of provinces and functions such as trade. Ngobila is the special administrator who controls the river. After 1700, however, references to the kingdom become scarce. Now the chiefs of the plains, especially Mboo, acquire legitimacy through the *nkobi* ideology, reflecting a rise in wealth from the influx of goods brought from Loango over the Tio-Laadi route and later a similar influx over Nkemi and Ntsei.[85]

Vansina also interprets the invention of the political *nkobi* to reflect the growing affluence of traders linked with metallurgy in the Abala area along the Alima river to the north of the Tio kingdom as well as in the Mindouli area. The *nkobi* were not given to the lords for political recognition of dependents so much as they were bought by them as "super-charms." Only wealthy lords could afford them, thus demonstrating their ties with the wealth of mining, forging, and trade.[86] To what extent this also explains *Lemba* may be determined by comparing the ingredients of both *nkobe* traditions. The similarity is striking. The Tio lords' *nkobi* contains kaolin, camwood, three other varieties of red obtained from stones, several types of shells, indeed shells from Lower Congo,[87] also metal objects such as hammers, anvils, and imported manillas called *ntsaa*, war bracelets and anklets fashioned in Nsundi and Loango, necklaces of beads and cowries. Around the *nkobi* shrine are found miniature bells, *mvaba* signs of authority, anvils, and full-sized bracelets, red copper *ngiele*, a ring of the *ntsii* chief, or ordinary *ngiele* and brass rings with relief worked at Loango, carrying the onia broom emblem of justice (see plate 12).[88] These objects are in many cases identical to the contents of *nkobe Lemba*, as fuller analysis in later chapters will reveal. For the Tio lords they reflected *unu* (power) and were all trade objects, expressing power gained from prowess in trade. *Lemba* was then a Western extension of the Tio *nkobi* system. The differences were that the Tio lords were attached loosely to a king, an *nkira* domain source, and the *nkobi* were hereditary. But in their function and much of their insignia they were identical to *Lemba*. Their rise in the mid-seventeenth century corresponds to the rise of an independent mercantile elite in the coastal kingdoms.

THE NSUNDI SYSTEMS

Nsundi (Sundi, Soondy, Masundi) in ethnographical and historical literature describes societies of both banks of the Zaire River, from the Matadi/Vungu area in the west all the way to the Pool in the east. The term also labels the important northern province of the old Kongo kingdom. It describes as well chiefdoms that spread north of the river during the seventeenth and eighteenth centuries, perhaps even earlier. Finally the term is the name of an important clan of the region. Each of these functions or entities needs to be examined here to understand the political organization on the southern periphery of the *Lemba* area, and its relationship to the coastal kingdoms and the Tio (see figure 3).

Nsundi, as the northern-most of the four original provinces of the Kongo kingdom, dates back at least to the fourteenth century. Some maps depicting this area suggest that the Nsundi province took in

Figure 3

Seventeenth-century Nsundi districts and their capitals, and eighteenth- and nineteenth-century Nsundi strongholds north of Congo/Zaire River (indicated by names within dotted-line boundaries). District names, mostly south of river, based on visits by Montesarchio (1650), Marcellin d'Atri (1697), Luc de Catalanossetta (1697–99), and Matheo de Anguiano (1706), as recorded in J. Cuvelier, *L'Ancien royaume de Congo*, 1946, pp. 341–50 and 362b (map). Eighteenth- and nineteenth-century north-bank sites based on author's field-work and colonial archival sources, Luozi.

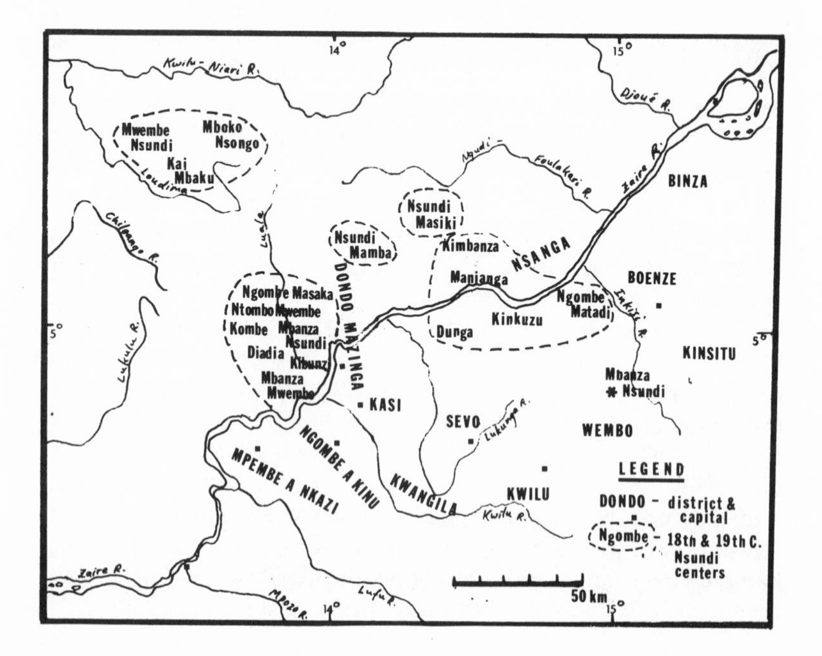

major areas north of the Zaire River, including the coastal kingdoms of Loango, KaKongo, Ngoyo, and Vungu.[89] Although the Kongo king did cite himself as ruler of these kingdoms in praise epithets and may have received gifts from them, it is unlikely that this represented significant hegemony over the north-bank region. By the early sixteenth century, when Europeans had begun to frequent the Congo coast for purposes of trade, diplomacy, and missionary work, the region north of the river under Kongo (Nsundi) control is depicted as a small area directly north of the Nsundi capital—no more than Dondo Mazinga and Nsanga districts—between Vungu and Tio territory.[90]

As the northern province of the Kongo kingdom, Nsundi was ruled by the Mani-Nsundi (MaNsundi) who was appointed by the Kongo king. Until the late sixteenth century, the MaNsundi was frequently the eldest son of the Kongo king, appointed to rule this key province before acceding to the Kongo throne. Nsundi's central place in the kingdom derived from several historical and economic factors. First, the original conquest of Nimi a Lukeni in the thirteenth century probably came from Vungu and Nsundi, so the Kongo king had natural allies there. Further, once trade between Mpumbu at the Pool and the coastal ports such as Ambriz had developed, Nsundi was strategically situated for the control of caravan trade routes running right through Mbanza Nsundi and Mbanza Kongo.

Nsundi's integral place in the early Kongo kingdom is evident from the well-known events and personalities involved in early contact with Portugal in the late fifteenth and early sixteenth centuries. Nzinga a Nkuwu was ruler of Kongo in 1491 when Portuguese explorer Diogo Cão visited his court at Mbanza Kongo. At this time Nzinga a Nkuwu's son Nzinga Mpemba ruled at Nsundi. When Nzinga a Nkuwu died in 1506, another brother Mpanzu a Kitima contended with Nzinga Mpemba for the throne. As is known to readers of Kongo history, Nzinga Mpemba had embraced the new religion of Christianity, whereas Mpanzu supported the autochthonous spirits. In the battle between the two brothers, the Christian Nzinga Mpemba killed the "pagan" Mpanzu. Nzinga Mpemba was inaugurated as Affonso I, whose long rule represents in many ways a high point in Kongo history. Trade with Portugal flourished, at least at first; diplomatic relations were opened with Lisbon; ambassadors and students were sent from Kongo to Europe; missionaries opened schools; and craftsmen came to construct churches in the capitals of Kongo. However, already during his reign Affonso witnessed the development of the slave trade and intrigue against his authority.[91]

Following Affonso's death the Kongo kingdom was further paralyzed by the take-over of Portuguese mercantile and political interests, by insurrections of vassals, and by the invasion of warriors who not only sacked the capital but also drove through northern and southern Kongo territories, establishing small but fearsome military enclaves. One of these military colonies was created on the north bank near or in the Mindouli/Mboko Nsongo mining fields, ostensibly for the control of trade and minerals which were becoming important in the coastal trade of the late sixteenth century.

The fluctuating stability of the Kongo throne after the death of Affonso affected affairs within the provinces; for example, the extent to which the king could dictate policies in the provincial governor's (*mani*'s) appointments, the choice of hereditary princes, and the extent of tribute to be collected. Nsundi continued to be fairly stable as is well documented by resident missionaries like Father Jerôme de Montesarchio. In theory the Kongo king was to be chosen by the electors of the royal family. He in turn selected the provincial governors from among candidates presented by local provincial clans. The king could also in theory nominate governors of the provincial districts, although in Nsundi this right was assumed by the provincial governor (Mani-Nsundi). Chiefs of the provincial districts were elected by matrilineal relatives of the incumbent.[92] In Nsundi there were at least twelve such districts whose names appear consistently over several centuries and still today as names of modern villages, towns, or clan estates: (from east to west) Binza, Kinsitu, Boenze, Nsanga (north of the river), Wembo (just south of Mbanza Nsundi), Sevo, Kwilu, Kasi, Ngombe a Kinu, and Mpemba Kasi, Mazinga (north of the river), Ntanda Kongo, Kilemfu, Lemba, and Nkanga Nsundi (see figure 3 above).[93] Each district had its Mani, representing the ruling local lineages. Each in theory paid tribute to the provincial Mani-Nsundi who represented the King. A centralized, hierarchic structure existed of the sort seen in the coastal kingdoms and among the Tio, although the scale here appears to have been greater. With the growing influence of the Portuguese, such titles as "duke" and "marquis" appeared in respect to the local offices and landed estates, as well as "*fidalgos*" for nonterritorial posts. These are little more than overlay on pre-existing office titles. The "duque" of Nsundi, given permission to nominate "marquises," appointed the marquis of Nsanga, Kifuma, Zimba, Ngombe, Mazinga, etc., officers already known to be *mani* of the various districts of Nsundi.

After the decline of influence of the Kongo kingdom in the late seventeenth century, trade shifted from just south of the river to the northern area and to the far southern area of Cassange and Loanda. Glimpses of Nsundi provincial structure thereafter suggest a continuing centralized polity, with the autonomous *n'tinu* MaNsundi being inaugurated with the regalia and the insignia of the leopard skin like neighboring groups, required to battle for his rights to the throne, to kill a matrilineal kinsman, and to pay his own consecration fees instead of receiving the nomination from Kongo. In the inauguration of the last MaNsundi, NaMenta, in the early nineteenth century, no mention is made of the Kongo king, or of any influence from Mbanza Kongo.[94] All is left to the *nkazi a nsi*, the "wife-clan" Mpanzu, customarily designated as the inaugurators and wife-givers of the Nsundi king-designate. Mpanzu "kidnapped" NaMenta early in his life to prepare him for his role. When he reached puberty they castrated him not only to keep him from fornicating with unmarried women but also to guarantee his symbolic "otherness." After collecting the coronation tax from Nsundi, Mpanzu and the candidate waged war with the other contenders to establish their right to occupy the *mbanza*. Having routed their opponents, they proceeded to decorate their candidate-king with the ingredients of the royal medicine, *kiyaazi* (from *yaala*, to rule), including chalk to anoint him and leopard skin upon which to place him.

> Then they placed a rod over NaMenta's shoulders, set a leopard-skin diadem on his brow, a necklace of leopard's teeth round his neck, a plaited cap (*mpu*) on his head, and a loin-cloth about his loins.[95]

A free-born woman of the Kimpanzu clan was brought before him and designated *n'kazi* or *nkama*, queen. Because of the king's sterility, she went to bed with the king's brother. This structure of the nonconsummated royal marriage resembles that in Loango and Sonyo nobility.

Because of widespread poverty in Nsundi by the early nineteenth century, the last Nsundi *n'tinu* was not given proper burial on his death in 1835 either by the combined supporters of the Mpanzu (the coronators [*n'kazi*]), by the children and grandchildren (*mayaala*) of the Nsundi, or by the Nsundi themselves. As in Loango, however, other types of offices and practices maintained the skeleton of hierarchic tribute and title exchange for a time, even though the royal office of king (*n'tinu*) had now lapsed. In a sense the kingship had already lapsed much earlier, becoming a mere expression of symbolic authority, the king being no more than a charm of power.[96] Elsewhere, closer to the north-bank trade which continued throughout the nineteenth century, the symbols of Nsundi authority and the titles that were conveyed took on new substance and even expanded.

In the region of the Manianga market along the trade route in the old districts of Sevo and Nsanga, the Nsaku clan carried on the practice of granting designation of the *Mpu* title of chiefship to local authorities in exchange for tribute in slaves, pigs, and cloth. It had been an ancient duty of an Nsaku (Nsaku Lau, Nsaku ne Vunda) autochthonous priestly class, "senior of the Kong clans," to ordain the Kongo king and to counsel him in his decisions.[97] Now in Nsundi, an Nsaku ruler named Ntotila Fuanda, born to his mother Matele in Kinkuzu, in the Sevo district south of the river, had received the *Mpu* from Ntete, governing at Kinkuzu, as had Kata Mandala at Dunga (also in Sevo) and Makita at Ngombe Matadi (just north of old Mbanza Nsundi). Fuanda crossed the river northward, establishing his rule at "Kimbanza," where he bestowed the *Mpu* upon subject chiefs in exchange for tribute in slaves, pigs, and cloth which he forwarded annually to Ntete in the south (see figure 3 above). The clans receiving the *Mpu* from Fuanda north of the river were Nsundi and Kingoyo.[98] As in several other instances the titles of chiefly office are bestowed upon a candidate by office-holders or priests of another clan. Here, the Nsaku priestly clan carries out this function.

The fundamental feature of such a structure of authority is the mutual complementarity of two exogamous clans, the acknowledgement of one as "royal" (*kimfumu*) providing the candidate, the other as providing the queen (*kinkazi*) and possibly the sacred emblems of authority (*kiyaazi*). A variation is that the one exogamous clan becomes "priestly," the other "secular." The regent must in this case be "detached" from his kin group through a ritual murder of a matrilineal kin, his castration, or ritual acts such as a series of taboos. Finally, there is always reference in Kongo chiefly and kingly power to the "children" (*baana*) and "grandchildren" (*batekolo*), who collect the offspring of males of the ruling house (the *mayaala*) who, themselves unable to accede to the royal throne, have a strong vested interest in creating and maintaining their "fathers" in authority. These are the elements of Western Congo social structure out of which centralized structures of authority have repeatedly been erected. The exchange of titles for tribute between the *mayaala* and *nkazi* on the one hand, and the *mfumu* on the other, assures the perpetuation of the system. But in order for the complementarity to work, the flow of tribute goods must be maintained. Where this depended on trade, it is apparent that fluctuations in trade set off crises in the structure of local authority.

The authority system that developed among the Nsundi clans northwest of Manianga perhaps as early as the late seventeenth century and early eighteenth century followed the structures outlined here. Historical and legendary accounts refer to Mwembe Nsundi as the capital of a complex of chiefdoms extending from the Zaire River northward into the copper mining area of Mboko-Nsongo, westward into Mayombe, and eastward as far as Mindouli.[99] Mwembe Nsundi's location is specified further as being in the watershed area between the Luala and the Luangu Rivers, which is the point where the northern Mpumbu to Loango caravan route crossed the copper-mining region.

The presence in legendary history and in contemporary place-names in the general Eastern Mayombe-Manianga region of the name Mwembe, and documentary evidence of several clusters of chiefdoms spawned by invading Nsundi clans in the seventeenth century and later, make appropriate its designation as a "Mwembe system." Recurrence of the name "Mbanza Nsundi" suggests that the north-bank Nsundi societies are the result of cultural migration in which entire place-name and authority structures were transported from a home region recreating new settlements from blueprints of the old, analogous to North American place-names such as New York, New Berlin, New Orleans, New Mexico, New Hampshire, etc. Mbanza Nsundi (Nsundi Center, chiefship) was used in the settlements created by those who rushed to the copper mines of Manianga and the control of lucrative trade along the highland caravan route from Mpumbu to Loango. Archival materials help us to describe one such Nsundi enclave around Mbanza Mwembe (see figure 3 above).

> At Mbanza Nsundi (north of the river, not to be confused with ancient Nsundi provincial capital) the Nsundi clan [in ca. 1700] divided and scattered to find a new land. One group settled in Mbanza Mwembe, attaching to its name Nsundi the term "Mwembe" to differentiate itself from the first group, with which it then married. At Mbanza Mwembe the clan prospered, adding numerous settlements at Ngombe, Ngombe-Masaka, Kombe, Diada, and others. Thus installed, the clan organized itself separately in the tradition from which it came. A chief was

> named to reside at Mbanza Mwembe; the villages put at their heads chiefs (*mfumu bwala*) or judges (*nzonzi*) to settle disputes.[100]

Instead of intermarrying with local autochthonous clans—whom the Nsundi oral historians sometimes allege were not there, the land having been "empty" when they came—they saw fit to divide the leading clan into two exogamous halves, permanently severing the "blood" through the sacrifice of a pig and a common feast. On the model of pre-existing Nsundi polities, they devised a system of local chiefs and judges. In due course the royal model could be recreated around a ruler and other basic elements, just as had been done in Kimbanza by Ntotila Fuanda.

> Nkombo Mafwana, chief of Mbanza Mwembe, who in the meantime found that the land of that region was not suited for him, left to found a new settlement at Ntombo. There he called a meeting of his chiefs and had himself named *Lulendo* (power) chief, with authority over the entire clan. He received the investiture from Mayombolo, chief at Mbanza Nsundi, and was succeeded in the *Lulendo* office by Mangovo Kabi, Nsango Lumba, Makai ma Diengila, Ngoma Ngonde, and Mazanza, the last of whom had just been inaugurated when the Europeans arrived.[101]

The inauguration ceremonies followed appointment typically by election of the incumbent *Lulendo* chief's brother, or maternal nephew within the royal house, and ratification by all the clans.

> In his new *Lulendo* enclosure of trees, the *Lulendo* chief underwent isolation. No member of his clan could see him, only his wives and the "children" (*bana*). A priest was attached to the investiture to teach him his prohibitions (*longo*). After the royal charm (*Bueno nkisi*) had been brought by the chief of Mbanzi Nsundi, the sword of authority (*Mbele a lulendo*) would be brought before the new chief, seated on his leopard skin. Two slaves who served as executioners (*bayala mabangu*, "rulers of the sword") would bring two of the new chief's matrilineal nephews. For the first and last time in his life he would take the knife and cut off his kinsmen's heads, bathe himself in their blood. He would then receive *Bueno*. Never again could the chief touch his sword; it was kept by his guards and used for the execution of criminals.[102]

The ritual murder of a kinsman indicated the intention to set the candidate apart from his lineage as well as the creation of an order of law and administration on a scale larger than any of the local clan estates. In the particular polity under discussion (Mwembe Ntombo), sources suggest that the Lulendo's duties centered on settling feuds through the intervention of his soldiers and holding an appeal court over which he was the supreme judge. His soldiers consisted mainly of "*bana*" born to slave-women and therefore totally dependent on him for their well-being. Sources say nothing of tribute, but it is hard to imagine a centralized polity with an "army" and a "court" lacking any type of tribute. It is known that Lulendo's powers were held in check by the children (*bana*) and dependents (*bamayaala*) who not only ratified his election from the ruling clan but also saw to it that he would not "take the clans with him" by dying of disease in old age; they choked him to death when he became too old to rule effectively.

In the sources on this Lulendo chiefship in the southern-most of the Mwembe Nsundi enclaves there is mention of a Kiasi chief akin to the autochthonous Kinsako priest of Kongo and Nsundi, or the Mpu priest, or the Bunzi priest in Ngoyo, a mediator of the local spiritual forces needed to legitimate the invading, conquering, military office. In Mwembe, the Kiasi bore the title of Ma Muene (lord); he also levied market tribute. Like the Lulendo chief, he was inaugurated by a priest from Mbanza Nsundi.

> When the seclusion was over the masses entered the Kiasi's enclosure to find him sitting on a leopard skin laid over elephant tusks. The chief of Mbanza Nsundi would give him his regulations of office, and trace in *mpemba* chalk on his body: a transversal line on the forehead, on the nose, and a line on each leg. Then he would be given the *miasi* emblems of office, a collar of leopard teeth, and bracelets of iron for each leg and arm, as well as earth from the burial grounds of the previous Lulendo and Kiasi chiefs.[103]

These Nsundi political systems were thus a series of loosely affiliated small conquest states or chiefdoms radiating out from a number of centers such as Mwembe Nsundi in the copper- and iron-mining area around Mboko Nsongo, situated on the highland Mpumbu to Loango trade route. The emigrating enclave that established itself as a small state sought legitimacy via a link back to its own traditional source (Mbanza Nsundi) or via the benediction by the autochthonous spirits of the earth (Bunzi, Bikinda, Mpu, Kiasi, for example). In all instances there seems however to be a concern for the establishment of a royalist model of governance. In this sense the Nsundi invaders differ from many other north-bank political traditions. *Lemba* constitutes the other major transformation of the basic structure of public authority legitimated by the autochthonous priesthood of the earth.

LIFE BETWEEN THE KINGDOMS: MARKET LAWS AND *LEMBA*'S MARRIAGE POLITICS

Between the kingdoms on the coast and the Teke federation, and where no Nsundi chief had asserted his local hegemony, there existed an acephalous political system. We may contrast it to the centralized model of the polity found in foregoing discussion by noting that there was no office created by either a ritual murder of a kinsman or through appointment by another central figure. There was generally no tribute payment to another chief. No grand judge could be found in the form of the N'tinu who acted as appeal court. There were no standing armies nor loyal dependents like the Lulendo chief's soldiers in Mwembe Ntombo to impose order. A colonial report in 1938 described the political system in the same negative terms as those used in ethnology of the time:

> As always, the "northern" region has shown itself more resistant. Not one *chef médaillé* has succeeded in imposing himself in these chiefdoms whose populations traditionally, for that matter, never submitted to the authority of one man. Well before our occupation the indigenous people lived in a sort of anarchy, not recognizing any authority other than the hardly effective family chief holding authority more often religious than political.[104]

A positive description of this political system would need to include the following characteristics: (1) several types of local chiefs, including the lineage or clan chiefs (*mfumu dikanda, mfumu nsi*) and the various types of judges (*nzonzi*); (2) several ceremonially-rich *min'kisi* which recognized authority, including *Mpu*, *N'kondi*, and *Lemba*; (3) the so-called "market laws" (*min'siku mia zandu*), a set of prohibitions and practices that spelled out the rules of peaceable trading, and regulated the measures of adjudication and punishment for their violation. These dealt with most public affairs such as trade, hunting, and marriage, and were maintained by councils of judges (*zinzonzi*).

The local chiefs were attached either to descent communities or residential communities and markets. These two types of polities or organizational principles interacted to provide a dynamic balance of power and a coverage of administrative function. The lowest level of lineage chief was the head of the *mwelo* "door" of the house. His role was not really titled unless as judge. Such an "elder" assured the well-being of his dependents: to provide them with land, trees, and other rights, and to see that they were properly married and cared for. The role of the "clan chief" (*mfumu dikanda*) was a more inclusive version of this; his duties as well covered the subsistence of kin dependents and their proper marriage relationships. His was the role of the men's hut chiefship where clansmen and their dependents gathered daily for eating and palavering. The clan chief had also to assure that the ceremonial duties of the local clan section were taken care of by the patrifilial children and "grandchildren," as priests of their "fathers."

The "village chiefs" distinguished between the principle of landed estates and the populace on it. The assumption was that one or two clans were landowners, claimants of the ancestral cemetery grove, thus the presumed autochthonous inhabitants of the immediate area. Several titles, reflecting regional characteristics and historical differences, belong here. All gave the titleholder the recognized acknowledgement of being a freeman. Perhaps the most widespread title for the role of head of such a landed estate was *mfumu nsi* (landed estate chief), a term in widespread use in the Mayombe. The term was also known in the Manianga region where the office holder wore a twisted copper bracelet that passed within the matrilineal line of succession. Such clans as Mazinga, Nsundi, Kikwimba, Bwende, Kimbanga, and others were noted *mfumu zinsi* of this region. In some areas the title *mfumu yetila* or *yetisi* was used, but it connotated chiefship of the village.

Comparable to the estate chief is the "crowned" chief *mfumu mpu*. Some informants in the North Manianga said it was identical to the domainal chiefship, reflecting freeman status in a land-holding local clan. The *Mpu* chief, like the others of this category, was inaugurated into office and supported by the collective "children" born to the clan's men. Through the isolation of the *Mpu* candidate from his matrilineal kinsmen, the patrifilial children were able to generalize the loyalties of their fathers, to broaden allegiances so that fractional differences within the matrilineal clan of their fathers would not destroy them as a landed, corporate group. *Mpu*-ship was often allocated to a person who was "sick." Structurally, the *Mpu* was situated in the free clan so that his consecration to ceremonial office was complementary with the structural positions of power elsewhere in the clan. The *Mpu* could be used as an appointed title in a centralized kingdom such as Kimbanza at the northern fringes of Nsundi, but in a neighboring acephalous setting, it would be generated from "below" to thwart political fragmentation.

Thus far the political structure of the *Lemba* region, as described, is not distinctive from low-level organization elsewhere in the general Kongo region. However, examination of the more inclusive levels of political structure reveals a striking contrast to the kings and prominent chiefs found elsewhere. The "laws of the market" (*minsiku mia nzandu*) and supporting roles, functions, and ceremonials, reflect a unique political system. The market system in north-bank society operated around the four-day week (see figure 4). Each market, located on an open plain between several villages, was "ruled" by a market committee of chiefs or judges from these surrounding communities. While the notion of a sovereign was absent in this system of acephalous governance of markets, the functions of large-scale government were very evident. The market was regarded as a "court," with the right to impose capital punishment. The market committee and its constituent communities constituted a "market area," which could combine with neighboring market committees to solve large-scale disputes. Often village or clan chiefs would have tenure in two markets for more effective regulation of disputes. The "laws of the market" thus regulated both trade in the markets as well as the fabric of society that kept the markets open and viable. Munzele has listed the major market laws from the Kivunda area:

1) Theft is prohibited on all paths.

2) Fighting is prohibited.

3) Beginning a feud in any village or market district is prohibited on pain of paying for it in persons.

4) A person may not enter the market area or sit there before the market heads have given the signal.

5) *Kimbanzia* grass, because it is sacred, may not be picked or removed in any way from the market; it stands for the health and prosperity of the clan, the benediction from God, the ancestors, and the clan.

Figure 4
Market areas and villages of the Kivunda region, Luozi (the Manianga); corresponds to Nsundi Masiki region in figure 3

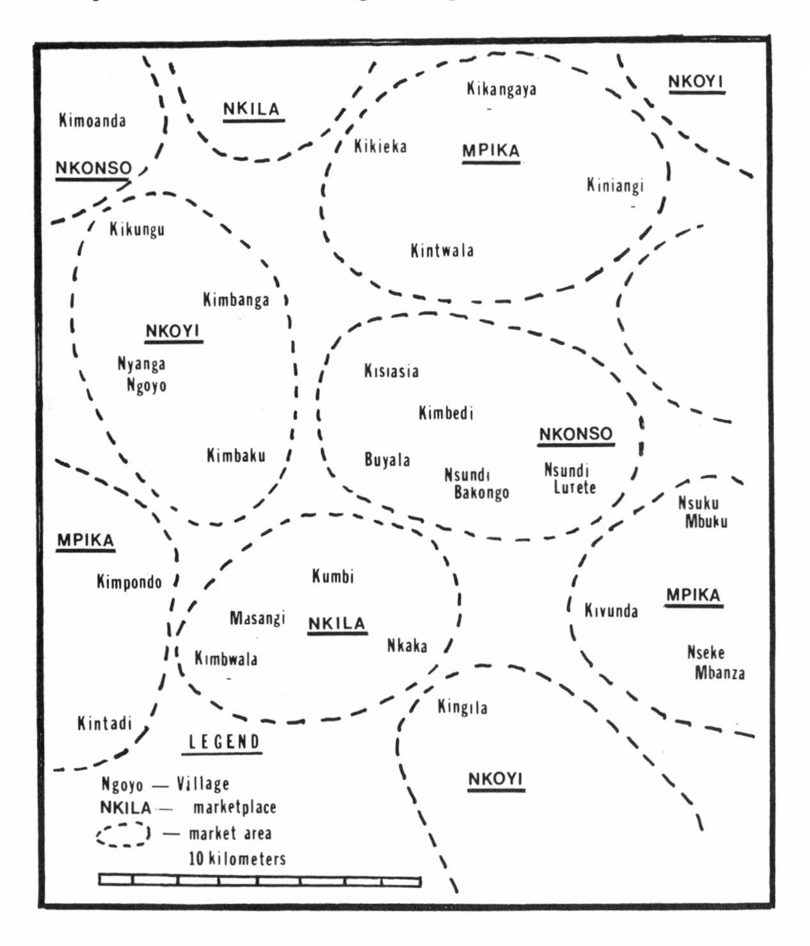

6) Only the market committee has the right to invoke the death penalty on a person.

7) A severe punishment falls upon any individual or clan who kills or harms a palm wine tapper, for palm wine is the ingredient of social intercourse.

8) A judge (*nzonzi*) or a messenger carrying the judge's staff may not be harmed or seized, on pain of being punished in the market place.[105]

The market chiefs would meet in the market center prior to trading to "open the market" while contingents of men, women, and children from surrounding villages waited at their respective entrances (see plates 2, 3). This committee determined what would be sold or exchanged, whether criminals—murderers, recidivist thieves, adulterers, or violators of the market laws—in any of the "entrance" groups (*mafula*) deserved being "planted in the market," a euphemism for the method of capital punishment whereby the victim would be mercifully given great quantities of wine, seated in a hole, and buried before a sharpened bamboo stake was driven into his head by his possessor or close superior. The market council might also decide that hostilities between groups were so great as to require canceling the market on that day. If and when trading was opened, it was done in the center of the market by delegate groups from the "entrances." Women and children were rarely permitted access to the center, for fear that they would be seized as pawns or hostages in on-going feuds, or as debt payment. Following a peaceful market, men would gather under a shelter to drink and talk.

Where feuds broke out between participants in a market group—over land, women, hunting accidents—the absence of central judicial institutions became evident immediately. Even the fabric of warfare reflected the lateral alliances rooted in the market structure and in marriage ties and descent, as well as in the organization of the landed clan villages with their clients and slaves. All of these social domains structured feuding and peacemaking, as the following example of the "War of Kidiba," fought in ca. 1880, in the Nsundi Lutete area, illustrates. (For villages mentioned refer to figure 4.)

> The "War of KIDIBA" between the people of Kisiasia and the people of Kimbaku took place on account of MFWEMO-MAYAMBI of the Mazinga-Kingila clan and his wife MANGEYE-KIDIBA of Kikwimba of Kimbaka. (MFWEMO-MAYAMBI was a slave at Kisiasia.) KIDIBA ran away from her husband; she didn't care to live with him any longer, even though they had two children, a boy, BANUNDA-DIATA, and a girl, KILENGO. When she ran from her husband she went to live with another man named MUNSWANGALA who lived at Masangi, of the Mazinga clan of chief KIODI. This angered MFWEMO-MAYAMBI greatly, so he gathered the people of Kisiasia so that they could go and seize a hostage (*bwila nkole*) at Kimbaku: a woman in replacement. Meanwhile KIDIBA had left Masangi to go to her lineage home at Kimbaku. When the people of Kisiasia saw that it was

MFWEMO's wife, they seized her and brought her to Kisiasia to her husband. But MFWEMO's anger was not satisfied: "We must go to war (*nwana muzingu*) with her uncles (*bankazi*) at Kimbaku." Our elders (here in Kisiasia) told him though "there is no need to go to war over your wife. Let us be satisfied that she is in our hands again." But MFWEMO would hear nothing of it. "We must go to war over the matter," he insisted. The elders then told him, "we cannot follow you in this matter; if you must fight, it is your affair."

Then the warriors (*makesa*, young men) of Kisiasia agreed to go to war as MFWEMO wished. They went near Kimbaku to wait for the lineage headman (*mfumu dikanda*) of the woman KIDIBA to warn him with a gun salvo (*sika bizongo*). The people of Kimbaku replied, "Never mind, we have warriors also and they know how to fight too." And so those from Kimbaku fought against those from Kisiasia.

Then other villages entered the conflict: Kintwala and Kimwanda were brought into the fight on the side of Kisiasia, and Masangi and Kumbi on the side of Kimbaku. MAZALA and MUNANU of Kintwala, of the Nsundi clan of BINKITA, were killed and hurt with a ball in the eye respectively. MANAKA of Kimwanda was killed too. When the people of Kintwala and Kimwanda saw that they had each lost a man, they went to Kimbaku and killed NZUZI, a sister of chief ZIONA of the Kindamba clan, who was in the same house with BAYEKULA of the Kisiasia. She [Bayekula] was unharmed.

Now, seeing all the killing, the elders and judges (*bambuta vo nzonzi*) sought to call it to a halt, and sit to talk out the matter (*zonza nsamu*). They agreed that KIDIBA was in the wrong for having left her husband. She was charged with payment of "one corpse" (*futa mvumbi*), that is seven people. Further, they judged that MUNSWANGALA of Masangi was also at fault for having taken a married woman from her husband. He too must "pay a corpse," or seven people (to the clan victimized), plus seven cloths (*mbongo*). MFWEMO was judged for having started the war, and charged with paying "one corpse and a half" in people (of his lineage), BILONGO, MAKWENIA, MIHAMBANTU, KIHENI, and he himself MFWEMO-MAYAMBI paid for the corpses killed in the war. They further paid their debt as follows: out of MFWEMO's lineage, KUKINGA went to MALEWO of Kisiasia where he became a slave of the Kimbanga clan; TEMBOSO, a woman, was sold to DIAKOKA at Kintwala; MAKUNDU, a male

> was sold to MUNDELE at Kimbedi. Further the members of the Mazinga line (MFWEMO's) sold the land they had bought (*kudisa ntoto*) to the Kimbanga clan of Kisiasia, to allow MFWEMO to pay his debt to Kimwanda for the man they had lost on his account.[106]

Seizing a hostage was a favorite manner of taking justice into one's own hands. Yet it was not one's direct antagonist from whom a hostage was taken, rather from another stronger community which, when informed of the strategic purpose of the kidnapping, could impose settlement terms on the original antagonist, its status subordinate. As in contemporary international terrorism, this method could also result in the embroilment of a dozen villages in many market units, and in numerous deaths. The laws of the market had extremely harsh recompense terms for the guilty, once the passion of the young warriors had subsided and the cool rhetoric of the judges had taken over. Not merely the *lex talionis* of an eye for an eye was invoked, but seven persons for every human casualty in the war. Thus Mfwemo's entire clan and its land were dispersed to pay for the three deaths inflicted in the war.

Another war in the same region in 1912 was provoked by an impatient hunter who had lost his dog to an errant ball from a fellow hunter's gun. In the settlement the aggrieved hunter shot at (but missed) the judge. The council of judges fined him eight pigs and other articles, to be paid to the market-area groups participating in the judgement, as directed by the laws of the market.

The judicial structure of both cases reflects the absence of a hierarchic appeal court. The conflict is absorbed through lateral alliances within which the judges from the very groups involved, and their neighboring judges, effectively impose upon the antagonist and their patrons radical and binding punishments. Given the strategic role of judges, it is not surprising to see in these regions, in connection with the market-law system, elaborate rhetorical usages, songs, proverbs, call-and-response sanctions, and rituals of conflict arbitration. The category of charm called *N'kondi* existed at the level of the clan, village, and market, as a ritual contract between persons or groups who vowed not to make war, or to seize hostages from each other's populace. Such *N'kondi* were canine or anthropomorphic wooden figures into which blades, screws, and iron nails or hardwood pegs were driven as the oath was sworn never to engage in mutual hostilities, or following hostilities, to arouse *N'kondi*'s anger (*mfunyia*

= ferocity = wedge) against the antagonist, thus sanctioning them to hold to their promises. Sacrifices of animals, usually goats, were made as the *N'kondi* priest drove "blood wedges" into *N'kondi*, and evoked promises from the two partners:

> Between your village and my village we have an accord, you may not seize hostages from us, and we will not seize hostages from you. If one of our people does something to the other group, we will meet to talk and will not fight.[107]

The other major charm of public order, beside *N'kondi*, was of course *Lemba*. It is described by Munzele as an *n'kisi* integrating people, villages, and markets (*Lemba i n'kisi wabundisa bantu, mavata ye mazandu*). It permitted persons from one market area to travel and trade in another market area. One who carried *Lemba*'s insignia—*nkobe*, bracelet, staff—conveyed the information that he had received *Lemba*'s instructions, and was therefore trustworthy. He must be received in the market, for he was a person of peace, a carrier of light (*n'nati a mpemba*). *Lemba* priests and priestesses were the prominent citizens. In the above narration of the War of Kidiba, the narrator's father, Nsundi-Mukila of Kintwala, freeman from Nsundi and a well-known judge, and his wife Kibuni, freeman of Kimbanga (Kisiasia), were initiated into *Lemba*. Likewise, Mundele-Mbenza, who shared in Mfwemo's "spoils," was a *Lemba* priest as was one of his wives. Mundele-Mbenza was a slave who because of his recognized intelligence and integrity had been elected by his masters to represent their interests; he was a prominent judge and *Lemba* priest.

The promotion of a slave figure to judgeship and *Lemba* priesthood reflects the crucial role of marriage politics as another, major, factor in the maintenance of alliances between clans, villages, and market areas in the "region between kingdoms." The landed estate system that extended from the Loango coast into Mayombe and eastward into Teke country found local villages comprising a major matrilineal clan with its *mfumu nsi* or *Mpu*. Client and slave lineages (clan fragments) usually comprised a type of hierarchy of exogamous sub-communities, closely intermarried. The dominant clan of the domain extended land and women to its client males, but needing their support in every way and receiving from them women and labor and political support. Most of the client lineages derived from women or girls who had been seized in feuds or traded for debts and then had married a male of the dominant clan. They usually came from neighboring free clans. In the Manianga region dominant lines married closely into their clientage, particularly during the first few generations of their habitation. Men of the leading clan, during the nineteenth century, could have from five to ten wives, mostly of slave origin. In order to assure plentiful progeny in the dominant line, its women were married to client men, thus keeping them at home with their children.

As has been seen in the review of coastal polities such as Loango and Mayombe, the women of dominant (noble or royal) clans had a sharply restricted progeny, thereby reducing greatly the number of heirs. In the acephalous political context, priorities were reversed. Preference was given in dominant *nsi* clans to marriage of their women with numerous client and neighboring free clans. Often elderly women of these lines would have had three or four consecutive husbands—serial polyandry—to maximize their effectiveness as alliance creators whose progeny belonged to the dominant group. A given dominant clan would thus maintain from five to ten key reciprocal alliance ties with neighboring clans to offset the tendency to become an isolated endogenously-marrying polity. Alliances between free clan sections and between a dominant landed clan and its more powerful, populous, client lineages were the alliances most often initiated, both husband and wife, into *Lemba.*

For example, in the Kimbanga village of Kisiasia, where I conducted fieldwork in the 1960's and 1970's, about six *Lemba* households had existed in 1920 at the end of *Lemba*: two representing Kimbanga freemen married polygynously to client women, two more representing Kimbanga women married to men of sizeable client clans. Several other Kimbanga women were married in *Lemba* to freemen of neighboring clans. These interclan alliances constituted traditions of permanent "blood reciprocity" (*mvutudulu a menga*) in which a son by marrying his father's sister's daughter or some classificatory equivalent returned to his father's clan the hereditary substance his clan had received when his father married his mother. In one instance *Lemba* slave priests perpetuated the spiritual tradition of their fathers where they had had no female progeny. *Lemba* was thus a symbol as well as a structure assuring the continuation of a descent line and corporate community through the correct exchange of women. *Lemba* represented the patrilateral flow between clans of an on-going alliance, binding clan to clan and extending the requisite network across the countryside to assure effective commerce. In the absence of any other centralizing structures, *Lemba* assumed the functional equivalence of the state.

In summary, it is possible to see underlying similarities in the *Lemba* region's political systems and the way they were expressed in sacred symbols. On the one hand there were everywhere polities linked to landed estates, many small-scale such as the domains of the Teke, of the Central highlands, and the Mayombe. A few such as the Tio king Makoko, the coastal kingdoms, and some of the Nsundi chiefdoms were larger in scale. But these territorial, landed polities were invariably legitimated by localized earth or water spirits such as Kwe Mbali of the Makoko and Bikanda or Bunzi farther westward. These were autochthonous spirits related to specific places, either waterfalls or tracts of land, as were the estates they symbolized. On the other hand there were the "moveable estates" linked to justice, trade, or conquest. The Tio lords and the *Lemba* priestly couples with their moveable shrines were consecrated to a variety of spirits, some of which derived from localized shrines such as the Tio local shrines or the western Bunzi; other symbols were legitimated in nonterritorial spirits and forces such as Bunzi's daughter Lusunzi, the trickster Mani-Mambu, the androgynous demigod Mahungu. All contributed to the estate of *Lemba*, created and sustained by exchange, alliance, and trade.

Chapter 3

Biographical Sketches of *Lemba*'s Demise

Introduction

An institution as widespread in scale and as deep in historical duration as *Lemba* cannot be made homogeneous by ethnological and historical reconstruction. Change, internal tension, regional variation, and the institution's disappearance must be accounted for. This chapter introduces biographies of *Lemba* priests and aspirants to show how the drastic changes that occurred at the hand of the Congo Free State and as a result of Belgian, French, and Portuguese colonialism of the late nineteenth and early twentieth centuries confronted individuals with alternatives leading to the fragmentation of *Lemba* and its ultimate disappearance from the cultural and political landscape of Lower Zaire.

The caravan routes that *Lemba* supported and controlled were used extensively to move the machinery and baggage of early colonialism from the coast to the Pool. From ca. 1885 the demand for porters drawn from local populations along the routes was accompanied with threat, seizure of family hostages, and meager payment. By 1887 the exigencies of the southern caravan route along the Zaire River had through death or desertion depleted the supply of porters. Many of the villages in the Ngombe area had fled north across the river.[1] More widespread labor recruitment became the practice in the Free State backed up by "in-kind" food taxes levied to support the armies and caravans. Labor recruitment for portage and for the construction of the Matadi-Leopoldville railroad became so heavy that numerous revolts erupted, and the loss in lives was high. Chinese laborers had to be brought in to supplement the African labor force. By 1896–7 portage along the northern route from Loango to Brazzaville reached the limits of its labor potential carrying a mission of ninety tons overland (3000 loads at sixty pounds [thirty kilograms] per porter). Here too there was a revolt, the "Sundi revolt," which was put down repressively. Completion of the Matadi-Leopoldville railroad by 1900 permitted the abandonment of portage on both banks, much to the relief of local African populations, reeling from epidemic diseases, high death losses, and famines from overtaxation on the time and resources for food production. Portage seems to have continued on a sporadic basis in the French colony until 1915 when the auto route was completed from Loango to Brazzaville. The Congo-Ocean railroad to Pointe Noire was completed in the late twenties.[2]

Although the cessation of colonial portage alleviated the heavy burden of labor recruitment, its total substitution by rail and auto-route transportation had the long-term effect of replacing *Lemba*'s economic function of three centuries, the revenue from which had generated *Lemba*'s ceremonial fund. Shorn of this traditional base, *Lemba* could only sustain its economic viability by cutting deeply into resources now claimed by the colonial taxes and *corvée* labor demands. Disenchantment with *Lemba* grew within the populace. One old Kivunda observer noted that *Lemba* priests and priestesses only met now to fatten themselves on pork. Colonial authorities perceived the competition for resources; thus French authorities banned *Lemba* in the early thirties for "exploitation and extortion of fees" destined for the colony's tax coffers.[3]

Other dimensions of the colonial intrusion affected *Lemba* adversely by dividing its ranks into competing interest groups. There were those who accepted the colonial chiefship and allowed themselves to be drawn into the taxation system. Those precolonial chiefs who refused, sending forward instead vassals, deputies, and even slaves to receive the medals, benefits, and supports offered by the Europeans, found their authority overturned by these one-time subordinates.[4] Colonial collaboration was now necessary to preserve one's influence, although it destroyed one's authority through taxation abuse.

Others abandoned *Lemba* to become mission catechists. There were those who might once have been drawn into *Lemba*, but for reasons having to do with the clash of old ceremonial demands and new colonial taxes, perceived *Lemba* as having become too expensive, although still the preferred ritual solution to their ills. Christianity offered a way out of the impasse.

Finally, there were those who acknowledged the apparent bankruptcy of the old rituals, but refused to play along with either the colony or the missions. Like Kimbangu, the Kongo prophet, they forged new African rituals, bypassing the foreign priests and pastors to create an African response to challenges of colonialism and competition of a strange world religion thrust upon them.

Accepting Colonial Authority: Ngambula, Mampuya, Sobisa

All three of these *Lemba* priests accepted colonial authority. Two (Ngambula and Luvuangu-Mampuya) became medalled "*mpalata*" chiefs under the Free State/Belgian colonial system. Another (Sobisa) was named chief by his clan, although still very young, because it was thought he could better cope with the intricacies and foibles of colonial officials. In all cases the colonial government imposed difficult choices on individual *Lemba* adherents.

Ngambula's life story, told by Bittremieux in the twenties,[5] reflects these pressures on a successful leader in the old system. Ngambula grew up a freeman of the Vinda clan in the Nkangu region of the Mayombe. After his childhood and adolescence in his father's village in the late decades of the nineteenth century, he entered the N'kimba initiation school, where his N'kimba name Tu Masungi was added to his childhood name N'lele Mbutu. For his recognized leadership he was chosen to be a local N'kimba master.

After his happy youth a series of crises appeared around him and in his life. A drought so severe occurred that the Lukula River near his home dried up. This, in addition to the hardships of colonial labor, led to famine. As if drought and famine were not enough, locust plagues descended on the area. Most significant for his personal future, however, was an experience that grew out of a court case involving his clan.

Ngambula remembered attending the palaver in the court of the great Yombe chief Mabwaka of Mazamba, in Kangu region. Many *mfumu nsi* chiefs came with double-gong musicians, staff carriers and special advocates, favorite wives and their servants. Nobility were seated on mats or leopard skins shaded by umbrellas. The debate was over livestock, women, and other issues compounded into a major confrontation between two clans. Speakers for the two sides would take turns, arguing eloquently and waving their arms about. Ngambula remembered particularly the musical chime resounding from the bracelets of the *Lemba* priests. After the settlement was reached and payment made in small livestock and wine, food was distributed, ending the adjudication on a festive note. Ngambula remembered the delicious mutton, and how he felt fortunate to be at so auspicious an occasion in the court of the great chief Mabwaka, with so many *Lemba* priests displaying their engraved copper bracelets while toasting the health of their wives.

But above all Ngambula remembered his great consternation when after the feast he was told that in secret bargaining he had been given to chief Mabwaka as a pawn in payment of his clan's debt settlement. He felt stigmatized, suddenly having been turned into property and a trade good. However he remained in Mabwaka's court and was well taken care of.

The next memorable event of Ngambula's life was Mabwaka's death. Succession deliberations by the clan counselors failed to identify a competent brother or nephew, so they turned to an outsider, and favor fell on Ngambula. According to the custom of the land, he could not become the MaKangu, chief in the Kangu dynasty; he had to be made an *mvuanzi* chief, whose own direct line is nullified. In an act of "chiefly incest" he took an *pfumu Vinda* wife from his own family, thus severing his own line of descent. He was now a member of no lineage, in order to be a chief over many. The people of Mabwaka accordingly consecrated him as priest of the earth cult *Mbenza*. Never again could he take *k'oze* (a dark fruit) in his hands, or climb a palm tree. On an *Nsona* day he was placed on a dais (*vunda*) with his chiefly staff in his hand; four palms were planted around him; and a palm canopy erected over him. He was placed on a leopard skin and anointed with white chalk (*pezo*) and red powder (*ngunzi*), and given a fly whisk, while a healer danced about him (*banguka*). He was given the new name of Mboma Simbi, designating his new status as an *Nkita* spirit devotee—perhaps even an *Nkita* spirit, notes Bittremieux. Amidst much dancing, drumming, and drinking, and made up with red and white stripes all over his body, he was brought from seclusion to his palace (*m'bongi*). He was now called the MaMboma, and his staff accompanied him everywhere.

The next important phase of Ngambula's life began with his head wife's request to become his *Lemba* partner. Initiation to *Lemba* would be expensive, but he agreed. The consecration was organized, and many *Lemba* priests and priestesses were assembled. Part of the ritual was held in the village, part in the bush, characteristic for *Lemba*. The *Lemba* shrine consisted of the *n'kobe* (to be elaborated in Chapter 7), a pair of small drums, and the copper medicine bracelets worn by the priest and priestess. Sacred *Lemba* trees were planted in the grove behind the house: *mfuma* the silk cotton tree, *lubota*, *nkumbi*, and *kuaku*, as well as other plants. Based on the proverb *menga ma tsusu, simba: kuambula* (chicken's blood, hold it and let it go), he received his *Lemba* name, Ngambula.

Ngambula was now N'kimba master, priest of *Mbenza,* the MaMboma chief, and priest of *Lemba,* all the roles of authority to which a turn-of-the-century Yombe could aspire. In the eyes of Belgian colonial officials Ngambula met the criteria of a nobleman. In the Free State and early Belgian Congo tradition of autocratic authority, Ngambula received from the colonial administration yet one more title, *Mfumu Palata*, the "medalled chiefship," linking him to the colonial state, making him eligible for protection, and obligating him to recruit laborers, collect taxes, and maintain order. Ngambula regarded the colonial chiefship as an enhancement of his authority. But the difference with this title was that the tribute collected in its name passed on to the central colonial coffers for the maintenance of a distant state. Where the tax was "in kind" (food, for example) it was used to feed soldiers and porters. But it was neither circulated in the market nor redistributed to the local populace in the form of a lavish feast.

Across *Lemba* territory, individuals like Ngambula struggled with this issue of collaboration with the colonial government. In Manianga, to the east, two other *Lemba* priests, Luvuangu-Mampuya of the Kingoyi clan in Kimata and Sobisa of the Kimbanga clan in Kisiasia, were typical of those who cooperated. Luvuangu-Mampuya had already received the colonial chiefship when he participated, with his wife, in the last regional *Lemba* inauguration at Nseke-Mbanza in 1919. He represented the type of figure who in due course becomes a *chef de groupement*, an administrative level created beyond traditional chiefdoms, to consolidate small-scale domains and clan chiefships of north-bank segmentary society. The creation of a tribunal with jurisdiction over the *groupement* lent this level of colonial administration a certain legitimacy in the eyes of the populace, and thus some sense of coming to terms with the new government. Meanwhile, Luvuangu-Mampuya retained his *Lemba* insignia, insisting as late as 1965 that he was still *nganga Lemba* and that therefore he could not talk of his secrets. He would die with his *Lemba* adherence, his ritual objects going with him to the grave.

The Kimbanga of Kisiasia, as has been pointed out in the previous chapter, had several *Lemba* priests in their midst at the turn of the century when the Free State's agents appeared. Nzuzi Pierre, clan-section head, suggested in 1970 that the thinking in 1915–20 on cooperating with the Belgians was that they would hardly disappear, so it was necessary to deal with them as resourcefully as possible. When taxes were first levied in 1910–15, a woman was delegated to organize this work since women had the groundnuts needed for the African soldiers. At the same time it became necessary to name a new clan-section chief, *mfumu dikanda.* Skipping over many older men who were eligible, clan counselors elected youthful Sobisa. Their reasoning was that since he knew how to read he would better understand the problems of the new era. But he was not the only one who could read. Their decision was also based on criteria exercised in initiating him into *Lemba.* The ideal *Lemba* man had courage, rhetorical ability, and sound judgement. Thus even though *Lemba*'s public functions were usurped by the colonial state, *Lemba*'s leadership criteria continued to be exercised. Still, the divisive forces of the new order drew *Lemba*'s initiates farther and farther apart as individuals accommodated themselves to new roles.

Populist Religion and the Missions: Katula

Ngambula discarded his ancestral medicines and charms in 1917, two years after he met Scheutist Fathers at Kangu mission, because he had a dream in which the white-robed Catholic priests surrounding him persuaded him to take up the "truth, the word of God." Despite the strength of the dream, he kept his *Lemba* name and identity, and postponed baptism until he was on his deathbed some years later.

Another *Lemba* priest who converted to Christianity, but unlike Ngambula became an active evangelist and teacher of the new faith, was Katula Davidi of Nseke-Mbanza in the eastern Manianga. Katula with his young wife had participated in the last *Lemba* inauguration of the region in 1919 along with Luvuangu-Mampuya and his wife. Whereas Luvuangu-Mampuya had stubbornly held to *Lemba* while joining the colonial administration, Katula was persuaded by the forceful preaching of Swedish missionaries to give up his *Lemba* insignia. He only kept the hollow *n'kobe* box as "souvenir" after discarding its contents. Reminiscing to me in 1965, he noted that *Lemba*'s membership criteria had been particularly important in maintaining a high level of leadership in precolonial society. What attracted him to Christianity, and particularly to Protestantism, was the possibility with a few years schooling of becoming leader of a local congregation and teacher in the local school, with literacy the key to interpretation of the Scriptures.

Although Christianity attracted many for this reason, it was in its way divisive. By the twenties, mission societies had divided up the entire Congo, and Protestant and Catholic missions competed everywhere for African souls. A friendly missionary priest or pastor was a powerful ally in dealing with the foreign colonial government. The tendency for Africans to identify with and support "their mission" and "their missionaries" led to the alignment of the foreign Catholic/Protestant schism with pre-existing African divisions and distinctions, precipitating numerous religious feuds.

Protestant populism particularly undermined the priestly class of *Lemba*. Although both Catholicism and Protestantism—indeed, *Lemba* as well—publicly maintained the ideology that their way was for all, Protestant missions were more prone than other religious persuasions in Congo to make everyone a "priest." Early converts were often slaves ransomed and brought up by the missions. Early translation and wide dissemination of KiKongo Bibles amplified this effect. Catholics handled access to religious truth more cautiously, insisting on properly consecrated priestly roles and graded Bible-story books and catechisms. Both types of Christianity drew many converts from the ranks of those who had aspired to the powerful traditional medicines and cults, but who for a variety of social or economic reasons had failed.

The Common Man's Dilemma: Ndibu

Ndibu, who at the turn of the century lived in Kingoyi, east of Mboko Nsongo, felt called to join *Lemba*, the highest ranked *n'kisi*. However even with the patronage of his clan he could not afford it, given the gradual shift of resources from kinship and ceremonial expenditures to colonial taxes. A feeling of blockage led him to Christian baptism. Ndibu's autobiography, written for Swedish missionary Laman, describes beautifully the situation of a common man.[6]

To begin with, Ndibu's marital status was complicated. In youth with the help of his father he chose a girl as his bride. Since she was too young to take immediately, he married an older woman first, again on suggestion of his father. The older woman died soon after. At the same time his father died, leaving behind two wives. Before the burial could be held, his father's estate and the fate of the two women and their children needed to be decided. Ndibu hoped to receive some money from his father's estate, but was informed that not only had his father left no money, but that the slave-women and children would become his. Ndibu reluctantly accepted this proposition. His clansmen comforted him that women would be better than money, which would be spent leaving him with nothing. A woman could be of help and solace.

The date for his father's burial feast was set. Mats, cloth, *pièces*, and other supplies were gathered, and the tomb prepared. Many friends came. Great quantities of gunpowder were consumed in salvos to make it an "honorable burial." Several elephant tusk horn ensembles performed to stimulate the dancing. The festival so strengthened Ndibu that he was able that night to go to bed with one of the women he inherited, and, as anticipated, she became pregnant.

Ndibu, on returning from drawing palm wine one day, found his neighbors gathered in his court. They announced to him that he had just become a father of twins, a girl and a boy. Under pressure from his neighbors he called the priest of Funza to initiate him, his wife, and their newborns to the twin cult of Funza. In the Mboko Nsongo region Funza is held to be a spirit in the *bakisi* class, the origin of all *min'kisi*. Nzambi is the invisible source of unity in the universe; Funza is Nzambi's visible and material side, patron of twins and the source of the multiplicity of powers. Parents of twins when initiated become not only priests of Funza but high priests of all the *min'kisi*, since their twin children are special spirit-children.

All this was awesome to Ndibu, but he went along with the initiation rituals. Each step of the initiation involved persons from the family and elements of the natural universe, both being sacralized with a song. The priest pronounced instructions for raising twins, such as not to treat them unequally and always to remember that they were spirit emissaries. And he stressed that Ndibu and his wife were the parents of twins, as the song for crossroads indicated:

I am the source of Nsimba;
I am the source of Nzuzi;
I have given birth to Nsimba;
I have given birth to Nzuzi—
Easily, easily,
Like the cricket, like the grasshopper.

Ndibu took his responsibility very seriously, doing all he must to abide by the codes of twin parenthood in Funza. But then disaster hit, leaving him fearful and disillusioned. He wrote:

> Look what happened. When the children began to grow up and to stand, one of them took sick with a swollen stomach and suddenly died. Oh! how sad. The little girl had been such a beautiful child. But we prepared it for burial in a grass mat, and dug a grave for it at the crossroads. As it was the female child that died, we mounted a *mukuta* basket, took Lemba-Lemba plants, and Nsanga-dinkonde and a Lubota tree and planted them on the child's tomb. Then we prepared a mortuary statue, assembled the medicines,and told the remaining child not to become angry because of the death of its twin Nzuzi. In doing this we hoped that the *bakisi* would leave our land alone, since they might have thought that the prepared *mukisi* was conveying a sign to seize parents of twins somewhere else. We also distributed a token of palm wine. . . . But then in 1912 the mother of the twins herself died. In that same year I decided to be baptized.

In spelling out his motivation for baptism to Christianity, Ndibu expresses less a religious conviction for his actions than an existential desire to clarify his muddled life situation, to find meaning in his sadness and relief from fear of *bakisi* that haunt parents of twins.

> When one gives birth to twins, one makes association with all the *bakisi*, and one should not fear a *mukisi.* When the *bakisi* call to go prepare them *n'kisi* medicine, you go. The instruction is to join the *bakisi* of the earth with those of the water.
>
> Only two of the *bakisi* refrain from killing parents of twins: *Lemba* and *Lumani*. These alone. *Lumani*'s priest has adequate drink and food and would never seek out parents of twins. *Lemba*'s owner, even if he were angry, would never harass a parent of twins. But to get this privilege, parents of twins must pay the extravagant sum of five or six pigs. Were this not the case, people would initiate only to *Lemba*. Especially parents of twins, for *Lemba* and *Lumani* are the only *bakisi* that do not harass parents of twins.

Even after baptism, Ndibu considers *Lemba* to be the ideal ritual solution for parents of twins. He blamed his lowly economic situation for his inability to make it into *Lemba*.

There were no doubt many more individuals like Ndibu who saw themselves alienated from the sources of power and protection offered in the traditional religious system. Populistic Christianity offered by the missionaries, backed up by some political protection and the hope of education, held forth a solution to many in Ndibu's rank. Others found this a new type of alienation and did something about it by participating in the prophet movement that broke out in the Lower Zaire in 1921.

Seeking Redemption in the Colonial Setting

Despite the drain on indigenous labor and resources of portage, railroad construction, and colonial taxes, and despite the gradual undermining of indigenous chiefship, the negative rhetoric of missionaries toward indigenous religion in Lower Zaire, for nearly a generation after the beginning of colonialism *Lemba* chapters continued to control exchange circuits, to play a role in peacekeeping, and to hold initiatory séances. In the thinking of the populace and *Lemba* priests with whom I spoke, the sudden appearance of African prophets, more than anything else, destroyed *Lemba*.

Luvuangu-Mampuya and Katula both walked to Nkamba and Kiese near the Zaire River to see for themselves what Kimbangu and the other prophets were doing. *Min'kisi* were being discarded *en masse*. What impressed people most was that whereas the old magicians and healers had only been able to heal, the new prophets could "raise the dead." Although few *Lemba* priests joined the prophets, many functions of the old, ceremonial organizations and of chiefship were adopted by the prophetic communities.

Who were the prophets of 1921, and why did they appear just then? This subject has prompted voluminous resarch; it must suffice here to review a few of the explanations I have developed elsewhere.[7] Of the new roles of leadership that developed in Belgian colonialism, the catechists who worked with European missionaries probably came the closest to acceptance in the knowledge and power of the new order. Their authority centered on access to the Bible, the sacred source of European authority (an *n'kisi*, in effect), knowledge of which, with the attendant skill of literacy, opened up new vistas. Despite their access to the source of European religion, it had become apparent to some catechists by the first decades of the century that their authority merely served European colonial superiority. Especially Protestant catechists, to whom full spiritual power had been promised, were liable to growing disenchantment. Complaints began to be heard about not being able to study beyond the second or third grade, to study medicine in Europe, or to earn the same salary for services rendered as the Europeans. The growing gap between expectations and realizations produced myths of secret or hidden knowledge kept from the Africans by the missionaries.

Kimbangu and his apostles, drawn from the ranks of disenchanted catechists or catechist-aspirants, were perceived to have been granted the true power of the Holy Spirit and the Bible, bypassing the mediation of European missionaries. Even though Kimbangu and his main followers were arrested after a few months of public ministry and exiled for life, their revolution destroyed what remained of the authority of the old political-religious institutions like *Lemba*. By taking upon them some of the trappings of authority such as the staff (*nkawa*, *mvwala*), and the redness, whiteness, ecstatic possession, the power of purification, and the power to heal and raise the dead, the prophets had laid claim to the symbols of the paralyzed traditional offices of authority. A new era had begun.

Part II

The Rituals of *Lemba*: Management of Reality

"Who can bring a clean thing out of an unclean? There is not one."
—Job in Job 14:4

"Those who suffer He rescues through suffering and teaches them by the discipline of affliction."—Elihu in Job 36:15

Introduction

The present section examines *Lemba*'s rituals and their role in *Lemba*'s influence over society and its material resource. The authority of *Lemba*'s adherents rested on the right of the most pure to levy fines for moral transgressions. The high level of rhetorical skill and influence of *Lemba* priests and priestesses created an effective governing order over a network of markets, alliances, and trade routes. The *Lemba* priesthood thus usually coincided with the bases of economic and political power in the wider society and with the possession of crucial knowledge. Songs, puns, legends, and rites indicate that the authority wielded by *Lemba* was rooted in an ideology of esoteric and mystical sources such as ancestors and spirits. Practitioners of *Lemba* thus consolidated its governing capability and coordinated public resources by manipulating ritual symbols effectively. This is why a closer examination of *Lemba* rituals, the task of this part of the book, is important for an understanding of *Lemba*'s overall impact on seventeenth- to early twentieth-century Congo coast society.

The major source of evidence on the *Lemba* rituals is a set of largely unpublished indigenous texts, with supporting evidence coming from ethnographies and the mute records of museum artifacts. These textual, ethnographic, and artifactual—art historical—sources will be presented in the form of four Lower-Congo, regional variants and a composite profile of *Lemba* in the New World. Chapter 4 presents the northern variant among the Kamba and the Yaa people living to the right and the left of the Kwilu-Niari River valley in today's Republic of Congo. Chapter 5 presents the eastern variant among the Lari north of today's capital of the Congo, Brazzaville. Chapter 6 depicts the central variant of *Lemba*, among the so-called Bwende and Nsundi peoples of the Manianga region of Lower Zaire. Chapter 7 provides the western variant from the inland Yombe and the coastal Vili and Woyo, the former living largely in Zaire, the latter in Cabinda and Congo. Chapter 8 presents the New-World extension of *Lemba* with material from Brazil and Haiti. Unique characteristics and problems in the source materials will be discussed at the opening of each chapter; a more general methodological and theoretical critique of the issues in analyzing rituals needs to be explored first.

One issue concerns the varied nature of the evidence and the random manner in which it was collected. A set of old ethnological questions may be asked: Are the variations spurious or significant? What are their underlying determinants? Are the varied song texts, ritual acts, and symbolic forms and combinations "free variations" which reflect individual creativity within a latitude of more structured limits? Or are they due to structural variations in social, economic, possibly even ecological zones described in foregoing chapters on the *Lemba* region?

The four regional variants are in part grounded in a quite self-conscious differentiation made by the indigenous writers between "schools" or "styles" of *Lemba* ritual. The author of Text 1 (northern variant) speaks of a distinctive "Kamba" style which is contrasted to a "N'tini a Mongo" style with which he is more familiar. Similar allusions are made in the indigenous accounts of "Yaa" and "Lari" *Lemba* rites which have, in the eyes of the authors, distinctive features. These "ethnic" diacritica will be used where appropriate, but cannot however be systematically applied. In fact they seem to be used by authors outside their home areas, and these latter, such as "Nsundi" and "Bwende," do not appear in the indigenous accounts, nor do "Yombe," "Vili," or "Woyo." It is possible that these ethnic designata, which I have critiqued in Chapter 2, were and are introduced by Europeans and are not part of the indigenous culture at all. Or if they are, they pertain to distinctive *Lemba* zones or stylistic characteristics.

Some stylistic variations not consciously announced by the indigenous writers are however significant in terms of structural variations in the societies of the *Lemba* region. For example, as will be explained in more detail later, coastal Vili and Woyo *Lemba* shrines reflect a less elaborate initiation rite and a less complex *nkobe* than is found farther eastward; this is combined however with an extensive backyard grove and sometimes a fixed "house" shrine. Such a gradual transition from the portable *nkobe* to the backyard shrine may be correlated with a gradual transition in local political structure from the market governing committee without chiefs, historically, to the presence of prominent local chiefs and even kings nearer the coast. The western variant of *Lemba* seems warranted then because of the unique set of symbols correlating with a specialized type of political structure.

Other variations of importance in understanding social change are not of a regional nature. All writers describing *Lemba* initiations meticulously detail the type and quantity of economic object exchanged. Thus it is evident how the economic levels of the initiations vary from the opulence of the Kamba area near copper mines and rich agricultural lands to the relative poverty of the Lari area on the sandy Teke plateau, and from dues paid in traditional goods to the use of colonial tax currency in the Western variant. Changes introduced with colonial currency are not to be explained as mere regional variations, they are part of the eroding exchange economy of the early colonial period in which *Lemba* had by 1930 been destroyed.

Another important variation in *Lemba* ritual which is not regional is the differential reference to widespread patron spirits such as earth goddess Bunzi, dualist demigod Mahungu, trickster Moni-Mambu, and numerous ancestral figures. It is not easy to account for alternating uses of these spirits in *Lemba* since they exist throughout much of the region in most local pantheons. Differential reference to the one or the other may reflect a "sectarian" preference, or the subordination of one figure to another.

To adequately capture variations bound both by regional considerations and those spanning regions or those having no particular regional articulation requires an analytical approach which can combine both local, concrete and more abstract issues. For this reason the chapters of this section will each begin with a portrayal of local rites based on textual accounts, but will then in the latter part of each chapter pick up themes which may figure more widely such as the social structure of clan alliance, the logic in *Lemba* medicines, *Lemba* naming, or the characteristics of *Lemba*'s patron spirits.

Related to the variation of *Lemba*'s rituals is the issue of the assessment of type and quality of data, and the determination of which is the best analytic framework for the uneven assemblage of lyrics, medicinal recipes, lists of rules, etiological myths, historical and ethnographic interpretations, and artifacts. In other words, which theoretical model best bridges all the textual, ethnographic, and art historical (artifactual) data? An initial determination of types of available data and their locations of origin was made in Figure 1 (see also the essay on sources, below). Sources were divided into "artifactual" objects derived from authentic *Lemba* settings and events; "etiological texts" derived from authentic *Lemba* events and explanations in KiKongo; and "ethnographies," that is attempts to describe *Lemba* and to relate it to its social and physical environment. Despite the high quality of these sources, they are of varied scope. The ethnographies of *Lemba* initiations range from those which are event-specific, probably even based in a few instances on eye-witness or participation, to those which describe norms or customs or even ideals. Among the lyrics, some appear to be highly original and individualized, whereas others, or parts of all of them, appear to be standardized phrases which occur widely. In the case of the artifacts, some are crude whereas others reflect great craftsmanship. It is necessary to exercise a critique of quality which delineates the type of data, its inner form as intended by the actor or as interpreted by the analyst, as well as its quality as an aesthetic object or performance.

These concerns for assessing the data and analyzing the various kinds of evidence of *Lemba* ritual will be met through the use, in each of the following chapters, of a limited number of *expressive domains* drawn out of textual and artifactual evidence. These expressive domains will for the moment be defined as areas or modes of behavior with a high degree of consistency in form and meaning and a considerable specificity in the vehicle used, because they are based upon a cultural consensus or are inherent in the sensory capacity of all actors. Expressive domains to be used in following chapters are: (a) the spatial and temporal distribution of events in the séances, that is the formal events structured by an apparent sense of the sacred; (b) the exchanges of goods and symbols in these events, tied to the local economy of subsistence production as well as the regional and worldwide commercial economy; (c) the social organizational idioms used in *Lemba*, often based on kinship, with special emphasis on modes of achieving public order; (d) the sacramental objects (*min'kisi*) composed for the séance and given meaning in the context of the culture's classification system; (e) verbal categories of ritual process as found in indigenous exegeses and descriptions of the institution; and (f) lyrical scores of songs and etiological myths of *Lemba*. This set of domains is not exhaustive. It excludes, for example, dance and instrumentation, both known to have been primary in *Lemba* but unavailable for analysis because of *Lemba*'s extinct status. Nor is this set of domains necessarily composed in the only manner possible. Colors could have been dealt with separately, as they have been by several authors.[1] However, colors are often part of a larger ritual code and have here been subsumed under the sacramental objects. The rationale for the present choice of expressive domains lies both in the demand for a consistent analytic format in the face of randomly composed data, and in the theoretical understanding of how a rite such as *Lemba*'s initiation generates meaning, affect, and social control. It will become clear that what I call expressive domains provides *Lemba* actors with a set of related yet autonomous vehicles of expression to deal with difficult issues and formidable contradictions. I shall illustrate this shortly.

The approach taken rests on several lines of analysis in the study of symbolism, metaphor, and communication, and it is appropriate to review these approaches very briefly. Proponents of the so-called symbolist approach to the study of expressive behavior have emphasized the many-layered "strands of meaning" in symbols and their expression of "deep meaning" or "dominant" themes.[2] In this view, a culture's basic values and themes, as well as its major institutional profiles, can be gleaned best through the study of ritual symbols performed in "total events" such as cockfights,[3] electoral campaigns,[4] divination séances,[5] festivals, pilgrimages,[6] healing and initiation ordeals,[7] and religious movements, to name a few. Criticism has been leveled at this approach for allowing arbitrariness and mere description to substitute for explanation of symbolic behavior. To counter this criticism, some proponents of the approach have emphasized that expressive symbols are always rooted in materialistic, sensorily observable areas such as the physiological, emotional, affective, and economic realms of human experience.[8] It is a strength of this approach that, indeed, the sensory and emotional can be combined with the cognitive realms of human life. These are appropriate emphases for a study of *Lemba* which for three centuries constituted a major north-bank institution and provided the context for dominant symbols and social ideologies. The fact that these symbols focused on illness and healing confirms the importance of a theoretical view rooting symbols in materialistic considerations on the one hand and in ideologies on the other.

Another scholarly tradition in the study of expressive domains has emphasized the structure of metaphor. In this view the linkages and associations between expressive domains are made the primary focus in analysis. Modes of expression such as sculpture, literature, myth, music, masking and the like are considered to each have their inherent, autonomous characteristics. Analysis looks at the combined, "orchestrated" media, and the structure by which combinations of media are joined. This line of analysis yields "root metaphors"[9] and "deep structures"[10] which articulate common principles across all expressive media. Although these metaphors and structures resemble the deep or dominant symbols of the foregoing approach, there is here a greater emphasis on understanding the manner by which a metaphor achieves "movement," the way in which one domain is associated with another or with the total social context to achieve evocative and emotional power.[11] In the study of *Lemba*'s expressiveness this approach is of considerable help. While the distinctive contribution of each mode of expression—be it song, proverb, medicine, fictive kinship, gift exchange, choreography—must be understood in its own terms, all must be related to the dominant metaphoric statement about *Lemba* alliances, economic ties, and healing. There is in *Lemba* ritual an orchestrated quality by which each "instrument"—each expressive domain—plays its unique music but contributes to the overall harmony of the major themes which are more than the sum of their parts.

The overall meaning of many levels of expression in a concerted performance is grasped best by a third approach which combines the sensitivities of the symbolists for the focal symbol and of the structuralists for the relationship of expressive levels in metaphor. This approach has been called "semiotics" by some,[12] and "communications theory" by others;[13] its varied proponents work in such a diversity of ways, however, as to render the use of these labels almost meaningless. Nevertheless, the analysis of multiple levels or modes of expression as approached by these scholars proceeds in a helpful way, for present purposes, by establishing a set of redundant messages along numerous expressive channels that point toward "meta-messages" or signification of greater generality than a single level or mode, thereby addressing the condition of the whole culture and its relationship to the natural world.[14] In this approach the dichotomy culture/nature, so much a tender nerve of contention in the whole field of performance analysis, disappears before the set of messages that range along the entire spectrum from genetic to kinesic to reflexive-muscular to verbal to behavioral to the self-conscious dramatic. In other words, there is no break between the cultural and the natural; there are only numerous idioms or vehicles of performance and communication, each with their sensory modes and their intangible signification. Also, the analyst is not held to be a human deity who possesses "etic" objectivity in the study of indigenous "emic" subjectivity. Rather, each mode or domain of expression has its "code" which permits the actor to work towards performance and excellence, and which helps the analyst to achieve understanding. Such codes do not, of course, fall ready made onto the researcher's notebook. He must construct them if they are not evident in the performance. In the analysis of performance in anthropology, folklore, drama, and criticism, and in social and behavioral sciences generally, emphasis in deciphering codes has been placed either on cultural genres with their own logic and meaning or upon universal sensory-perceptive capacities. In the present study the codes of expressive domains will provide insight into mostly cultural and social rules and principles, although there is in some areas such as reproduction and spatial/temporal ordering of events, as well as in the therapeutic framework of the entire initiation, evidence of noncultural constraints.

The basic units of analysis of *Lemba*'s expressiveness in the present study will then be (1) the domains—space and time in the initiation rite's layout, exchange of goods and symbols, social organization, medicine and the therapeutic, verbal categories of ritual action, and the lyrical—(2) the domains' codes, that is the regularity in terms of which variations make singular sense, and (3) the relationships between domains, in particular in whole situations with a clear context. Some of the codes will be derived from the persistent and widespread interpretations given in native exegesis to such symbols as the *Lemba* drum or bracelet, or explanations derived from verbal categories such as *handa*, "to initiate or consecrate a medicine," and *handa n'kisi*, "to enter a cure in the consecration of medicine." Other codes will be derived from recurring types of events or acts at particular places in the space-time order of the séance, or from the regularity of certain kinds of exchanges between leading figures such as father and child, husband and wife, or the initiated and the noninitiated.

Once such order has been determined within a domain, and its explanatory code established, it will be possible to perceive the metaphoric links between domains. For example, while the exchange of goods, gestures, and words builds up a fabric of reciprocal obligation between the neophyte, his kin, and *Lemba*, the lyrical domain characterizes in song and declaration the heroes of the past or spirits in whose name events and persons receive legitimation. Thus, as the neophyte's kin receive an offering of pork stew and manioc bread, the neophyte priest and his wife (or wives) receive from the *Lemba* priesthood their symbols of authority; the metaphor (or shifter) is the statement that "gods' food" is the medicine of the new *Lemba* couple. The exchange of human food against offerings of trade goods occurs contrapuntally, as it were, to the distribution of medicines. The priestly couple's political authority is established amongst the patrifilial children and the local public, while they rise in the *Lemba* order. All this activity in the social and economic domains sets the stage for the reconstruction of reality in the lyrical domain.

Culture heroes such as earth goddess Bunzi, trickster Tsimona-Mambu, androgynous demigod Mahungu, to name a few, span the gap between a distinct *Lemba* consciousness and the conventional religious culture of the region. In conventional narrations these heroes are often entangled in dilemmas of human life, showing scenes well known to students of African oral literature. Human tragedy is frequently transformed into animal parody in which monstrous animals, ghosts, or familiars take up the plot as if they are dancing out a cleverly concealed psychoanalytic transference. In *Lemba*'s etiological narratives, by contrast, these heroes avoid such traps and entanglements, taking lengthy narrative bypasses to reach what is heralded as "the *Lemba* solution." In effect, *Lemba*'s ideology attempts to resolve complications enacted in the conventional narratives. The problematic, thus blocked out of *Lemba*'s lyrical domain through possible resolution, is however brought back into consideration in other expressive domains such as the spatial ordering of séance events, the ceremonial exchanges, and the composition of medicines where action and object are better able to articulate contradictions and to mediate symbolic resolution. Thus the methodology of expressive domains permits us actually to see the alignment of alternatives in a culture with the intent of bypassing implacable problems.

The opening *Lemba* initiation variant from the Kamba (Chapter 4) will offer the context in which to establish the analytic technique's usefulness. This reference text is the longest and most detailed as well as internally the most consistent of all accounts of a *Lemba* rite at our disposal. A short discussion of *Lemba* from the Yaa to the north of the Kamba stands in sharp contrast to it.

The eastern variant, based on a number of texts and accounts (Chapter 5), tests the method's capacity for identifying reportorial errors and gaps, as contrasted to simple ethnographic variation. An important element in this test is the use of the notion of "code" to explain each domain. Additional variants of the rite will allow further testing. For example, in the domain of spatial and temporal ordering of séance events, it becomes clear that an inner logic requires mediation of the village with the world beyond: the bush, forest, river, and cemetery. This rhythm between the inner household world and the outer world of "powers" is found everywhere, even in Haiti in the New World. Accounts which omit it may be considered erroneous or partial. Elaboration of a domain's code thus lends the analysis its most effective criticism of the quality of textual material.

The central variant (Chapter 6) permits development of the analytic issue of the *Lemba* etiological text in relationship to non-*Lemba* myths in the conventional Kongo-language oral literature. Mahungu, the hero to whom *Lemba*'s origin is attributed in the central region, is compared to other Mahungu myths.

The western variant (Chapter 7) extends the analysis of hero mythology—the lyrical expressive domain—to another common figure, trickster Tsimona-Mambu. Common structural features in Mahungu and Moni-Mambu myths within and without *Lemba* permit generalizations about the "ideological" manipulation of consciousness in *Lemba*, from the "tragic" endings of the conventional narratives on these figures to the "heroic" or "resolution" endings in *Lemba* narratives. Because the vehicle of *Lemba* resolution of social contradiction is the *Lemba* medicine, the drum and the bracelet, and because of the high concentration of collected *Lemba* artifacts in the western region, full analysis of the expressive domain of "medicine" is deferred until the chapter on the western variant.

The New-World variant, concluding with Price-Mars' account of a *Lemba*-Petro séance in Haiti (Chapter 8), offers a final test of the validity of codes discovered in the expressive domains. There is at least a 150-year divergence between New-World and Old-World *Lemba* expressiveness. Not only do the Lower-Congo ritual codes and variants assist in the identification of authentic *Lemba* elements in the Haitian variant, but also the converse is true. This latter identification, which reflects an earlier level of *Lemba*, suggests the presence of "proto-*Lemba*" structures, symbols, and metaphors at the basis of both African and Afro-Caribbean culture. These features exhibit a greater emphasis on fertility than on the trade and mercantilism so prevalent in the late-nineteenth- and early-twentieth-century Congo manifestations of *Lemba*.

Chapter 4

The Northern (Kamba, Yaa) Variant of *Lemba*

"That which was a 'stitch' of pain has become the path to the priesthood."—Kwamba, Text 1.94

Introduction to the Sources

The northern account of *Lemba* is based on two textual sources: the first from "Kamba" country, by Kwamba Elie,[1] an excellently detailed rendering of an initiation and healing, with insightful comments on *Lemba*'s organization and its theory of power; the second from "Yaa" country, by Lunungu Moise,[2] a briefer report of the rituals but with more extensive discussion of the pollution and purification theories in *Lemba*. The two authors were members of the group of sixty catechists who at the beginning of this century formed the teaching staff of Swedish missionary-linguist-ethnologist Karl Laman. At their workposts throughout north-bank Kongo they collected responses to Laman's ethnographic questionnaire. The *Lemba* texts are a small portion of the overall catechists' corpus of 23,000 pages.[3]

Very little is known about the catechists' ethnographic instructions, although the list of questions around which Laman's well-known Uppsala series *The Kongo I–IV* was organized indicates that all texts on *Lemba* come from answers in the section on "*min'kisi*," consecrated medicines. It is also apparent that neither Kwamba nor Lunungu are in their home territories, since in prefatory remarks not translated here they distinguish *Lemba* as they are witnessing it with *Lemba* "at home," or they state that it is just the same as "at home." Nevertheless, their incorporation of technical "native" terms is noteworthy, suggesting that they had no difficulty with the language.

The translation I offer is as literal as possible. Further exegesis and commentary follow in the second part of the chapter in keeping with the method of "expressive domains" outlined earlier.

The Lemba *Séance Near Mboko Nsongo (Among the Kamba)*

Text 1

RECEIVING THE LEMBA CURE FOR LEMBA ILLNESS

(1) *Vo muntu una handa Lemba, buna una teka baka kubela kwa ntulu ye kihemi mu ngudi ntulu sangama.*

If a person would receive *Lemba*, first he must get a chest cough, the stitch, or breathe with difficulty.

[(7) *Nkianguna Lemba wazensila mu nitu andi mu mubedisa.*]

For *Lemba* manifests itself in his body by making it ill.

(2) *Buna yandi una fidisa mwana ye nsusu ye malamu kwa nganga Lemba.*

Then he must send a boy with chicken and wine to the *Lemba* priest.

(3) *Nganga una vitula mpolo yena mu nsaba ye fidisa kwa mubedo.*

The priest will mix *Mpolo* [earth] into a small pot and send it to the sufferer.

(4) *Mubedo bu kanwini Mpolo Lemba bio kahodidi buna weka Mwana ma Lemba ye nganga weka Tata ma Lemba.*

When the sufferer has drunk the *Mpolo Lemba* and improves he then becomes a *Lemba* Child and the priest a *Lemba* Father.

(5) *Buna una fila nsusu zole kwa Mwana ma Lemba kasukula mu nwa Mpolo kampodisila ye banzila mpe lumbu kiantula Lemba mu nitu.*

Then [the Father] sends two chickens to the *Lemba* Child whose mouth was cleansed with the *Mpolo*, and instructs him in considering a day for putting *Lemba* into his body [for initiation].

(6) *Kadi wonso wanwa Mpolo una handa; yandi kidi kabiala mu mbongo.*

For whoever drinks *Mpolo* will be initiated; he must be in command of fortunes.

(8) *Idiodio Mwana ma Lemba una kubama mu keba ngulu zazingi, nsusu, mbizi bia ndia biankaka bialumbu kia mpandulu mboko fila ntumwa kwa Tata ma Lemba kiza kahandisa mwana.*

Therefore the *Lemba* Child will begin assembling many pigs, chickens, and other edible animals for the day of initiation. Then he sends a messenger to the *Lemba* Father that he should come initiate his Child.

THE FIRST GATHERING OF THE PRIESTS

(9) *Yandi Tata ma Lemba una bokila nganga zankaka bende nandi mu handisa Lemba kwa mwana wambikisi.*

The *Lemba* father then calls the other priests to help him initiate to *Lemba* the named Child.

(10) *Bu bizi bakatumisa buna una sola makambu manata kwa mwana ma Lemba bonso buzolele Tata ma Lemba kwa yandi mu mpandulu, mbo nanguna biabionsono bivwilu mu nkisi wa Lemba ye nata.*

When the invited come then he elects a delegate to send to the *Lemba* Child expressing to him the *Lemba* Father's wishes regarding the initiation; all who possess *Lemba* come and bring it with them.

(11) *Bu bizi tula kwa Mwana ma Lemba buna Tata una sika ngoma ye mikonzi ku fula dia bula.*

When those who will initiate the *Lemba* Child come, then the Father sounds *ngoma* and *mikonzi* [drums] at the village entrance.

(12) *Ye makambu una kwenda kwa Mwana ma Lemba mu ta vo:*

The messenger [from the priests' ranks] goes to the *Lemba* Child and tells him:

(13) *Bonga malamu ma Tat'aku ma Lemba ye ma mimbanda wabakotisa ku lumbu lwaku.*

Fetch the wine for your *Lemba* Father and his wives and bring it to them in your enclosure.

(14) *Buna yandi una nanguna biabio ye hana kwa Tata ma Lemba, mbo kotidi mu ngudi hata dia Mwana.*

Then the Child will hold all up and present it to the *Lemba* Father as he enters the court of the Child's village.

ENTRANCE INTO CHILD'S COURTYARD; INSTRUCTIONS OF MPOLO CURE

(15) *Bu kakotidi una tangununa ebu:*

When [the *Lemba* Father] has entered, he sings this song:

(16) *Ko-ko-ko? Ko!*
Wanunga Lemba wanunga? *E—Lemba!*
Will you gain *Lemba*? Yes—*Lemba*!

(17) *Kiazinga Lemba,* *Kuyusaul Lemba*
What *Lemba* gives, *Lemba* takes away;
Kiasa ntangu, *Kuyusula ntangu.*
What the sun gives, The sun takes away.

(18) *Ndozi binunu kalotwa,*
You may have dreamed of ancestors,
Milunga mianganga miakwangi kalotwa,
The copper bracelets of priests he has dreamed.

(19) *Ngulu zanusinguku*
Pigs to assure
Kima kiabwa mu mamba
That the thing [causing illness] may fall into the water,
Katwizidi.
That's why we've come.

(20) *Ko-ko-ko? Ko!*
Wanunga ngeye wanunga? *E—Lemba!*
Will you win it? Yes—*Lemba*!

Mboko una bonga nkunga ena:

Then [the *Lemba* Father] takes this song:

(21) *Dibedi vwamva,*
That which was the fawn,
Diankabi lolo.
Is today the adult *nkabi* antelope.

(22) *Dibweni mulengo ma Lemba?* -*A-ma Lemba!*
Have you encountered
difficulties with *Lemba*? A-a-ma *Lemba*!

(23) *Mbe kifwanga kiaseha*
Oh! It is that which dies, which laughs
na bambwa.
with the dogs.

(24) *Nieka tadulu dia kanda*
Become guardian of
ma Lemba. *A-a-ma Lemba!*
the *Lemba* clan. A-a-ma *Lemba*!

(25) *Bana Lemba kukandila*
Children of *Lemba*, protect them;
Ku zumbu kinzinga;
And their forests and fields;
Bu kiahanda ma Lemba. *A-a-ma Lemba!*
Those who initiate to *Lemba*. A-a-ma *Lemba*!

(26) *Mbota tatu bungidi wo*
Three *mbota* sticks you broke
Handa nasumika lusaba
Initiate, and I apply the (*lusaba*) medicine pot
ma Lemba. *A-a-ma Lemba!*
of *Lemba*. A-a-ma *Lemba*!

(27) *Nabonga mandala minatula*
I took palm arches and installed them,
ye mandala;
And palm branch arches;
Mbwangi mu lusaba lwa Lemba.
And put copper bracelets in *Lemba*'s (*lusaba*) pot.

(28) *Nayika Tata ma Lemba*
I became a *Lemba* Father
ma Lemba! *A-a-ma Lemba!*
of *Lemba*! A-a-ma *Lemba*!

(29) *Tata ma Lemba bu keti sa bobo buna ha kimosi ye Mwana Lemba keti longuka ye banganga bumosi beti sa bu beti sumika lusaba luanzensila makaya.*

As the *Lemba* Father sings this he is together with the *Lemba* Child who is learning from the priests when to apply the *lusaba* pot and to cut plants into it.

(30) *Mpimpa yoyo bana kina nkununu yanene nate ye bwisi bu kiedi.*

This same night all dance a big *Nkununu* dance that ends at the break of day.

(31) *Banganga bu bana swaka mwana ma Lemba, mbo yambula kina.*

When the priests have washed the *Lemba* Child, the dancing ends.

GOING TO A DISTANT PLAIN

(32) *Lwaka mpila mosi, kwenda nseke nda mu vwota nsokia vo mbongo zina mana mu moko maku;*

Then they go to a distant plain to don *nsokia* grass skirts so money will [not] be depleted in their hands;

(33) *kansi butuku vwikidi mulunga wankwangi mu koko bubu weka nganga yantela mu Lemba.*

but that access to the copper bracelets will be forthcoming to him who would become a priest in *Lemba*.

(34) *Nkiangunu wonso una kuta kimpela buna ukusumuni mu diodio Lemba kana kuhanina mbongo ye una mana yandi.*

Whoever desecrates him will spoil *Lemba* because of this, and must be charged a fine thereby furthering the neophyte in his initiation.

NEOPHYTE'S DUES PRESENTED; INSTRUCTIONS CONCERNING PROFANATION; LEMBA "MARRIAGE"

(35) *Bu bavutukidi ha hata, buna makambu una kwenda ye mwana ma Lemba ku lutengo mu mukamba biayenda na Lemba vo muntu swakulu bonso ena: ngulu yamimbanda, ngulu tanu zanganga zanatwa kwa Tata ma Lemba; ngulu tatu zanene zambudulu ngungu ye Tat'aku ma Lemba.*

When they return to the village, the priests' delegate takes the *Lemba* Child aside and informs him that those initiating to *Lemba* owe the following at this point: a pig for the priests' wives; five pigs for the *Lemba* priests—which are brought to the *Lemba* Father—three pigs, large ones, to the *Lemba* Father for the drumming of the *mukonzi*.

(36) *Buna una hana ngulu zazonso bonso butudi makambu; mboko honda ngulu ye mwangisa menga mu muzumba kinzungidila madiedie kansi ngulu tatu zambulu nkungu zina kebo zamoyo nateye nganga zazo zenzi, mboko honda zo.*

Then [the Child] gives all the pigs, as the delegate instructed. Then they kill the pigs and spread the blood in a circular trench. But the three pigs of drumming the songs are kept alive until all priests have spoken, then they are killed.

(37) *Tata ma Lemba bu kahondidi zo, buna una bonga menga ye zunga ha bunsaba.*

When the *Lemba* Father has killed them, he takes the blood of an *nsaba* pot measure

(38) *Mboko tula ku nima nzo ye ha mwelo.*

and puts it behind the house and on the door.

(39) *Mboko bana kwenda ye Mwana ma Lemba ha nima nzo mu kaba ngulu zozo ye kunkamba vo: tala mpala nkute kimpela.*

Then they go with the *Lemba* Child behind his house to distribute these pigs and to instruct him in guarding against strangers who would disrespect him or profane him.

(40) *Buna una tomba mono yakubela makambu mu kufutisila dio kidi watala bonso nganga Lemba kasilanga nkasu mu dia mbongo za Lemba.*

Then [instructs his *Lemba* Father] you will call me to show you how to demand the fine, so you can see how the *Lemba* priest exhibits vigor in collecting *Lemba*'s money.

(42) *Mukento bu kena mu mamba vo bakala una kulumuka ye lembo kunkamba katomboka mu mamba kaluta, buna una futa.*

If a woman is at a stream, and a man descends and speaks to her, and ascends together with her, he must pay.

(41) *Nga ti ndonga yamwana buna lomba malamu kaka.*

[For this instruction] a single "wine" is request from the ranks of the neophyte.

(43) *Mbo bana nwa malamu koko nima nzo ye mimbanda miatata ye mwana ye sika minkonzi ye nkunga ena:*

Then they drink this wine behind the house together with the wives of Father and Child, and drum *minkonzi* for this song:

(44) *Tata na Mwana basunda ko,*
Father and Child will succeed in all,
ma Lemba. *A-a-ma Lemba!*
of *Lemba*. A-a-of *Lemba*!

(45) *Kibedi kununika*
He who perseveres
Malenge kieka,
Becomes successful before
Singu diatubisa Bunzi
The curse thrown by Bunzi
ma Lemba. *A-a-ma Lemba!*
of *Lemba*. A-a-of *Lemba*!

(46) *Dibe kanga diesama*
That which was a barren plot
kiekimpwaka ma Lemba. *A-a-ma Lemba!*
has become fertile—by *Lemba*. A-a-by *Lemba*!

(47) *Ndozi bata buyakwama*
Dreams of *Lemba* Fathers
ma Lemba. *A-a-ma Lemba!*
when they tortured me. A-a-of *Lemba*!

(48) *Ko-ko?* *Ko!*
Wanunga Lemba wanunga? *E—Lemba!*
Will you gain *Lemba*? Yes—*Lemba*!

(49) *Tata ma Lemba nwa malamu mankunga za Lemba.*
The *Lemba* Father drinks the wine for the *Lemba* songs.

(50) *Nata mikole mu hembo;*
Wear the band over the shoulder;

(51) *Mwana wabaka mbongo zalunga;*
The Child found sufficient funds;

(52) *Dieka bobombo,*
And later he will gain
wiza wambindula.
access to *Lemba*.

(53) *Nkundidi ku nsi,*
I supplicated the earth,
Nkundidi ku zulu.
I supplicated the sky.

(54) *Wanunga Lemba wanunga?*
Will you gain *Lemba*?
Ko-ko bwe Lemba?
Ko-ko what is it with *Lemba*?

Tata ma Lemba vo:
The *Lemba* Father replies:

(55) *Kubedi bunganga*
That which was difficult

(56) *Matondo ya ma Lemba, ma Lemba,*
In gratitude from *Lemba*

(57) *Weka kungwamu mutumbi mabinda*
Has become a source of healing power, that
Nyiaka bana, ti nionzi zakula;
Heals the children,
makes *nionzi* fish grow big.
Bihambi vunza tolo ma Lemba.
Those who wait get a portion in *Lemba*.

(58) *Mboko bonga milunga ye sakumuna mio.*
Then [the Father] takes the bracelets and blesses them.

(59) *Lwika mimbanda mia Mwana ma Lemba mu nsoko umosi umosi ye hambana, bu kameni bieka Mwana ngang'andi.*
When he has consecrated his neophyte priest, he takes Child's wives and each receives a copper bracelet one by one.

NEOPHYTE'S FIRST PROFANEMENT

(60) *Lumbu biankaka bu biahioka, buna watubwa kimpela kwa mpala mu diba, yandi Mwana ma Lemba buna ntumbu tumisa Tata ma Lemba kiza kansonga bonso kana lomba mbongo zanzensidi mu kimpela kwa Lemba.*
Sometime later when he goes out and another person drops something from a palmtree on him, the *Lemba* Child quickly

sends for his *Lemba* Father to show how he must exact the fine of profanement.

(61) *Tata ma Lemba bu kizidi, una sika ye yimbila vo:*

When the *Lemba* Father comes he drums up and sings this:

(62) *Ko-ko-ko? Ko!*

Wanunga Lemba wanunga? *E—Lemba!*

Will you gain *Lemba*? Yes—*Lemba*!

(63) *Yebedi mfwenta yeka*

He who was lazy, has become

mbukuni i mbumba

industrious—

mvamba ma Lemba! *A-a-ma Lemba!*

paradox of *Lemba*! A-a-of *Lemba*!

(64) *Mukonzi nasika kwandi*

The *nkonzi* drum is sounding

u-nkembo ma Lemba. *A-a-ma Lemba!*

for the festival of *Lemba*. A-a-of *Lemba*!

(65) *Kayika biyadi mfuba nzamba*

He has become a harvester

of the *nzamba* field,

muna nzo ami kwandi

in my house

mubuyangi. *A-a-ma Lemba!*

in happiness. A-a-ma *Lemba*!

(66) *Mbo una lomba malamu mamunungusu Lemba kwa muntu wa ta kimpela kwa Mwan'andi ma Lemba ye ngulu ya nkonko Lemba ye buta kwa nkonko Lemba ye ngulu ya binganini bia Lemba ye ngulu ya mimbanda.*

Then [Father *Lemba*] requests the "wine of achieving *Lemba*" from the one who profaned his *Lemba* Child, and a pig for the *nkonko Lemba* drummer and elder of the *nkonko*, and a pig for the *Lemba* host, and a pig for the priestesses.

(67) *Mboko futa ngudi nzonza mu muntu vo kumi dia ngulu ye ngulu yansweki ya Tata ma Lemba buna muzita Lemba una mona ye tambudila sungama.*

Then [the debtor] pays the chief speaker a bondsperson or ten pigs and to the *Lemba* Father a "secret pig" so that the Child's *Lemba* statue will see and respond well.

(68) *Mboko mwana ma Lemba una sumba ngulu yina fwa mitete mitanu mu yandi mbongo yambundukila.*

And the *Lemba* child pays a pig of five *ntete* baskets of raphia cloth for his redemption.

(69) *Bu kasumbidi ngulu tumisa Tata ma Lemba ye nganga zankaka biza bamanisa Lemba ye yokila wo kuni ngudi nkobe ye kaka nzo mu mbiekolo yazimunina mu mpandulu Lemba.*

When he has the pig ready he summons his *Lemba* Father and the other priests to come complete *Lemba*, dry the wood for the *Lemba* box, and "secure" the house for the final consecration of the *Lemba* initiation.

ASSEMBLY OF PRIESTS FOR CLOSING RITE

(70) *Nganga zazonsono bu zizidi bana bikula vo:*

When all the priests are on hand they proclaim:

(71) *Ko-ko-ko! Ko!*

Wanunga Lemba wanunga? — *A—Lemba!*

Will you gain *Lemba*? — Yes—*Lemba*!

(72) *Dibe disu diatia*

That which was a spark in the fire

Dieka nkama ye makumi

Has become a hundred and ten

ma Lemba! — *A-a-ma Lemba, wansila bo!*

of *Lemba*! — A-a-ma *Lemba*, do it like that!

(73) *Wahanda Lemba, sika mukonzi,*

If you would receive *Lemba*,
You must beat the *mukonzi* drum;

Wasa na mbongo ma Lemba. — *A-a-ma Lemba.*

And pay *Lemba*'s wealth. — A-a-its wealth.

Wangula mu yoko mbau.

Cleansed in the fire.

(74) *Mboko Mwana ma Lemba bongidi ngulu tatu, bahondidi zankielolo.*

Then the *Lemba* Child takes three pigs and they are slaughtered.

(75) *Mpimpa yamvimba yimbila nkunga vo:*

All night long this song is sung:

(76) *Wahanda Lemba*
You who have received *Lemba*
Sunga tolo nge twangembo
Be alert like the bat
Muna bubu ma Lemba.
In the night of *Lemba*.

(77) *A-a meka ngie maluboko-yongo,*
Be evasive like the night-jar,
Mbo wayene ma Lemba.
So you will see *Lemba*.

(78) *Mukento wakikundi nakutula*
Put away your mistresses
Muniku nungu ma Lemba.
So you can keep access to *Lemba*.

(79) *Mboko mu nsuka bana honda ngulu yina yanene ye kwanga mankonde mamingi, biobio bina lamba kwa bala babutu mu kanda diodio diaweti handa Lemba.*

Then in the morning the big pig is killed, and lots of manioc bread and plaintains are cooked by the patrifilial children of the clan receiving *Lemba*.

(80) *Bala bu beti sala bobo, buna banganga benzi nseke nda.*

While the "children" are preparing the meal, the priests go to a distant plain.

(81) *Bu bena kuna bana ta kwa Mwana ma Lemba vo: bu tuna vutuka mu bula, buna ngeye una leka mumbanda wa Tat'aku ma Lemba, ye yandi una leka n'kento wawaku mpe.*

As they go they say to the *Lemba* Child: When we return to the village, you shall lay with the priestess-wife of your *Lemba* Father, and he shall lay with your wife too.

(82) *Buna mu diodio una kia meso mu lomba mbongo kwa muntu utubidi kimpela ye ta sa mina mia Lemba bonso miena mu ngolo kwa nganga.*

In doing this your eyes will be opened to ways of requesting goods from those who profane and transgress the laws of *Lemba* that give the priest his power.

(83) *Bu bameni kumutela bobo, mboko tota makaya mama: mumbwangu-mbwangu, mundanda-nzila, ndimba, minkwi-sa-mianseke, nuila-mwindu, mulolo. Momo mana kanga ha lubongo mboko vutuka.*

After this has been stated, the following plants are collected and mixed: *mumbwangu-mbwangu*, *mundanda-nzila*, *ndimba*, *minkwisa-mianseke*, *nuila-mwindu*, *mulolo*. These are wrapped in a raphia cloth and then they return.

(84) *Bu bavutukidi ku nseke nda viokakana ku mpemba mu bonga mukuyu wanduka mu nkobe mu bedi bakulu bandi, buna bonga kanga (tadi dia butoto) ha bulu (zindiama).*

On their return from the far plain they pass by a burial place to fetch a wise *n'kuyu* spirit from amongst his ancestors by taking a clod of earth from the grave; it is put in the *Lemba* box.

(85) *Bu batukidi ku bikinda bobo, buna bana kwiza mu kaka nzo mandala ye mandala—mbwangi.*

When they have returned from the cemetery they enclose the house with many palm branch arches.

(86) *Mboko bana ledika lukaya lumosi-lumosi mu momo matukidi mau ku nseke nda momo mandala maba, ye mboko fuka milele miamingi kunzunga ye kotisa mumbanda mia Tata ma Lemba ye mia Mwana ma Lemba.*

They take one from each plant from the plain and attach them to the palm branch arches, and wrap many cloths around the "lodge"; a wife of the *Lemba* Father and one of the *Lemba* Son are brought into the lodge.

(87) *Batuta makaya momo matukidi ku nseke nda mu matadi.*

They then take the plants brought from the plain and mash them together on a rock.

(88) *Bu bameni tuta makaya momo buna Tata ma Lemba ye Mwana ma Lemba ntumbu kota nganga zankaka zina sika mikonzi ye minkunga ye makinu ku mbazi.*

After the leaves are mashed Father and Son *Lemba* enter the lodge quickly while the other priests are drumming *mikonzí* and singing and dancing outside in the courtyard.

(89) *Buna bau bole bana solana bakento baluku umosi umosi mbo lekana bo.*

The Father and Son have each chosen the most beautiful wife, and have intercourse with them.

(90) *Bu bameni ngiela yoyo bana kubasona namanga-manga, kidi nganga zankaka zazaya vo Tata ma Lemba ye Mwana ma Lemba makiolani.*

When they have done this they make designs on the women so the other priests will know that the *Lemba* Father and Son have had coitus with them.

(91) *Buna bana bonga bidiu bilembi bala kilambu ye kwenda ku nima nzo mu kaba kio ye handa Mpolo Lemba.*

They take the food cooked by the patrifilial children—the *kilambu* meal—and go behind the house to distribute it and to compose *Mpolo Lemba* medicine.

(92) *Buna banganga bana kaba kilambu kiokio kwa bala batuka mu kanda diodio babonsono.*

The priests distribute the *kilambu* meal amongst all the patrifilial children of the [initiate's] clan.

(93) *Kilambu bu kilungidi, buna bana sika mukonzi ena:*

When the meal has sufficed, the "Children" drum this *mukonzi*:

(94) *Kuka-kuka* [sound of drum]
Kibe kihemi
That which was a "stitch" pain
Lweka lukula banda manganga he.
Has become the path to the priesthood.

(95) *A-a kieka kimakisa*
A-a he has caused to rise
Ntangu ma Lemba.
The sun of *Lemba*.

(96) *Kimfwila kiami kiaba*
My death has occurred
Na Tata ma Lemba
In the *Lemba* Father;
Ku mukula moyo ma Lemba.
Now there is life in *Lemba*.

(97) *Mbokò bonga makaya momo mabatutidi mu vula kia milele*

ye hesona kanga dibe ku ndiamu soba hanionso mu bulu ku nima nzo mu mamba ye malamu, mbo tula mu nsaba,

Then they take the plants pounded together in the village, take them from the raphia cloth, and take grave earth, and mix all this together with water and wine in an *nsaba* pot which is

(98) *buna yeka Mpolo Lemba yilenda fidusu kwa wonso bwilulu kwa Lemba, ye nsaba yoyo kukangila mu lutumbu koko nima nzo ntangu zozo.*

inserted in a hole behind the house. This prepared *Mpolo Lemba* can then be sent to whoever is struck by *Lemba*.

(99) *Diaka bana bonga nkobe ye tula kanga diodio momo buna dieka mukuyu.*

Again they take up the box and put the sack in it thus binding in the ancestor spirit.

(100) *Tula tukula ye kolwa biamakaya mabedi ku nseke nda matuta mimbanda mu ngudi nkobe;*

Tukula red and the bundle of plants from the plain are mashed by the *Lemba* wives and put in the center of the box;

(101) *ye mfumbu zabundwa kwa nganga zazonsono zazi: milengi, nsala zamoko ye nsalu, nkongi, mikenzi mianlele miankulu mianzo muntu-muntu.*

also a package of the following from each priest: hair, finger-nails and toenails, eyebrows and pieces of old cloth from each one's house.

(102) *Mbo mimbanda mia Mwana ma Lemba mina kanga mizita mu lukongolo lwankobe mina kala dimbu kwa mulumi au vo mumbanda sumukini mu miau, buna una tala mizita kani miena bonso bumi a tudidi.*

Then the wives of the *Lemba* Child tie the statues together in the circular box as a sign to their husband. If the wives profane themselves the husband can inspect the statues to see if they are still in place.

(103) *Kansi vo muzita watengama buna wasumunu.*

If a statue is leaning on the side, this indicates profanation.

(104) *Mboko bana nanguna nkobe Lemba ye kwenda yo kotisa mu ngudi nzo a yulu lwa mbatu ye mbo nianika mikonzi lwandu ha mwelo nzo.*

Then the *Lemba* box is ready and is placed inside the house on a shelf; the *nkonzi* drum is placed over the door of the house.

THE POWER OF LEMBA IN HEALING

(105) *Lulendo lwa Lemba lwena mu bakisa muntu kubela mbo mpe kumpodisa, kidi ka baka mbongo mu yandi bu kameni kuntula mu nitu.*

The power of *Lemba* manifests itself in seizing with sickness an individual, also with healing him and taking his money after it has been put into his body.

(106) *Bilongo bina sadulwa mu mbukulu a mbwidulu a Lemba i bina kaka bibasoka mu mbungu: bieka nkumbu Mpolo Lemba.*

The medicine used in healing those struck by *Lemba* is only that which has been put in the cup: consecrated, it is called "*Mpolo Lemba*."

(107) *Nkiangunu nganga una nianguna nsaba ye katula bina findambu ye nwika.*

Therefore the priest will open the *nsaba* pot and remove a small portion and give it to the patient to drink.

(108) *Bu keti katula Mpolo, buna una tangumuna mpe ena:*

When he removes the *Mpolo*, he will chant this:

(109) *Kitukidi mu ntangu*
That which comes from the sun
Kukatula ntangu;
The sun takes away;
Kitukidi mu ngonda
What comes from the moon
Kukatula ngonda.
The moon takes away.

(110) *Tata ma Lemba*
Father *Lemba*,
Wambuta, wandela.
He gendered me, he raised me.

(111) *Zangata mansi*
Praise the earth,

Wazangata mayulu.
Praise the sky.

(112) *Kadi nayikidi*
For I am enhanced.
Nyenda nseke-nseke
I have gone far.
Nanseke watwawalula
From far I brought it back.

(113) *Ubafimba mu ndonga*
Search in the ranks
Yabala babutu
Of the patrifilial children
Mu luvila lualu.
Of your clan.

(114) *Ko-ko-ko?* *Ko!*
Wanunga Lemba, wanunga? *E—Lemba!*
Will you gain *Lemba*? Yes—*Lemba*!

(115) *Yambula mumbedo waniaka,*
Let go of the sufferer so he may be healed,
Kidi wakotisa mwanzole mbongo
He will bring the goods accordingly,
Fiwansakila nabangang'aku.
Thereby offering a gift to your priests.

(116) *Mbo kana bonga nkula ye ndimba, kusa mu usoso zameso ye kila mamoni mpe mu moko, kidi vumi kia kinganga kaluta monika mu yandi.*

Then he takes *nkula* and *ndimba* red and rubs it around his eyes and in lines along his arms so that the respect due the priesthood will be made manifest in him.

THE LAWS OF LEMBA

(117) *Nga mina mia Lemba miena kwa nganga kaka ye mimbanda miandi.*

The laws of *Lemba* apply only to the priest and his wives.

(118) *Lemba una katuka mavumba, katuka ngolo tina ye lembo kala diaka.*

But *Lemba* may lose its scent and lose its strength permanently.

(119) *I mu diambu diamizita miatulwa mu lukongolo lwa nkobe bukahandu vo kiokio kina kaka dimbu kiampandila ma nitu kwa Lemba vo sumunu kwa muntu.*

The figure-statues placed in the circular box at initiation are a sign of the presence of *Lemba* in case of transgression of the laws by the person.

(120) *Ikiangunu, nganga kana sweka muntu umusumuni ye lembo mu dia mbongo ko.*

For this reason the priest cannot ignore the profanation and refuse to take the fine payment due him.

(121) *Vo mumbanda una sweka, buna mizita mitengamani Lemba sumukina, tinini, weka kizekele, kifwa mbombo ye makutu.*

If the *Lemba* wife tries to hide a sin, the statues will indicate *Lemba*'s profanation, its loss of scent, and its deafness.

(122) *Diela dimeni mvu-mvu yikatuki mu yandi weka kifwanga.*

Its spirit will have left it forever and the one associated with it will die.

(123) *Lemba uhandungu kwa bakala dimosi mboko bieka mimbanda miandi mu keba mina mina bakila ulumi'au mbongo mu Lemba.*

Lemba is received by a single man and his wives are consecrated to keep each of the laws so that their offspring may be preserved in *Lemba*.

(124) *Nga yandi wabiekwa Lemba kwa ngudi a nganga bu kabwilu kwa Lemba kibeni kidikalunga mu kanda dia mase mandi mu baka mbongo nkiangunu una wo zaba nsadulu ye mbukulu ye mpandusulu ye mpandulu ye bilongo kwa ngudi nganga mina tuka miomio miamionsono.*

He who is consecrated in *Lemba* by the high priest, when he is possessed by *Lemba* he will go request money in his father's clan in order to learn healing and initiating and the initiation and the medicine before the appropriate high priest, whence all this comes.

(125) *Buna Mwana ma Lemba zebi bonso bwena nzila mu yandi Lemba.*

In this wise the *Lemba* Child will know the way of *Lemba*, and its laws.

(126) *Nganga Lemba kana mona mpene vo yanga nkento nganga ko!*

A *Lemba* priest may not see a nude woman nor lay with the wife of another.

(127) *Kana dia mbongo zabalembolo kuntela kimpela ko!*

He may not take fines other than those arising out of profanation.

(128) *Mutima ngulu kana dia Tata ma Lemba bu kakidi moyo ko, kansi ufwiti kala wa Tata ma Lemba wampandisa.*

The heart of the pig may not be eaten by any *Lemba* Father, it must be the *Lemba* Father who initiated the neophyte.

(129) *Kalenda dia ntoba mpe.*

He may not eat *ntoba* manioc stew either.

(130) *Kalendi dia biabiomba ko.*

He may not eat anything unclean.

(131) *Kana lomba mbongo za Lemba ye ka lembolo nganga ko.*

No one may ask for *Lemba*'s goods without being a *Lemba* priest.

(132) *Vo sumukini kina kimosi mu biobio, buna una tumisa nganga zankaka biza kaka nzo ye honda ngulu mu udiangolokolo kwa Lemba.*

If any of these laws are transgressed, then that one will call other priests to erect a lodge and kill a pig to renew *Lemba*.

(133) *Buna nganga veedidi ye vutukidi kala bonso kana ntete waduna wakondwa bunkuta kwa Lemba diaka bu kabanza vo una hondwa.*

Thus the priest is purified and returns to the former state, not fearing the wrath of *Lemba* as before thinking he would be killed.

(134) *Nganga Lemba ka sadilanga kinganga mu kwenda buki yonso ntangu kazolele ko, kansi ubakilanga mbongo vo bete dia malamu dinsotonini muntu wankaka, buna didi zo kwa yandi, vo titi kianguba, vo titi kia yaka, vo fikanga.*

The *Lemba* priest does not use his priestly office to go heal any time he wishes, rather he collects fines only if wine is spilled on him by another—then he charges for it—or a peanut shell, or a bit of manioc, or some earth.

(135) *Ye wena nsisi bu keti zieta mu mavata malembolo Lemba.*

He is greatly feared as he travels in villages without *Lemba*.

(136) *Mukawa kaka kana nata ye nlunga wankwangi mu koko; nkuutu ye nkalu yansekola malamu bina natwa kwa kilezi kitalanga vo kololo ye bansumuni, buna yandi una kamba vo nanguna mamba.*

He will carry only a staff and a copper bracelet on his arm; the satchel and a calabash for tapping wine will be carried by a youth who watches that he is not made drunk or profaned, in which case a fine will be imposed.

(137) *Tata ma Lemba wena diswasani ye Mwana ma Lemba, kadi Mwana ma Lemba kaka mu diedila bantu katubukidi dio kansi Tata ma Lemba wena kundu ha ntandu a kinganga kiandi.*

The *Lemba* Father is different from the *Lemba* Child, for the *Lemba* Child can use his intelligence on people only to heal, whereas the *Lemba* Father has *kundu* power surpassing that of the Child.

(138) *Mu diodio Mwana ma Lemba una lembana kala detila ye Tata ma Lemba mu vumi.*

For this reason the *Lemba* Child will be unable to surpass his *Lemba* Father in honor.

(139) *Kadi Mwana lenda tina vo si kafukisa kanda diandi mu dia ye ngudi a nganga.*

The Child can leave his clan if it is threatened with decimation and "eat" with the high priest.

(140) *Lemba kalendi zimbakana kanda diateka kala ngang'andi ko, nkiangunu kana bwila muntu vo katumbulu banzila mu hingana mu kala nganga ko, mfumu a Lemba bu kafwa.*

Lemba will not decimate a clan which already has one of its priests, and it will not possess a person who has thoughts of being a priest when a *Lemba* chief dies.

(141) *Ikuma habedi nganga Lemba, nganga una hingana hoho, kidi mbongo zasensisa Lemba mu kanda kazidi katuka mu kanda diodio ye zimbala.*

Therefore *Lemba*'s priesthood is inherited with the wealth given to *Lemba*. *Lemba* is then in that clan and it will not be extinguished.

Lemba in Indo (Among the Yaa)

Text 2

THE LEMBA PURIFICATION

(1) *Mpila ankaka a nkwedolo i mu Lemba, mbiekolo a bakento ku nkisi a Lemba mu lembwa yanga. Mu nsi yayi mpe mwena nkisi wau nate bwabu.*

Another way of marrying is in *Lemba*, by consecrating women who wish to be pure in *nkisi Lemba*. The *nkisi* continues in this country till today.

(2) *Buna tuka nsi ankulu, buna fu kiaki kiena mu mbiekolo yayi ya ngiobosolo kwa banganga zihendi Lemba.*

Since ancient times there is this custom to consecrate through cleansing from priests initiated to *Lemba*.

(3) *Vo bakala dizolele, vo bwabu nkento ami ka una vutuka yanga ko, buna buketi mona beti handa Lemba bahaika ha bwala, kadi bonso zeyi Lemba diena finhandila ku mfinda, kansi mambu mamakeke, buna bakwiza mo maninga ha bwala.*

If the male wishes it, and if "now my wife desires to remain pure," then it is considered necessary to compose *Lemba* outside the village, for *Lemba* is composed partly in the forest, and partly also composed on the return to the village.

(4) *Ikuma Lemba buditotokele ha bwala. Mu handila, buna nga nkento una wawana ye banganga vo bana sukula nkento andi ye yandi beni, kidi kana vutuka yanga ko.*

Lemba is brought out first in the village. To initiate, the woman and her husband meet with priests to cleanse the woman and himself, so there is no return to adultery.

(5) *Nsukulu yena bonso bwabu. Banganga bana kanga lukongolo (i.s.v. nkangulu yavandumuka) buna bana sukulu ye zinganga bana kota nsi a lukongolo, mboki banganga bana kubasikula mu mbwasulu (mbwangulu) anlangu mu bisafi.*

The purification is like this. The priests create a circle (themselves standing in line) for cleansing and the priests enter the circle, then they rinse them off with a water-soaked sprinkler of palm fronds.

(6) *Tula nlangu mu longa mboki bondika safi biobio mu nlangu, mboki banda mu nitu zau, nate tesobukilungidi bahaikidi kwau.*

They put water in a basin then they dip the frond in water, and strike it on their bodies until it is sufficient, then they come out.

THE PADDLES OF PURIFICATION

(7) *Mboki bobo basukulu, buna nganga una kuvana fibaya nkento ye bakala. Vo bakala wena ntalu a bakento baya, buna babo bafwiti sukula ye yandi, kidi bakento bandi kabana vutuka yanga ko. Wanga nganga uvana ntalu bimbaya-mbaya bonso bwena ntalu bakento. Kadi mu bimbaya-mbaya biobio momo mwena dimbu kianzaila vo bwabu nkento umeni yanga.*

When they have all been washed, the priest gives a small wooden paddle to the woman and to the man. If the man has several wives, then each one must be washed with him so they will not lapse into adultery. The priest will distribute as many of the small paddles as there are women. The meaning of these paddles is that they are a sign that the woman will no longer practice adultery.

(8) *Lumbu kibabiekongo, vo sukulungu ikiokio, nganga ubumbikanga makasu ha kati diabaya bonso bwabu mboki vwidi nkento bu kamwani ti makasu momo masumukini ye lomba buna ntumbu zaya vo nkento yengi.*

On the day of the consecration after the washing, a priest ties a vine around the middle of the paddle  so that the owner of the woman when he sees the vine torn will know the woman has been violated.

(9) *Buna vwidi nkento ntumbu tumisa zinganga mu kwiza mona kwa tata (i.s.v., samanuka bakala dilele yandi). Ibobo bwena bila kiabaya.*

The woman's owner will quickly call the priests to come be seen of the father (i.e., expose to the male her cloth). This is the nature of the paddle.

(10) *Bakala diayanga nkento wabieko ku Lemba fwiti futa ntalu beni: muntu mosi ye bibulu ye mbongo kwa vwidi nkento.*

The man who has violated a woman consecrated in *Lemba* pays a stiff fine: one person, animals, and money to the woman's owner.

(11) *Mboki yandi kibeni vwidi nkento fwiti vana nkombo mosi yibana dia zinganga. Mboki diodio bu dimeni buna nganga una vutuka tula vo fula diaka makasu mamona va baya.*

Then the owner himself of the woman must pay one goat kid to the priests. This is for the purpose of the priest returning to put a new vine around the paddle.

(12) *Ibobo bwena dimbu kiabaya diakento. Nga mu baya diabakala, buna kadiena mu diambu diayanga ko, kansi mu kundu diandi, kidi kana kwe lokingi bantu na mpimpa ko, kadi wenda ku loka, buna fwa kaka.*

This is the nature of the woman's paddle. The man's paddle is not for indicating adultery, but on account of his mystical power, so he will not curse people in the night; for whoever is cursed, dies.

(13) *Ikuma vo yandi kibeni bakala fwidi, buna mu baya diodio dina ta kimbangi kadi vo bakento bandi banhondele bu baswekele nsamu wu balekele ye bakala diankaka, kani vo yandi yandi kibeni.*

If the man himself dies, this wooden insignium will be a witness as to whether it is his wives who killed him for hiding their affairs with other men, or whether he himself was responsible.

(14) *Bu bameni tala mabaya moso namabakento bandi, vo nkento. Bu batedi vo mabakento mandi vo diankento ka disamukini ko, kansi diayandi beni disamukini ye lomba pinda, buna kabalendi vutuka kwamisa nkento ko, vo ngeye didi toko diaku, kansi buna kundi diandi dindidi.*

They then investigate the paddles of his wives, or his wife. If they see that his wives or wife did not commit profanation, but he himself profaned and called for evil, they will not come back and harass the woman alleging "you ate your man," for that would mean she had "eaten" her companion.

PROHIBITIONS OF LEMBA

(15) *Nkento bu kameni sukulu ku Lemba, kalendi vutuka simbwa kwa babakala ko. Ulenda kunsebuna nkasi andi ye mwana nkasi buko ye tat'andi.*

A woman who has been cleansed in *Lemba*, may not be touched by men, except of course she may be near her maternal uncle, her nephew, and her father.

(16) *Nga mu babakala bakimi, buna futa kaka mu simba kubasimbidi.*

But when men show themselves off and they touch her, they must pay.

(17) *Nlele andi kasimba ko, nga buna futa.*

If they touch her clothes, they pay.

(18) *Wasumbuka nti ukadieti, futa.*

If they step over a log where she has walked, they pay.

(19) *Kuhiole, vo kwena kini kiandi wahiokila ko, futa.*

If they linger and do not withdraw where she dances, they pay.

(20) *Kulendi kuntela mbila ko, nga futa.*

If they stare at her for any reason, they pay.

(21) *Kulendi kuntuba loko ko, nga buna futa.*

No injury may be spoken against her, or they will pay.

(22) *Vo muntu weti bula (teta) nkandi kantimbudila sula futa kaka.*

If a person is breaking palm nuts and one ricochets and hits her, that person shall pay.

(23) *Mu nsi ankulu yakwaku (Indo) buna mfutulu yaluta kala mu bantu bole bole mu futa, muntu ndiena sumuni nkento wasukulu ku Lemba. Bantu nkatu, buna futa mbongo.*

In earlier times in this region of Indo, payment of two people was the main way of handling the profanation of a woman cleansed in *Lemba*. If no person was available for payment, money was used.

THE COMPOSITION OF N'KISI LEMBA

(24) *Mpandulu a Lemba kizeyi ko vo yena diswasana ye mpandulu ye ya Bakongo. Kadi mina miankaka, buna mpila mosi kwandi (i.s.v., ku beti handila muntu wankaka ka lendi ko kwenda, mboki mfutulu ambongo zazingi zingi, buna mpila mosi, kadi kundambu nsi eto buna difutulwa mbongo zazingi mu handa).*

I do not know whether the initiation to *Lemba* is different from that of the *Bakongo*. There are some rules that are the same (e.g., during initiation another person may not pass by, he will be taxed much money; also the same as in our country, the initiation itself costs much money).

(25) *Mboki mu zingi, buna mpila mosi, kadi kwaku, buna zingila beni bazingulanga.*

With the ceremony, it is the same; here they simply dance around together.

(26) *Lemba mu nsi yayi, mbaduku, buna i nsukudulu.*

Lemba in this country, initially, consisted of the cleansing.

(27) *Mboki bukazole handa nkati handa, buna ukwendanga ku mfinda ye nganga mu handa nkati nsalu. Kadi mpandulu a Lemba yena bonso nkisi miankaka miaminene, b.v., teba longo kimosi mboki yimbila nkunga. Mboki, longuka mbukulu ye longuka ndwenga zankaka mu kiloka.*

When they want to initiate to it, they simply go to the forest and the priest does the composing. For the composition of *Lemba* is like any other large *n'kisi*: that is, teaching a rule, then singing a song. Then, learning therapeutics and techniques for saying spells.

(28) *Kadi wonso ukwendanga ku beti handila Lemba vo muntu una kwenda koko, buna ntumbu kunhonda mu kiloka.*

Whoever strays into the area where they are composing *Lemba*, he will be killed by spells.

(29) *Vo ka bazolele kunhonda, buna ntumbu kunsa zengi kiamionso-mionso nsamu tambudila kwandi, b.v., kina, tambudidi kwandi mu kinda, yimbila wayimbila kwandi, mboki vova monso-monso mambu.*

If they do not want to kill him, they create some special effects to acknowledge him, such as dancing, receiving him into the cemetery, singing, or speaking about any affair whatsoever.

(30) *Mpila nkadulu yibikwangwa Mayingi, ka lauka nadede ko. Nga kifwani kialauka. Nga lenda kwenda konso-konso mpe.*

This treatment produces a state called Mayingi; it's not exactly madness, although it resembles it, and a person can go any which way from it.

(31) *Nga Lemba diandambu yayi balenda dio handila kwandi ha bwala, kansi mu nkubu a nsusu bakwendanga ku mfinda mu handa.*

Lemba in this country can be composed in the village, but usually at the first cock's crow they go to the forest to compose it.

(32) *Nga bu beti handa ha bwala, bahanda beti handa kwau;*

mboki bankaka mu dia ye nwa malafu mau ye kina kwau, kadi mpandulu a Lemba yena lumbu biankungi.

When they compose it in the village, they just do it among themselves, while others drink their wine and dance their dances, for the initiation to *Lemba* is a matter of days of festivity.

(33) *Nga nlunga wakinganga kalendi vwikulwa ha bwala ko, ku mfinda; ye nkobe a Lemba yena bilongo ye mfusa ye betota biankaka, buna kayinde lekulwa kuhendi dio ha bwala ko, kansi ku mfinda bana dio tundila ha moko mandi.*

The bracelet of the priesthood may not be put on in the village, it must be the forest; the *Lemba* chest bearing medicines, chalk, and other assorted items are thought not to be validly composed in the village but in the forest. In the forest the bracelets are placed on [the priest's] arms.

(34) *Mboki bateka kumbufanga beni bonso bubazolele. Mboki bu kana vutuka ku bwala, buna ku nsi a nlele kana vaikila ku bwala. Ibobo bwena mankaka mampandulu a Lemba mu nsi yayi.*

They first dine mightily according to their desires. When they return to the village, they are shrouded under a cloth; they come out from under it in the village. This is how *Lemba* is composed in this country.

The Expressive Domains and Their Codes

THE SPATIAL AND TEMPORAL DISTRIBUTION OF EVENTS

This domain is quite explicit in Kwamba's account of a *Lemba* initiation. Turner and other scholars of Central African ritual have noted the participants' tendency to express their ritual actions spatially. In North Kongo the reason for this is obvious, for the village constitutes a cosmological space and an ideological unit lending symbolic structure to all rituals held in its confines.

Kwamba's *Lemba* séance begins as the priests gather at the village entrance (elsewhere it is a crossroads). Both places are auspicious sites of ritual attention, for the burial of twins, or protective medicines, the exchange of gifts, or the rendering of sacrifices. The village entrance is the main opening to the "social body," and stands in isomorphic relation to bodily openings. Thus when, in the village entrance (*fula dia bula*), the *Lemba* novice receives medicines of *Lemba*, "it enters his body" (Text 1.5), and after gifts are exchanged, the priests "enter the center of the village" (1.14). Sixty years later lemba-lemba plants used in the "opening" (*bonzo*) part of medicine in Kongo are planted at the entrance to villages, markets, and near houses associated with twins. The spatial zones demarcated in the *Lemba* rite are classificatory analogies to other aspects of the ritual cosmology such as the human body, social relationships, plants, and special words and names.

The village courtyard (*ngudi hata,* "mother," source, center; also *nkanu*, court) is the site of several key phases of the rite, such as initial instructions to the neophyte, an all-night dance, a ritual cleansing, part of the *Lemba* "marriage" as well as its "consummation." The North-Kongo village courtyard is a public place, even when a ritual event occurs there. It is also thought of as a "male" place; the men's house (*mbongi*) is found either in its center or at one end. Villages of the region usually consist of two parallel and facing rows of houses. If the village is on a ridge, as is often the case in this hilly region, the parallel rows are straight. Otherwise, they may bulge to form a circle. "Behind" the houses are cooking hearths and kitchen huts; this is "female" space. Beyond that are gardens, domestic fruit trees, trash pits, and drying racks, and then the bush or forest, considered "wild." All these zones—entrance, courtyard, house, hearth, garden, bush—become important in *Lemba* (see figures 5 and 6).

After the first large meeting in the courtyard on the first day, and the dance of the night (1.15–31), the activities move out to a distant savanna clearing (*nseke nda*). It is unlikely that Kwamba observed these activities, since he devotes only a few lines (1.32–4) to what must have taken much of the morning of the second day. Also his explanation of the purpose of the savanna phase is mostly interpretation, rather than observation. It is understandable that he should stay away, if not a *Lemba* devotee. *Lemba* rhetoric stated that a profane person who wandered near these sacred savanna or bush areas would be beaten, fined, forcibly initiated, or even killed. Other accounts suggest that what occurred within the *Lemba* group was the first instructions—as Kwamba intimates—on how to act like a *Lemba* priest. The first phase of the initiation was thus evenly divided between village and savanna clearing, a clear spatial ceremonial rhythm.

Following the priests' return from the savanna on the second day—the celebrants having stayed up all night—the neophyte couple

Figure 5
Spatial zones of *Lemba* ritual
as described in Text 1 by Kwamba

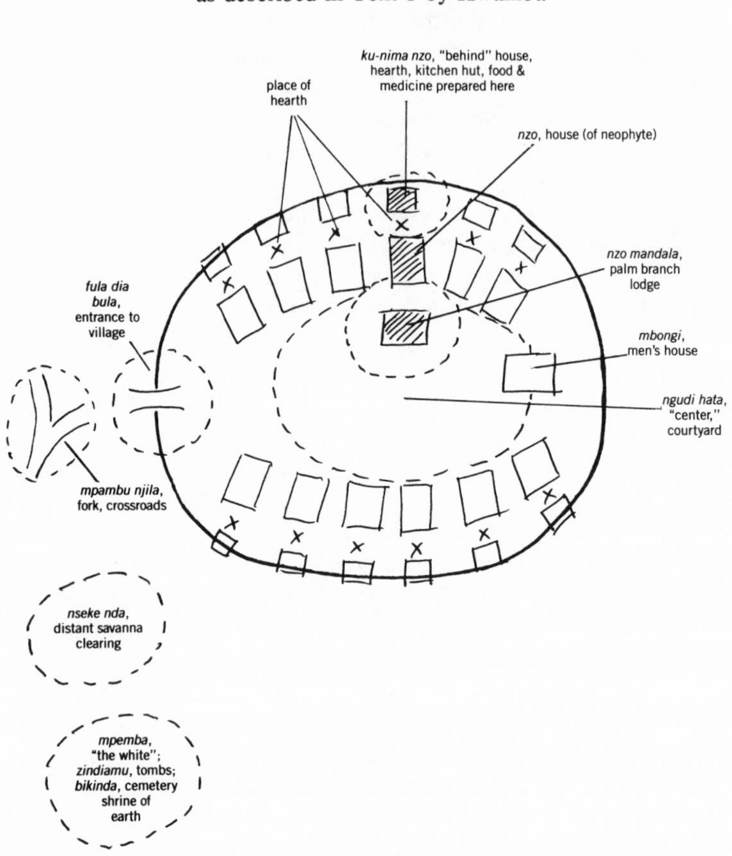

receives its copper bracelets in a ceremony in the courtyard. The neophyte or his patrons have paid the dues in pigs, which are now slaughtered, and their blood is poured in a circular trench at the door of the neophyte's house, approximately where the lodge will be built later. Sometime later priests and the neophyte couple move to the kitchen area behind the house, where more pigs are slaughtered. The couple is instructed in the ways of guarding against defilement, and the *Lemba* priestesses sing their song. The neophyte couple puts on their newly consecrated bracelets, and they, as a couple, are blessed. Pigs' blood from an *nsaba* pot is spread on the door of the house facing

Figure 6
Spatial and temporal organization of events
in Kwamba's account of *Lemba* inauguration.
Numbers refer to lines in Text 1.

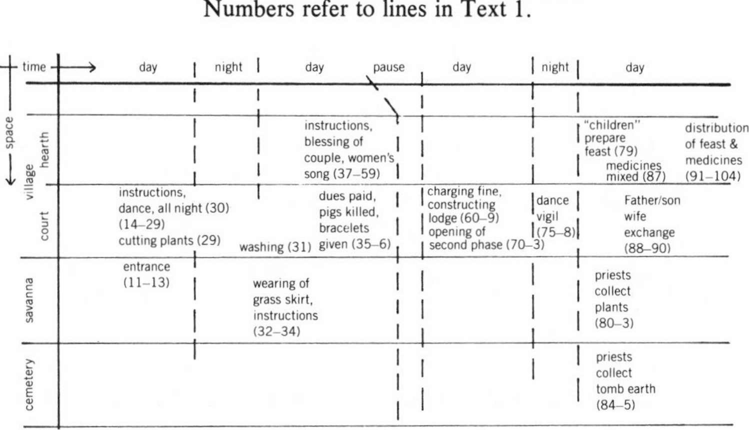

the hearth. The slaughter of so many animals suggests a distribution or feast at this point. The first half of the rite is now completed.

The rite has moved full cycle, from village to savanna and back to village. Within the village, the complementary opposition of courtyard and hearth has also been established, and in connection with the latter opposition, that of male and female has been made isomorphic. The "marriage" ceremony, the exchange of pigs for the bracelets, and further slaughter of pigs for the consecration of the bracelets suggest a sort of step-by-step movement through the ritual zones, a sacrifice or exchange at each crucial place. From this first phase of the rite the analyst must conclude that ritual here is anything but amorphous antistructure. If anything, it is superstructure, in which all available codes are made available for the creation of a cultural, cosmological statement. This is further in evidence when Kwamba notes that the priest, having been taught his prohibitions and consecrated, goes out for an indeterminate period of time to be "profaned" at some undetermined spot. Daily life is profane, its placement is hardly possible. Only when the neophyte priest is profaned—by a verbal assault, a drop of spilled wine, etc.—and notifies his *Lemba* father is the initiation rite reconvened at a determinate location and time.

The second phase of *Lemba*, concerned with restoring the new priest's purity and showing him how to maintain it, is in broad lines like the first phase in that the same spatial zones of courtyard, kitchen, savanna are again covered. Several additional zones and groups are added in the second phase. The patrifilial children—the neophyte's matriclan's male members' children, collectively—occupy the site behind the house where they take charge of the feast preparations, the usual role of patrifilial children. Simultaneously, in the courtyard before the neophyte's house, a palm arch (*mandala*) lodge is erected. During this preparatory work, the *Lemba* priests march off with the neophyte priest to fetch plants from the savanna and earth from a tomb for the neophyte's shrine box (*n'kobe Lemba*). Kwamba is not explicit about which cemetery is visited, again suggesting that he was not present. However, Kongo ritual structure would allow it only to be his father's clan's cemetery, where he would be a patrifilial child "priest," where he would be mediator, and where he would receive his spiritual identity.

On the priests' return from savanna and cemetery, the front and back of the neophyte's house become sites of accentuated symbolic charging. Whereas previously these zones had been given "male" and "female" charging, they now are made the poles of a series of exchanges between the *Lemba* father and son, and the two clans they represent, as well as between the son's clan and his patrifilial children. *Lemba* presides over this double layer of patrifilial relationships centering on the new priest. First the *Lemba* father and son "exchange" wives in the lodge before the house, that is, they have coitus with them. (The symbolism of the semen of this exchange coitus becomes clear in other regional variants, especially the eastern variant dealt with in the next chapter.) The neophyte's patrifilial children, meanwhile, are preparing the feast of real human food, while the *Lemba* priests, acting a parallel role with regard to the medicines, fictive ritual "cooks" so to speak, are preparing for the neophyte couple their fictive "food," that is, their medicines. The two levels of food symbolism are striking. Ordinary human food is gotten from the perpetrator of profanement; sacred "food"-medicine is gotten from the savanna and the ancestors. Similarly, the two levels may be seen in the distribution. The medicines are prepared in the sacred "kitchen" of *Lemba*, in an *nsaba* pot in a hole in the ground somewhere in the hearth area. At the same time, the feast of human food, prepared by the neophyte's children, is distributed by *Lemba* to these same children, dependents and supporters of the neophyte's clan, and to the general public.

The spatial and temporal coordinates of the rite have shown the central role of the village/savanna, courtyard/kitchen dichotomies, and the day/night/day temporal rhythm of the sessions. Within these ritual axes, other social and cultural signifiers such as male/female, father/son, and food/medicine are manipulated to achieve a full statement of enormous condensation and power.

ECONOMIC AND EXCHANGE STRUCTURES IN THE RITE

The exchange of material goods such as manioc, pigs, copper bracelets, and the like—items used in the regional trade—should be considered under the same rubric as the "symbolic" exchanges such as father and son's coitus with each others' wives. All goods, services, and symbols exchange hands within one and the same social matrix. There are not two economies, but rather a single social structure in which numerous media get exchanged to create or maintain statements of value. In clearly orchestrated progression these media follow exchanges between *Lemba* son and father, *Lemba* and the public, the *Lemba* son and his patrifilial children, and the like (see figure 7). The first phase of the exchange, during the first meeting of a day/night/day, appears to be a fairly straightforward exchange of material goods from the neophyte-sufferer to the *Lemba* father for ceremonial goods such as medicine, instructions, baths. The second phase entails, as has just been shown, several levels of exchange of various types of "food," including medicine as a sort of mystical food, requiring a more nuanced reading of the ceremonial economy of *Lemba*.

It is important to recognize that the neophyte does not pay more than a small portion of the overall amount of goods circulated and consumed, and that in the first phase in connection with receipt of the medicine and the bracelets. The greatest portion, that which opens the second phase, is paid by the "perpetrator of profanation" who comes up with at least fifteen pigs, a considerable sum indicating *Lemba*'s influence in the Mboko Nsongo region even as late as 1915. It is, furthermore, important to recognize that this sum is not consumed by *Lemba*'s priests in an exploitative fashion, but is redistributed through *Lemba*, to the neophyte priest's patrifilial children and the general public (1.92). As important as the volume of consumption appears, in such a séance, it cannot be explained in terms of an easing of the burden of growing biomass in an ecological niche, as New Guinea "pigs for the ancestors" feasts have been explained.[4] *Lemba* exists in an open-market situation of considerable volume in trade, as Chapter 2 has already shown. What then is the function of the profanement tax and the redistribution so clearly described in Kwamba's account?

Figure 7
Exchange structure of *Lemba* séance:
goods, services, symbols, persons

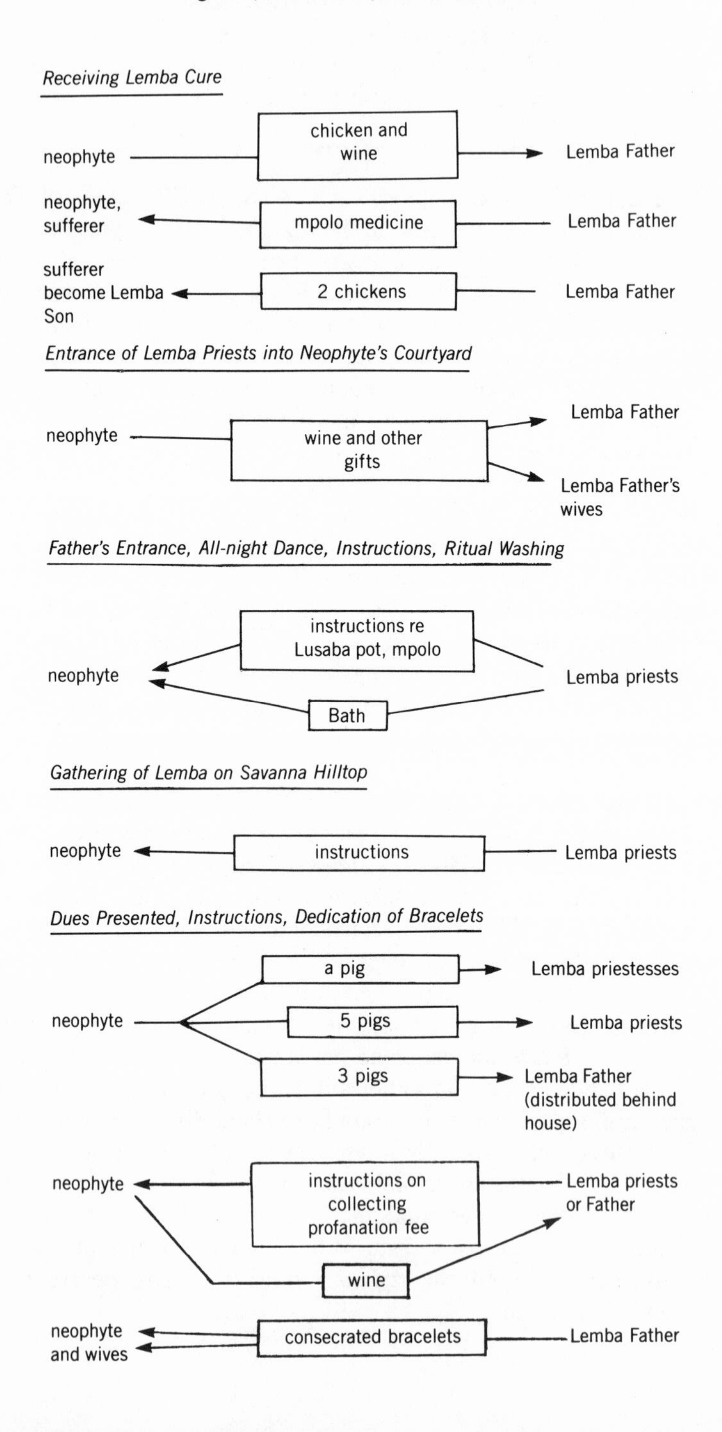

Figure 7 (cont'd)

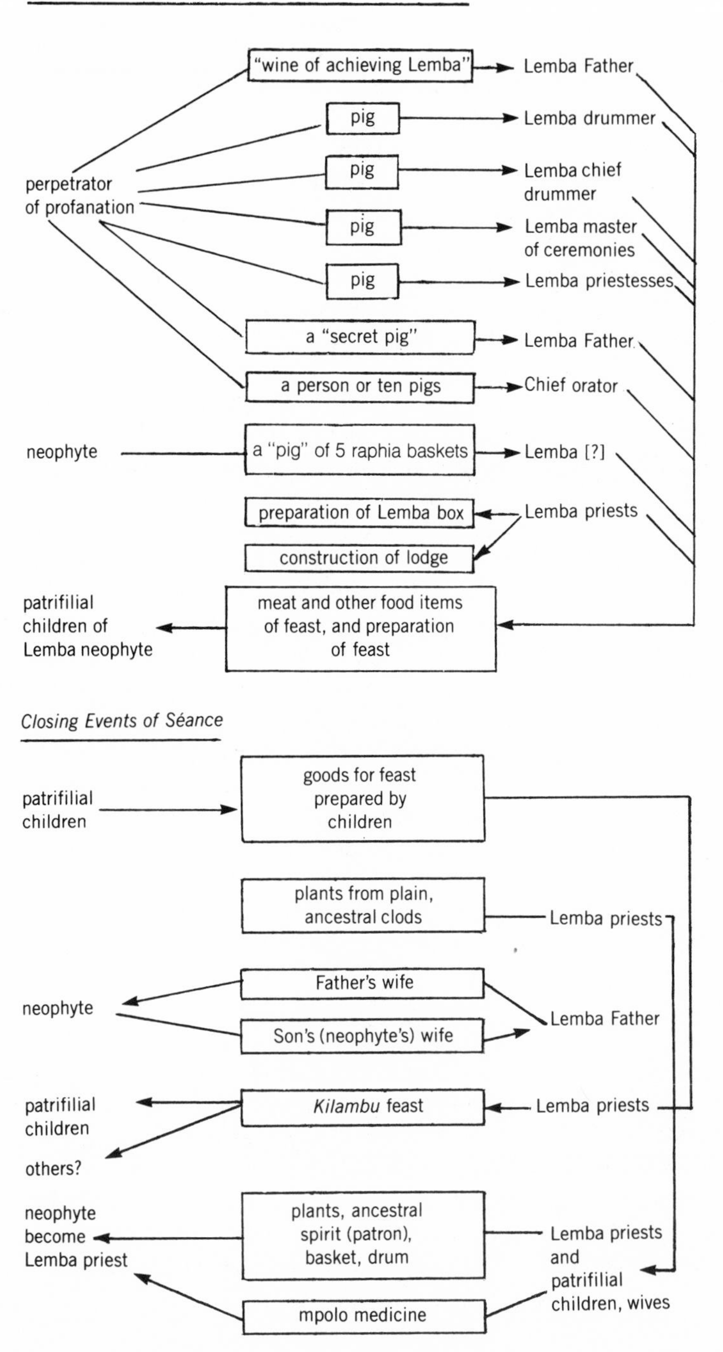

Lemba's economic function here would be the stimulation of the exchange structure over a local, perhaps "market," area, and the generation or renewal of authority symbols within that context. The exchange network brought into play in this account is the same as exists in a major marriage, funeral, or chiefly inauguration, with the difference that *Lemba*'s priestly couples from a wider area participate. From a local region, perhaps a market area or two, these prominent couples, themselves linking key clans, function as a local elite network; therefore their ties as couples, and as a collective elite, are renewed. The neophyte and his spouses are brought into this collectivity during the ceremony. Of equal importance is the group of the neophyte's patrifilial children. As a collectivity they represent dozens of localized groups, clans, who have potential reciprocal relations to him and to *Lemba*. The patrifilial children of the neophyte represent a redundant set of ties already present to a degree in *Lemba*. Thus the fabric of regional alliances is charged, and given special merit.

Where there is exchange, there is social cohesion. Distribution generates authority. Thus the connection of the feast to the neophyte's medicines is not hard to understand. The medicine, his *nkobe* as symbol of authority, is a paraphrase of the exchange and the cluster of obligations it establishes with the patrifilial children. In stimulating distribution to the children, who represent, it must be emphasized, dozens of neighboring clans, *Lemba* is merely using conventional alliance-building mechanisms available in North-Kongo society. But this alliance network is activated by the levying of a fine from some profaner "out there." Thus *Lemba*'s authority is made to extend over the profane world, creating a fan of wider legitimacy than merely those of marriage and patrifilial children. *Lemba* broadens the scope of gifts a "father" can use for the beneficence of his "children," who are also his supporters and allies.

SOCIAL ORGANIZATION: *LEMBA*'S CEREMONIAL KINSHIP

Since the overall social structural setting of *Lemba* has been discussed in Chapter 2, what may be emphasized here are the unique characteristics of the present variant. Little is said of the organization of *Lemba* as a translocal entity, although it may be assumed that someone was the master of ceremonies, the convener, and the manager. Other variants develop these features. Kwamba's account is most insightful in explaining how conventional kinship ties of father to child and husband to wife were specifically shifted by *Lemba* to maximize their translocal political integration.

The Father/Son (*se/mwana*) dyad in *Lemba* is defined as a mystical hierarchy. The *Lemba* Father has greater *kundu* power than his *Lemba* Son (1.137), and, reciprocally, the Son must give his Father greater respect (*vumi*) (1.138). The son may heal, once he is inaugurated, whereas the father may heal and govern, destroy witches, and use his *kundu* mystical power to destroy individuals for the well-being of a collectivity. But this hierarchy is a relative or situational matter, since every son is also a father, as is the *Lemba* neophyte to his patrifilial children. In certain conditions two individuals and clans will be reciprocally patrifilial, to each other "father" and "son," a situation that elicits much good humor and the ambiguity out of which profound African rituals are made. It is, in the *Lemba* séance as described by Kwamba, the structural logic behind the convergence of ritual roles in the kitchen: the neophyte's children prepare the feast; the *Lemba* priests, the medicines for the neophyte couple. To understand the social structural possibility of this mutual patrifiliality of two clans, closer attention must be paid to the *Lemba* marriage, and its unique qualities.

Kwamba and other writers on *Lemba* all emphasize the extreme morality of the *Lemba* household. Deleval in the Kavati-Mayombe, Bastian in Loango, Lunungu among the Bayaka to the north, all contrast the *Lemba* household's enduring permanence to the instability of other types of households. The rules binding the *Lemba* couple to a rigid code of purity, in Kwamba's account, are striking. *Lemba*'s laws apply specifically to priests and priestesses (1.117), not to just anyone. A *Lemba* priest may not see a nude woman or commit adultery (1.126). The figurines placed in the *n'kobe* are a sign of *Lemba*'s power in the case of profanation (1.111). Further, the stated purpose of receiving *Lemba* is so their offspring may be "preserved in *Lemba*" (1.123). According to this set of prohibitions and qualifiers, the *Lemba* marriage is a secondary, "super" marriage singling out certain alliances between clans for special attention. A clue as to which alliances so qualify for attention, which have this high priority, is given in the presence of the two-tiered set of father/child dyads in the *Lemba* séance: The *Lemba* Son and his initiatory relationship to his *Lemba* Father, and this same son's relationship as father to his patrifilial children. There is here a concern for the maintenance of an unending patrifilial chain such as exists in the permanent and enduring alliance between two clans in which every generation's son marries back into father's clan, or in which there is the mutual patrifiliality spoken of above. The emphasis on the patrifilial chain is present in the convergence of roles in the kitchen, where *Lemba* representatives and the patrifilial children of the neophyte each "cook": the latter, feasts; and the former, medicines. Elsewhere we will see these two categories of preparations blending together even more. But the kingpin of the system, as it were, is the singling out from the neophyte's polygynous household one wife for special attention—one who is "separated" (1.59)—presumably one who has the right alliance for *Lemba*'s emphasis and the ritual exchange of wives between the *Lemba* father and son (1.89). This exaggerated act—*Lemba*'s form of "royal incest"—highlights the great preference in the *Lemba* worldview for patrifilial exchange, colloquially known as "blood reciprocity." The specific form of marriage that most effectively embodies this preference is the patrilateral cross-cousin marriage, already described in Chapter 2. Linking isolated villages and markets, reinforcing the patrifilial chain across more than two generations, it establishes a permanent relationship of complimentary reciprocity between exogamous groups. The father/son wife exchange commemorates the convergence of the two classes of relationships that allow a segmentary society to function effectively: (1) the father/son tie as the model of hierarchic relations; and (2) the extension of this relationship to the corporate level in which two exogamous groups of equal status exchange women, that is the husband/wife relationship.

SACRED MEDICINES

The *Lemba* medicines, called *min'kisi* because they are consecrated, consist of the bracelets worn by the priest and priestess(es), the drum or drums that are used in the couple's inauguration to *Lemba* and kept on their house wall, perhaps as an identifier, and the large *n'kobe*, a cylindrical bark box approximately forty centimeters tall, within which is kept a variety of symbolic substances collected during the initiation ceremony and used later either for purification or for the *Lemba* priest's own future healing activities. The ingredients of these "medicines" are collected in much the same way as the exchange items discussed above—food, livestock, drink—and passed along the same social channels. The two sets of objects are distinguished by the fact that the one—the exchange items—is assembled, distributed and consumed, whereas the other—the medicines—is assembled and kept, as a sacred "documentation" of the ceremony. Exchange items are for the most part in the charge of the patrifilial children, resulting in a huge feast; the medicines are in the charge of priests, following a course roughly epiphenomenal of the exchange. Both, therefore, stand for human relationships. The food brings people together, the medicines remind them of their common lot in roles and groups.

The difficulty with the analysis of the medicine objects is that their meaning at the time of ritual use was filled with multiple connotations. By contrast, verbal accounts of 1915 may be approximately understood in light of current KiKongo usage, which has not changed beyond recognition. Social structure and exchange patterns, similarly, have remained quite constant. But the medicines of the early twentieth century have gone out of fashion, and few if any individuals can give reliable exegetical account of their use sixty years ago. Thus, although Kwamba faithfully relates the collection of ingredients for the medicines of *Lemba* in 1915, he hardly hints at their meaning to the initiands.

The analytic strategy to be employed on the medicines of *Lemba* will be to compare slightly diverging accounts with the help of what exegetical and contextual meaning can be gotten. As in the other expressive domains, additional variants will allow insight into the cultural structure that gave rise to the particular cases. Kwamba's account of *Lemba* medicine will be given only a contextual examination here; further interpretation will be possible in light of other variants examined later in the work, especially in Chapter 7 on the western variant.

The basic *Lemba* medicine is the *mpolo-Lemba*, a small pot of chalk used by the *Lemba* priest to treat or purify the *Lemba* sufferer. When the treatment is considered effective, a father/child relationship is opened that becomes the *Lemba* patrifilial relationship. One of the ingredients of the *n'kobe Lemba* box is the neophyte's own *mpolo* medicine. It should be noted that *Lemba* healing or initiatory séances are accompanied by drumming (for example, 1.11) or singing and dancing. As in most Kongo ceremony, these expressions transport the ritual action to another plane: drums are the voice of ancestors; the songs articulate the medicine's significance (for instance, Kwamba's *mpolo* song 1.108–15).

The copper bracelets, mentioned repeatedly in songs early in the ceremony's first phase (1.18, 33), are given to the neophyte couple at the end of the first phase (1.58). These bracelets, made everywhere especially for the individual priests and priestesses, when donned give them their first public insignia of their new rank. The bracelets seem to be the culminating symbol of the first phase of the initiation, and ceremonies leading up to the actual blessing and donning of the copper arm rings mention them as the artifact for either showing moral purity (1.32–4, 1.135–6) or of exercising authority in collecting fines. The bracelets are also used to differentiate the *Lemba* wife or wives from other wives, in a polygynous household (1.59). The copper bracelets constructed of red ore from Mboko Nsongo and Mindouli are not only beautiful in color, but also their resonant tone, when striking other metals, contributes much to the aesthetic appeal they had and to the collective dances reported everywhere in *Lemba*. A dancing group of *Lemba* priests and priestesses would have sounded like a chorus of voices combining soft chimes and small double-tone drums. At some point early in the initiatory séance—Kwamba does not specify it—the neophyte couple receives its small *nkonzi* drum. This too is an object of prestige and beauty; it is displayed over the door of their house.

However the major part of *Lemba* medicine is the *n'kobe* box and its ingredients. The ingredients are collected throughout the second phase of the ceremony, that is after the neophyte has been "profaned" and is being led into full membership. Five sorts of savanna plants and earth from an ancestor's tomb are brought into the ritual events of phase two of the rite. In a raphia cloth bag they are hung on the lodge during the "wife exchange," then they are taken to the "kitchen" beyond the house, prepared with mortar and pestle, and mixed in a pot (1.83, 86, 87, 97) with other ingredients such as *tukula* red (100). The apparent contextual meaning of these plants is their movement through or across all the zones of *Lemba* ritual attention: savanna, courtyard, hearth. In much North-Kongo ritual plant use, however, significance is lent the particular plant through a pun on its name, such that a verb fitting its name gives it an action appropriate to the ritual situation. Thus *mundanda nzila*, "path follower," might be used because the symbolism of paths is appropriate. But unfortunately, Kwamba's text is silent about such plant-name meanings, and they cannot usually be reconstructed because they are not pancultural in Kongo territory. They are like proverbs which have an opaque meaning until the particular intention is known or explained. The meaning of tomb earth and *tukula* bark powder in this context is not as likely to vary from the conventional understanding. Tomb earth, *tobe* (when mixed with wine), conveys purity and spiritual continuity. *Tukula*, a red ochre, conveys transition and mediation with the beyond or across social roles. Water, palmwine, tomb earth, and *tukula* go into the neophyte's new *mpolo* medicine pot, stored in the *n'kobe*. The satchel of plants as well enters the *n'kobe*, perhaps as a memento of the ceremony of initiation. Another satchel filled with hair, eyebrows, nail parings, and old clothing rags of the *Lemba* brotherhood and sisterhood also enters the *n'kobe* (1.101), perhaps as a sign of collective identity in which the neophyte couple shares. Finally, the statues of the wives, bound together and inserted also into the *n'kobe*, are given the significance of a sort of moral watch or reflector (1.102). The bundle if upright denotes purity, if toppled over denotes profanement. These bear some relationship to the prohibitions binding on the *Lemba* wives not to commit adultery.

Much is left unsaid in Kwamba's treatment of the medicines. Later chapters will deal more fully with this part of *Lemba*.

VERBAL CATEGORIES OF RITUAL ACTION

The two texts reveal a clear and consistent language of ritual action, both defining in standard Kongo cultural vocabulary the manner of charging and using symbols, as well as indicating the structure of ritual space which results from the manipulation of charged ritual symbols. This vocabulary varies somewhat from account to account, and region to region, but, as in the verbal punning on plants, the significance of patterns remains consistent.

The key verbal category of ritual action in *Lemba* is *handa*, meaning variously to initiate, to compose, or to identify a person with the consecrated medicine designated by his treatment or by the diviner's judgment. *Handa* appears in phrases such as "*handa Lemba*" (1.1; 2.2–3), that is to "compose *Lemba*," as well as in the form of initiating someone to *Lemba*, *handisa* (1.9). This distinction of composing the medicine and initiating the neophyte also is carried over into the nominative forms of *mpandulu* (1.69, 1.124; 2.24) and *mpandusulu* (1.124). Another major category of ritual action which appears in the first two texts is *bieka*, to consecrate, as applied to either persons taking up special commissions or ritual objects being activated (1.69, 1.106, 1.123; 2.1–2). Another well-known category of ritual action appearing in these accounts is that of *loka*, the utterance of power words, spells, curses, and the like, for both beneficial and malevolent purposes (2.12, 2.27–8). Less well-known categories of ritual action include the following: "securing, protecting the house with palm frond arches," *kaka nzo ye mandala* (1.69, 1.132); "tying a knot," either in a literal sense around the ritual object representing the purity of the *Lemba* priestesses (*bumba makasu*, *tula makasu*, 2.8), or in a less direct sense of appropriating power to obtain something for *Lemba* (*sila nkasu*, 1.40), or even in the abstract sense of the *Lemba* community surrounding the neophyte couple during their ritual bath to "absorb" them into their purity (*kanga lukongolo*, 2.5). A comparable ritual action is the process of "opening the eyes" of the neophyte to give him greater effectiveness in his mission (*kia meso*, 1.82).

These general ritual acts, labelled by standard phrases, may be called acts of effecting *Lemba*'s—and Kongo ritual's—more nuanced states of being, again both positive and negative. In the course of the descriptions of *Lemba* by Kwamba and Lunungu, terms are used to identify the positive ritual actions of *purification* the end goal of which is the achievement of *power*. Alternatively, through *profanement* power may be lost, as well as through the violation of clearly-defined *prohibitions*. This structure of ritual space, made of both actions and states, permits a host of particular incidents and experiences to be given meaning under one rubric: *Lemba* control of reality.

Positive ritual action clusters around the healing and purifying of the neophyte and his wife or wives. The initial *mpolo* medicine "sucks out" (*hola*, 1.5, 1.105) impurities, the dirt of his disease, from his body, and "heals" (*mbukulu*, 1.124) the neophyte. Throughout North Kongo the cupping horn, *n'kisi mpodi*, exercises this function in a less collective manner. Later in the initiation the neophyte and his wife or wives are "bathed" (*swaka*, 1.30; *sukula*, 2.4–6, 2.15; *ngiobosolo*, from *yobila*, 2.2), another ritual practice with widespread therapeutic connotations in Kongo medicine. Later when the neophyte couple experiences profanement, payment of the fine renders them "redeemed" (*bundikila*, 1.68). the experimental profanation and the related repurification described by Kwamba, brings the neophyte again to the purity of his original initiation (1.133). This striving after the ideal of purity (*vedisa*, 1.133) implies a state of the pure (*veela*, 1.133). The *Lemba* priest is taught how to seek the contrast between purity and its opposite; purity opens the path to power, whereas profanation is the loss of power.

Profanement terms are numerous in these *Lemba* accounts, beginning with the general term *sumukini*, or *samukini* (1.34; 2.14) which Christian missionaries translated as "sin" (*masumu*). For the *Lemba* wife profanement is defined in terms of sexual congress with other men, or their inclinations to approach her with sexual or flirtatious insinuations (*yanga n'kento wabieka ku Lemba*, 2.10, literally, "have congress with a *Lemba*-consecrated woman"). The wife's profanation is believed to be signalled by the "loosening" of the vine tied around the "purity paddle" (2.8) or by the upsetting or undoing of the statues in the *n'kobe* shrine representing the wives or the couple (1.102–3, 1.119). The husband's profanation is more inclined to come as a result of the misuse of his ritual powers for private gain (1.127) or of his mystical powers to harm others (*lomba pinda*, 2.10, literally, "call up darkness"; *lokinga bantu na mpimpa*, 2.12, literally, "curse people in the night"), whether intentionally or unintentionally through his superior mystical powers (*kundu*, 2.12). Profanement is not something the priest can ignore or disregard. It may strike him unawares and destroy his relationship to his wives and their clans (1.122) or even kill them (1.22; 2.13), and, in any case, unless it is attended to through propitiatory sacrifices and payments, it diminishes the *Lemba* couple's power (1.118; 2.13). Similarly, the priest and priestess must continually be on guard against inadvertent profanement by those around them who "throw at them something or speak foul of them" (*ta kimpela*, 1.60, 1.134, 1.13). Their life is described as a struggle to maintain purity in the face of profaning situations; their goal is to strive for ascetic power released through purity.

Explicit rules binding on the *Lemba* couple articulate the boundaries of the moral-legal and ethical code, just as the visible mementos—purity paddles, statues in the shrine—express profanement. Such concrete embodiments are necessary where the thing expressed is as abstract as purity and profanement. The figures "by their life" indicate the extent of profanement of the priestly couple; so the rules (*mina*, 1.117–31; 2.15–23, also prohibitions, laws, codes) sketch ethical constraints governing numerous public relationships in the *Lemba* order and across the society at large. Numerous rules govern male-female relationships, the backbone of the *Lemba*-buttressed network of the region (1.126; 2.15–22). Others regulate the governing or "taxing" function of *Lemba*, forbidding anyone other than an authorized *Lemba* priest to take *Lemba* fines (1.131) and conversely forbidding the *Lemba* priest from taking money other than that associated with his *Lemba* prerogatives (1.127). Some rules govern strictly internal *Lemba* relationships and postures, such as those forbidding the eating of unclean food (1.129–30), and those, again often articulated by food prescriptions, defining the father-son relationship (1.128). The purpose of the rules, suggests Kwamba, is to give the priest and priestess their power, to define their prerogative in society.

The power-terms in *Lemba* theory are perhaps more abstract than the other sectors of the ritual structure. They are not embedded in concrete action, but used to spell out a quality, an idea, or a state that links the subject to mystical sources. Thus, in delineating laws *Lemba*'s power (here *ngolo*, 1.82) shows a social referent. In affliction and healing (here *lulendo*, 1.105) it has a mystical and physical referent. In the use of cosmetic decorations such as red earth color it takes on an aesthetic referent, making manifest the priest's "glory and prestige" (*vumi*, 1.116). Redness also shows an element of the mystical in that it refers to the threshold between the visible world and the other world of invisible spiritual powers. Finally, the power of *Lemba* is defined in distinguishing the mystical authority (*kundu*, 1.37;2.12) and the prestige (*vumi*, 1.138) of the *Lemba* Father and Son, the former always possessing more than the latter, in the unending chain that makes every Son a Father, with his own neophyte-Son.

The verbal categories enunciated here portray the social nature of power in *Lemba*, and by extension much of the Congo Basin. The terms are dynamically related so that a transformational process is apparent, moving the subject. Purification and power are positive; profanement and prohibition, negative. Purification and profanement are categories of action, whereas power and prohibition are attributes or qualities, states. The rites of purification remove the neophyte from the ranks of the common, profane, and "open" him and his wife to initiation. Purity is the ritual action requisite to power. The right to levy fines, learned in conjunction with the "experimental" profanation, tests the neophyte's ability to seek purity. But the power is concretized best in the porhibitions. Violation of prohibitions put the priest(ess) into contact with the polluted, profane world, weakening the priest(ess) and making it necessary to go through purification rituals again to regain strength and power.

THE LYRICAL AND ITS MESSAGE

The "lyrical" combines verbal narrative with musical performance. Nowhere better than in its songs does *Lemba*'s style or sense of special reality emerge more effectively than in the initiatory séances. Kwamba's account gives songs by the *Lemba* Father to several initiatory groups, by the wives of *Lemba* Father and Son, by the *Lemba* priests, by the patrifilial children on the day of the feast, and by the neophyte *Lemba* priest after he begins his practice. The lyrical domain has a strikingly consistent structure, which facilitates analysis. Each song is announced or "framed" by being "drummed up" with the small hand-held, two-tone drum (*n'konko*, *n'konzi*): the call "Ko-ko-ko!" (sound of drum), which is answered by "ko." A phrase call such as "Will you gain *Lemba*?", and the reply, "E-*Lemba*!" introduces the lyrics proper and closes them. The body of the song consists of a series of couplets that may be repeated in sets of two or three for hours on end. Kwamba's version gives these songs only once, but in performance they must have been repeated each twenty to thirty times over. For example, the song sung "all night" is only two phrases long. There appear not to have been set *Lemba* songs across the entire region; rather, local variants develop comparable themes such as the neophyte's illness, his progress through the initiation, *Lemba*'s strength, the joy of the patrifilial children, and so on. Common images and symbols such as the bracelets, the role of certain natural objects used in the medicines, recur throughout the area.

The lyrical couplets which are developed between the opening and closing frames invariably combine images in one of several ways. One common association creates the substitutable referent in an action setting, as in this phrase:

> What *Lemba* gives, *Lemba* takes away.
> What the sun gives, the sun takes away. (1.17)

Lemba's action is defined by substituting the sun in its place. The sun's action of rising and setting, perhaps emitting or controlling light and heat, is made comparable to *Lemba*'s action, perhaps that of creating and controlling power. The couplet may also state a sort of "transitive" association, in which the substitution of terms suggests a fusion or identity of the two objects, as in this phrase:

> The neophyte dreamed of ancestors,
> The neophyte dreamed of copper bracelets. (1.16)

Ancestors and copper bracelets are brought into a relationship of identity, or identity representation. A third type of lyrical combination may focus upon some process or observation in nature suggesting a transformation, as in this phrase:

> That which was the fawn,
> Has become the grown antelope. (1.21)

The transformation of fawn to grown antelope refers here to some process within *Lemba*.

As already suggested in the introduction to this part of the book, these lyrics may be studied both as symbol and metaphor. Symbols are seen in the nouns—neophyte, ancestor, bracelet, sun, fawn/antelope—as well as in the verbal actions—dreamed, give/take. Symbols are distinguished as perceptible to the senses at one level, and at another level conceptually or ideologically charged. In the *Lemba* lyrics natural and human objects, things, are repeatedly associated with ideological and moral assertions, values, and expressions. Lyrical metaphors emerge then in the associations made within and across expressive domains. It is possible to speak of both verbal and nonverbal metaphors, and of multimedia metaphors. Ritual symbols are always polysemic, with multiple, necessarily contradictory, meanings. For example, the cluster of terms, objects, and connotations surrounding "*Lemba*" are understood both as sickness and health, both bane and blessing. Multiple and contradictory semantic structures such as this serve the purpose of allowing movement, or the possibility of movement. Structures of metaphoric relations identify members of a class, they link similars and oppose differences, and they range units on scales of ascending value. Perhaps the most common metaphoric structure in *Lemba* expression is that which takes elements from the hierarchically arranged series of beings "animal/human/supernatural," and associates with these elements a contrastive set of "human type A" and "human type B." A series of allusions or expressive metaphors links the two series, establishing a matrix of movement, most often of the neophyte and his household.

Some analysts of narrative genres have insisted that reality-defining lyrics such as these in *Lemba* be called "myth." In the *Lemba* setting I would reserve this term for tales told about the heroes and their relationship to humans. The distinction of such tales and lyrics is made by *Lemba* adherents. Whereas the lyrics are an important part of the ceremony, in concert with drumming, the tales are not told in the *Lemba* setting. However, as shall become clear in subsequent chapters, heroes and human figures mentioned in the ceremonial lyrics of *Lemba* may also be the figures of the tales. Therefore, an analytic method is required which can move from the one "genre" to the other.

The present analysis, which covers both lyrics and tales, can benefit from a simple rewriting procedure which identifies the principal nouns, verbs, and objects of narrative sentences—the elements of verbal metaphors—and arranges them so as to facilitate the recognition of "movement," such as transitive, causative, reflexive, or gradual, long-term, and permanent syntagmatic transformation of a figure, be it the legendary hero or the human neophyte.[5]

The *Lemba* Father's opening song in the courtyard may be rewritten in the following manner to sketch metaphoric relationships.

	NOUN	VERB	OBJECT
(1.17)	{*Lemba* / sun}	{gives / takes}	*X*
(1.18)	neophyte	dreamed of	{ancestors / copper bracelets}
(1.19)	[payment of] pigs	supports	X's falling into water

The first couplet, as already suggested above, associates *Lemba* and the sun with the verbs giving and taking. The KiKongo phrase indicates that an object is involved whose identity is not clear in the context of the couplet alone. The broader context of the *Lemba* initiation hints that the object (*X*) is the force or spirit in *Lemba*, the attacking, harassing illness, the malaise. Later songs will show that this "hidden referent" is being "moved." The third phrase of the song (1.19) states the condition of this movement. If the *Lemba* child pays or sacrifices pigs, *X* may be neutralized or removed into water. Other Kongo *n'kisi* phrase the hold of an illness upon the sufferer in this way. Thus here the first couplet defines the general context of *Lemba*'s order by relating it to the sun, and both to a hidden object. The neophyte's dreams are acknowledged, in which ancestors are represented in copper bracelets. The conditions of release and fulfillment are stated in clear causal terms: pay pigs, *X* will disappear.

In his second song, which is sung through the night of the first phase of the ceremony (see figure 13 below), the *Lemba* Father introduces further images of movement, both those drawn from nature—the fawn which becomes the grown antelope—and from his own initiation.

(1.21)	fawn	becomes	grown antelope
(1.22)	*Lemba*	causes	difficulties
(1.23)	{X which dies / dogs}	laugh(s) at	neophyte?
(1.24)	*X*	{guards / protects}	{*Lemba* "clan" / children / property / novices}
(1.25)			

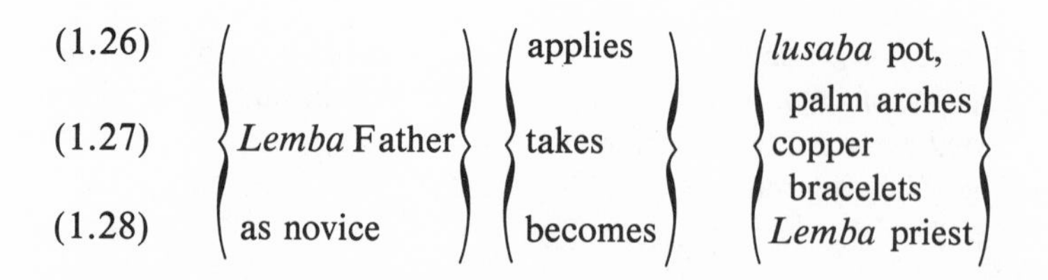

At least three levels of movement are suggested in this song. The fawn becoming a grown antelope is the most obvious natural symbol on which all else is hung. From lines 22–25 *Lemba* or the hidden referent *X* moves from causer of difficulties to protector and guardian of *Lemba*-associated clans, children, property, and novices. Dogs have an interesting relationship to the spirit world, in that they are able to see invisible spirits, and dogs are often taken as signs of mediators, pointers to the beyond, as their role in hunting hidden animals strongly suggests. A third movement occurs in lines 26–28 where the *Lemba* Father recalls his own progression as a novice and the pertinent ritual objects—the *lusaba* pot's medicine (*mpolo*), the arches of the lodge, the bracelets—thereby sketching for his own *Lemba* Son the movement anticipated in the latter's ceremony. This song, especially lines 22–25, and part of the previous song, especially line 17, introduce a pattern in the way *Lemba* expression handles ambiguity and contrast. The passages speak of a given force or power causing both positive and negative effects: giving and taking away, causing difficulty and protecting. They thus demonstrate the concern with shifting the force of *X* from threat to beneficial ally. In the song of the *Lemba* priestesses—the *mimbanda Lemba*—sung behind the house in the kitchen hearth area at the end of the first phase as the bracelets are consecrated and the *Lemba* couple blessed, this hidden referent is identified as Bunzi.

The song of the priestesses is more a rejoicing over father and son's perseverance in their quest than an agonized introspection of the son-neophyte's dreams.

(1.44)	{father / son}	will succeed	in *Lemba*
(1.45)	he who	{perseveres against / is successful with}	Bunzi's curse
(1.46)	field	{was / is}	{barren / fertile}

(1.47)	dreams about *Lemba* Fathers	persisted	
(1.50)	child	wears	shoulder strap [of *Lemba* *n'kobe*]
(1.51-2)	child	{ found will gain }	{ money access to *Lemba* }
(1.53)		supplicate	{ earth sky }

In accordance with the interpretation introduced above about the tight juxtaposition of ambiguity with spiritual force, here Bunzi, earth deity, *simbi* spirit or land, territory, and water spirit, is related to barrenness and fertility. The overriding theme of the song however is not Bunzi but the beauty of the patrifilial continuity of father and son, and unending dreams by sons or children about fathers in *Lemba*. The neophyte has gained access to *Lemba*. He is already pictured as wearing the *n'kobe.*

The presiding *Lemba* father replies, while consecrating bracelets and blessing the couple, in lines that define the *Lemba* transformation in yet more ways.

(1.55–57a)		{ was has become }	{ difficult source of healing power }
	Lemba	{ heals causes to grow }	{ children nionzi fish }
(1.57b)	those who wait	get	portion of *Lemba*

Here, as in other songs above, the *Lemba* Father spells out virtues of *Lemba* members. *Lemba*'s power helps the novice to heal, to cause growth and prosperity. Essential personal virtues of the *Lemba* priest and priestess are patience, perseverance, persistence, clarity.

The power of *Lemba* and the virtues of the novice-priest are lauded in even more spectacular terms when the test profanement has occurred and *Lemba* priests and priestesses reconvene for the second phase of the initiation. The *Lemba* Father opens the sénce (1.63 ff) and the priests and priestesses reiterate, in an evening and all night celebration (1.70 ff), the virtues and characteristics of *Lemba* adherents.

(1.63)	the lazy one	has become	{ industrious
(1.65)			harvester in "*nzamba*" field }
(1.64)	*nkonzi* drum	assembles	festival of *Lemba*

The *Lemba* Father praises his Son for industriousness. The "harvest" undoubtedly has reference to the amount of tax in ceremonial goods levied on the perpetrator of the profanement. *Nzamba* may refer to a type of harvest net or a type of grass of which the net or basket is made, but this "field" is almost certainly allegorical, referring to the operations of the *Lemba* priest in society, his ability to rule and levy morality fines, to be a noble person and an effective one. In later texts (8.3) references criticizing laziness and lauding industriousness and work will appear in similar rubrics.

The *Lemba* brotherhood's evening and night songs define the virtues of the *Lemba* adherent in more exotic ways. The mood of the following songs is clearly festive:

(1.72)	spark	has become	"a hundred and ten" (a raging fire)
(1.73)	receiving *Lemba*	requires	{ beating *mukonzi* / paying money / cleansing in fire }
(1.76)	*Lemba* recipients (like) bats	are	alert
(1.77)	(like) night-jar	(can "see")	evasive (insightful)
(1.78)			"faithful" (no mistresses)

Lemba witnesses with whom I spoke told of huge fires at these final *Lemba* initiatory festivals. To define the quality of *Lemba* productivity as a "spark" is quite natural, one which jumps from "one" to "hundred and ten." The image is a powerful one suggesting offspring, political effectiveness, enrichment, and the like. As insightful are the further character traits of *Lemba* recipients, alertness, evasiveness, insightfulness, faithfulness. Creatures of the "night of *Lemba*" are drawn into the metaphor-making process. No analysis can recreate the expressive content of these verbal terms. An entire night of singing and dancing around a fire, in the company of regional leaders, with the promise of effective recruitment to leadership and a banquet on the following day, hints at the background of these song texts. The bat is lightning fast, able to veer and dart instantly. The night-jar, another nocturnal creature, is able to catch insects on the wing by darting about rapidly. These character traits of prowess in the midst of social and political life define the *Lemba* adherent. Then, they are summed up as "seeing" in the dark of life just as the nocturnal bat and bird "see" in the night. Such virtues of the public realm are combined with marital fidelity.

Kwamba gives no songs for the morning afterwards. It is very likely that an esoteric *Lemba* lyrical tradition existed for the portions of the ritual in the savanna clearing and even in the long walk to the cemetery to collect tomb earth. The song of the patrifilial children of the neophyte (1.94–96) is brief but poignant. It is sung in connection with the combined feast distribution and preparation of medicines in the kitchen area. It reflects the "movement" of the other songs in its acknowledgment of the neophyte's early obstacle-ridden status outside of *Lemba*, and his new status as successful priestly mediator.

(1.94)	*X*	{ was has become }	{ "stitch" of pain path to the priesthood }
(1.95)	*X*	caused	dawn of sun of *Lemba*
(1.96)	novice	{ died rose to life }	{ in *Lemba* Father in *Lemba* }

Several powerful classes of metaphors are combined here to chart the ritual movement of the neophyte. Once more the ambivalence of a domain—pain/priesthood, life/death—is in juxtaposition with the hidden or unnamed referent. This power is transformed. In the most characteristic symbolism for an African drum of affliction, the force of the pain becomes the force of priesthood. Allusions to the "sun of *Lemba*" combine outer cosmic references, where the sun circles the earth, with the inner cosmology in which the individual is born and dies. Thus, a multiple metaphor of cosmological proportions emerges such that pain-becoming-priesthood is like the sun's rising, which in turn alludes to the metaphysical rebirth of the *Lemba* neophyte through death in his patron-father. The patrifilial children in *Lemba* would be analogous to the chorus of a Greek drama, defining the cosmic connections and proportions of the protagonist's life course. These motifs reappear in other variants even more forcefully.

A final lyric in Kwamba's account is the new priest's chant used in his own healing séances (1.109–115). It brings *Lemba*'s ritual full circle, demonstrating sufferer turned healer, his analysis of himself as sufferer now projected upon a new sufferer. It opens with the creation of a ritualized context in the natural and social universe, following which the force causing the suffering is addressed.

(1.109)	{Sun Moon}	{grants takes away}	
(1.110)	*Lemba* Father	{bore gendered raised}	me
(1.111)		Praise	{earth sky}
(1.112)	I	{am enhanced have gone far}	
(1.113)		Search	{patrifilial children's ranks}
(1.115)	*X*	release	sufferer
	{Sufferer Priests}	{will bring will receive}	gift

The ritual function of the songs is to encourage the sufferer-neophyte through the tortuous path from illness to health, from conflict to clarity of purpose, from being victim of an attacking spirit to its beneficiary. Each song suggests at least one type of encouragement, from a variety of sources—his *Lemba* Father, the priests and priestesses together, the *Lemba* wives, the patrifilial children—

moving him from negative to positive ritual status. The father is concerned with the terms of the movement from harassed sufferer to one who is protected by *Lemba*, in touch with its powers. The priests reflect this in their song, but emphasize the character traits of the complete *Lemba* adherent. The *Lemba* wives mention the transition from barrenness to fertility as a result of effective patrifilial continuity. The patrifilial children of the neophyte recognize movement from illness to the priesthood, from "death" in the *Lemba* Father to "life" in *Lemba*. A host of specific natural symbols are related to these ritual conditions, symbols such as the fawn becoming a grown antelope, the sun and moon's setting and rising, dogs laughing, fish growing, harvest, fire sparking, fire purifying, bats being evasive, night-jars being alert, and the like. By "rooting" the mystical themes in these very familiar and concrete natural movements, the deeper truths of *Lemba* emerge, easy to understand, sharp and plain. Most difficult of all seems to be the articulation of the invisible mystical force behind the ambiguity of the sufferer's condition. Mostly hidden, or buried, the unnamed referent crops up most frequently when the descriptive signifiers in the lyrics are contradictory and contrasting. This may be an attempt to clarify ambiguity through sharper contrast, even exaggerated contrast. Or the contradictions of life are stated clearly so as to push the neophyte toward the positive pole of ritual experience, helping him to control his own reality more effectively. In Kwamba's account the mystical referent varies from the vague unnamed "*X*", to simply "*Lemba*," to the "curse of Bunzi" identified by *Lemba* priestesses. In variants to follow pre-existing figures are used much more frequently.

The metaphoric structure of lyrical expressiveness may be followed in two other directions, into the ritual objects such as bracelets and medicines, or into the structure of social-role relations lived in by the *Lemba* Father, Son, wives, patrifilial children, the clans, and *Lemba* itself. Further chapters shall explore these possibilities.

Chapter 5

The Eastern (Lari) Variant of *Lemba*

"Their women gather to beat drums and clang bracelets in great celebration."—Kimbembe, Text 3.25

Introduction to the Sources

Lemba's eastern variant is represented by four extensive accounts and several different types of commentary, ranging from a turn-of-the-century catechist's observations to the work of several missionary ethnographers and an account and analysis by a modern Brazzaville African writer of the region.

Kimbembe, the catechist, offers a description of a *Lemba* séance dating from about 1915. It will be given in full and used as the point of reference for the Lari variants of *Lemba*.[1] Kimbembe's description concentrates on the public portion of *Lemba*.

Stenström's account (1969) is a synoptic reconstruction based on several sources gathered in 1929 in the Madzia region.[2] The esoteric portion of the séance is better represented here but since it is not interpreted to any degree it presents serious problems for use.

Andersson's account (1953) is based on information given by a hunter at Madzia and catechists at Musana in about 1930–31.[3] Like the account by Stenström, this is a synoptic reconstruction, collating several disparate versions. Madzia in Lari country is fifty kilometers distant from Musana in Nsundi and Kongo country. Internal analysis is required to identify regional sources in the data.

Malonga's account of *Lemba* (1958) is also synoptic in that it speaks for the entire "Lari" region and people, all of *Lemba* and, indeed, the whole ancestral past, which is regrettably being drowned out by Western European influences according to the author.[4] Malonga's description is internally coherent, however, reflecting a skillful synthesis of the main lines of emphasis, gleaned from one locality or related localities. In apologetic style, Malonga calls *Lemba* not only the "biggest *n'kisi* of the past," an assertion made once by Fulbert Youlou, but also "one of the most important sociopolitical organizations of the Lari." In his essay he endeavors to articulate the ideas and customs of this major institution, insofar as this is possible given *Lemba*'s extremely effective policy of secrecy over esoteric aspects of the rite.

Malonga's lucid analysis of *Lemba* as a conscious political institution of the traditional elite (*bitomi*), who understood the manipulation of symbols of healing, contrasts markedly with the Europeans' focus on the mythic origins of *Lemba*. Questions of how *Lemba*'s adherents understood their role will be taken up here and in Chapter 10.

The Lemba *Séance at Madzia (Among the Lari)*

Text 3

TAKING BONZO MEDICINE

(1) *Lemba diyokidi mikisi miakaka mu bunene ye mu ntalu.*
Lemba is bigger and costlier than all other *mikisi.*

(2) *Kadi nti muntu bakidi yuku-yuku diankokila lumbu kasidi lumbu buna bana kwenda kwa tata dia Lemba mu nwana bonzo.*
When a person catches evening fever a day is set to approach a *Lemba* Father to drink the *bonzo* medicine.

(3) *Bu kemusila bonzo tala yasidi buna basidi laki nti diankoyi bemusana (buka).*
When the *bonzo* has been given then they need to set a time to complete the healing.

THE FIRST DAY OF INITIATION

(4) *Lumbu cina bucitula buna bankwezi zandi bana twala malavu.*
On the day it is done [the initiates'] in-laws bring wine.

(5) *Bantu bana bakila nkuni zazingi zazingi.*

Other folks bring lots and lots of firewood.

(6) *Tata dia Lemba yandi katuvila monika vata, ka ku fula kana yakala nate ye mwana ma Lemba una tambika nsusu zole kwa matwala malemba (wele landa nganga).*

The *Lemba* Father may not see the village; he will stay at the entrance till the *Lemba* Child brings two chickens to the masters of ceremonies who fetch the priests.

(7) *Matwala bu kakwe twadi biabio buna tata dia lemba kulumukini ku vata.*

When the masters of ceremonies have arranged all then the *Lemba* Father descends to the village.

(8) *Basabo nitizabizi yidika nabanganga nandi.*

They are told what will happen; the priests may begin.

(9) *Bu meni yidika tiya nibikula bekabikula nti*

When the fire is going the call goes out;

(10)	*Widi*	*Widi*
	Do you hear?	We hear!
	Tala	*Tala*
	Look.	Look.
	Mona	*Mona*
	Do you see?	We see!
	Kia nunga?	*Lemba!*
	What will he earn?	*Lemba*!
	Banganga	*Ko! Ko! Ko!*
	Priests.	[sound of drums, bracelets]
(11)	*Widi?*	*Widi!*
	Do you hear?	We hear!
	E lutundulu nui'n'wandi	
	The *lutundulu* ant, his mouth	
	Kadila wele kindula.	
	Devours the sweet fruit ravenously.	
(12)	*Widi?*	*Widi!*
	Do you hear?	We hear!
	E nsibisiulu,	
	O the *nsibizi* rat,	

Mudimba kadila wele kindula.
In the low places he roots ravenously.

(13) *Widi?* *Widi!*
Do you hear? We hear!
E nsibisiulu
O the *nsibizi* rat,
Mudimba kadila wele sengola.
He devours the very land that is his grainery.

(14) *Widi?* *Widi!*
Do you hear? We hear!
Yoka vindumuki kwaku
Go! Rout out here.
Kani vakanga sina kubwanina.
I'll find you on a termite mound.

(15) *Widi?* *Widi!*
Do you hear? We hear!
Mwini Malamu mu mukonzi
Sir Malamu in the *nkonzi* drum
Tata bwanga wa nyieni mo
Father is drumming, he leads me with it
Yenda lundi mafunda
To go store up treasures
Tata bwanga wa kidi moyo!
Father drums, he is alive!
Na nso kuzimbakana *Buna bamubikudidi.*
What was forgotten, Shall be remembered.

(16) *Widi?* *Widi!*
Do you hear? We hear!
Mwikwa wamukazi
The pubes of the *mukazi* wife,
Kadi kasidi sonyia.
It causes embarrassment.

(17) *Bu bamana sa bo, mimukunga una wantete, ubabadikilaka babatikidi nti: tata na mwana bakina kwau—E yaya e-e!*
When they have sung the opening song, Father and Child dance together—O yeah!

SORTING THE MEDICINES

(18) *Bu basa bo bakielolo na teye mbazi padi bu baso dia ngulu zole benzi kwau, kadi biau bio ni bilongo kwau bizi mu tangisa ye ngudi a Lemba ku nkula (ntwala) biakidi.*

When they have done this, they wait till the cock's crow at dawn, when they eat two pigs. For it is their medicine which they count out into the core of *Lemba* where they put *nkula* red.

(19) *Masuku bu mavioka basidi malaki (bilumbu) nti ta nwatu masuku makemana (makaminisa) Lemba matudidi (lweke).*

When the leaves have been brought out into the festive place then *Lemba* has been assembled (has arrived).

PRESENTING THE PATRIFILIAL CHILDREN AND LEMBA WIVES

(20) *Buna suku (lumbu) dina buditudidi nkwezi malu matatu ye mupata.*

When day breaks, the in-laws [of the neophyte] give three palm wine portions and 15 francs (5 mupata).

(21) *Nkumbu biaubio biabionso bibakutanga bibikwanga mpunza za Lemba.*

Collectively, the name of all these bringing something is "*Mpunza za Lemba*"—the paternal gift of *Lemba*.

(22) *Basidi bo bena mu ndambu yo bizi kina kwau ye kielolo bwisi bwamvimba.*

Those who are there dance by themselves and wait for the others.

(23) *Banganga bubizidi bana yidika tiya ku fula, mboko matwala malemba una nata nsusu nana ye mutete wabikwanga ye malu matanu.*

When the priests have come they build a fire in the entrance; the masters of ceremonies bring nine chickens and five baskets of manioc bread.

(24) *Bu bameni zo dia ku fula, buna bana kwiza ku bula.*

When they have eaten in the entrance, they move into the village.

(25) *Bakento bau bana kubabwana ye sika mikonzi ye betisa mulunga mu nkembo wawingi.*

Their women gather and beat drums and clang the bracelets in much celebrating.

(26) *Buna bau bubasa bo bizi vwanda muntu mankulu andi zakala.*

When they are through, the old people sit down.

(27) *Bu bani yidika tiya, buna bantu bantete bana tekila kina.*

When they have lit the fire, the first people begin to dance.

(28) *Tata Malemba mboko mwana malemba ye bakaka mbo sibalanda mwe kina.*

The *Lemba* Father, then the *Lemba* Child, and all the others follow in dancing.

(29) *Kukina na mukento andi bu ke bonga kito kiansusu umudikidi, buna yandi wo vwendi.*

Each dances out with his wife holding a chicken which he then extends to the one who receives it.

(30) *Nsusu yantete buyikuba basididi bala bamfumbu ye basodidi mpe bambanda.*

The first chicken is extended to the representative of the patrifilial children (*bala bamfumbu*); the neophyte's chosen wives are also there.

(31) *Bala ye mimbanda bu bameni solobo, buna mwini wamvimba kuseva pele, nga nsusu kana futa kwa bangudi zanganga.*

When the children and the *Lemba* wives have been presented, all day they dare not laugh, or else a chicken is paid to the high priests.

CONSTRUCTING THE PALM-ARCH LODGE; THE "DEATH" AND "RESURRECTION" OF LEMBA NEOPHYTE

(32) *Ntangu nsinza buyitula buna bayidikidi bala bamfumbu, mwana nzo wamandala kunima nzo ye bambanda ku mwela nzo.*

In the afternoon the patrifilial children construct for the Child a palm-frond arch lodge behind [his] house and for his wives one before the house.

(33) *Ntangu malengola beteka mamba ye tedika mfumba ye bu betedika zo, konso kinzu kiteka bila batedi mulolo ye balundidi zo nate ye fuku diakaka.*

At the appropriate time they fetch water and boil the big kettles; every pot is filled so they cook for everyone; the portions are stored till the next morning.

(34) *Fuku dio bu dibwidi, buna bakubudi yandi una vanda Lemba, ye banganga bavovanga nti fwidi-fwidi.*

When morning falls, then they strike the one initiating to *Lemba*, and the priests speak about that he has died.

(35) *Bu basa bo, nifula (fwekisa) beka kubafula, ye bubafulukidi nimilolo beka ta ye kubula mfula.*

Then, they blow [in his ear] with wind, and when they have resurrected him they raise a shout of joy and fire a gun salute.

THE KILAMBU MEAL AND THE DONNING OF BRACELETS

(36) *Buna badidi kilambu ye bwisi bubukia beso vonda ngulu iya.*

Then they eat the *Kilambu* meal, and have four pigs slaughtered.

(37) *Ye bu bekoma mimbanda milunga benzi kwau ka tata malemba una sala lumbu kimosi nate ye beso dia ngulu yamivambanu ye mwana malemba, mbo bavambani.*

And when they then have fitted the wives' bracelets the *Lemba* Father remains another day to eat the pork and then he takes leave of his *Lemba* Child.

The Expressive Domains and their Codes

THE SPATIAL AND TEMPORAL DISTRIBUTION OF EVENTS

All four accounts of the eastern (Lari) variant indicate it lasts three days at least and two nights (figures 8–11). Kimbembe and Malonga describe it as if there is a pause sometime after the taking of the initial *bonzo* medicine, during which resources are collected for the full ceremony, and the neophyte receives intensive instruction. Malonga says this may take six months to a year; Stenström's account also suggests such a time lapse. Only where the neophyte and his supporters dispose of all necessary resources at the outset may the séance occur in one staging, as Andersson's account suggests.

All four accounts suggest, further, the common feature of a rhythm between ceremonial location in the village and outside the village, in the savanna or near a stream. As was clear in Kwamba's account of the northern variant, the rhythm is indicative of the relationship of *Lemba*'s public and esoteric worlds. The eastern variant under consideration is especially clear in demonstrating how these two

Figure 8
Spatial and temporal distribution of events in Kimbembe's account of eastern *Lemba* inauguration. Numbers refer to lines in Text 2.

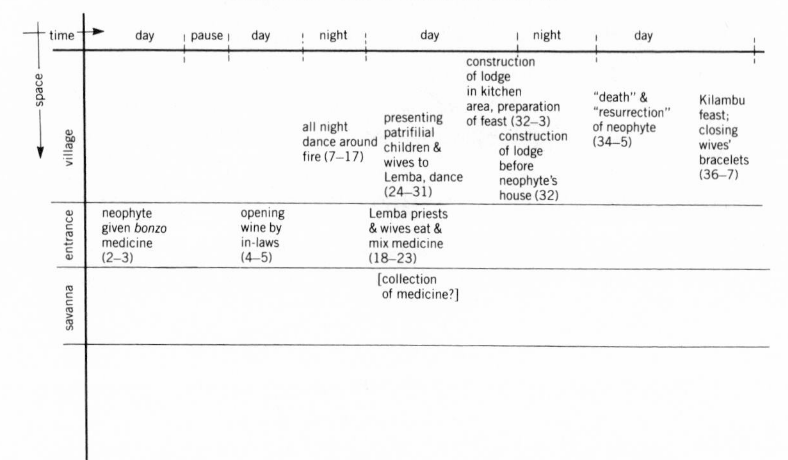

Figure 9
Spatial and temporal distribution of events in Stenström's account of eastern *Lemba* inauguration (Stenström, 1969)

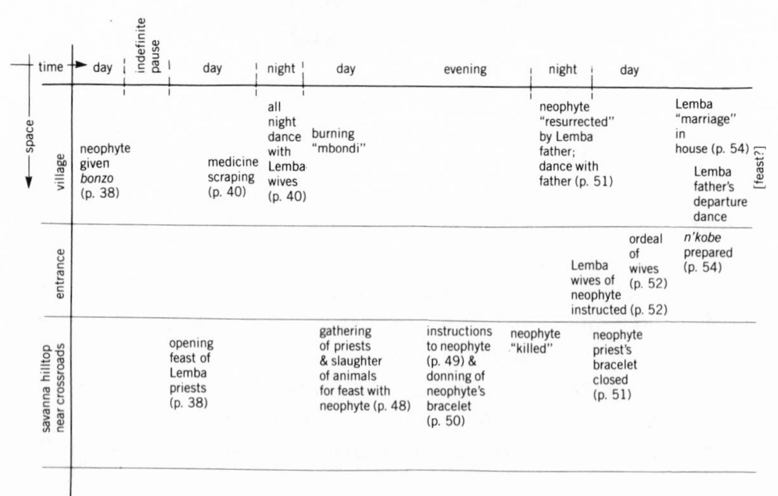

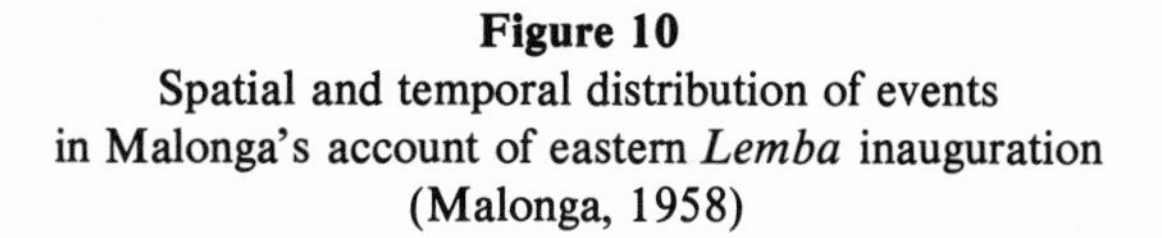

Figure 10
Spatial and temporal distribution of events
in Malonga's account of eastern *Lemba* inauguration
(Malonga, 1958)

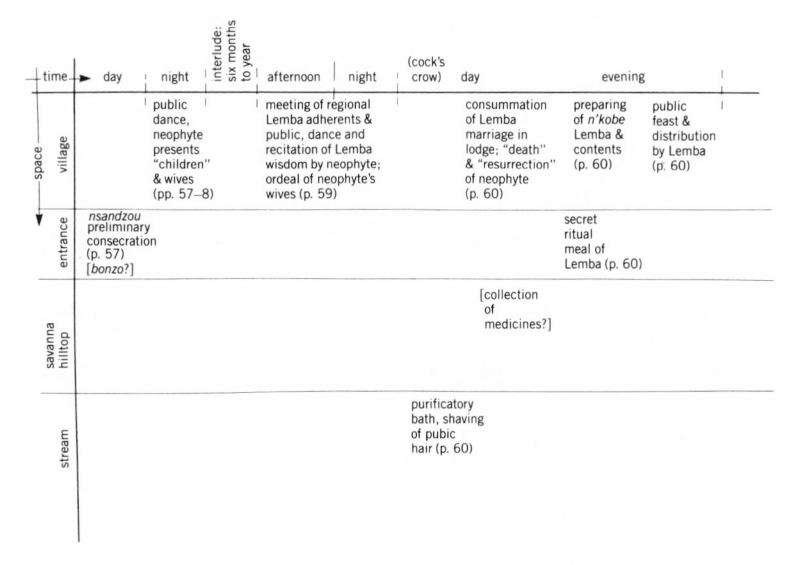

Figure 11
Spatial and temporal distribution of events
in Andersson's account of eastern *Lemba* inauguration
(Andersson, 1953)

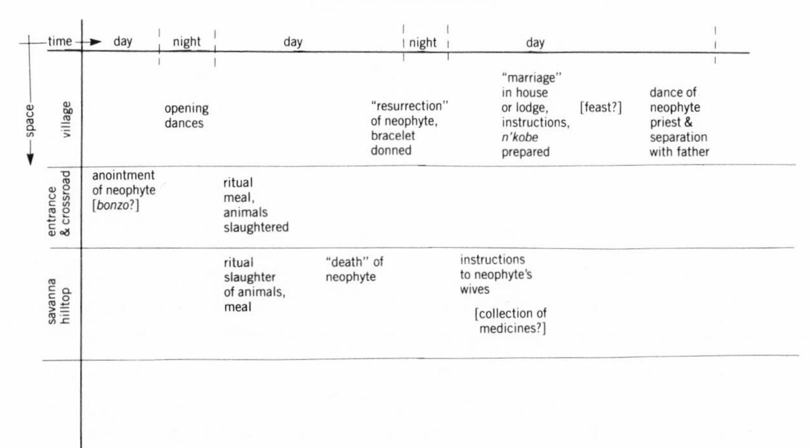

spheres—public/esoteric, village/nonvillage—come to be inverted near the close of the initiation, so that the public space around the neophyte's house, hitherto the scene of conventional dances and feasting, becomes the location for the *Lemba* marriage and its special ritual qualities. Of the four accounts, only Malonga's has the clear spatial-temporal organization and rhythm present in Kwamba's account in the foregoing chapter, with the ceremony divided into two phases, each touching savanna and village, and within the village dividing activities clearly between courtyard and kitchen.

The effect of such rhythmic integration of public and esoteric spheres, so common in Equatorial and Central-African ritual organization, is to charge or load symbols by juxtaposing contrasting poles of meaning: savanna/village, day/night, courtyard/hearth, and so on. The accounts show the movement of the ceremony, for example, from the entrance or hilltop area at the outset into the village square for a public dance, corresponding as well with the contextual movement from daytime to night, light to darkness. Also, in the ritual "death" and "resurrection," Andersson and Stenström describe this process moving from the esoteric setting of the savanna hilltop to the public setting of the village square. Several of the accounts also recognize the court/kitchen opposition in the marriage, as was the case in Kwamba's northern variant. Kwamba indicated that the conventional meaning of court was its public, male significance, and that of the kitchen its semiprivate, female significance, but that this was inverted when the courtyard lodge became the site of the "wife exchange," and the kitchen the site of the preparation of medicines. In several of the eastern variants, this same inversion occurs: the court becoming the site of consummation of the *Lemba* marriage, the kitchen the site where *Lemba*'s ritual food, or medicine, is prepared. To understand the implications of this spatial rhythm and the inversion of conventional spatial and sex-role definitions, we must examine other expressive domains.

ECONOMIC AND EXCHANGE STRUCTURES

Only Kimbembe and Stenström offer systematic information on the nature and quantity of exchange goods in the eastern variant of *Lemba*'s inauguration. A glance at figure 12, which summarizes this information, suggests that these quantities are only a fourth of those reported by Kwamba in the Mboko Nsongo region: six pigs are consumed, instead of the twenty-six in Kwamba's account. The final grand Kilambu feast, emphasized by Kwamba, and Malonga in

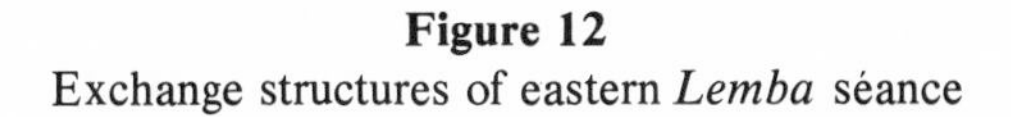

Figure 12
Exchange structures of eastern *Lemba* séance

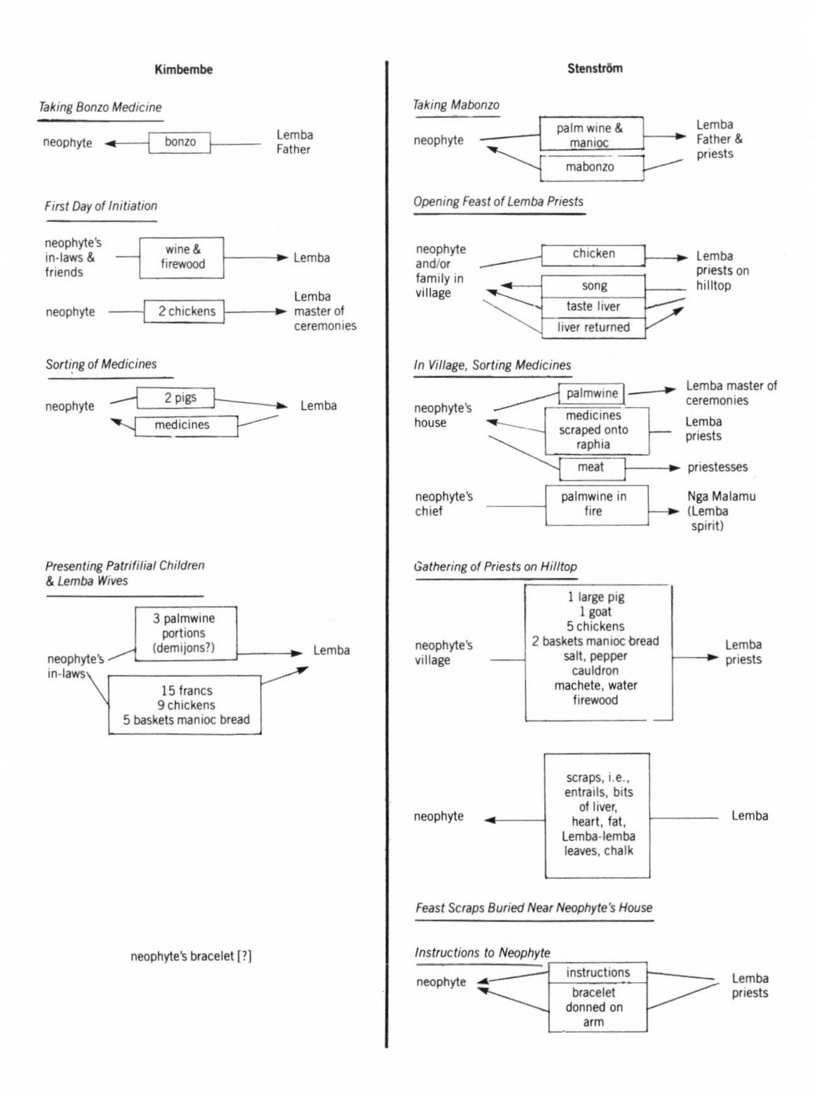

Figure 12 (cont'd)

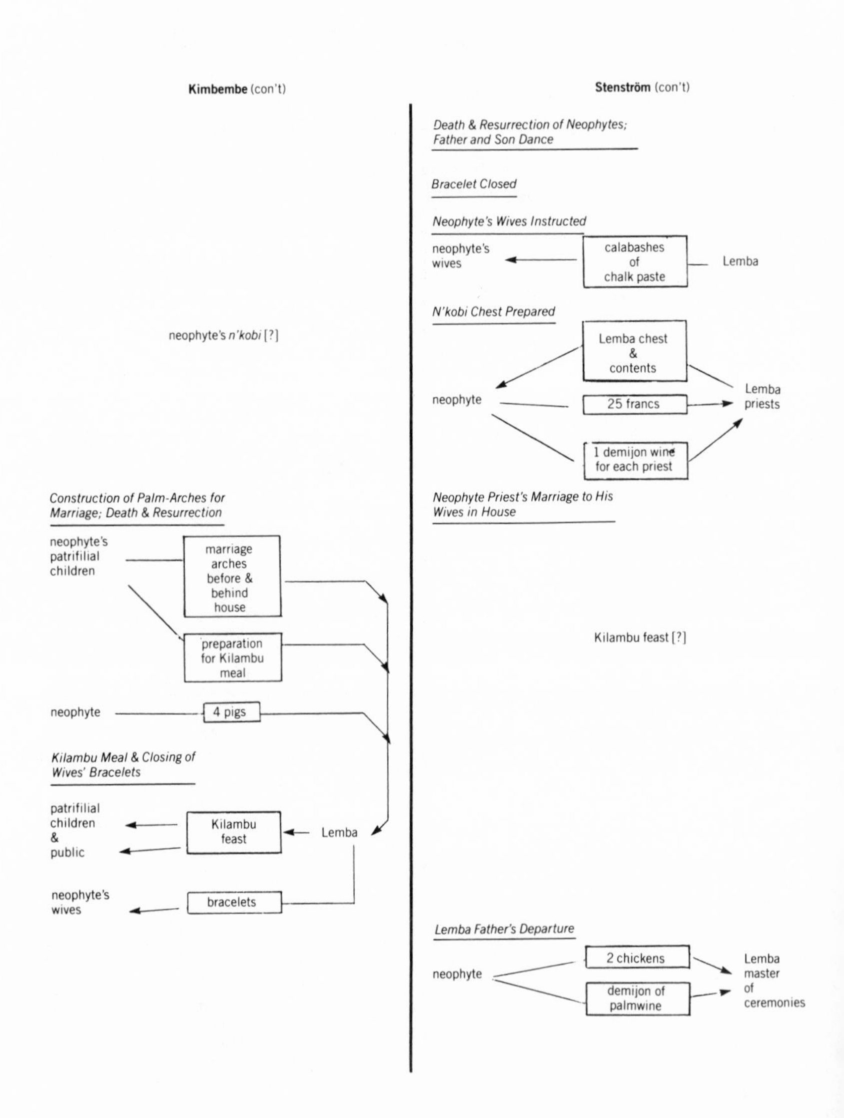

eastern reports, is totally missing from Stenström's account. Although this might be an ethnographic oversight, it might also indicate hard times, the absence of a ceremonial fund in the early colonial period due to heavy taxation, the decline or absence of trade goods or other sources of local wealth. There is no question in the four accounts of *Lemba*'s high status in the Lari region, thus ceremonial funds would not have gone to another *n'kisi*. The proximity of the Lari region to the colonial capital of Brazzaville suggests that by 1915–30, the time of the reports under consideration, *Lemba* was at the very final stages of existence as a public institution, still highly esteemed but economically being choked out of existence. By 1930, suggests Stenström, *Lemba* was decreed illegal by French colonial powers because it was consuming too many resources.

The overall structure of exchange is comparable to the northern account of *Lemba*'s inauguration. The sufferer approaches a *Lemba* priest seeking a "cure," and when the *bonzo* has been administered, the priest becomes the sufferer's *Lemba* Father. After the *Lemba* Son has assembled the requisite goods and patronage, he and his kinsmen—of his own clan and village, as well as his wives' clansmen —then the regional *Lemba* adherents are notified. Numerous exchanges occur between *Lemba* and these groups identified with the neophyte, with *Lemba* presenting the *n'kobe* box and the bracelets, drums, and other paraphernalia he and his wife or wives will keep. At the close of the séance the neophyte's lineage's patrifilial children prepare the Kilambu feast, which is distributed to the local public in attendance. *Lemba*'s secrets, wisdom, and medicinal mementos are given the neophyte's household. One important difference in the exchange pattern here is the absence of a massive infusion of goods from a "profanation" tax.

KINSHIP AND SOCIAL ORGANIZATION

Throughout the accounts a clear status opposition is seen between the neophyte, called "sufferer," "sick man," "deacon being initiated," "*Lemba* child," and the "healer," "senior priest," and "*Lemba* Father." There is some disagreement on the exact nature of the tie between these two figures. Malonga states that an individual prefers to be initiated to *Lemba* by his true father, or if his father is deceased, by his father's brother, his *parrain naturel*. A man is thus encouraged: "Initiate yourself to Lemba while your father is still alive, oh rich one, so that you won't lament him when he is no longer there."[5] Indicative of the emphasis on patrifiliality was the phrase, *mouana kou mbouti ko, kou ntombolé mpemba'ko*, "if the child is not engendered by me, he does not receive the white chalk," that is, the blessing. Or, from the son's view, *mpemba tata mpèni moyo*, "whiteness given by the father, gave me life."[6]

Cognatic ties, on the other hand, were recognized in the *Lemba* system only in the combination of groups in the public part of the ceremony: the neophyte's matrilineage, the matrilineages of his wives (his *affines*), and the fragments of matrilineages present in his own clan's patrifilial children. Some of these groups played special roles in the *Lemba* ceremony. For example, the neophyte's clan's patrifilial children (the *bala bamfumbu*) became the pages, cooks, and partial priests for the inauguration. His in-laws, collectively called the *punza dia Lemba*, or the clans behind the co-wives in the *Lemba* household, brought wine and firewood, according to one account. The *Lemba* inauguration or renewal brought together these many descent groups, stimulating interlineage and village exchanges.

The idea of marriage, which links these various descent groups into an extensive network and maintains it over time, is then at the heart of *Lemba* as an institution. *Lemba*'s marriage code, reflecting the importance of the affinal and patrifilial ties to extensive networks, is spelled out in rules given the neophyte priest and his wife or wives. He is warned that if he commits adultery he will be stricken by *Lemba*'s illness. He must live in accord with his wives, preferably eating with them—a custom not common in Central Africa. The *Lemba* wife or wives are instructed not to have extramarital affairs and to resist the advances of other men as strongly as they resist insults during initiation (Andersson, Stenström's account) at the hands of established *Lemba* wives.[7] During the height of the *Lemba* "marriage" the wives' faithfulness is tested.

The neophyte priest and his favorite wife are brought to the palm-branch lodge before his house. There, under the eyes of the patrifilial children, the *Lemba* marriage is "consummated." At the instant Malonga terms "psychologically right" the neophyte's genitalia are struck so that he momentarily loses consciousness. *Lemba* theory has it that the quicker he revives, the more faithful are his wives. If he fails to revive quickly, his wives will be called to confess their infidelity. During his unconsciousness sperm is taken and mixed with the wife or wives' pubic hair for a preparation of a powerful symbol in the memento, the *mizita* figurines.[8]

The quality of the *Lemba* marital relationship is also suggested by the structure of participation of the *punza dia Lemba* group, the cowives of *Lemba*, in exchanges. Their payment to the *Lemba* ceremony constitutes a sort of reverse bride payment—perhaps a ritual dowry—uncommon in conventional Central-African exchange, which tends to equalize obligations between the neophyte's and his wives' clans, making the *punza* copartners in the *Lemba* household.

The patrifilial children (*bala bamfumbu*) like the descent groups of cowives (*punza dia Lemba*) constituted a network of several communities supporting the neophyte. Those present at the inauguration, at least in eastern accounts, appear to be selected representatives of the entire group of the neophyte's clan's patrifilial children. As in general Kongo ceremonial life to the present, the patrifilial children presided over the kitchen behind the neophyte's house, served in the dance, and acted as priest during the "death" and "resurrection" of the neophyte, as they preside over all transitions between the two worlds of the living and the dead in their fathers' clan.

In an important sense the patrifilial children are the source of their fathers' power. As has been seen in the northern variant and to a degree in the eastern account (see figures 7 and 12), the patrifilial children receive and redistribute the final feast as the neophyte receives, from *Lemba* priests, the symbols of authority and power. The patrifilial children offer their loyalty and support, thus becoming the continuation of the line that *Lemba* father and son have established. The three-tiered polity that results is mirrored in the eastern *Lemba* etiology myth in which Nga Malamu, Kuba, and Magungu are the succession of priests to have originated the idea of continuous *Lemba* insight. The final section on lyrics in this chapter returns to this matter.

The patrifilial alliance, extending a political network over space and continuity over time, broke the isolation of landed matrilineages as effectively as some of the chiefly traditions of the Lower Zaire. Malonga's, of the four eastern accounts of *Lemba*, gives extensive insight into just how *Lemba* governed on a day-to-day basis. *Lemba* was holder of truth, the source of laws. Its *matwala*, like major ministers of the regional séances, initiations, and renewals, were responsible for the maintenance of *Lemba*'s control of regional resources, both the materials that flowed through the markets, as well as the knowledge held by the various specialists, such as smiths and healers. The *matwala* often went out under disguise to collect formulas and techniques, both beneficent and malific, from magicians. *Lemba* appropriated all knowledge in the society to itself; only in this manner was it able to presume to combat witchcraft, that is, antisocial powers and persons. The neophyte's socialization into the deep understanding of society occurred during the six months of the year after his initial medicine, and before his inauguration.[9]

In order to maintain such a monopoly of resources *Lemba* needed to assure the recruitment of the "brightest and best" men and women to its ranks, those who constituted a natural basis of power in society. Reluctant leaders were harassed through mystical threats or promised great wealth and power. Despite the persistent rhetoric of illness and healing, there was no specific "*Lemba* illness," states Malonga. The idiom of illness was used to speak about social disorder, and specific episodes of suffering were used to advantage to extend *Lemba*'s network among the qualified. Malonga makes it very clear that *Lemba* maintained a highly conscious public image, manipulated behind a front held in common secrecy by priests and priestesses. The regional *Lemba* elder, the *munkukunyungu*, held the "high priesthood" as a sort of senior, honorary title. The chief treasurer and minister, the *matwala*, was a position of power. He, along with the other *banganga Lemba* and their *mimbanda* wives, constituted the local elite of every region. They were the links in the continuous network of market trade and peace-keeping.

The explicit ideology which used the idiom of illness and healing to maintain public order was in the eastern variant embodied in the role dichotomy of the *bitomi*, the pure and initiated, and the *bihinga*, the profane. (*Tomi* derives from *toma*, to excel, be superior or pure; *hinga* from to beg, supplicate.) It is important to understand this rhetoric of purity in *Lemba* not as an entrenched power of a continuous elite but as a mode of ritual in a segmentary society. All sources emphasize that *Lemba* membership could not flow within the matrilineage. Offices could only be perpetuated by extending the patrifilial link, which in turn stimulated exchange. Priests and priestesses were buried, when they died, with their bracelets and paraphernalia. Everywhere *Lemba*'s wealth returned to the localized village supporters in the form of the lavish feast distributed by the patrifilial children of the neophyte. *Lemba* was thus a stimulation of exchange between exogamous groups, rather than a hoarding association within an endogamous, hereditary elite.

MEDICINE OF *LEMBA*

It should be apparent that the expressive domain "medicine" is the nonverbal articulation of social structure, the exchange of goods and gestures, words and songs. The clay, hair, fingernails, plants, and bits of wood designated as "medicine" (*bilongo*, contained in the *n'kisi*) contain little intrinsic meaning, but they are imbued with meaning through words or songs uttered in their collection, mixing, and the social context in which they are used. A type of verbal punning is widespread in Kongo cultures whereby words spoken in the séance correspond to the plants received by the sufferer—thus, for example, "*lemba, lemba*" (peace, peace), describes the action of the plant *lemba-lemba* (*Brillantaisia patula T. Anders*) given in the oral potion. As I have argued elsewhere, this type of verbal composition principle need not exclude an understanding of the chemotherapeutic effect of plants, especially where such medicines are taken orally or applied to the skin.[10] Nor should the possibility be excluded that a few of the ingredients, particularly the bodily fluids and exuvia—hair, semen, feces, blood, fingernails—carry a powerful connotational, even iconic, impact. But even here the precise meaning of the bodily object is given in word, song, or social context. This is very well illustrated in the eastern variant's exchange between "food" and "medicine," already hinted at in the analysis of the northern variant.

At the outset of the ceremony the neophyte and his supporters give food and drink (chicken, wine) to *Lemba* in exchange for *bonzo* medicine (chalk, etc.). At the second stage, food is again offered the *Lemba* priesthood by the neophyte, and medicines are sent back in exchange. At a later stage the *Lemba* priests are presented with an even larger quantity of food, a lavish feast, for which the neophyte receives medicine, but this time mixed with scraps of food from the priests' meal, specifically the chicken "giblets" of heart and liver. The bracelets for the neophyte and his spouse(s) are prepared during the episode of death and resurrection, and further medicines are developed as the bracelets are consecrated. During the consummation of the *Lemba* marriage, the groom's semen and the bride's shaven pubic hair are mixed into a medicine. The final stage constitutes a complete inversion of the opening, in terms of the exchange of food and medicine. *Lemba*, through the beneficence of the patrifilial children of the neophyte, distributes the Kilambu feast to a general public. The *Lemba* priests and priestesses, now including the neophyte and his wives, partake of a medicinal "feast," made up of food bits from the Kilambu, but heavily enriched with "medicine" such as semen and pubic hair from the marriage ceremony and dried excrements of *Lemba* adherents.

Commenting on this final meal of the *Lemba* pure, Malonga notes that "the symbol of this rite, revolting to the profane, is a key to the indissolubility of the *Lemba* order. It consecrates that feeling of fraternity uniting all the pure (*bitomi*). They must consider themselves as constituting one body whose trust they may not betray."[11] In terms of the code that is followed, this exchange and mixing of medicine and food is expressive of an abstract view on purity and profanity. *Lemba*'s purity is defined by its exposure to the neophyte's impure social context, his "illness." Profane filth collected around the neophyte is first absorbed by mixing chalk (*luvemba*, whiteness) and *lemba-lemba* herbs (calmness) with it, then by having the *Lemba* priests and priestesses eat the neophyte couple's sexuality, impurity, dirt, excrements, and the like. As Mary Douglas has so correctly observed, ritual power is generated by the absorption to the sacred of dirt, the ambiguous, death, sin, and the impure.[12]

All this, and more, is borne in the permanent "documentary" symbolism of the *n'kobe* and its contents and in the drum and bracelets, which, taken together, are expected to conserve the values of exchange, well-being, purity, peace, and political loyalty lauded in songs, speeches, rules, and instructions. In the eastern variant, as in the others, *Lemba*'s permanent medicine is composed in two phases: the first in connection with the initial *bonzo* (elsewhere called *mpolo*), the second in connection with the novice priest's own *n'kobe*. Each will be dealt with briefly here. Chapter 7 will consider medicines in fuller, and comparative detail.

Stenström's account offers the ingredients of the *Lemba* high priest's *bonzo* (pl. *mabonzo*), or opening medicine, intended to clear the way for the new status which is to follow.

Lemba-[*lemba*] herb
Nsangu dia dinkondo (seeds) (*Ocimum bazilicum*), with pungent odor or aroma
Makala manzo mbongi (*sic*), "charcoal from the hearth of menstruating woman's house" [This cannot be correct, for *mbongi* is the "men's house."]
Mpemba, white chalk
Lutundu, herb with red fruit
Mansunsu (*Ocium arborences*), an aromatic plant
Nkukidila niaṃba, leaves, twigs, silt, etc., thrown onto river bank during flood
Muyitu, ashes of herbs and leaves from sweat bath
Ngasi zasombo, small palm nuts cracked by teeth
Nsala zankuka, feathers of the *nkuka* bird (*Turacus persa*.)
Nsangi, a small fish[13]

These items are recorded to suggest that they are wrapped in the skins of two antelopes, the small red *kinkululu* and the *mbambi* water antelope. However, it is not clear which ingredients are associated with which skin, nor what the verbal definers are of the articles in the context used. It cannot be assumed that the meaning of such items is consistent in northern Kongo cultures, thus an interpretation or dictionary meaning given in one setting cannot be carried over to another. Stenström has conflated several informants' lists of ingredients, and it is impossible to analyze them effectively. Some of the same ingredients appear in the second phase of medicinal composition for the *n'kobe*, in which context their lyrical definition is fortunately given (see figure 13).

N'kobe ingredients begin to be collected in the "scraping" ceremony at the time the *Lemba* couple and their pages and patrifilial children are presented to *Lemba* officiants early in the first phase (see Stenström's account, figure 9; Kimbembe, figure 8, Text 3.18–19). These ingredients, in Stenström's account, are placed onto two skins, of the *nkumbi* rat and the *musimba* wildcat respectively, and after they are tied shut they are hung temporarily on the neophyte's house until the end of the initiation. As they are scraped, the plants or substances are "charged" with verbal meaning by the priest. For example, the *nsangi* fish is cut up to the singing of the following phrase:

> *Nsangi, nsangi mu mbanda e ké é*
> *Nsangi* fish, *nsangi* fish, be mixed—cause to
> jump, dance—the *mbanda* wife, eh, eh.

As the *lufumbu* vine is scraped, the priest sings:

> *A muti ambumbu, tata walembo kina, ka ulamo ko*[14]
> Oh *mbumbu* tree, father doesn't dance, he won't dance.

The objects are so to speak given life and meaning in the context of the performance. This situational attribution of meaning may vary greatly from one locale or initiation to another, and from one set of medicines to the next, for all but a few of the classic Kongo or Central-African ritual symbols, which seem consistently to retain their underlying meaning from context to context, region to region, even decade to decade.

Thus, *mpemba* chalk, present in all *bonzo* openings, symbolizes "whiteness" and is a sign of purity, correctness, loyalty, innocence, and truth, synonymous virtues in *Lemba*. *Lemba*'s cure, as many

Figure 13
Eastern *Lemba tukobe* and ingredients

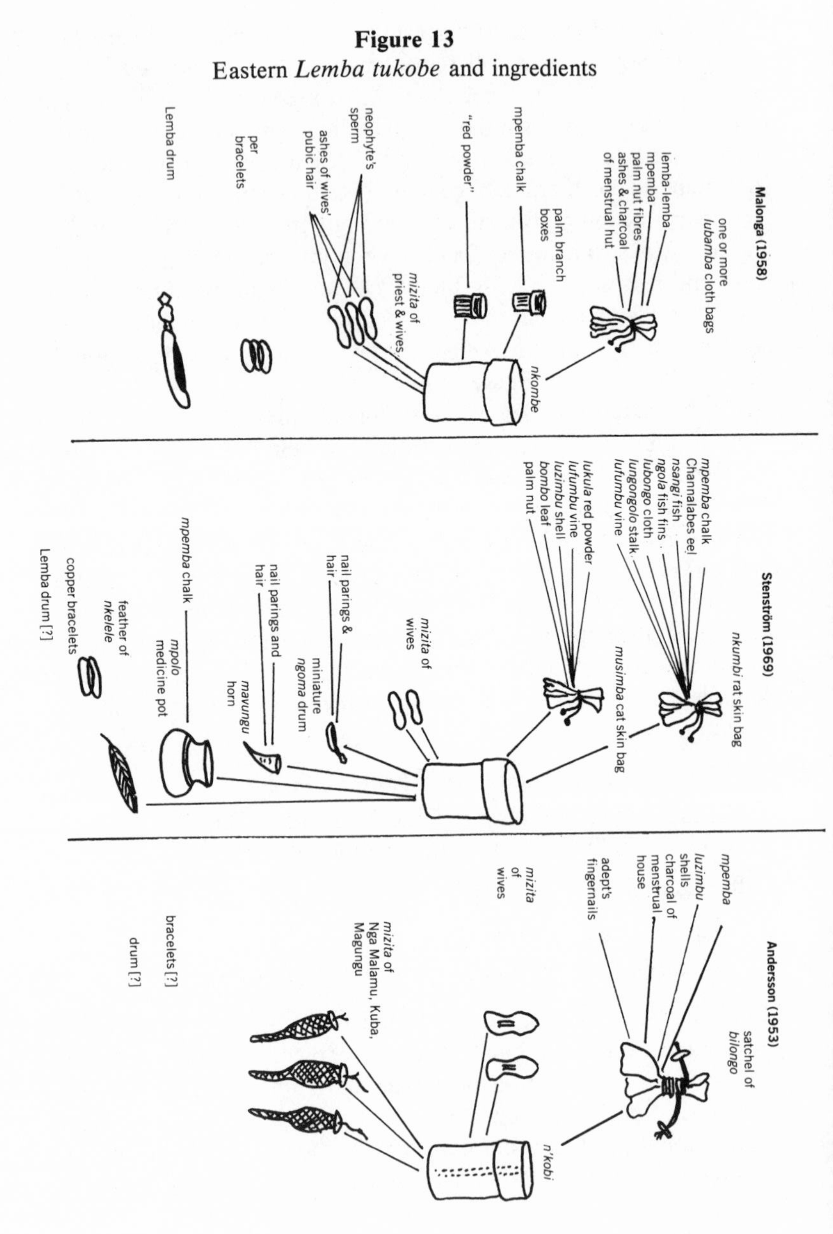

others, contains *mpemba* chalk because of the ready contrast it offers with states of sickness and impurity.[15] Thus, in a rather predictable interpretation as they add chalk to the medicines, the *Lemba* priest sings

> *mpemba batata mpedi moyo e é*
> With *mpemba* the fathers gave me life;
>
> *mpemba tata mpedi moyo e é*
> *mpemba*, father gave me life.[16]

Another pervasive classic ingredient is *lukula* or *tukula*, red powder of the *tukula* tree (*Pterocarpus cabrae* [*el soyauxii*]), which is usually used in conjunction with *mpemba* chalk to designate contrasting but related qualities. In the eastern *Lemba* accounts, *mpemba* in the *n'kobe* denotes life or power in the neophyte priest's life, and it is kept in the skin of an *nkumbi* rat (see figure 14, Stenström and Malonga). *Tukula* red, kept in the skin of the *musimba* wildcat, signifies the benediction of the ancestors upon the *Lemba* couple.[17] The juxtaposition of *mpemba* and *tukula* in nearly all *Lemba tukobe*, in connection with virtues of the *Lemba* priest and priestess respectively, suggests that there is here a basic metaphor. Indeed, it reappears in all regional accounts of *Lemba* from the Teke-influenced Lari in the eastern variant, to the Mayombe and coastal accounts. The elements of the metaphor are drawn from what is known to be widespread in Equatorial-African cosmology and thus characteristic of a widespread ritualization process. The sex roles of the *Lemba* male and female are first of all defined by whiteness and redness, the first denoting purity, contact with ancestors, virtue, the second denoting power, fusion or mediation, sometimes danger. The sense of these substance and color symbols is made crystal clear by their containers in the *n'kobe*. The male "whiteness" is placed in the skin of the *nkumbi* rat, a striped rodent whose underground burrowing skills are widely lauded. He stands for contact with the underground domain of *mpemba*, the land of the dead. Female "redness" is contained, in Stenström's account, in the spotted skin of the *musimba* cat, a tree animal, whose characteristics thus suggest skilled human interaction, especially in the realm of relations between the sexes and in fertility. The fragment of the *Lemba* metaphor might be sketched as in figure 14.

Malonga's exegesis of other *n'kobe* ingredients explicates some of the other common ritual items found in *Lemba*. The fibers of the palm nut—variation may be palm nut, palm branch—convey the wealth of

Figure 14
Sketch of *Lemba*'s dominant metaphor,
based on eastern variant

sexual roles and identities	substance and color	animal order	cosmological space
male	whiteness *mpemba*	*n'kumbi* rat	burrows underground
female	redness *tukula*	*musimba* cat	runs on ground, climbs trees

the palm in Kongo societies: oil, wine, cloth (= money) are all derived from it. Inclusion of a bit of the palm draws the neophyte into association with the productive realm of society.[18] Ashes are the symbol of the hearth that every respected man must possess. The *Lemba* priest has a sacred obligation not to become isolated, without hearth or household, wives and children. Charcoal is the "allegory of discretion," denoting that what is hidden in obscurity is difficult to uncover. Discretion is a virtue of every *Lemba* person, every *butomi*. Charcoal is a sign of the ability of magicians to render invisible from profane eyes and minds their intentions and methods.[19] Menstrual blood associates *Lemba* with the moment of a woman's greatest fertility and reproductive potential. Menstrual symbolism complements the male element in *Lemba*, advocating multiplication and productivity, life.

These medicinal ingredients (*bilongo*) are attached, by words and connotations, to the active norms and ideals of the *Lemba* couple and *Lemba* as a wider social institution. Some of them also gain their meaning out of the functional context in which they are used in productive life. Others, as suggested earlier, may have a direct iconic derivation having to do with the body of the initiate or of the corporate body of *Lemba*. Bodily clippings, exuvia, fluids, and parts find their use in expressive efforts to represent unity of individuals. Thus the *mizita* figurines present in all accounts (see figure 13) contain ashes of the wives' pubic hair and the husband's semen, mementos of the transcendent "moment of truth" in the consummation of the marriage when the groom is knocked unconscious ("dead") so he may be raised ("resurrected") to the new unity in *Lemba*. The *mizita* may have individually colored beads to represent each wife, but their contents denote permanent transcendence of individuality in the new life of *Lemba*.

The unity of the larger corporate body of *Lemba* is represented in the nail-parings and hair (elsewhere, rags from old clothes) clipped from each priest and priestess and placed into the miniature *ngoma* drum or *mavungu* horn (figure 13) that are inserted into the *n'kobe*. Whether these drums are called *ngoma*, *nkonzi*, or *nkonko*, they are called the voice of the ancestors or spirits, representing the corporate collectivity. Thus in one song (Text 3.15), *Lemba*'s legendary founder Nga Malamu is addressed:

> *Mwini Malamu mu mukonzi*
> Sir Malamu, in the *n'konzi* drum
>
> *Tata bwanga wa nyieni mo*
> Father is drumming, he leads me by it.

In another, Kuba:

> The *ngoma* goes *mbwe*! *mbwe*!
> Don't you hear it?
> Oh Kuba!
> I move to it![20]

No less than the bones or hairs of martyred heroes of Western Christianity inspire the church in shrines, or ancestral chiefs' bones are revered in the ancestor baskets of clans in Central Africa, these bundles of fingernails, hairs, etc., of the *Lemba* community iconize the disparate individuals into one communal body, joined with distant heroic ancestors. But *Lemba*'s icon, it must be recalled, is not hereditary but must be renewed by initiation of new couples.

THE LYRICAL

The lyric sense was already present in the previous section, defining or sharpening the meaning of inchoate medicinal ingredients or other ritual objects. In this section I want to illustrate the full form of the lyrical in one important song and the etiological myth of Nga Malamu, Kuba, and Magungu present in a fragmentary way in most of the eastern variants of *Lemba*. It is now apparent that the ritual objects such as clanging bracelets, throbbing drums, burrowing rodents, semen and pubic hair ashes, food and the like lend social interaction a sensory immediacy of great power. On these objects, as we have seen with such cases as the miniature drums, the bracelets, and other articles, metaphors of esoteric reality are constructed that embody less tangible but no less real statements about the human and supernatural world. In the *Lemba* setting, social relations are often linked with the realm of spirits and deities, and both are concretized in ceremonial objects.

This type of linkage of the human, material, and spiritual realms is evident in a favorite eastern *Lemba* song type about two types of animals, one of whom is an effective, the other an ineffective burrower for food. Kimbembe (Text 3.11–16) and Malonga[21] offer comparable texts.

KIMBEMBE	MALONGA
	A! Lou nkouma-nkouma tat'e, *lou na loua koumini ngoudi* *a nganga.* Oh, my son, the truth resides in the words of the chief priest.
E lutundulu nuinwandi, *Kadila wele kindula.* O the *lutundulu* ant, his mouth devours the sweet fruit.	*Ma tondélé nkoumbi, na* *mayelo ma tembélé.* Whatever causes *nkumbi* rat to rejoice, makes his moustache dance (twitch).
E nsibisiulu, mudimba kadila *wele kindula.* But oh the *nsibizi* rat, in the deep places he devours with ravenous appetite.	
E nsibisiulu, mudimba kadila *wele sengola.* Oh the *nsibizi*, he even devours his own granary!	*A! ntsibizi zoba, dimba ka dila* *meni sengola.* But the stupid *ntsibizi*, he burrows up the ground that is his granary!

Yoka vindumuki kwaku kani vakanga si na ku bwanina Go! Roll up! I'll catch you on a termite mound.	*E! Yenda, vindoumouki kou'akou!* *Kani ghakanga tsia na ku bouanina.* Go! Roll up! I'll catch you on a termite mound.
Mwini Malamu mu mukonzi *Tata bwanga wa nyieni mo.* Sir Malamu in the *nkonzi* drum, Father beckons, he leads me by it.	*A! Bou kouenda bou kouenda, yenda yenda na nkouma na ngou'andi a diambou.* On your journeys, see that you are accompanied by the "word of truth" (proverb and message).
Yenda lundi mafunda *Tata bwanga wa kidi moyo.* Go, store up treasures Father beckons, he lives!	
Na nso kuzimbakana *Buna bamubikudidi!* What was hidden, Shall be revealed!	
Mwikwa wamukazi *Kadi kasidi sonyia.* The *Lemba* wife's pubes, Cause embarrassment.	*Taba dia nkazi* *Ka sidi bèmba.* Il s'est certainement frotté à la 'garniture' de sa femme eu venant.
	Didi nkoukou hou koukoum' anga. Il a mangé le coucou qui bégaie.

The texts characterize sets of natural creatures: Kimbembe, the *lutundulu* ant and the *nsibizi* rodent; Malonga, the *nkumbi* rat and the *nsibizi*. All are burrowing, digging, or wiggling creatures. As suggested earlier, *nkumbi*, with striped skin and joyful twitching whiskers, appears in many *Lemba* contexts, his burrowing highly lauded, his skin taken as a container for the white chalk symbolizing the *Lemba* neophyte's mystical and rhetorical abilities.

The songs also speak of the *Lemba* Father and Son, the high priest, *Lemba*'s founder Nga Malamu, and the *mukazi Lemba* wife. The *Lemba* Father is depicted as an animator, reviver of the Son, who puts him in touch with the powers, secrets, and wealth of *Lemba*. Not only are mystical links intended here but also the power of words, skillfully used as an access to power. Thus, Sir Malamu speaks to the *Lemba* Child through father's drumming on *n'konzi*. Similarly, the neophyte priest is told to take with him on his journeys the essence of truth, "the word"—probably special proverbs or oratorical techniques. The songs move from the natural object concretizing truth, to the less tangible qualities defining access to *Lemba*'s powers.

There is in these songs, as in many of the couplets studied in the northern variant, a sense of the hidden referent, probably given in the *Lemba* context some esoteric meaning. Here, as in the songs of the previous chapter, the hidden referent—"that which was hidden, shall be revealed" (Kimbembe)—occurs in the face of a contradictory or dichotomous situation. At one level this contradiction is visible in the set of creatures, one of whom is successful, or skilled, the other of whom is unsuccessful, stupid. In the first song by Kimbembe, *lutundulu* reaches his sweet fruit, whereas *nsibizi* destroys his food source and gets caught. In the second song, *nkumbi* is successful, *nsibizi* stupid. *Nsibizi* is caught on a termite hill, itself full of pores and tunnels, as he rolls himself up in a ball, thinking he has protection. The successful creatures are the *Lemba* priests who can reveal secrets, know and use rhetorical words to great effect. They can handle truth. The unsuccessful "diggers" are the profane, lacking truth and power.

There seems to be a further sexual-political signification in the songs relating the burrowing animals to the *nkazi*-wife. The "successful" digger understands fertility, the secrets of reproduction, and replenishment of the earth, whereas the "unsuccessful" digger destroys, like the metaphoric *nsibizi*, the very source of his food. Instead of children and followers, he effects destruction and loss of human resources. He is politically inept.

The movement of the *Lemba* neophyte and his wives into touch with these truths appears to have not only a practical consequence in their political and economic effectiveness, but a metaphysical connotation, formulated in the eastern region by the idea of a succession of *Lemba*'s spiritual substance (*kitswa*) from one generation to the next. Many of the references in the songs and incantations, as well as the *mizita* figures and the *mavungu* horn in the *Lemba* chest (figure 13), refer to Text 4, the eastern etiological myth of *Lemba*, which follows.

Text 4

> According to the version from Madzia, the creator of *Lemba* was a man called Nga Malamu—Nga designating the status of chief. As a man, Nga Malamu composed the first *n'kisi Lemba* with the inspiration of a protecting spirit (*kitswa*) of a deceased kinsman. When, in his turn, he died, he became the patron spirit (*kitswa*) of *Lemba*. Now Nga Malamu is considered to be a supernatural being, according to his name, immortal, one who endures, who is and subsists. Nga Malamu it is who gives force to *Lemba*. Kuba, who followed him, fell ill. Nga Malamu healed him, and he became the first priest of Nga Malamu. The third founder and protector of *Lemba* is Magungu. These three personages act in *Lemba* and by *Lemba*. *Lemba* is so old that generations have been born and have died without anyone recalling a time when *Lemba* did not exist. According to some, the founder may have been Yaya Mwaya.[22]

The figures of Nga Malamu, Kuba, and Magungu occur repeatedly in the ceremony in songs, alongside the creatures and ritual objects such as *nkumbi* rat and whiteness. Their characteristics thus come to be defined more exactly. A few examples suffice to convey this integration of etiological heroes, medicinal objects, and social roles of *Lemba*. Thus, in one account of the savanna ceremony early in the first phase, the priests and priestesses sing "Tremble before Mavungu."[23]

Mbokidi makondo
Kneel, spy
Ka mbakidi akina ko
I have been unable to dance
Wauleno Mavungu
Tremble before Mavungu.

Later, during the scraping of medicines ceremony in the village square, the song "Nzambi-God passes" is sung.[24]

Widi, widi
Hear, Hear
Mpemba tata mpedi moyo
Mpemba chalk, father gave me life
Lembolo mpemba, kadi nganga ko
Without chalk, one isn't a priest
Mpemba nkima yikwenda nami
Chalk is what accompanies me
Bandama kwaku
So bow down
Wadi Nzambi kayoka
For God is passing
Nzambi watele vunguteno
God has said: murmur hum, hum
Nsunsu ka kuba ngumbi kwa kudi
Chicken to Kuba, partridge
Nkonso kidi ngolo
Whoever would be strong
Kidi ntedi Kuba diamwana Lemba.
Then Kuba became the *Lemba* Child.

This song recalls the transfer of the *kitswa* protecting spirit from Nga Malamu to Kuba, the second priest. Ritual substances such as white chalk and auspicious sacrifice objects such as chickens and partridges are mentioned. Nzambi's passing is an indicator of awesome sacred power. A little later in the all-night dance the participants sing "Kuba in Ngoma Drum," already cited above. Following a song of gratitude to the *nkumbi* rodent, successful striped burrower with joyful quivering whiskers, another song is sung on the savanna hilltop lauding *Lemba* with its unique humming tone: "God has said Hum."[25]

Tuidi bamintiobo
We are like worms
Ga tutambukila kweto
Here we will burst
Nzambi wasidi, vunguteno
God has said, hum, hum

Tuidi bambwetete
We are like the stars
Ka tuwaka lutangu ko
We are without number
Wauleno Magungu!
Glory to Magungu.

At once an alliteration of the peculiar *Lemba* low humming "grumble" and the name of the third *kitswa* of *Lemba*, the song expresses satisfaction with the banquet of pork, in terms befitting a well-fed *Lemba* priest.

The foregoing textual evidence from diverse sources can be brought together in a single metaphoric structure to depict the movement present in the eastern variant of *Lemba*. Social roles, medicines, and supernatural heroes or deities are joined to create a semantic fabric within which direction is apparent. Frequently it is the descriptive traits of the medicines—*nkumbi* rats, white chalk, lemba-lemba plants— that do the defining, with the help of short couplets or phrases uttered during their use. The effect of this ritual action is however to move the power of the *Lemba* Father into the *Lemba* Son and on to his wives and patrifilial children, in the same terms as *kitswa*, the spiritual substance in the etiological myth, moves from Nzambi to Nga Malamu, to Kuba, and to Mavungu (figure 15).

Figure 15
Metaphoric association of domains
as depicted in eastern variant of *Lemba*

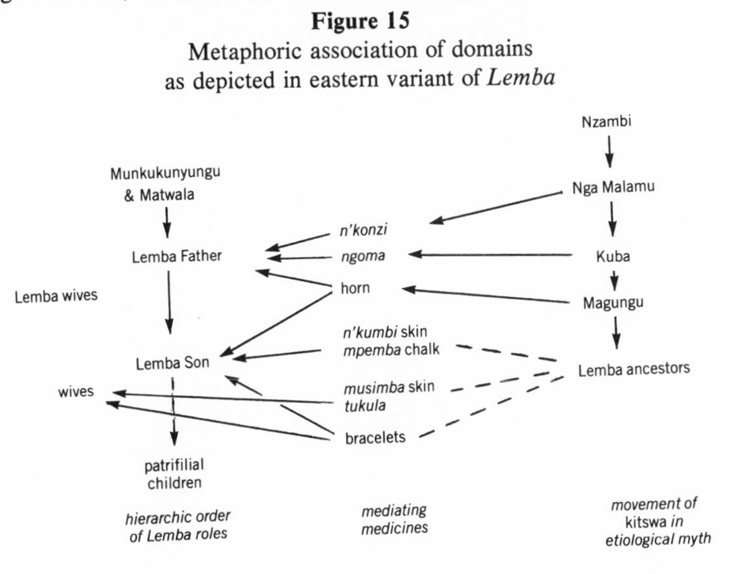

Chapter 6

The South-Central (Nsundi, Bwende) Variant of *Lemba*

The Lemba *Séance in Nseke-Mbanza*

The south-central variant of *Lemba*'s inauguration ceremony is based on an account by Fukiau, recognized MuKongo writer and educator. Because this account, representative of much of the Manianga region, has been published in Fukiau's Kongo cosmogony (*Nza Kongo*),[1] I need not offer it here but shall proceed with an analysis of the expressive domains related in it. A few introductory comments are in order about Fukiau's *Lemba* account and the conditions of its compilation, because it has come under serious attack by a fellow Maniangan author, Batsikama ba Mampuya.[2] Batsikama charges Fukiau with having invented a personalistic view of Kongo cosmology and perpetrated it for self-aggrandizement. It should be noted that Batsikama originates not far from where Fukiau is at home, and there is more to this attack than its scholarly content. Without wishing to join in or rehash the debate, I might note that Fukiau could have averted such charges by acknowledging his considerable debt to *Lemba* priest Katula of Nseke Mbanza. Later in this chapter I shall return to a few of Batsikama's specific criticisms. Here I should clarify the conditions under which Katula's account of *Lemba* was gathered.

Early in my fieldwork in 1965, Fukiau and I spent an entire day with Katula. Katula was well aware of the stringency with which some *Lemba* priests kept the secrets of *Lemba* decades after its demise as an active institution. Although he shared with them a great admiration for it, he believed the secrets deserved to be told for posterity. As an educator (see Chapter 3), he frequently spoke of the ancestral past to his students. As speaker (*nzonzi*) for his clan, the Kikwimba of Nseke-Mbanza, he utilized his remarkable oratorical skills in a way that reflected his *Lemba* training. When Fukiau and I suggested a thorough coverage of *Lemba*, Katula willingly consented to meet with us.

The "interview" was held, at Katula's request, out in the high savanna bush and at the outskirts of Nseke-Mbanza where the last séance of the region had occurred in 1919. Although Katula felt unsure speaking about *Lemba* in general, he related with ease and remarkable memory the séance of 1919. Fukiau's account reflects this specificity. My own KiKongo was quite rudimentary at that time, those parts of the interview pertaining to esoteric features of *Lemba* songs and symbols passed me by, but Fukiau took extensive notes of them all, as his published account shows. Answers to some of my questions also appear in Fukiau's account. Fukiau's published account of the Nseke-Mbanza *Lemba* inauguration may thus well be the most exact and authentic account on all of *Lemba*. What errors exist in the account are distortions having to do with extraordinary detail of some aspects alongside mere hastily-covered generalities of others.

The spatial-temporal distribution of events in the séance is accurate because of Katula's *in situ* presence where the 1919 event occurred. The logic of the stages, presented by Fukiau with KiKongo glosses, reflects this precision. Similarly, the visual details of ritual space are exact. Katula sketched for us the precise details of various *Lemba* altars, symbols, dances and ceremonious actions as carried out in 1919. He told us what had been esoteric knowledge, beyond the range of observation by the uninitiated (*bihinga*). The significance to our analysis of some of these details will become apparent in Chapter 8 on *Lemba* in Haiti, where they reappear, slightly altered, in the séance reported in the thirties of this century by Price-Mars.

Fukiau's account of *Lemba* gives mythic hero Mahungu a central position, not only in the *Lemba* etiology legend, but in the "Kongo cosmogony." The role of Mahungu in relation to *Lemba* varies from region to region, just as Mahungu's identity is variable, around the persistent motif of duality. In the foregoing chapter, Mahungu was third priest of *Lemba*, represented in a hunting horn. In Fukiau's (Katula's) account of *Lemba*, Mahungu becomes the central androgynous deity, source of *Lemba*. The present chapter examines at length this figure Mahungu, hero of complementarity, both as represented in *Lemba* etiologies and beyond *Lemba*. What in foregoing chapters was analyzed as a "hidden referent" of *Lemba* causation, in this chapter becomes the study, at closer range, of the composition of a deity. In addition to the Mahungu text provided by Fukiau (Text 4), three further Mahungu tales from a Nsundi enclave in Cabinda, told by Nitu (Texts 5, 6, 7), offer materials for this analysis of a mythic hero reaching across *Lemba* territory from east to west.[3]

Detailed materials on the figure of Mahungu make up for gaps in information on *Lemba*'s social and economic context, material already studied in the northern and eastern variants.

The Expressive Domains of Lemba

SPATIAL-TEMPORAL DISTRIBUTION OF EVENTS

Fukiau distinguishes the sites of stages of the *Lemba* initiation that dealt with the neophyte as still profane (*bihinga*) from those sites and stages that saw him either partially initiated or fully initiated.[4] The first phase, the "tying of knees" (*mbundulu a makoto*), refers to the neophyte's attachment to a *Lemba* priest, his first consecration. It takes place at a crossroads (*mpambu a nzila*), an auspicious location suggestive of the change occurring in the life of the neophyte. As elsewhere, the reasons for entering *Lemba* that are given by Fukiau are diverse. The neophyte may be afflicted, or there may be a *Lemba* position in a clan that needs to be filled. After sacrificing a chicken and some wine, over a fire, the *Lemba* Father "jumps" (*dumuna*) the child three times in a common form of blessing, and he is consecrated (*biekwa*).

When the neophyte has acquired a pig, the local *Lemba* adherents are contacted, and the next phase of the initiation may occur. It is called *ku sinda*, or the "rubbing of the bracelets" (*kusa n'lunga*) and the "holding up to the sky of the staffs" of the priests, signs which suggest that the *Lemba* brotherhood is cohesive and together, that the new priest will join their ranks. The pig is slaughtered and eaten in a festive setting, not far from the savanna lodge site.

The initiation moves directly into the next phase of instructions at the lodge of *Lemba* (*ku londe*) in a clearing in the bush. Here the neophyte priest is given the laws of *Lemba*, such as prohibitions against pollution, through eating, acting, or being demeaned in specific ways. The consecration and instruction of the neophyte's wife or wives is described separately by Fukiau. It appears to have occurred parallel to the neophyte priest's consecration and instruction.

Fukiau's account suggests the scheduling of the *Lemba* inauguration in two major phases, separated by a pause of indeterminate length (see figure 16.) This corresponds to the broad lines of the inaugural reported by other observers in foregoing chapters. One eyewitness of *Lemba* in the north Manianga suggested that the entire *Lemba* initiation took up about two four-day weeks after the neophyte had been given the initial blessings. Nkila and Nkoyi, according to this witness, were "*Lemba* days" and auspicious points of beginning for the first full cycle. One may speculate that the two day/night/day cycles comprising the inauguration each opened on the same day of the week, Nkila or Nkoyi, leading the first time into a limited-scale event with only *Lemba*'s priests and priestesses present, and moving from there into a full-scale cycle with all affines and patrifilial children present.

In any event, the second cycle opens with double sets of feasts. At the savanna hilltop lodge, a banquet is served the *Lemba* priests (and priestesses?), whereas the neophytes receive crude "unsalted" (lacking in meat) "feasts," as a type of ordeal to test their patience. Meanwhile, in the village, another feast has opened with dancing and eating. This double feast suggests the food dualism of other accounts, in which conventional food is mixed at times with medicinal food or has a closely structured relationship to it. While the village festival is under way, the priests take the neophyte(s) to the confrontation with the *Lemba* ancestors down at a stream, via other phases of this mystical penetration at the savanna lodge (*londe*). This corresponds to the ritual "death" of the neophyte in other accounts, as well as to the visit to the cemetery to fetch earth from a tomb. This process of direct encounter with the forces of *mpemba*, the beyond or the dead, was the terrible high point of the initiation, surrounded by much awe and fright. The neophyte needed to be especially consecrated at the savanna lodge prior to the "descent to *Lemba*" (*nkulumukunu a Lemba*).

The "descent to *Lemba*" is situated in Fukiau's account within the terms of his Kongo cosmology. In this view, the village and the beyond are opposing poles of a cosmic opposition, the former being the realm of humans, the latter the realm of ancestors, spirits, and Nzambi-God. The former is symbolized by the color "black" and is represented with charcoal; the latter is "white" (*ku-mpemba*) and is represented with *luvemba*-chalk. This Kongo world is shaped like two inverted disks, suggesting a type of terrestrial knoll floating on a cosmic water called Kalunga, within or beyond which is the realm of *mpemba*. To establish contact with this source of power, a human being must know the role of the priest. The priest, in turn, must know how to relate to the

Figure 16
Spatial and temporal organization of events in Fukiau's account of *Lemba* inauguration (Fukiau, 1969)

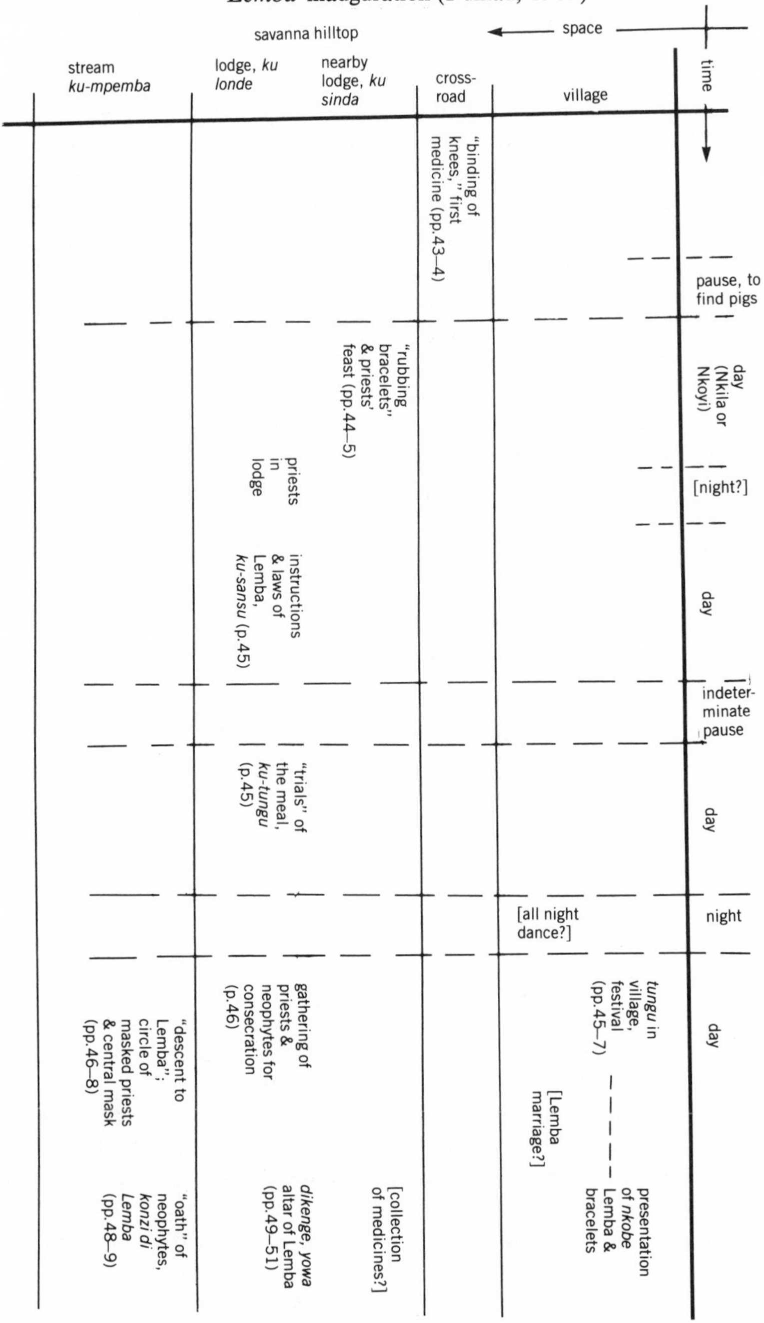

space
time

savanna hilltop

stream *ku-mpemba*

lodge, *ku londe*

nearby lodge, *ku sinda*

cross-road

village

"binding of knees," first medicine (pp.43–4)

pause, to find pigs

day (Nkila or Nkoyi)

"rubbing bracelets" & priests' feast (pp.44–5)

[night?]

priests in lodge

day

instructions & laws of Lemba, *ku-sansu* (p.45)

indeterminate pause

day

"trials" of the meal, *ku-tungu* (p.45)

night

[all night dance?]

day

"descent to Lemba"; circle of masked priests & central mask (pp.46–8)

gathering of priests & neophytes for consecration (p.46)

tungu in village, festival (pp.45–7)

[Lemba marriage?]

"oath" of neophytes, *konzi di Lemba* (pp.48–9)

dikenge, *yowa* altar of Lemba (pp.49–51)

[collection of medicines?]

presentation of *nkobe* Lemba & bracelets

ancestors who are in turn in contact with God (Nzambi), ultimate and unitary power. The gradual initiation moves from mundane blackness, through red transition, to terrifying *mpemba*-brilliance. Prior to their encounter with the white the neophytes are consecrated. After their encounter they must take an oath and again consecrate themselves at the altar of *Lemba* (*dikenge, yowa*). Finally, their *nkobe* and bracelet and drum represent mementos of their encounter.

Fukiau's description of the neophytes' encounter with *mpemba* and the following events merits closer examination because he offers exact drawings—given by Katula—of the ritual spaces, the choreography, of these events. In the "encounter with the white" the neophytes find themselves face to face with a masked figure on a pole, decorated in white, red, and black. Surrounding them are the *Lemba* priests, now wearing similar masks. The priests are playing their instruments—probably *nkonzi* drums, the "ancestors' voices"—and singing such lyrics as the following:[5]

O! Tala!
O, Look!
Tala matebo!
Look at the shades!
O n'kuyu!
O demon!
E Mpungu-tulendo!
God Almighty!
Banganga, ka tuswama ko e?
The priests won't be afraid.
Bakulu ku mpemba!
Ancestors in the White!

At the propitious moment loud salvos are fired from guns nearby and a priest in the outside circle pulls a string animating the masked central figure, all of which has the effect on the psychologically-prepared neophytes of terrorizing them so that they want to flee.

Trembling with fright, they are brought to a nearby site called *Konzi dia Lemba* (the "drum" of *Lemba*) where they are told what has just befallen them. It is a classic initiation sequence of mystery and fright followed by clarification. A *Lemba* song they have heard before, in earlier stages of the ceremony, is sung to explain the episode:[6]

Ntondele kwami
In gratitude
Na mayedo ma nkumbi
The whiskers of *nkumbi* rat
Me'tèmbil'e
Wiggle, twitch
Wanga mbil'e
Be attentive to the call
Mahungu e
Of Mahungu
Wanga
Be attentive.

Further clarifications are given, how this experience is like the life of the *Lemba* priest and that he can expect situations like that which he has been through. Then he swears an oath of loyalty to *Lemba* and its secrets.

Priests and neophytes now move to the savanna hilltop lodge of *Lemba*, but before they enter it they circle it thrice, symbolizing the "life of man" (*luzingu lua muntu, zingu* = circle), singing the song comparing the endless circle of life to this circle. The Kongo cosmology is expressed clearly in this: the path of the sun around the earth being analogous to the path of life from birth to death and then to rebirth. One might note that this episode is situated in the same moment of the inauguration as the "death" and "resurrection" events in other accounts.

At the lodge a ritual space is prepared, called *dikenga* or *diyowa*, which replicates the dichotomy this world/the beyond with that of neophyte/priest. The term *dikenga* suggests a place of circling, the center of a circling motion, or the hill around which one circles, here representing the life-cycle process referred to above. *Diyowa* suggests *yoba*, to bathe or anoint, and is here as in other Kongo ritual definitions indicative of the boundary between this world and "the white." The cosmogram suggested in the combined features of *dikenga*, place of the life cycle, and *diyowa*, place of anointment to the beyond, commemorates the encounter with the terrifying mask in a more serene and detached manner. The encounter at the stream was the genuine confrontation with power, now the neophytes are shown how to relate ceremonially to the abstract reality of power and the beyond. The priests enter the *dikenga* circle on one side, the neophyte on the other. On the priests' side is planted the "tree of life," and alongside the central pit or cross-like trench at the circle's intersection are further symbols of mediation with the beyond, a small jar or pot of palm wine and a sack (or sacks) of *mpemba* chalk and *tukula* red.

The procession of *Lemba* now divides into three groups. The *Lemba* Father presiding over the séance enters the cosmogram on the side of the tree; the neophyte(s) on the opposite side; all other adherents surround the cosmogram in a circle. Father and son face each other across the cross-like trench, the son holding his staff with two hands, the father with one, over the *diyowa*, sign of swearing. The father, before the witnesses surrounding him, swears to his son that if he has any doubts about the uprightness of his father-teacher, that *Lemba* may punish him. The father puts together a packet of nine sticks (*vua*) constituting "men," and nine more representing "women" (*mizita*)—the *Lemba* wife will receive these later as well. Now the *Lemba* Son recites a similar oath to his father before the surrounding witnesses, as the father pours wine into the *diyowa*, and passes the knife thrice under the neophyte's throat. With the two packets of sticks in his hand, the neophyte swears:[7]

Nge' tata
My father
Va lukongolo
Before this circle
Tutelamane
We stand
Ngatu yakuwila
If I hear
Maniungu-niungu
Rumors, gossip
Ngatu n'samu wambi
or evil reports
Vo lufwa
May death come.

The neophyte now kneels and rubs his mouth in the *kitoba* mud of palm wine and dirt in the cross trench and passes the knife thrice under his throat. After another affirmation or call of the *Lemba* Father to the twitching whiskers of Nkumbi and the completeness of Mahungu, the neophyte is marked with white clay and red powder. Then the group eats and drinks at *nkonzi* and returns to the village. There, in connection with the final feast that Fukiau mentions but does not describe, the bracelets and the *nkobe Lemba* are given the neophyte *Lemba* couple(s).

MEDICINE, MEANING, AND THE CATEGORIES OF RITUAL ACTION

The Fukiau/Katula account of *Lemba*'s inaugural in the north-Manianga region does not give specific ethnographic data on the exchange of goods and symbols in the rite, nor does it delineate very well the social roles of all participating in the rite. Since these features have been dealt with in previous variants, it is appropriate here to analyze in more careful detail the medicines of *Lemba* and the implications of their composition in ritual acts. Ritual has appropriately been defined as the manipulation of symbols. In the *Lemba* ceremony depicted by Fukiau, the ritual symbols that are used in the séance reappear in the ingredients of the *nkobe*, as synecdochic representations of the processes out of which they arose. Fukiau tends to explain this process in terms of the "Kongo cosmogony" which constitutes perhaps the dominant metaphor of ritual action. That figure, the opposition of the profane human world to the sacred world of the beyond (*mpemba*) and its powers, offers a generally correct explanation of the rite. The neophyte is introduced to the priesthood of controlling powers in society. He learns, in *Lemba*, to manipulate the signs of power, and understands its effects in rhetoric, ritual, and political and economic action. Some of the supporting significations need to be amplified, however, because they suggest a rich and nuanced symbolic understanding in north-bank Kongo culture.

Fukiau's list of ingredients in the *Lemba nkobe* is based on Katula's own *nkobe*, as he related it to us. In most instances these ingredients define both the ritual actions of *Lemba* as well as the ideal characteristics of the *Lemba* priest and priestess.

The small pot of *mpolo* medicine included in the *nkobe* was usually a mixture of whitish ash from the hearth and *luvemba* chalk. It constituted a type of lime which retained qualities of cohesiveness and stuck to the body in ritual settings, and it also had uses as a substitute for salt. In *Lemba* the *mpolo* medicine was used as an initial purification, and at the end it entered the neophyte's *nkobe* for his own treating. It was thus representative of his own status transformation. It symbolized power (*wisa, lulendo*), sanctity (*n'longo*), and clarity (*kia*). Whenever the *Lemba* priest appeared wearing or using *luvemba* or *mpolo* medicine, he was understood as a bringer and wielder of justice, consecration, and victory over obscurity and confusion.

The use of *tukula* red powder, and its representation in the *nkobe* in a small satchel, set forth a cluster of qualities comparable to, yet contrasting with, those in "whiteness." Whereas whiteness represented absolute sanctity, redness was seen as another type of sanctity which people feared. The *Lemba* priest had powers of life *and* death, and he was a judge who could perceive the inner nature of things and events. In many ritual settings both white and red were used, suggestive of the duality of power in society: its legitimacy on the one hand, its fearfulness on the other.

Salt was included in the *nkobe* as a practical preservative. But as such it also signified the *Lemba* priest's use of "righteous indignation" (*sinsu kia nganzi*) at the right moment. Indiscriminate anger is seen as destructive in society. Precise, well-aimed anger is a valuable rhetorical tool in the conservation of society. Salt is contrasted, in rhetorical theory, to oil, a substance for smoothing over.

Nsaku-nsaku leaves and bark (*Cyperus articulatus L.= Cyperaceae*) when mashed produce a pleasant incense-like aroma. The *Lemba* priest, in like manner, should be pleasant, agreeable, a person desirous of peaceful relations with others.

As in many Central-African rituals, Fukiau's *Lemba* séance has further plant symbols. There is the "tree of *Lemba*" planted within the circle of *n'konzi*. This tree is a banana sapling which represents the renewal of life, the rebirth of the neophyte, and the source of human multiplication. Perhaps the most important in terms of its inclusion in the *nkobe* is the palm tree (*ba—Elaeis guineensis*). Throughout the ceremony palm wine is present as an offering, as a drink both refreshing and slightly intoxicating when turned, and as a symbol of transcendence. Called *nsamba*, from *samba*, to "cross over," "transcend," another derivation of which is *sambila*, prayer, palm wine is used in the *n'konzi* ceremony to prepare the *toba* mud in the cross-like trench for the oath of *Lemba* before the ancestors. Palm wine is the pan-Congo liquid of prayer and sacrifice. The palm is a central feature in several of the etiological myths later in this chapter. Several parts of the palm enter the *nkobe* to signify this all-purpose resource of the land.

The palm nut (*sombo*) in the *nkobe* represents the multiple attractions of people to one with resources. At one level there is the recognition that palm trees are resources vital to the survival of humans.

The fibers give cloth; the wine is refreshing and nourishing; the clusters of nuts give oil; the nuts may—by the time of *Lemba*'s political zenith—be traded for goods and money. At another level, the palm nut is recognized because it attracts ants and termites. Thus, in Fukiau's interpretation, it represents healing among men, the opposite of illness which destroys human association.

For related reasons, the palm fiber, raphia, is also included in the *nkobe*. It symbolizes the *Lemba* priest's authority to travel across local territories others might find hostile and dangerous. A frond of raphia tied to the staff was supposed to indicate the *Lemba* priest's power, his legitimate right to trade and travel. It must be recalled that throughout the history of the coastal trade the raphia cloth or *pièce* constituted the main currency (*mbongo* = money).

The cowrie shell (*lusungwa*) was either inserted in the *nkobe*, or mounted atop the *nkobe*'s lid (see plate 5), or engraved upon a copper *Lemba* bracelet (plate 7). Fukiau suggests that its significance was that of reminding the *Lemba* leaders of the importance of people, individuals, and the origin of all persons in childhood. Thus the prominent should not abuse the weak and the infant.

A final essential ingredient of the *n'kobe* was the double statue of Mahungu, whose male facet, Lumbu, was tied to or joined with the female facet, Nzita. In other variants the figurines of the wives are called *mizita*. Sometimes they are combined with figures or emblems of the etiological deities such as Kuba or Nga Malamu. Here the representation of mystical origin and femaleness are joined into one object, Mahungu, whom Fukiau interprets as primarily a representation of the complementarity of opposing forces in the universe—male/female, strong/weak, violent/peaceful, and so on—required to maintain an effective, stable social order.

Although all the foregoing objects are by their presence in the *nkobe* given a symbolic prominence and cohesiveness, it is possible in the lyrics of the ritual to identify a dynamic metaphoric movement behind their composition. That is, they are not just isolated symbols with a given meaning but moving elements in a coherent universe of domains, like that which was identified in other variants already examined (see figure 15).

Songs introduced in the opening stages of the "Binding of Knees" (the first anointment or medicine) and repeated throughout the subsequent stages of the ceremony amplify this universe of domains. The first song outlines a relationship between humans, ancestors, and Mahungu.[8]

Kubèle bakulu
In the time of the ancestors
Kubèle bantu
In the time of humans
Nsôngo na nsôngo
Scores of copper bracelets
Se zibètana
Chimed
Tuaniungut'èno kwèto
So let us do our humming
(distinctive *Lemba* hum)
Kubèle bakulu
In the time of ancestors
Kubèle bantu
In the time of humans
E Mahungu e!
Oh Mahungu!
Nge' bahungila'
You preserved them
Badianga
So they could eat.

The structure of the song is one of double couplets in which an initial phrase is repeated in each couplet and followed by different actions: copper bracelets chiming and Mahungu preserving life. As already suggested in the analysis of the songs of the northern variant, such substitutable referents constitute the shifting or moving action in a metaphor. We could then rewrite the song in the following manner.

<table>
<tr><td>bracelets</td><td>chimed</td><td>in time of</td><td>ancestors</td></tr>
<tr><td>Mahungu</td><td>preserved</td><td>life of</td><td>humans</td></tr>
</table>

Bracelets chiming would stand in a relationship of metaphoric movement to the action of Mahungu preserving the society of humans. The verb *hungila*, describing the action of Mahungu, suggests verbal punning. The verb designating the unique low throaty hum of *Lemba* singing—*nunga* or *hunga*—ties the pun and the metaphor together another way. It is likely that *Lemba* priests had developed other esoteric meanings for these suggestive formations.

The opening rite contains two further songs, one defining Mahungu in relation to the *nkumbi* rat, the other seeming to link the entire ritual to the "passing of God." The text of the first song follows:[9]

Ntondele kwami
I am grateful
Na mayedo ma nkumbi
That *nkumbi*'s whiskers
Mè tèmbil'e
twitch
Wânga mbil'e
Listen to the call of
Mahûngu e
Mahungu
Kuwânga ko / buna bwasisa bakulu beto
Don't you hear, what our ancestors left us?
Kuwânga ko e
Don't you hear?
Wânga mbil'e
Listen to the call of
Mahungu e!
Mahungu
Wânga
Listen.

This song could be rewritten as follows:

nkumbi's whiskers	twitch
(*Lemba*)	rejoices
ancestors	have told us
Mahungu	calls

The implied meaning would be that *nkumbi*'s whiskers stand to *Lemba* in the same relationship as the ancestors to Mahungu, perhaps suggesting that *nkumbi* is a sign or referent of the spiritual power of the ancestors and Mahungu. The opening episode ends with the other song "God passes."[10]

Bândama
Bow down

Nzambi kayoka
God passes
Nima na môyo
On the back as the abdomen
Luse na môyo
On the face as the abdomen.

Fukiau's interpretation of this song, chanted as the neophyte is smeared with *luvemba* white and *tukula* red, is that God is consecrating the neophyte, but that God is so almighty that no ordinary mortal can see Him with his own eyes. To "see" the power of God, the neophyte must bow down and cover himself "with fear" lest he die.

A metaphoric statement emerges like that in the eastern (Lari) variant (figure 15). A hierarchy of powers ascends from humans to ancestors, to Mahungu, and to God. Within the human world a clear dichotomy is made between the *Lemba* priests and priestesses on the one hand, and the neophyte couple on the other. Mediating ritual objects such as masks, the *nkumbi* rat and its twitching whiskers, the objects of the *nkobe* such as *luvemba* chalk and *tukula* red, and the bracelets are poised between the two (figure 17).

These songs and ritual objects tell us which powers *Lemba* sought to organize and control. In the next section the myth-making process itself is examined, in terms of a number of Mahungu texts, the first used by Katula to explain the orgin of *Lemba*; the others from a non-*Lemba* source which clarifies the nature of Mahungu as mythic figure in the rigion with which we are concerned.

THE LYRICAL: THE MANY DUAL FACES OF MAHUNGU

In ritual representations, lyrics, and myths throughout the *Lemba* region Mahungu's identity varies from that of third priest of *Lemba* represented in a hunting horn *n'kisi* (eastern variant), to a set of hunter-brothers, to the hunter and the hunted, to healer and sufferer, to androgyne (Fukiau's account), husband and wife, and father and son. Whatever else this mythic figure may be, it is definitely a creature embodying duality and complementarity.

Efforts to identify Mahungu through etymological exercises have not been very successful. First of all, across the region the presence of the varying /h/, /g/, /v/, /b/ phoneme creates enormous problems of a purely formal sort. Furthermore, in the lyrical context of word use new meanings are constantly being created, as is clear from the songs

Figure 17
Metaphoric association of domains
in south-central variant of *Lemba*

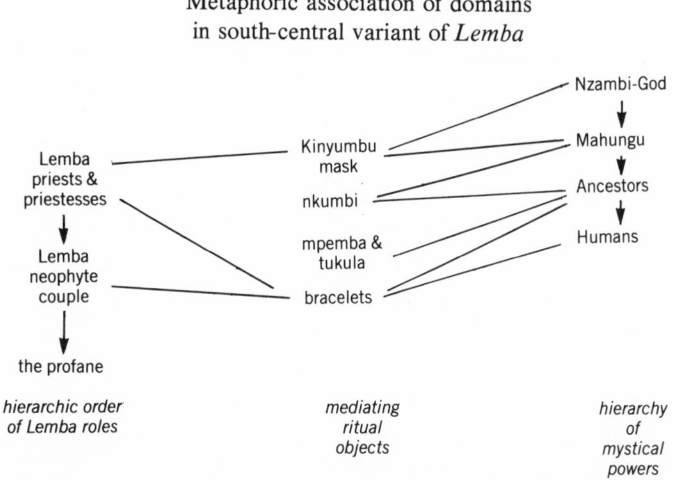

just analyzed. Thus, Mahungu is said, in Fukiau's account of the *Lemba* ritual, to preserve (*hungila*) the *Lemba* order, while a pun or rhyme is made in the same song on the murmuring hum of the priests (*tuaniungut'eno*).[11] Phonological analysis has usually followed the same method in order to ascribe a word's meaning as the method native speakers and singers use to invent new meanings. But such analysis can at best lead to circularity and confusion. Thus, to explain Mahungu, Laman uses the verb *hungula*, an exchange which sets in motion a ritual or relation, bringing two persons or groups together. But there is, for Laman, another derivation, *vunga* (syn. *wunga*), which may mean to blow or cause noise, as air blowing through trees.[12] It is this latter understanding on which Fukiau has focused, in which terms Mahungu becomes the double being whose spirit either "blows softly" as a creative force or "blows violently" as a destructive force. Mahungu, he concludes, is a being who thus embodies contradictory and opposing forces.[13] Batsikama invokes the term *hungu* (syn. *wungu* or *vungu*), force or power, thus Mahungu is he who holds force or power. For Batsikama, Mahungu (Mavungu) is the ancient priest who consecrated the rulers of the kingdom of Vungu which once held hegemony over north-bank societies.[14]

In ritual, lyrical, and mythical contexts, all of the foregoing meanings of Mahungu appear, therefore it is this contextual usage which must be further analyzed. First, Fukiau's *Lemba*-related

Mahungu text[15] will be studied; then, three somewhat less closely linked to *Lemba* will be examined.

Text 5

(1) *Ntangu yayo yavioka, Mahungu wakala mu kiese kialunga.*

In times past, Mahungu was in complete happiness.

(2) *Kakala ye mpasi nkutu ko; wakondwa mpisulu mu keto; wakondwa nadede mpisulu mu nzinunu; wakala walunga mu mamonsono.*

He had no pain; he knew no jealousy; he had no knowledge of hatred; he was complete in every respect.

(3) *Wakondwa konso banza mu luzingu; wakondwa banza mu nsatu zazo zena zakangama mu kimuntu.*

His life caused him no cares ("thoughts"); he had no concerns for the needs in life known to man.

(4) *Mu kinzungidila kiakundwa kwa Mahungu mwamena n'ti wabikwa vo "mutie-mpungu" vo "ba-dia-Nzambi".*

In the surroundings where Mahungu lived there grew a tree called Mpungu's tree or God's palm.

(5) *Nti wau wajaka wabsusu bèni mu nsemono ya muntu; mu wau mwavaika mpila ngolo zakala ye lendo beni ye zalenda vambisa nsemono ya muntu eto wantete.*

This tree was greatly feared in the human creatures; from it there emanated a special force; it had special power in the division of our first created man.

(6) *Lukufi ye n'ti wowo ka vafinama konso lekwa kiamoyo nkutu ko, kadi buna i nsisi kwa kiau.*

Close to this tree no living thing dared to approach; for it was an aweful thing for them.

(7) *Mu kuma kia mpeve yalebakana (ya nkento) yena mu muntu, muntu wazina moyo mu finama ye n'ti wowo, "ba-dia-Nzambi," mu mona ye bakula mankaka mu wau.*

Compelled by the feebler spirit (female) in man, man desired to approach this tree, God's palm, in order to see and understand more of it.

(8) *Mahungu wasindusulwa kwa ngindu zozo zalebakana mu zungana kinzungidila ye n'ti.*

Mahungu was driven by these weaker thoughts to circle around the tree.

(9) *Kansi mboki, bu kameni lungisa nzunga yantete ya n'ti wam'vimba, wapamuka kadi wamona vo kasidi diaka mosi ko, kansi bole mu mbonokono zole zanswaswani: nkento ye bakala.*

When he had made the first full circle of the tree he was horrified, for he saw that he was no longer one, but two beings of different natures: female and male.

(10) *Wonga ye kiadi kiababwila bu kabalendi kala diaka se umosi ko.*

Fear and sorrow came over them when they could no longer be one.

(11) *Batalasana napii, bayindalala.*

They regarded one another pensively, and reflected.

(12) *Lumbu (bakala) wakitala ye banzila ndambu andi ya kikento yatina ye bobo Muzita (n'kento) wakisuna mpe ye tomba ndambu andi ya kibakala yatina mu yandi.*

Lumbu (male) saw and thought about his female half that had left him and Muzita (female) longed also and sought her male half that had left her.

(13) *Bu bameni yindula, bavovasana mu zungulula ba-dia-Nzambi mu lusunga lutalane ye lwantete.*

After reflecting on this they decided to return around God's tree in the opposite direction.

(14) *Nzunga yoyo bu yimeni, basikila bole kaka bonso bateka kala: n'kento ye bakala.*

This circle completed, they remained two beings: female and male.

(15) *Tuka ntangu yoyo bau bole batombasana: n'kento watomba bakala kad'i ndambu andi; ye, bakala n'kento.*

Since that time woman and man seek each other; woman seeks man because he is half of her, and man seeks woman.

(16) *Nzinunu zakota mu muntu, mu ntombasani yoyo, mpasi vo bana vutuka kala va mosi se umosi, mu nkadulu au yantete yan'longo.*

In this original mutual longing for each other, they tried to return to be one, the being they had first been in purity.

(17) *Muntu wakitula mu lufimpu lwanene mu solula mvutu yifwanene kwa n'samu wowo wa mvambunununu a muntu wantete mu bantu bole banswaswani.*

Man set out on a great search to find an adequate reply to this puzzle of the division of the first man into two different persons.

(18) *Muntu wayenda kwanda ye mabanza mandi ye, va zimunina, wabwa mu banza dia nkwedolo: bundana landila ngwawani a tuzolo tole tuanswaswani.*

Man sought far in his thoughts, and finally came up with the solution of marriage: the union of two separate beings in mutual trust.

(19) *Landila nkabununu a Mahungu mu nsemono zole zaswasana, n'kento ye bakala, n'kento ye bakala bayika kinsona mpe.*

Following the separation of Mahungu into two creatures of distinct natures, man and woman felt alone.

(20) *Yenge ye luvuvamu biatina mu bau.*

Joy and hope had eluded them.

(21) *Bau bole batombasana ye bavwa n'kinzi a nsalasani va kati kwau.*

The two sought each other and had need of mutual help between them.

(22) *Bakala, mu kibakala kiandi, wakivanga kesa ye kinwani va kati kwa semwa biabio; n'kento wayalwa kwa wonga ye lebakana.*

The man, in his "maleness" was inclined toward violence and aggressiveness amongst all things created; the woman was overcome by fear and weakness.

(23) *Ndieu, n'kento, wavwa n'kinzi a lusanusu lwa bakala bu ka kalenda zinga mu kinsona ko va kati kwa mavanga mansisi ma nsemono yayonsono.*

Thus the woman had need of the man to be able to live without fear amidst the terrifying acts of all creatures.

(24) *Wanama mu tambi bia bakala mu kum'vana lwaka lusadusu; bau bole bakunda va kimosi: bakwelasana.*

It is a trait of the man to give her this help; the two lived together: they married.

(25) *Mu kuma kia tezo kia lusadusu lwanata muntu-muntu mu mbundani yoyo.*

This is the measure of help each brought the other in their union.

(26) *N'kento wayika n'sadisi kaka kwa bakala diandi.*

The woman became the helper of her man.

(27) *Mu kuma kia nsemono au yakala diswasani, bau bole bazayana ye mboki, n'kento wayaka (wabaka ntunda) ye buta.*

Because of their creation according to difference, the two knew each other and the woman conceived and gave birth.

(28) *Mu bila kiokio, n'kento wabika bakala diandi, n'lumi ye bakala wabika n'kento andi m'buti, kadi yand'i "m'buti-a-m'fuma, ye mindimba" (mbuti a bakento ye babakala).*

For this reason the woman called her husband genitor and the man called his wife genitrice, for she is the "mother of the *mfuma* and *mindimba* trees" (females and males).

(29) *Mu nkalasani yayi, nkwedolo, muntu wamona nkièvo vo watungulula nkadulu andi yantete yan'longo yavila tuka nzungununu a ba-dia-Nzambi vo mutie-Mpungu ye, mu yau, nkwedolo, muntu wasolula nzila yanayaki-yaki mu niekisa n'kun'andi mpe.*

In the state of marriage, it was as if man had recreated the original sacred condition that he had lost in the encirclement of God's palm or the Mpungu tree; in marriage, man discovered the easiest way to multiply his family.

(30) *Muntu wavisa vo nkwedolo i nzila yaluta mbote mu niekisa kanda diandi.*

Man understood that marriage is the best way to multiply the numbers of his clan.

(31) *I mu bila kiokio, mu n'kunga miandi, wabadika sevila nza ya bibulu yikondolo nkwedolo.*

For this reason, in his song, man began to mock the world of animals lacking marriage.

(32) *Ya nsusu na kakwela? / kakwela ko / Muntu na muntu / kwela kwandi / kakwela ko.*

Does the Chicken marry? No, it doesn't marry, each the other. Does it marry? No, it doesn't.

(33) *Ya mbulu na wan'kwela? / Kakwelwa ko / wonso ka wonso / kakwelwa / kakwelwa kwandi / kakwelwa ko.*

Does the jackal marry? No, it doesn't marry. Anyone can marry it, it doesn't marry, it doesn't marry.

(34) *Na-nsinsi na'wan'sompa? Kasompwa ko / konso ka konso / sompa kwandi / kasompwa ko.*

The wildcat, who married it? It doesn't marry, anyone, yes anyone can marry it, it doesn't marry.

(35) *Na-nsesi na'wan'yula? / Kayulwa ko / wonso ka wonso / kayula kwandi / kayulwa ko.*

The little red antelope, who asked for it? It hasn't been asked. Anyone, yes anyone can ask it, it never gets asked.

Although Fukiau uses this text to explain the origin of man and human society, its immediate referent in the *Lemba* ceremony is the *n'konzi* oath enactment during which *Lemba* "sons" follow their "fathers" around the tree to seal their initiation to the mysteries. A comparable rite is held for the neophyte wives. In addition, the bound figurines of Lumbu and N'zita depict the male and female parts of Mahungu, and the complementarity of sexes in the *Lemba* marriage.

The myth introduces an important further dimension into the relationship of father to children, and male to female, that of the unfolding of complementarity from androgyny. As most Kongo myths, this one is constructed in three stages: (1) an original condition of homogeneous authority, self-sufficiency, purity; (2) a lapse of time, passage over space, or some differentiation such as the dispersal of clans or here, "dispersal" of the sexes; and (3) an actual contemporaneous condition, human awareness of present flaws in view of past perfection, some attempt at solution. Fukiau argues that the aim of the myth's representation by two bound figures in the *nkobe* is to seize the moment of greatest tension and dynamic strength in their relationship, the moment of greatest complementary opposition between male and female, strength and weakness, creativity and destruction. At this moment the "powers are bound" (*ngolo zabunduswa*), synthetically restoring the vision of Stage 1, the original perfection, of the myth.

In ritual contexts, these principles are clearly expressed in the rotational pattern of dancing. There is no agreement over the direction of Stages 1, 2, or 3, but if clockwise dancing is used to depict the separation of powers or qualities from an original unity, then counterclockwise dancing will indicate the attempt to reintegrate these powers or qualities. In contemporary Kongo ritual both directions are used. Healing prophets dance around their sufferers one way to "undo the illness," then the other way to restore health. Funerary ceremonies dance one way in the village, then the opposite way in the cemetery.

Dance directions and stages in narrative have the identical purpose of articulating the relationship of unity to diversity, the processes of endogeny ("within one") to exogeny ("between two"), and in *Lemba* this was seen with regard to marriage. But at a philosophical level the problem was more general, addressed to the relationship of the one to the many, of peace to violence, of strength to weakness, of social order to disorder, and similar issues. This approach to cosmogony is characteristically Bantu. Unitary power must somehow be related to, and preserved in, diversity and multiplicity. In the next Mahungu text, the problem of endogeny and exogeny is depicted with reference to the culture of food: who eats whom, and what this has to do with social order.

I have already suggested that Mahungu, an important north-Kongo deity of duality, existed in local cosmologies across the entire *Lemba* area. Three texts from eastern Cabinda represent this wider corpus.

Text 6

(1) *Va kala muntu evo bantu bwadi; kifu kiau kwe vondanga bantu bangana badi muntsi.*

There was once a man or two people whose custom it was to kill other inhabitants of the land.

(2) *Bu bameni ku vonda, ku sasa muntu wowo; batunga bianga biodi.*

When they had killed someone, they cut him into pieces, and divided

(3) *Bu batunga bianga bibiodi, bu ba meni kubasa muntu kukaba kutula kikuku va kianga kinka dedi.*

the meat into the two baskets they had made, and dried it over the hearth fire.

(4) *Buna babasalanga pila yoyo bayolukanga bayolukanga: "nanie? nanie? wo? nani e?"*

As they would be treating their victims thusly, passers-by would call: "Who is there? Who?"

(5) *"O mi Mavungu é Manga nsitu, muna m'manga diambu ngie kuviokila mu dikubu."*

"Ah, it is Mavungu the ogre of the forest. To avoid trouble pass by in the trees beside the road."

(6) *Batu Banka "é é yisa, nkwenda kwama ko yayu."*

Some would say, "I'll not go to the side."

(7) *Yuwa ti mi Mavungu ukituka buyoba kumanga kwaku, ku viokila mu dikubu.*

The answer would come, "Listen, it is Mavungu; you're crazy to come here, pass by the side."

(8) *Mi yisa nkwenda kwama ko, evo mi yisa ku kwenda kwama ko.*

And again they would say, "I'll not bother to go to the side."

(9) *Di bakala be dio dibeki diela bu vioki tsi kwandi. Ba sala pila yoyo.*

Wise men would pass by to the side. And so it continued.

(10) *Buna muntu nka bwesa vioka. Bu bayolukanga kuna "Nani nkolukanga kokwé?"*

Then another person came along, and he too called out as he approached: "To whom am I calling out there?"

(11) *Ti o mi Mavungu.*

It is Mavungu.

(12) *Titika biyobwé. Nkwe yendanga kuna.*

He was foolish, and went there.

(13) *Nkwe sa basika vana, ka bianga bibiodi, bisa nsimbidila.*

When he arrived there, he saw two baskets; he was grabbed,

(14) *Kwitsa va kala va befu yinu bonso.*

and told: "come stay with us here together." (He did)

(15) *Buna bavingila fwati ni kilumbu ki sa kwila ko. Muntu waka vana.*

They waited a little and one day they saw another person arriving.

(16) *Bembi mu ntubanga vo "O mi Mavungu, utitika biyoba manga diambu vioka mu kubu.*

And they said, "we are Mavungu, do not be foolish. To avoid trouble, pass by the side.

(17) *Buna befu tu kedi kwitu vavé nandi befu yau é. Tu nvondanga bantu babé.*

We are ourselves here, we are who we are. We kill people.

(18) *Buna kiange kiki kiame kiangé kiki kiandi.*

This is my basket, that is his."

(19) *Buna bianga bibiodi ngie nzitu ti é yimweni; a buna nandi ti tidi kwenda ti é é tubantu vava.*

Then they saw that their two baskets were empty; and he said they would need to get some more people.

(20) *Befu yinu ti befu tu nvondanga bangana, buti ngie wa n'nanguka kwaku wa nkwenda ku bwala; mi yibesa ku kamba kwaku ko ti mi Mavungu ukituka buyoba viokila mu dikubwé.*

We will go by ourselves to kill some more, you may go to the village [for other food], but don't tell about us, that here is Mavungu who warns people to pass by the side.

(21) *Buna bakala vana babakanga bababwadi.*

[When they heard] they went and seized them both.

(22) *Ah! Befu na kubalanga ti bantu banvinha ko be mu nvondanga bantu.*

Ah—we are not madmen to have lived here killing other people.

(23) *Bababwila babanata bababwadi bayenda peleso.*

They fell upon them, and carried them both to prison.

(24) *Pila mweka. Pila mweka befu yinu bana ba Nzambi ba nka.*

And so it happened. So it is with us children of God on earth.

The violent antisocial side of Mahungu, merely alluded to in Texts 4 and 5, here[16] becomes the focus of the tale. BaKongo storytellers frequently generate such antiheroes to illustrate a social norm of which the negative figure is the inversion. Not having heard of

Levi-Strauss's concept of the "symmetrical and inverse" possibility of myth, they call these antiheroes "*diabolos*," referring to the apt metaphor of the photographic negative, which reveals the mirror image inverted in every way. Real witches, less comfortable to speak about, have the same qualities. The tale of Mavungu the ogre of the forest was undoubtedly meant to entertain as well as teach, and to frighten just a bit. Nitu's narration has numerous ellipses in it, as if everyone present knew the story well enough to fit the pieces together around the gaps.

There is no historical evidence that BaKongo were cannibalistic; however such tales as this confused missionaries and travelers. BaKongo did, and still do, use the figure of speech "eating" to speak about consumption of all kinds, whether it be food, medicine, money, or another's physical and psychic energy. An overabundant consumption, or an inappropriate consumption, is defined as witchcraft. In terms of this very abstract understanding of "eating," the present tale defines propriety by illustrating its negative inversion. Mavungu lives in the forest; human beings live in villages. Mavungu eats the flesh of his own kind, and only that; humans eat flesh of animals and a variety of other foods. It is not clear from the text whether there is one or two Mavungus, and if the latter, whether the traveler who joins Mavungu perhaps becomes the second. It is evident, however, that this traveling middle figure mediates the civilized inhabitants of the village and the cannibalistic ogre of the forest.

In this text, as in the foregoing, the two Mavungus (Mahungus) who are otherwise so dissimilar have in common their initial endogyny—in sexual identity, in "eating" their own kind—and the way they are transformed into figures of exogeny—sexual differentiation and marriage, and prohibited cannibalism, the tacit enactment of which would be eating other species and foods. In the next myth text,[17] even more complex dualities will be heaped upon Mahungu.

Text 7

(1) *Ba tunga bwala. Bu ba tunga bwala ba buta bana, bau badi vo bwala.*

They built a village, and when they had built their village, they had children.

(2) *Buna bu ba buta bana, unka u kamba a mwayi:*

Then, a certain one said to his fellow:

(3) *"Bwabu mi buta bwisi mbote ko, pana dionga diaku pasi ye lotsa bibulu du nsitu buna unvana dionga diandi."*

"My weapon is inadequate, give me your spear to go hunt wild animals in the fields."

(4) *Bu ka uenda u mona zinzau beti dia; ubonga dionga ubanda mu nzau.*

He went out and saw some elephants eating. He took the spear, and hit one.

(5) *Nzau unata dionga.*

The elephant carried away the spear (lodged in its side.)

(6) *Kunlanda menga kulanda menga, we bwa mu nlangu u n'neni wenzi kwandi.*

He followed the trail of blood until it disappeared in a large river.

(7) *Ah! Pila kiadi dionga di mwayi di ma zimbala.*

Oh, what sadness, the spear of his fellow was lost.

(8) *Buna uyitsa kwidi nzadiandi: "Mwayi, dionga dicimbidi; ti tala mwayi ti dionga diama disi mbakana kwe?"*

Then he returned and told the owner, "brother, the spear is lost! How will I find it?"

(9) *"Diambu vé komb'aku yi yi kwela ngie ku kwela komb'ami, mi ku kwela kombaku."*

"Do not worry. I'll take your sister in marriage [as payment], and you will marry my sister, and we shall be intermarried."

(10) *"Ka diambu vé komb'aku yiyi kwela, ki lendi kuwa ko!"*

"I cannot hear of marrying your sister!"

(11) *"Ka diambu evo ku botuka, ka botuka kwandi naté mi yi m'mona dionga diama."*

"Either that, or I shall leave, unless my spear is found."

(12) *Buna kiadi kibwa kwidi nzadai'ndi nandi nzadi'ama ma tsutika mu dionga, ulambalala mu bwilu.*

Then great sadness came over his brother, the one who had lost the spear, and he went to sleep for the night.

(13) *Buna ulotu ndosi.*

He dreamed of a voice saying,

(14) *Baka ngenge yoyo kileko kiyolukanga kio buna kwenda mu nzila kuvulanga ngenge bantanguninanga kuvulanga kileko, "Yayi nzila yenda kwami?" Buna m'mona na kanvwena "swi, swi" wakayenda.*

"Take this hunting bell *ngenge* and go on a journey asking it to answer questions: "Shall I take this road?' And if you see that it says '*swi, swi*' do not take the road.

(15) *Kansi buna m'mona kunkuvula, "Yayi nzila be mi yenda kwami e?" buna nandi si ka tuba "nge, nge, nge, nge" yenda mu nzila yoyo.*

But if you ask 'shall I take this road?' and it speaks '*nge, nge, nge, nge*' then take the road.

(16) *Buna bu ka yenda nzila yoyo utumamana bonso bu nkamba ndosi.*

If you follow these instructions, you will see your dream fulfilled."

(17) *Buna bu ka yenda mu nzila umona divambu.*

Then he took to the path, and soon came to a fork.

(18) *"A ngenge, yayi nzila yenda kwami e?" "Nge, nge, nge, nge, nge, nge."*

"Oh *ngenge*, shall I take this path here?" "*Nge, nge, nge.*"

(19) *Buna ka diata, ka diata kwe sadilanga pila yoyo zinzila ziazio uvuka kwandi.*

Then he walked and walked, approaching all paths he came to in this wise.

(20) *We bata nlangu un'neni bwatu bwidi vovo, "A a ngenge, yi kandama mu bwatwe?" "Nge, nge, nge, nge."*

At long last he came to the great river, and saw a boat. "Oh *ngenge* shall I launch out in the boat?" "*Nge, nge, nge.*"

(21) *"A ngenge yenda ku mongo nlangwe?" "Swi, swi, swi."*

"Oh *ngenge* shall I go upstream?" "*Swi, swi, swi.*"

(22) *"A ngenge, kwidi yenda? A ngenga yenda ku wanda nlangwe?" "Nge, nge, nge, nge."*

"Oh *ngenge*, which way? Shall I go downstream?" "*Nge, nge, nge.*"

(23) *Buna nandi bu ka yenda, buna ubonga nti evo dilemo uvwila. Buna uyimbilanga "Mavungu palabanda, é Mavungwe palabanda, é Mavungu palabanda, é Mavungu palabanda, é Mavungu palabanda.*

Then he took the oar as he departed, singing "Mavungu going downstream, Mavungu going downstream, downstream, downstream. . . ."

(24) *Buna bwatu bweti diata ngolo buna bu ka diata, ubaka va kielo kinka batu bapwedi bisanzu bidi vana.*

Then he was moving along rapidly in the boat, when he came upon a dilapidated house with many people in it.

(25) *"Mavungu!" Mavungu "nhinga!" "O witsa mu diyamba yitsa kwaku yitsa tapuka. Kanga bwatu, witsa mwa kwaku diyamba."*

"Mavungu" he heard. "What?" "Come over here to smoke some hemp with us. Tie up your boat and come smoke hemp."

(26) *"Vé minu a, a ngenge yenda ye nwa diyambé?" "Swi, swi, swi."*

"Oh *ngenge*, he asked, shall I stop to smoke hemp?" "*Swi, swi, swi.*"

(27) *"Yenda ku wanda nlangu?" "Nge, nge, nge, nge, nge."*

"Then shall I continue downstream?" "*Nge, nge, nge.*"

(28) *Buna udiata usala pila yoyo. Buna udiata, uyimbila lwimbu lwandi "Mavungu palabanda."*

Then he continued in this manner, singing as he moved along his song "Mavungu going downstream."

(29) *Buna udiata ke basika va dikabu di ba kieto bandumba, buna "ti una vioka vava kulendi baka ndumba evo nkietu u ulenda sakana yaku ko?"*

Presently, as he moved along, he came upon a band of young women who called out, "can't you cross over here and take one of us to amuse yourself?"

(30) *Buna nandi uyuvula ngenga. "Yenda kwama kuné?" Swi, swi, swi.*

Then he asked *ngenge*, "Shall I go over there?" "*Swi, swi, swi.*"

(31) *A ngenge, "Yenda ku wanda nlangu?" "Nge, nge, nge, nge."*

And again, "Shall I continue downstream?" "*Nge, nge, nge.*"

(32) *"Té u manga mu mavanga mamo ma bantonta u manga."*

"Not until you reject everything offered you."

(33) *Buna uyenda umona va tapukila nzau na menga.*

Finally he saw, as he went, the place where the elephant trailing drops of blood had gone ashore.

(34) *"A ngenga yi tapuka vavava?" "Nge, nge, nge, nge." Buna u yenda vana.*

"Oh *ngenge*, shall I go ashore here?" "*Nge, nge.*" So he pulled ashore.

(35) *Ngenge yandi u yolukanga "nge, nge," pasi ba zaba ti nandi nganga: "nge, nge" "a mboti tata, mboti, mboti, mboti."*

There *ngenge* sounded ahead of them so that others should think him to be a healer. "*Nge, nge.*" "Oh, greetings, sir, greetings."

(36) *"A ngie widi nganga?" "Nhinga a ko." "Kwidi bedi ko yi bedi, katsi mi nganga yineni beni yidi.*

"Oh, are you a healer?" "Yes indeed. A very famous one, a very famous healer indeed."

(37) *Buna ó fefu fumu bwala baka bazebi ko muntu wowo vo nandi u ba na dionga diandi. Uba na dionga di ka tsuma nzau ka banzei kwau ko, buna "befwé mutu widi vava boba yenzi ku ku dié banvengi pasi kuné.*

The village chief did not know that this was the man attached to the spear that had injured the elephant and so he told him, "With us here is a person who was injured and he is in great pain."

(38) *Buna ti ngie widi nganga ti ulenda botula nsongu wou, beju si tu ku futa.*

"If you are a healer you could remove his suffering. We would pay you."

(39) *Ye nandi mboti kwandi. A ngenga, "yi lenda kwami buka nsongu wou?" Ngenge, "Nge, nge,*

"All right," he accepted. Asking *ngenge*, "May I help this sufferer?" *Ngenge* said, "*nge, nge.*"

(40) *"Ti mu kwa nkisi ama bu ka ntubanga ti ó a benu bwabu mi ya mbuka nsongu wou."*

"In listening to my instrument, I can tell you that I shall heal this sufferer."

(41) *Buna a ngenga, "ti bapeni bi dia yi lenda dia kwami e? Pasi yi buka nsongo?" "Nge, nge, nge, nge."*

Then he asked *ngenge*, "What they pay me for healing, may I take it for myself?" "*Nge, nge, nge.*"

(42) *U yoluka. Buna landila diodio nandi u yenda mu nzo u tala nsongo wou ti "é benwé bonso mwa ku u lu weti sia?" "Ah! E mamé é mamé, kadi kwica, kadi kwitsa. Ti lwitsitsi si ka fwa.*

Then he entered the house to look at the patient, asking "Which one of you in there is the sufferer?" "O *mamé*, O *mamé*, come, come quickly, or I shall die," he heard.

(43) *E a tata sala kwaku. Buna nandi uyenda u ye kota ku nzo. Na nzau yoyo u mona va kotila dionga u bonga bilongo bonso (datolo) ou (nganga) u tula vana pasi dionga di lebila. Buna ubwata pila yayi ngolo.*

To the father he said "wait," and he entered the house. There he saw the elephant injured by the spear; he took medicine and like a healer put it on the spear wound to diminish the pain, and he pulled hard on the spear.

(44) *"E mamé, é mamé, é mamé" dionga di vodikanga divodikanga. Buna nandi u tuba a beno pananu kwala bwabubu mambu mameni.*

"O *mamé mamé*," he cried as the spear slowly came out. "Now," he said, "find a wrapping for the wound, the case will be over."

(45) *We twala kwala ka luzibula twala vava divudu ka, luzibula. Buna nandi banvana kwala kuna nzo u zinga pasi u zinga dionga dio diaka monika kwidi bantu.*

And they brought him a wrapping which he wrapped around the wound, instructing them not to open it. He also wrapped the spear so it would not be seen by the people.

(46) *A a "ngenga zibika mesu mau." Buna ngenga u zibika mesu ma babo. Buna nandi u nata dionga diodio kwe sweka kuna tsomo ku ka yizila muna bwatu kwe tula, buna u vutuka.*

"*Ngenge* close their eyes," he said. Then *ngenge* closed their eyes, and he secretly carried the spear over to the boat and laid it there, then he returned to them.

(47) *"Bwabu mue futi" "E befu twa kufuté. Bonga tsanga kitebi be yo.*

"Now you can pay me." "Yes, we will pay you. Take this banana sapling.

(48) *Kwe vata ya muna kilumbu bonga tsanga kite be yo kwe vata ya muna kilumbu ku mena muna kilumbu kubuta."*

On the same day as it is planted, it will bear fruit, on the very same day."

(49) *Buna banvana mikailu minkaka u yitsa kwandi. Buna ka mana ku lwaka vovo u vuka pe pila mosi. Bantumisa mu ndambu na ka zola kwenda ko.*

They gave him other gifts also to honor him. Then he returned in the same manner as he had come, but he had been so honored he hardly wanted to leave.

(50) *Buna ulwaka kwidi nzadi'andi, a a polo ti ndamba mwayi, "nzadi, twala dionga diama."*

When he arrived at the place of his brother to whom he had a debt, this one asked "brother, where's my spear?"

(51) *"Ti dionga disiko di sa bakana ko." do, "ka tuna tuban zipolo ko."*

"I didn't bring the spear" he feigned. "We cannot discuss the debt," the other replied.

(52) *Buna nadi "mwayi bonga dionga diaku." Buna u tuma nkietu'andi twala di kieta, vata tsanga yoyo.*

So he said, "brother, take your spear." He also sent his wife to bring kola nuts and the banana sapling.

(53) *Tsanga yo ba tsimbukulu yi ma kumbu mena yima buta. "Ah! ah!"*

They planted the sapling, and in one day it produced ripe bananas.

(54) *Nzadi, "siala mboti mi yima kwenda ku diangala ku ku kangala. Siala mboti u keba bwala. Keba na ci komba ciaku mi yi ma kwenda ki diangala."*

"Brother," said the one, "I am taking a walk to the forest. Farewell, guard the village, and watch over your sister, I'm off to the forest."

(55) *Buna nandi bu kayenda ku diangala, mwana mamatoto kite kio kibenga: "mamatoto, mamatoto!" udila, udila, udila.*

So when he had left for the forest, a child in the village began to cry for banana stew: "Banana stew, banana stew!"

(56) *A ukamba n'nuni'andi ye bongila mwana toto. Mwana wandilanga ngwandi katsi nandi unata kitebi*

The man instructed the baby's guardian to bring it banana stew. The child cried for its mother but was brought bananas.

(57) *Nandi dibakala dio u bitala kulubuka bonga ngie veka é ngie dibakala bemweni tidi kwaku kuvonda mwana bonga toto, buna uyenda.*

He looked at the bananas before him, but she scolded him, "You alone are aiming to harm the child by taking those bananas."

(58) *"E ka diambu ko, totu eyi kite ki nzadi'ami, kizi ko mambu." Buna udokula toto.*

"It doesn't matter," he said, "these bananas belong to my brother," and he tore one off.

(59) *Bu kamana kudokula toto mwana udia, bu kamana kudia toto batsimbukula kitebi vie vie, ki ma tina.*

When he had done so, the child ate of it. But as the child ate, the banana bunch disappeared completely.

(60) *Bu kitina nandi ku diangala kukayenda utuba. A bwau bwabu a yi tidi kwenda. Diambu dia kavana bwala mwayi nzadi u yi bikici diambu diaka vana.*

When this happened he went to the forest to tell the owner, who, upon hearing of the disappearance of the bananas, quickly returned.

(61) *Buna uyitsa. Bu ka yitsa, utala kite mwayi: "kamba kitebi konso ku ki yenzi. Tiwitsa kamba ko a mwayi pila kiadi mu kite kiama Kamba kite kiama konso ku ki yenzi."*

And he came. When he arrived, he looked at his brother, "show me the banana tree, and tell me how the bunch disappeared. Oh what sadness over my lost bananas."

(62) *E a mwayi, ndenvukila minu, mwan'aku ka zie nandi ubedila lukufi ku fwa. Buna mi yi lokuni toto yiveni mwan'aku kazi mi yisa yi dia kwama ko ve, vangi mwana. Kansi nandi udidi. Buna minu bu yiveni udidi buna kite kitinitsi.*

"Believe me, brother, your child was in agony, and close to dying of hunger. So I took the bananas and gave him some. I myself ate none, he alone. So truly, when I gave him the bananas, and he ate, the entire bunch disappeared."

(63) *Mwayi, diambu pe tu ntuba va kite kiama yitidi. Twala kite kiama ka diambu ko mwan'aku evo mwan'ami kansi kite kiama yitidi.*

"Brother, it does us no good to discuss the bananas, just bring me the missing bunch. No matter if it was your child or mine, just return the bunch."

(64) *Buna ununguka kiambu diodio diyitsa kwidi nandi. "A Mavungu, yi Mavungu, a Mavungu é." Bwabu ngie makiekulu mu kitebi." "Nhinga."*

Then he slept on the matter and someone spoke to him "Mavungu," "I Mavungu?" "You Mavungu. Now you shall find your bananas." "Yes."

(65) *"Bonga ngenga ye vatakana, ye vanga bonso buvanga nzad'aku. Buna uyenda utakana bwatu bobwau. Uyuvula kwandi keti va nzila. Uyuvula ngenga "yenda mu ndambu yo? Swi, swi" bokwa bwau.*

"Take *ngenge* and do as your brother did." So he went out toward the boat. He asked which path to take. He asked *ngenge* "shall I go this way?" "*Swi, swi,*" reject it.

(66) *Ye tula mu bwatu a ngenga "Yi kandama mu bwatu?" "Nge, nge, nge." Ka kandama mu bwatu lumbu lo kwa lwau, "E Mavungo é palabanda, E Mavungwé palabanda." Buna uyenda.*

Shall I take this way in the boat?" And *ngenge*, "*Nge, nge, nge.*" So he took off in the boat singing "Mavungu going downstream, going downstream." He heard a voice:

(67) *"A Mavungu, Mavungu é yiza nwa dyamba." Buna utapuka uye nwa dyamba. Bu kamana kunwa dyamba usia nkaka ubasisa mwisi.*

"Mavungu, Mavungu, come over here to smoke hemp." And he crossed over to smoke hemp, soon to be obscured in a haze of smoke.

(68) *Kansi kazimbukulu we kavana bwala, vana bwala bu ka fuma.*

He lost his way, and before he realized what had happened, he was in the place from whence he had come. In the village they shouted,

(69) *"O mwayi ma kwiza!" "Ti é é nkieto é nandi kadi nata kitebi." "Mwayi ma kwiza é é"; "kitebi kiami?" "A mwayi, yi sa ki baka ko!"*

"Oh, brother is back. Woman, come carry the bananas." "Brother has come!" "What, my banana bunch?" " Oh, brother, I didn't find them."

(70) *Ulembakana mu diambu bakutumisa mu mavanga mapwedi na kwe tapukanga. Buna ulembakana kubaka kitebi kiokio mu diambu di buvulu bwandi ki bila nkisi wowo ulenda vanga kwidi wonso-wonso ukuntumamanga.*

He failed because he let himself be distracted by the many seductions along the way; because of his own foolishness; and because he did not follow the magic of *ngenge* which could have guided him wherever he needed it.

(71) *Kansi nandi bu ka manga tumamana nkisi wowo ye mpila yoyo buna té bafundana na veka dikanda kiandi. Ba kana kivika kwidi mutu wowo.*

Because he refused to be guided by this magic, they accused him even within his own clan, and they abandoned him to slavery.

Of the several substructures that are woven into the foregoing Mahungu myth, the following will be examined in detail: (1) the relationship between two brothers, who are Mavungu's two sides; (2) the opposition of hunting and cultivation; (3) the interaction of the human and the nonhuman (animal) realms; and (4) the distinction between successful and failed mediation.

Relationships between the two brothers are initially couched in terms of equality and familiarity; the one calls the other *mwayi*, fellow, brother, confidant, kin (7.2). As their relationship becomes one of greater distance, they become *nzadi* to each other, a term which while still denoting "brother" can also refer to in-law, or someone of a collateral group, of the other part of a settlement or social unit (7.8). By the end, this relationship has been transformed into one of status differentiation, the one having become a successful healer and mediator, the other a slave, *muntu mu kivika* (7.71). The myth directly addresses the issue of social unity and difference, the one and the many.

Loss of a spear (7.6) is the narrative element introduced to discuss the differentiation in society that results from ambiguous relations of technique, subsistence, and ownership. If the spear cannot be returned to a brother, what is its equivalent. The original spear owner proposes that a sister given in marriage would suffice. The spear loser rejects the proposition as "unthinkable," whereupon the first brother threatens to leave the village—to segment. The reason for the refusal of a sister exchange on the part of the spear loser is not made explicit, but the lines of the dilemma are sufficiently like real life in Kongo society that it may be inferred. To accept a sister in exchange for a lost spear would confuse the lines of descent, ownership, and marriage. At one level it would be incestuous since the social unit of shared and borrowed tools is the descent group, the matrilineage, within which marriage is prohibited. The classic Kongo social-structural question is raised, of how an undivided, descent community of goods, can be divided. The well-known ritual of sacrificing a pig to "kill the descent of one blood" (*vonda ngulu a luvila*) is often invoked as the solution to the problem. In actual practice, it is rarely resorted to, but is said to have been used in the past where dominant single-lineage communities like the Nsundi invaders needed to set up polities of their own kind. A minimal exchange duality could be created in this wise. In the myth, the spear loser is thus faced with several options, each with clear consequences. If he finds and returns the spear, he maintains descent ties with his brother, or if he ignores the spear and exchanges a sister, he must break descent ties. The metaphor of goods and blood is clear, and may be graphically presented:

return spear	:	maintain descent ties	::	give sister in marriage	:	break descent (blood) ties

The group whose members borrow from one another—the matrilineage—seeks its spouses beyond its own confines, but to make this the group of marriage exchange (by severing blood ties) would render the unit of exogamous alliance very limiting. The rejection by Mavungu (the spear loser) of the tight exchange model is an implicit affirmation of the wider exchange model. This appears to entail another consequence in his actions. Having rejected alliance with his brother, yet not wishing this latter to segment, he resorts to a mystical solution to solve his problem: find the spear and establish contact with "the world beyond." Although there is no evidence that this myth was related to *Lemba*, structurally it does so relate by negating the isolated endogamous community, and establishing a preference for effective mystical mediation. It is at this point that hunting symbolism becomes significant.

Mavungu (the spear loser) is cast as a hunter and successful mystical mediator; the other Mavungu, whom we may call the banana bunch loser, is put into the role of the cultivator and the ineffectual mediator. One specific object relates hunting to effective mystical mediation. *Ngenge*, the bell hung under the belly of the hunting dog, leads the hunter through tall grass and forest to the game. African dogs do not bark. Their bells announce their presence to the hunter while not frightening away the game. This perception of the bell that smells out game is lifted and used as a metaphor for the effective diviner and mystical mediator. In the present myth *ngenge* is thus the near-living instrument of effective magic. Metaphors pile up in short order as Mavungu, spear loser but effective mediator, sets out on his journey to track the elephant. At one level the quest is a simple hunter's pursuit of a wounded animal. But the "path" of this pursuit is a wide river, suggesting a mystical journey. At another level the quest is indeed a dream, in which *ngenge* the hunting bell, by deft analogy, takes the figure of Mavungu (spear loser) on a mystical course to a correct solution of his problem with his brother back home.

There are two conclusions to the myth: one having to do with the consequences of effective mystical mediation, the other having to do with the outcome of relations between the brothers Mavungu. In the first, Mavungu (spear loser), as successful mediator, becomes a renowned healer with an ability to "hear" magical messages. *Ngenge* leads him to his goal, the "wounded elephant," who, transported to a mystical plain, becomes a human sufferer whom he cures. Hunting is a wide-spread metaphor for healing in Kongo culture, in which the hunter relates to animals (the hunted) approximately as the healer relates not to the sufferer but to the illness. The healer seeks out the affliction and finds it, in order to eradicate it. The healer is like the hunter in another sense. He goes out into the wilds of nature and brings back the plants with which he treats, just as the hunter goes out to bring back food for humans. In Kongo thinking, wildness possesses power and is the source of man's strength. Thus it is understood that Mavungu (spear loser turned healer) brings the banana tree back from the wild for his home and for his brother. Hunter and healer straddle two sides of the continuum from domestic to wild. The hunter begins in the village, but his field of action is in the wild. The healer's origin is outside in the wilds, but his field of operation is domestic society. In the present myth, the hunter chases the animal from the domestic field back into the wild, whereas the healer brings back plants from the wild. The two domains, the domestic and the wild, inversions one of the other, are mediated by *ngenge*. Again, although there is no mention of this text as *Lemba*-related, the central ritual function of a small bell is appropriate for *Lemba*. Numerous references from Dapper's 1668 account, several from the western variant, and that from Haiti describe such a bell. In the present text, this central mediating role may be sketched in the manner on page 222. In structuralist analysis, there are several columns of oppositions which are mediated by a middle operator, or which operate upon each other. *Ngenge*, the magical voice of the bell which moves between the village and the wilds, transforms the hunter into the healer, who heals the wound he has inflicted. His spear is transformed into an object of medicinal attention, for which he is rewarded a palm sapling. Finally, he is given power over mediation, the power of treating illness in society and ruling. That such a structure or set of procedures exists in Kongo thinking, is clear from examining the herbaria of *banganga*. There is, for example, "corpse hunter" (*munkula mvumbi*), a small tree growing at the edge of the forest, used to treat side pain and cramps. As the hunter goes into the wilds to kill in order to live, so the healer, with his origin outside of society and his mystical roots elsewhere, chases death from the domestic scene.

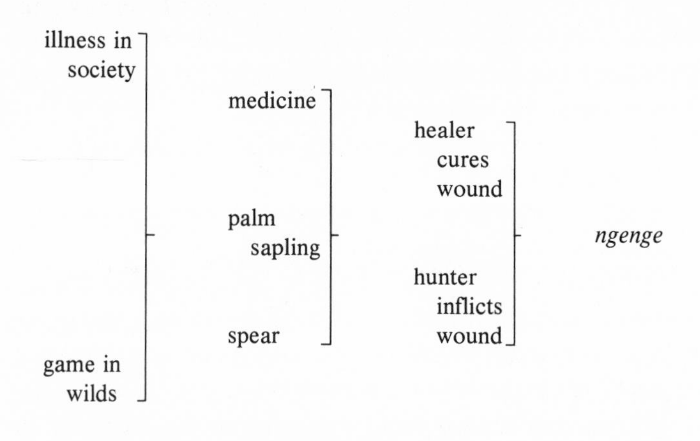

It is of course the different attitude of the two brothers Mavungu toward *ngenge* that determines their relationship to each other, and their status in society. Mavungu (spear loser turned healer) becomes the model of the priest, faithful to his "voice," and the recipient of high status. Mavungu (banana bunch loser) is depicted as the least disciplined person around, who is seduced away from the "straight and narrow" for a shallow "high" of hemp smoking. There may be a commentary here on some tendencies in *Lemba*. In the artifactual record of *Lemba*'s western variant there are numerous pipes identified either as "*Lemba* pipes" or "hemp pipes," some nicely carved, others large water-filled gourd pipes.

The composite picture of Mavungu in this text suggests something of the culture hero, bringer of messages from the beyond and of the banana tree to man. The dualistic play on two sides to every issue or question dominates. The text is set up as a double confrontation with the same challenge: to find the lost item—spear or banana tree—received from the other. The fact that both protagonists carry the same name, Mavungu, emphatically drives across this point of minimal differences in similarity, that is complementarity. Even the conclusion is suggestive of this: whereas Mavungu (spear loser turned healer) is lauded, Mavungu (banana bunch loser) is ridiculed and made a slave.

In the next text,[18] Mavungu is again a two-in-one figure, father/son, for whom the complementarity of two-within-one becomes a tragic dilemma.

Text 8

(1) *Mwana unka dizina diandi Mavungo ma. Mavungu kadi sala; bana be, kadi salanga.*

There was once a child named Mavungu. Of all the children, he worked the least.

(2) *A pila mwana, be u ngie kadi sala; nandi kadi sala kisalu kiandi kuvola kitimba kalendi sala ko.*

Oh! What a manner of child that he would not work. His only work was to suck on his pipe. Regular work he would not do.

(3) *Ngundi ye disia baluta kuzola bana bobo basalanga buna nandi ukalanga kwandi va bwala.*

Mother and Father loved the children who worked, but Mavungu was usually alone in the village.

(4) *Buna mu kilumbu kinka ukota ku nzo ununguka, bu ka nunguka: umona nkieto u kitoko beni uyitsa kwidi nandi.*

One day when Mavungu went into the house to sleep he dreamed: In his dream he saw a beautiful woman speaking to him.

(5) *"A ngie Mavungo, yuwa mayintuba, minu kivana meni."*

"Oh Mavungu, listen to what I tell you."

(6) *"Kubonga mbedi, kulengula mani; buna nkwitsa va tsitsi nti nhoka yo bantanguninanga ti mboma umweni. Mboma kutin'ani boma ko. Kupasula mboma yoyo si umona diambu dilenda kukusadisa, dilenda kukuvana moyo, vo mutu unvwama."*

"Take a knife and sharpen it. Then come to the foot of the tree indicated and you will see a python. Do not run from it in fear. Cut open the python and you will see something which can help you, give you life, and make you rich."

(7) *Buna bu kakotuka yimeni, Mavungu ubonga mwa mbedi ulengula, bantu bayituka beni! "O Mavungu, ti ka salanga ko. A bu bwidi kanlengudila mbedi?"*

So Mavungu took a knife; the people were greatly surprised. "Oh, Mavungu the one who never works! How will he sharpen a knife?"

(8) *Ulengula, ulengula, uyenda ku diala ku nsitu wo unkamba ndozi. Uyenda va tsitsi nti, umona mboma uyilama vana.*

He sharpened and sharpened, and went to the forest shown in the dream, and to the field indicated, where he saw at the foot of a tree a python.

(9) *Ukimba monho, usimba mboma, upasuna, ka zimbukula nkietu O be kwe nkamba ndozi ma kitoko beni.*

He seized the python, and cut it open as instructed. There he uncovered the very beautiful woman who had spoken in the dream.

(10) *"A Mavungo, ngie ngie mbadi, mbakidi kibwa kimbote ti O yizebi nduko kuna."*

"O Mavungu, partner, I've a good place, come with me there," she said.

(11) *Buna bu bayenda kuna nkieto wowo uyimbila: "Ye ditete a Mavungo minu bu ngina vanga monso mangina vanga mu ngieu.*

Then he followed her there, and as they went she sang: "You cannot believe what I can do for you.

(12) *Bidi, bidi té lufwa lwaku, siaku bonso bwa kwitsa bela pila disia diaku kumona (na) pe befu evo be yandi, kina kilumbu mbo mu m'monana be yandi é kianvutuka, Mavungu Ma Kata Mbamba, bonso bu u teka kala va mwelo nzo siaku. Yu wutswé?"*

Only you must promise that until your death, your father will not see you, and you will not see him. On the day that you should meet with him, you will return to your prior state, MaKata Mbamba, a nobody, as you were before. Understand?"

(13) *"Ti yuwutsu kwama."*

"I understand."

(14) *Buna bu bayenda va kibwa kiokio kimboti beni kikineni kimula uyimbila: "Mavungu makuvu utomba lwangu*

lukubia-dila; lwangu mbi ka mbiadila lwalu." Buna katsimbukulu beti sola.

As they proceeded to the village the woman sang to conjure up water to reside by: "Mavungu wants to live by the water, let there be water." And they found what they sought.

(15) *Uyimbila mu lumbu lolo ka zimbukula tsi nzo. Uyimbula mu lumbu lolo, katsimbukula va kakibanga kitoko beni kia kavana. Buna Mavungu umona n'henzi.*

She then sang a song, and they discovered a vast piece of land. She sang a song for every beautiful thing they came upon, and Mavungu was very happy.

(16) *Buna kayimbila lumbu waka ku nlangu makumbi ye bisalu binkaka bikwizilanga mu tangu mindela binkwiza mo dikumbi kwiza kota ku nzo unvwika, zisapatu uvula mivwatu miandi mi kabela mu zipasi evo mu kiadi unvwika mivwatu mikitoko.*

Then she sang another song and steamers appeared on the water in great hosts, with white men in them; one came near the house and they entered the house, giving him new shoes and replacing his old clothes with new beautiful clothes.

(17) *Buna Mavungu uyangalala beni ye di nka buvulu buwombo bu bayandi zingindu.*

Then Mavungu rejoiced greatly at his own good fortune, imagining his own folks' great awe in knowing of it.

(18) *Buna zingulu zio ziyendanga ku bwala bu tat'andi kwe dianga mayaka mangana. Buna siandi utuba, "a ngie n'tela, yenda we tala zingulu ziozio zindianga mayaka."*

One day Mavungu's pigs strayed to his father's village where they ate much manioc out of the field. His father spoke to a hunter, "go and find these pigs that are eating all the manioc."

(19) *Buna n'tela wowo uyenda u bakuka bakuka. Uyenda, ubasika va bwala bubuneni.*

And the hunter found where they had rutted the field. He pursued them on and on until he discovered a large town.

(20) *Ubaka boma. "A pila kiadi minu, n'tela yinkwitsanga tangu katsio mu nsitu wau, buna bwala bubunene kwe bu basikidi?"*

He was seized with fright. "How curious! A hunter comes into this forest regularly, yet suddenly there is a vast town here.

How has that come about?"

(21) *Kansi nandi n'tela utuba, "A a mi ka kina tina kileko ko, ki yi kambu monanga mu meso ko."*

But the hunter thought, "I cannot flee from something just because I haven't seen it before."

(22) *Uyenda kuna bwala beni uyuvula, "Nani beka bwala bubu?" "O Mavungo." "Mavungu mbi?" "O Mavungu Ma Kata Mbamba." "A mwana tata uzimbala tama kotso nandi makwitsa vanga ma pila yiyi."*

So he went into the village and asked "Whose town is this?" "Why Mavungu's." "Which Mavungu?" "Mavungu Ma Kata Mbamba." "Then this is the child that father lost long ago. How has he come to this present position?"

(23) *Buna u ye basika kwidi nandi unata nandi bu ka ye mona siandi uvana kio.*

Then Mavungu brought gifts to send to his father in the hunter's hands.

(24) *"Kedika Kedika Mavungu mweni." Ti nandi, "Yi mweni, tata, yimweni tata, yi m'mweni mu mesu mami."*

"Truly, truly I saw Mavungu. I saw him, father, I saw him father with my own eyes."

(25) *Buna landila Mavungu ukubika nzila mu kwe mona mwan'andi naveka ubonga ndusi.*

Then Mavungu (the elder) prepared to journey to see his child whom he called "Ndusi" (homonym).

(26) *Bu kayenda mu nzila buna nkietu wo utala a Mavungu: "Kadi kwenda kwidi siaku, kansi kwenda buna nkietu wo ukubika binuanunu. Uvanga bobo.*

As he was going the woman warned Mavungu (the younger), "When your father comes, do not meet him. Stay with me, for I am preparing the weapons to battle against him." She did this.

(27) *Mu kilumbu kinka, Mavungu uyindula: "A bwe tulendi simbidila nsamu wo ko bwabubu miyaka kisina yibeki. Bileko bipwedi, tata kalendi kubimona ko?"*

Mavungu thought to himself on that day, "How can this be handled? I have received many riches. But is my father not even allowed to see them?"

(28) *A mi didi "Mboti Tata!" kamona ku sa ntsibikila ku nzo utola nzo mu ngolo ziandi.*

When he arrived and greeted them the woman closed up the house with all her strength to keep Mavungu inside.

(29) *Nkieto uyenda kukunuana kadi zaba ti n'nuni'ama widi mu kwiza.*

She went out to fight with him knowing it was his father coming.

(30) *Buna uyenda "a u tata?" "Ti a u Mavungu?" "A mboti tata, mboti!" Nkietu waka mu kudila mu diambu di muina ukavana.*

But he came and greeted his father, and his father greeted him. The woman began to weep on account of the prohibition she had given.

(31) *Buna bu kadila pila yoyo wa vutuka. A Mavungu, buna nandi nkieto wowo uzola kikwezi kiadi beni, yi unkanina.*

When he heard her cry thus, Mavungu returned to her. He thought, "if she feels this way, and likes her father-in-law, I might compromise her rule."

(32) *Ubanza vo bika yivana ndambu lusadusu pasi kasadila mu fitangu-tangu. Kasi evo kadi yizebi kwa ti bisalu bia ntina.*

He thought, "let me go ahead and give some of my wealth to my father," thinking it would not disappear.

(33) *Buna uvana siandi ndambu lusadusu; basimbana mu mioko: "O yonso tangu kwiza pasi tumonana."*

Then he gave his father some gifts, and they embraced: "Any time you may come so we may see each other."

(34) *Ye bu basiala kumbusa a dibakala bu mengi kwa mambu mami: "Si uvutuka, Mavungu ma Kata Mbamba, si uvutuka va lukalu lwaku lu uteka ba."*

When this happened, the wife disapproved in these words: "Mavungu ma Kata Mbamba, you will revert to what you were before."

(35) *Dibakala diodio udila, udila, udila. Kalendi kunlenvukila ko. Buna samba bo bwau Mavungu makalu wutomba lwangu lukabiala biabio bi bavana bwala bimana kutina.*

The man (Mavungu) wept and wept, but she would not forgive him. All the wealth he had sought as well as the town suddenly disappeared.

(36) *Mavungu udila udila. Bu kadila kazimbukula nsitu uma boe kwelakana bo bwau bu ubela.*

Mavungu cried and cried. As he wept he found himself suddenly in the field where they had "married."

(37) *Buna nkietu mpe waka mu kudila mu diambu dikiadi buketi bundimina. Buna udila pila yoyo.*

The woman was also now sorrowful because of the impossibility of their union.

(38) *Udedakana Mavungu uyesingama va nti va katwama singamanga.*

Her farewells were as fond as his by the tree where they had met.

(39) *Buna zimbamba zivutakana bana mbi yayo yikala mu nandi yivutakana mu nandi.*

And all of the misery of his former state returned to Mavungu.

(40) *Buna mu kiadi ki pila yoyo, Mavungu ukituka bonso bu kateka kala. Buna mu kiadi ki pila yoyo ufwila vana.*

And with such sadness, Mavungu changed back to what he had formerly been, and in sorrow there he died.

The prohibition imposed on Mavungu (the younger) that he must reject forever his father to have a good life with a wife, creates a tragic dilemma for him. He must choose between accepting his father, at the cost of remaining politically impotent, or going with the woman to have material rewards but without being able to exchange them with his father. In this conceptualization of Kongo society the central juridical corporate institution, the matrilineage, is left unmentioned. Rather, the society is conceived in terms of the relationships an individual may voluntarily emphasize: patrilaterality and alliance. This text, like the preceding, seems to exaggerate the mutual exclusivity of the alternatives, and in so doing actually demonstrates the importance of integrating the two in a workable view of human society. It would appear that one of the main characteristics of these Mavungu myths is their internal analysis of society's various complementarities: male and female, age-different siblings, modes of subsistence, different aspects of kinship such as patrifiliality and alliance.

Every case of exaggerated or disjunctive complementarity contains its own solution, its unique form of mediation. Above I formulated this in terms of endogenous and exogenous process, or attempted solutions within one and achieved solutions between two. In the *Lemba* origin myth about Mahungu (Text 5), endogyny was expressed in the primal androgynous state of the hero, and exogeny was created by first exaggerating sexual difference, then by resolving it in the complementarity of marriage. In Text 6 about Mavungu the forest ogre, endogyny was expressed in the character of a radically antisocial hero who lived in the forest and ate only human flesh, and exogeny was emphasized in the arrest of the cannibalistic ("species endogastronomic") Mavungu and his incorporation into a noncannibalistic ("species exogastronomic"), law-abiding community. Text 7 about Mavungu (spear loser turned healer) and Mavungu (banana bunch loser turned slave) demonstrated several themes of endogyny becoming exogeny. The two brothers were initially of one status. With the loss of the spear, internal exchange of wives (sisters) and segmentation were proposed, but rejected. Original endogynous solutions to property, alliance, and descent were shown to be unacceptable. Exogenous solutions stated in the outcomes of the myth were status differentiation between the two brothers, and the differential access to mystical mediation resulting from differential subsistence roles of hunting, cultivation, and healing. Also, the desirability was underlined of mediation between the human and the "other-human" world of animals and spirits.

In Text 8, about Mavungu father/son, the exogenous solution is left unmentioned, or one might say it is mentioned by the exaggeration of endogenous alternatives—remaining with father and being weak and lazy, or leaving the identity of father and benefiting from the rewards of an alliance with the "other": in this case, trade at the oceanside and great political success, as seen in the grand city. The implicit exogenous solution is not hard to uncover. If Mavungu's "death" is due to the mutual exclusivity of patrifiliality and alliance, then "life" results from the complementarity of these two types of relations. This latter is, of course, the *Lemba* solution to the excessive endogyny of isolated settlements, marrying internally, thereby weakening trade and peace networks across the countryside. Any marriage "out," but particularly a "return blood" marriage such as the patrilateral cross-cousin marriage, accomplishes the feat of structuring patrifilial continuity together with alliance.

Numerous literary works have taken up this problem. Malonga's novel *M'pfoumou ma Mazono* is the story of a woman who is forced to flee her husband, a prominent chief and her cousin, after an illicit affair with her husband's slave.[19] In a vision her maternal grandmother tells her that the child she carries is her husband's. This comforts her greatly, but she dares not yet return and becomes a renegade, taking up life in the wild. There her son is born, and with his mother grows up in a cave by a lake. He teaches himself all the arts of human survival, especially hunting. This life in the depths of the wild is interrupted by two hunters from the husband-father's community, who as runaway slaves find the cave. The son, meanwhile, has become a strong and capable youth and invites them to join the forest settlement. This "wild" society of renegades grows into a vast city based on principles of egalitarian democracy instead of status differentiation, including slavery. Ultimately the healer-magician of the group, himself a runaway slave, divines the necessity to re-establish contact with civil society. Under the leadership of the youthful son, they move their mysterious community into the midst of other villages and establish a market to trade with them. At first threatened to the point of challenging war to regain lost slaves, the established society selects as its negotiator the husband-father. Father and son recognize one another, which of course permits father and mother to be reconciled as well, restoring peace to the region. Father conveys upon son a legitimate political office in the form of an inauguration to a ritual order (*Lemba*?). Each now has his own independent community, and they continue as allies in trade and war, closely intermarried.

The theme of the wilderness settlement recurs in mythology and lore, as well as ritual. Sometimes the inhabitants of such a settlement are ghost and spirits (*matembo*, *minkuyu*, *bisimbi*), at other times they represent a type of human community, different from but potentially related to the human community as a whole. Invariably these wilderness settlements are sources of contrast and of renewal, and powerful sources of wealth and danger, simultaneously. They embody peripherality and marginality, the power that comes from liminality and contrast. Often the mystery community represents an inversion of human society (Mavungu as the forest ogre) or an exaggeration of contradictions within the human society (Mavungu's city of wealth by the sea, Text 8). There is thus the theme of mediation achieved or mediation failed which runs through all accounts. One of the techniques of mediation in myth, ritual, and institution-building is to devise mediatory symbols such as *ngenge*, rivers, journeys, burrowing *nkumbi* rats, *tukula* red, and *mpemba* white, as well as composite mythic-religious figures such as Mahungu and the python-woman in the tree. These mediatory symbols and figures vary from the more-or-less human to the more-or-less natural (nonhuman). Sometimes, as in the case of the python-woman, this variance occurs in the midst of the text. The tendency to disguise or convert a hero into a natural or animal object, to remove him/her from the human realm, seems to correspond to the degree to which a social contradiction is consciously acknowledged. Thus, in Text 7 (Mavungu as the two brothers) and Text 8 (Mavungu father/son) the hunter is a significant mediator who stands in close relation to the natural world. Moving across the human/nature opposition, he is able to illustrate the differences as well as the interdependencies of the two realms. Mahungu as hero of complementary opposition often expresses contradictions in political and social life. The most interesting case of mediation failed is that in which the wife is couched in the form of a python (Text 8). Mediation achieved is portrayed in Text 5, and to a certain extent in Texts 6 and 7.

Insofar, then, as renewal, restoration, or regeneration of society is achieved the mediating symbols are of a humanizing quality in the myths. But insofar as these harmonious states are not achieved, the mediatory symbols tend to become naturalized. The importance of this issue for theories of myth analysis is great. It moves analysis beyond the point where all myth functions as a "logical model capable of overcoming a contradiction"[20] to the realizaton that societies are able to perceive the tragic dimensions of these contradictions and to understand that they cannot be overcome. Or, if they can be overcome, just what institutional alternatives must be followed, and which must be avoided because their consequences are tragic. These issues will be taken up in subsequent chapters, as will be that of how recognition of social contradiction relates to the medicines of healing in *Lemba*.

Chapter 7

The Western (Yombe, Woyo, Vili) Variant of *Lemba*

Introduction to the Sources

The western variant of *Lemba* is based on a great quantity and a wide diversity of sources because of centuries of coastal contact with Europeans. However, despite the extensive work by such ethnographers as Bittremieux and the Loango expedition, only the Laman catechists have described in any detail *Lemba*'s rites in this region. The two texts which follow, from eastern Mayombe, describe respectively the modes of recruitment to *Lemba* through "dream, curse or possession" (Text 9)[1] and the initiatory séance (Text 10).[2] An etiological myth from the forest region of the Mayombe near Kangu (text 11) features Kongo trickster Tsimona-Mambu as culture hero, bringer of *Lemba*, providing a basis for the analysis of the lyrical domain in the western variant. Trickster myths from outside *Lemba* (Text 12) offer contrastive material of the same range as that presented on Mahungu in the previous chapter.

The western variant demonstrates major points of differentiation between the Yombe forest and the coastal kingdoms and peoples. Although the eastern Yombe versions of *Lemba* resemble areas already studied, the coastal accounts change in an important sense. Art-historical expressions of *Lemba*—bracelets, drums, shrines—become more ornate. Among the coastal Vili, and possibly inland among some Yombe, Bembe, and Kunyi, the portable *nkobe* disappears in favor of a fixed shrine-house in the back yard "pantheon." Charm-jewelry appears in the form of miniature drums, figurines, shrine doors, necklaces, and elaborate bracelets in cast or engraved copper and brass. These objects permit a fuller analysis of the expressive domain of consecrated medicine.

The Lemba *Séance in Eastern Mayombe*

Text 9

RECRUITMENT TO LEMBA

(1) *Lemba i nkisi wena mu nkonko yifwanene bonso nlunga.*
Lemba is an *nkisi* in the form of an *nkonko* drum or a bracelet.

(2) *Nkisi wowo ubanzwa vo wambaki mbongo zazingi zikalenda tudulwa kwa bakulu.*
It is thought of this *nkisi* that it requires greath wealth to get the ancestors to bestow it.

(3) *Yandi wavangulwa mu ntinta yampemba isokwanga mu mpandulu andi.*
It is enacted with white chalk, given during its consecration.

(4) *Mboki, longo (bongo?) biandi biambukila biena muna mpe.*
Also, a marriage ceremony constitutes part of it.

(5) *Yandi Lemba ulotuswa ndozi mu bakulu.*
Lemba itself is presented in a dream from the ancestors.

(6) *Yandi ubikwanga vo nkisi a bakulu. Yandi ukwendanga ku mpemba ye ku bwala.*
It is called an *nkisi* of the ancestors; it mediates the land of the dead and the village.

(7) *Ikuma kakomwanga mu ndotolo a ndozi ye mu mpinunu a mafina ye mu mbwanunu a minkuyu.*
Thus it is activated by dreaming, by nightmares of suffocating by a curse, or through spirit possession.

(8) *Mboki mpandulu vo nkebolo a Lemba zena zazingi beni.*
For this reason initiations and initiands to *Lemba* are many.

(9) *Bankaka bakebanga Lemba mu nlunga a koko.*
Some keep *Lemba* in the bracelet on their arm.

(10) *Nlunga una mpe sadulwanga mbatu bonso nkonko a Lemba.*
A bracelet is sometimes used like the *nkonko Lemba* drum.

(11) *Vo bakondolo nkonko, buna i nlunga balenda komina nloko mwankaka.*
If they lack the drum, they use the bracelet to strike certain spells.

(12) *Balutidi sadila nlunga wanzongo mu tula mu koko.*

Copper bracelets are mostly used, worn on the arm.

(13) *Mboki nlunga wowo ukalanga na nganga Lemba; vo fwidi mpe ka ulendi katulwa ko.*

So the bracelet of the priest remains with him; if he dies it may not be removed.

(14) *Mboki kansimbi muntu wankaka ko walembwa dio vanda.*

Thus [*Lemba*] will not seize another person if it is not transmitted to another initiand.

(15) *Nga vo una simba mu diba, buna fwanane mu futa vo nsusu mosi kwa nganga Lemba.*

Even if one is seized, it suffices to pay a chicken to a *Lemba* priest.

(16) *Ndiena wavanda Lemba diandi usanga vuvu vo bakulu bandi babana bana fwa ku mpemba balenda kwiza kuntudila mbongo.*

The one who composes his own *Lemba*, hopes that his ancestors in Mpemba will provide him with funds [for the initiation].

(17) *Yandi Lemba lenda heha mbongo zena kwa bakulu ye zena kwa bamoyo mu diambu dialenda kiandi kiena kwandi mu twadisa mbongo kwa mfumu andi kadi bu batombulanga wo, buna bahehanga mu mafula makwizila mbongo mpasi bantu bakaka mambu Lemba basinduka mo mana bakamana mbongo za Lemba.*

Lemba is capable of exchanging wealth of the ancestors with the living so that it may be at their disposal, providing wealth to a person's lord so he may receive it; thus they exchange in the entrances whence comes wealth, and those who are in *Lemba* with their problems receive *Lemba*'s wealth.

(18) *Nkisi una mpe wena ye nkazi a Lemba.*

The *nkisi* also has a *Lemba* wife.

(19) *Ukotanga wo yandi i kundi ku nima nkisi wowo.*

She enters it to be the "friend" behind the *nkisi*.

(20) *Vo muntu una bwana nkuyu kansi ndinga yuzikamani buna nganga Lemba una bonga lutete lwansudia vo lwa tende.*

If a person is possesssed by a spirit but his speech is blocked, the *Lemba* priest will take a lutete gourd seed.

(21) *Vo yandi mbevo una lo tota, buna ngudi a nganga una kunkamba vo: "Yoya, monso mamweni, samuna."*

If the sufferer cracks it open [with his teeth], the chief priest tells him: "Whatever you see, tell it."

(22) *Buna mbevo i ntumbu badika vova vo kakedi vova ko, buna yandi una samuna makamweni.*

Then the sufferer immediately begins to speak if he has not already and tells all he has seen.

(23) *Vo nkuyu kamweni vo unkembi mambu, buna yandi una ntumbu samuna ye zaikisa yayonsono.*

If a spirit has appeared or spoken, he will reveal it and make all known.

(24) *Bobo i salu bia Lemba.*

This then is *Lemba*'s purpose.

(25) *Mboki nkisi wowo ukembwanga mu nkela.*

This *nkisi* is kept in a box.

(26) *Nkela yoyo ka ilendi talu wankaka mu ngudi ko.*

No one [beside the owner] may look into it.

(27) *Mboki nkisi wowo ukebwanga ku vinga kia mu ngudi a nzo, kuna vinga kiokio ka kikoti muntu ko.*

It is guarded in a special room in the interior of the house where no one may enter.

(28) *Buna una kubwa, nga vo ka bwa ko, buna una tekwa mu mbongo za Lemba.*

Should someone do this, he would be sold for the benefit of *Lemba*.

(29) *Fisidi Lemba nga diena mwamu. Konso diodio disadulwanga kwa babingi.*

Perhaps this is all about *Lemba*. Many use it in this way.

(30) *Ka diafwidi ko nate ye bwabu.*

It has not died out till this day.

Text 10

PRESENTING MWEMO-A-LEMBA MEDICINE

(21) *Fu kia zinganga za Lemba, vo bamweni muntu wena kimvwama, buna i ntumbu kunkamba vo nwa mwemo a Lemba, i.s.v., makaya ma Lemba-lemba.*

It is a custom of *Lemba* priests, when they see a person of means, to tell him he must drink *Mwemo-a-Lemba*, that is, leaves of the lemba-lemba plant.

(22) *Kansi vo muntu vumbidi vumu, buna si bavela munsumbi ye si bavela wa mu nkumba a Lemba.*

But if a person has a swollen stomach, they give him *munsumbi* leaves.

LEMBA CHILD BARGAINS FEE FOR COMPOSING NKISI

(23) *Mwana nganga i ntumbu bonga mpata ye kwe bwanisa ngudi nganga kuna fula.*

The neophyte priest next gives his high priest five francs at the village entrance.

(24) *Zinganga zazonsono zavanda Lemba mu tini kiansi kiokio, bu buwilu nsamu vo Lemba si dwandusu ku kingandi, buna bana kwina, kidi babaka zimbongo mu mpandusulu au.*

All priests who have been consecrated to *Lemba* in the surrounding area, when they hear of the *Lemba* affair, they make their way hither in order to enrich themselves by their initiatory expertise.

(25) *Ngudi a nganga si katambula kumi evo kumi ye mpata tanu.*

The chief priest will receive 50–75 francs (10–15 *mpata*).

(26) *Mboki zinganga zankaka zazono kani 30 vo 40 si zasola mwala (nzonzi) au mu kwe kubalombila zimbongo.*

Thirty or forty other priests will send their representatives forward to request payments of money.

(27) *Buna mwala si kateka tambula kani mpata mole vo tatu.*

The representatives will receive 10–15 francs (2–3 *mpata*) each.

(28) *Mboki si katangunanga nganga vo: ndieu ebu kadilanga, mboki mwana nganga si kavana ndiana ntalu yayi katambulanga ye yandi i ntumbu futa bonso buvovele nzonzi nate ye babonsono bameni futa.*

The priests will be told: the one who has requested *Lemba*, as *Lemba* child will be told the fee for receiving it, and he will pay whatever the spokesman says, until all have been paid.

(29) *Mboki i ntumbu vandisa nkisi.*

Then his *nkisi* will be composed.

(30) *Nkama Lemba ufutwanga ngulu ye mpata tatu, minkwala zole, mpidi zole zambongo.*

The chief priest's wife is paid a pig and fifteen francs, two *nkwala* mats, and two *mpidi* baskets full of raphia cloth.

COMPOSING NKISI LEMBA

(1) *Lemba i nkisi watudulwa mu mwila a tola.*

Lemba is an *nkisi* which is put in a cylinder.

(2) *Mu ngudi a mwila wowo mwasokwa mafutu mole mami-nkanda miabulu, nkumbu a futu diabakala: "Nsasa Lemba."*

Inside it are placed two sacks of animal skin, the name of the male bag being: "*Nsasa Lemba.*"

(3) *Va diau vatulwa bilongo.*

[In] On it are placed medicines.

(4) *Singa kiakala mu mbu ye mpemba biau biatoma kangwa va futu diankanda mbala.*

String is wound tightly around it to better contain the *mpemba* chalk in this bag of *mbala* antelope skin.

(5) *Futu diankaka dia nkanda nkumbi divwilu kwa nkama Lemba; va diau vena bilongo: n'nanga ye tukula.*

The other sack, made of the *nkumbi* [rat's?] skin, is the *Lemba* wife's; on [in] are put medicines: cauries and *tukula* red.

(6) *Futu diodio dibikwanga nkumbu "Mpemba Lemba."*

This sack is called "Mpemba Lemba."

(7) *Lemba biekwa ku Nsona.*

Lemba is consecrated on Nsona day.

(8) *Nsuka lumbu mpaikulu au kumbazi, bakala si kateka bonga Nsasa Lemba ye bonga mpemba ye teka tula mampemba mandi va futu diodio; mboki sonika mpemba mu mpenga ye mu mvamba miamoko.*

Next morning they go to the square; the male [initiand] first takes the *Nsasa Lemba* bag and puts chalk onto the bag's skin; then he inscribes chalk on his temples and his hands.

(9) *Mboki nkento mpe si kakutula funda ye sonika tukula mu mpenga ye mu moko.*

Then the woman [initiand] also removes *tukula* red from her bag and inscribes it upon her temples and hands.

(10) *Mboki bau bole ntumbu vaika.*

Then the two of them come out.

(11) . . . *buna kabalenda zieta vo sala mu lumbu kiokio ko, kansi si bavundila kio kaka.*

. . . they may not walk or work on this day but must sit the day out quietly.

(12) *Lembama kiokio, bau bana baka kimbevo vo kifwa.*

Failing to obey this, they may take sick or die.

(13) *Mafutu matulwa mu nti.*

The bags are hung in a tree.

(14) *Bilongo biankaka batudulwa mu ngudi a mwilu: dingongo, makayi kwa Lembe.*

Other medicines are placed into the cylinder: *dingongo* nuts and *Lemba* herbs [calmants?].

(15) *Lekwa kiokio i nsuki zatebwa ku ntu a ndieu wavanda Lemba ye zakangwa va nsi a nkanda nsesi ye nkaka ye nkanda a kubu, wakangwa mpe zinsuki zamwana nganga ye za ngudi a nganga.*

[Another] thing is hair from the head of he who has composed *Lemba*; it is tied into skins of *nsesi* antelope, pangolin, and *kubu* antelope; also in it are hair of the neophyte priest and the chief priest.

(16) *Nkanda wowo batambulanga wo mu lumbu kina kiteki mana vanda nkisi wowo.*

This skin [?] is brought along on the day when they have completed composing the *nkisi*.

(17) *Mafunda momo miatatu miabikwa "minkunda."*

These three bags are called "the abode."

(18) *Batulanga mpe bikengi.*

Bikengi water plants are also put in it.

(19) *Nkisi wowo wena mpe ye funda dibikwanga "kikundu dia Lemba": va diau batulwa bilongo biampila mu mpila—mweba, ntutu, cizika, munsumbi-nsumbi, nkuku-nona, ye nionzo ye makaya manlolo.*

The *nkisi* also has a satchel called "*Lemba* power" into which is put a variety of medicines—*mweba, ntutu* bark, *cizika, munsumbi-nsumbi, nkuku-nona, nionzo* and *nlolo* leaves.

(20) *Nkisi wowo wasadulwa mu mayela ma mpila i.s.v., vumu, ntima, ntu, lubanzi.*

This *nkisi* is used for a variety of illnesses such as those affecting abdomen, heart, head, side.

THE MARRIAGE CEREMONY BEHIND THE HOUSE

(31) [illegible] . . . *buna i ntumbu kunata ku mbusa nzo ye nkento andi.*

[the initiand and rite objects] are carried behind the house with his wife.

(32) *Ngeye n'nuni Lemba, keba nkazi aku Lemba bwambote; si bakamba mpe kwa nkento, ngeye nkama Lemba, keba n'nuni aku Lemba bwambote.*

[The priest intones] "You *Lemba* husband, guard your *Lemba* wife well"; they advise the wife, "You *Lemba* wife, keep your *Lemba* husband well."

(33) *Mu nzo a Lemba ka mulendi kota muntu wankaka ko.*

"No other person may enter the *Lemba* house.

(34) *Vo umweni muntu dieti nkwalu yiwena, buna kamba nuni aku evo umweni mpe muntu viokele mpe evo diata mu lwi nkulu lwa nzo aku, buna kamba nuni aku.*

If you see another person do so, tell your husband; or if you see someone leaving or walking near your house, tell your husband."

WHEN THE PROFANATION OCCURS

(35) *Buna vo muntu si kasumuna mina miomio dia Lemba, buna si ka futa mvika; kansi mu ntangu yayi lenda futa kani mpata 4 evo bonso buzolele nganga.*

When a person violates the prescriptions of *Lemba*, he must pay a fine; however nowadays [ca. 1915] it may be 20 francs or whatever the priest decides.

(36) *Bu beti wo vandisa, buna nganga ye nkento andi mboki mwana ngo ye nkento andi mpe; buna babakala si bateka vwanda vo ntandu a buku biole bianti.*

When it is composed, the priest and his wife, then the "leopard child" and his wife [are present]; the men first sit on the bark of two trees.

(37) *Mboki bankaka bana kubafuta ku nsi a vunga napi ye zinganga zankaka zeti sika zinkonko e zindungu ye beti zimbila nkunga wau:*

The others come to pay them remain silently beneath a blanket while other priests beat *nkonko* and *ndungu* drums, singing this song:

(38) *Wavanda lemba, kusuka kwamoyo.*

He consecrates to *Lemba*, let him cleanse his life.

(39) *Lemba diami dia bumpati bwa nganga*

My *Lemba* enclosure is the glory of the priesthood.

Mayamona mu Lemba ndiadi

Behold this *Lemba*!

Sukula ko!

Cleanse it!

(40) *Bu bameni diodio, i ntumbu vaika ye bakento ntumbu kwe vinganga ye diatasana minlembo ye simbasana moko ku nsi a vunga ye minkunga ye zinkonko mina tamana bonso busilulu babakala nate ye kani lokula biole, mboki vaika.*

When they have done this, [the priests] leave and the women present "walk" over one another with fingers and hold hands under the blanket while singing and drumming the *nkonko* drum like the men did it, until the two are cleansed, then they come out.

FINAL RITE IN THE FOREST

(41) *Landila bilumbu biole tata nganga kunata mwana nganga ku mfinda.*

Two days later the *Lemba* father takes the *Lemba* child to the forest.

(42) *Kuna mfinda bavwandila va mfuma ye makuku, bisoma mole va nsi bau biekanga—i.s.v., Mpemba Lemba ye Nsasa Lemba.*

There in the forest they sit upon an *mfuma* cotton tree and a set of termite mounds respectively, the ground beneath them consecrated as "*Mpemba Lemba*" and "*Nsasa Lemba.*"

(43) *Mbangudulu a mambu momo i vo bakala evo nkento andi wena sita buna si kabuta mu diambu diakameni vanda nkisi ko.*

The meaning of this is: if the male or the female is sterile, they may give birth because they composed this *nkisi*.

(44) *Mbangudulu a makuku i vo bana sibutwa.*

The meaning of the termite mounds is that children will be born.

(45) *Bu si bakola nyo a nonia ye kuntentika yo va mbata a ntu andi, binonia biobio bu beti kunzanzala ye kuntatika ku ntu, buna kalendi yaula vo nikuka nkutu ko.*

When they take one with termites in it and place it atop the head when the termites begin to crawl out and bite the head, they must not cry out or squirm.

(46) *Nga vo si kanikuka vo kubula binonia, buna i mabuta kakubudi, si bana kumbika vo ndoki.*

If they squirm or slap the termites their own offspring are struck and they will be called witches.

(47) *Bonso bwena ntalu a binzulu biobio bieti kunzanzala, i bobo buna kala ntalu a nkun'andi mpe.*

As is the number of these termites [ants] so shall be the number of their offspring.

(48) *Mwana wantete vo bana buta vo wankento, una bikwa "Mpemba Lemba;" vo bakala, "Nsasa Lemba" bonso bwabiekwa bisama biabiole zinkumbu.*

If the first child born is a girl, it will be called "*Mpemba Lemba*"; if a male, "*Nsasa Lemba*" corresponding to the names of the consecrated signs.

(49) *Landila diodio, si banika ngunzi ye mpemba mboki kwe biosonikingi mu nitu mwana nganga yamvimba matona-matona mampembe ye mambwaki.*

Following this, they grind a mixture of *ngunzi*-red and *mpemba*-chalk and trace the whole body of the neophyte priest with white and red spots.

The Expressive Domains

SPACE AND TIME: FROM PORTABLE TO FIXED RITUAL SYMBOLISM

Most characteristic of the western variant's spatial-temporal domain is the transformation of the symbolism of ceremonial ritual into the symbolism of permanent architecture and garden (figure 18). The richness of both rite and *n'kobe* diminish. The rite described by Babutidi (Text 10) lacks the elaborate rhythmic flow between village, savanna, forest, and stream of the northern and south-central variants. The western-Kongo landscape is largely forested, and villages and towns and fields cut and burned out of the forest constitute the only clearings. *Lemba*'s ceremonial rhythm spans this simple dichotomy of forest and village clearing. Across the Mayombe, *n'kobe* and reference to a "house"-shrine are both present in varying degrees of elaboration. In Babutidi's account, for example, from the far eastern Mayombe, the *n'kobe* is as complete as farther east and north, although one of the satchels within it is called the *Lemba* "house" (*minkunda*, 10.17), and although there is this reference to a "house" (10.33), the final ceremonies are held in the forest. Farther west, on the coast and in Loango especially, the *n'kobe* disappears entirely. The *Lemba* shrine becomes a fixed installation at the intersection of the forest and village, an elaborate "kitchen" behind the hearth, a garden grove of trees, filled with other objects.

Ethnographies from the Mayombe and Loango describe this *Lemba* "house" and details of the fixed installation. In the Kangu area of Mayombe, Bittremieux described the *Lemba* couple's yard as a wooded grove (*bikulu bia Lemba*) of wild shrubs and trees transplanted to the domestic area between house and shrine, and surrounded by a fence. The trees included the *mfuma* cotton tree (*Eriodendron anfractuosum*), *nkumbi* (*Lannea Welwitshii*), *lubota* (*Milletia*), *kuaku* (*Oncoba sp.*), *nsanga-nsanga* (*Ricinodendron africanum*); smaller plants included *lolo kitseke* (*Annona Senegalensis*), *mvuila tseke* (planted together, perhaps suggesting their association with the human world (= savanna, *tseke*) in contrast to the ancestral world (= forest), *ditambi-tambi* (in association with the *lubota* tree). By themselves in a small enclosure behind the shrine house were *mutsanga-lavu* and *dilemba-lemba* (*Brillantaisia alata*). The whole arrangement suggests a floral cosmogram fixed to a spatial location much as the *n'kobe* eastward contains a miniaturized cosmogram of plants collected from the zones of savanna, forest,

Figure 18

Spatial and temporal organization of events in Babutidi's account of *Lemba* inauguration. Numbers refer to lines in Text 9. Outline of *Lemba* shrine based on allusion by Babutidi (9.33) to "*Lemba* house," and on fuller indications by Bittremieux, 1925; Bastian 1874, pp. 170–3; Güssfeldt, 1879, p. 71.

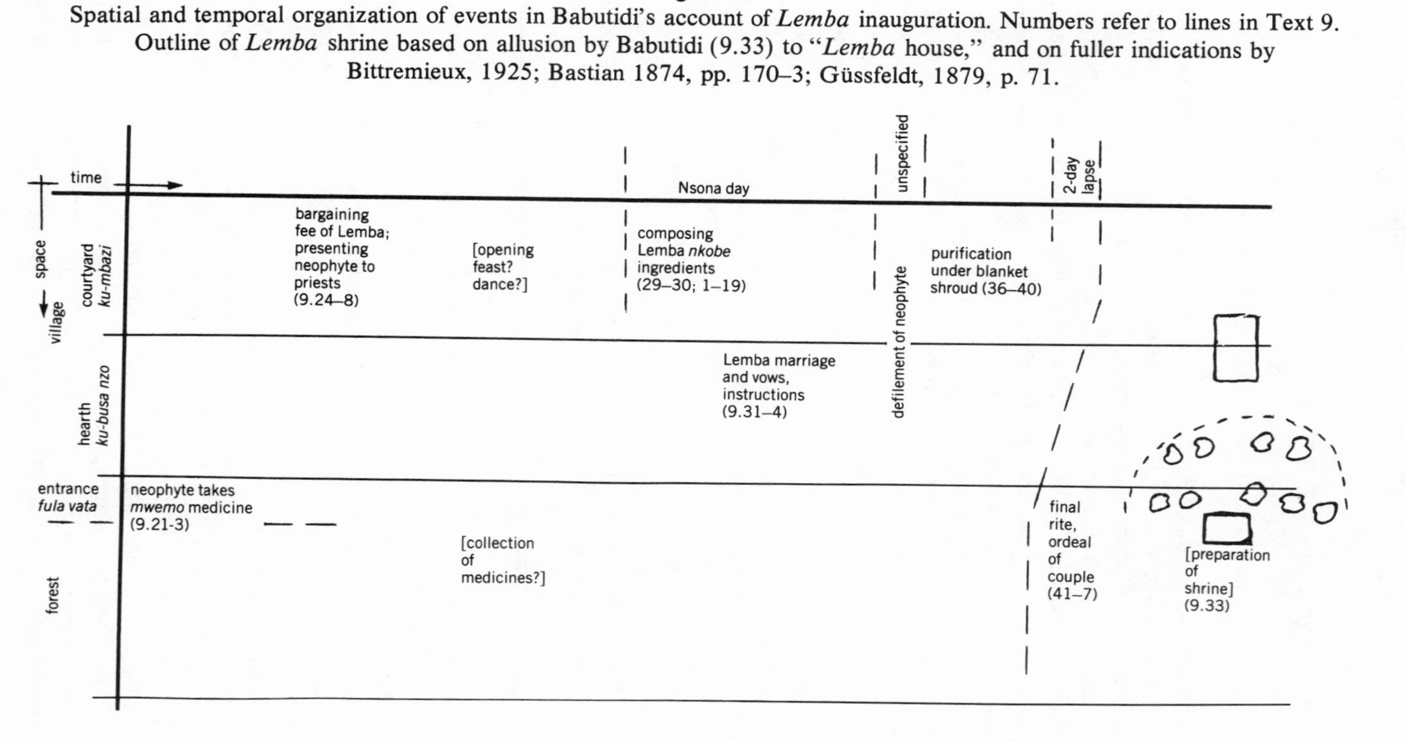

village, water, and cemetery. The purpose of bringing all these plants from the wild to be represented in the shrine grove, states Bittremieux, is to assure that the *Lemba* couple will be genuinely "other," truly changed (*baluka*),[3] permanently liminal.

The *Lemba* shrine-house is described by several writers. In the Mayombe Bittremieux reports that on its gable there is a sculpture made of woven *nsoni* grass of the *ndimba* snake (*Psammophis sibilans*, or *Leptodira Duchesnii*),[4] and a representation of the *lolo* and *mvuila* plants. Loango coast expedition writers report that the *Lemba* house in that area is situated in the forest well away from the houses, surrounded by a papyrus fence, and is used as a treasure house by the *Lemba* couple, secluded, locked with fanciful door locks.[5] Its décor is such that only the wealthy can afford it. Between the two front doors, one for the *Lemba* husband, the other for the *Lemba* wife, are planted respectively a *baobab* tree and a *mfuma* silk cotton tree.[6] Surprisingly little of this fixed architecture has survived, either in museum holdings of sculpture or in photographs and drawings.

More is known of the shrine context of the *Lemba* house. *Lemba*, where it appeared, was evidently the major shrine installation in a pantheon of *n'kisi* figures and objects. In the back-yard shrine-garden of Yombe chief Ngambula, whose life and *Lemba* priesthood was depicted in Chapter 3, *Lemba*'s shrine was flanked by other *min'kisi*, including: *Simbu*, in an *nzungu* pot, deity of time; a small *ndubi* statue with a mirror in its stomach (*kundu*); a *lukatu* statue in a pot, also with a mirror in its midsection; *Mbudila*, an *n'kisi* figure related to time and to the reign of the Mamboma chief; and a variety of others called *Mambinda*, *Maluangu*, *Mangaka*, and *Nzola*, either represented by a pot, a statue, or another object.[7]

The transformation of *Lemba*'s symbolism in the western region corresponds, then, to a general shift from moveable to fixed estates; from hunting and shifting cultivation to fixed landed domains; from segmentary polities to kingdoms and chiefdoms; from caravans traversing vast stretches over trails to endpoints, ports, and commerce at the coast.

ECONOMIC AND EXCHANGE STRUCTURES

A brief perusal of the exchanges in Babutidi's account (Text 10, figure 19) suggests an important difference from exchanges in other accounts already examined. Here the main payments are made in the currency of the late Free State and early Belgian colony. Only pay-

Figure 19
Exchange structure of *Lemba* account, after Babutidi (Text 10)

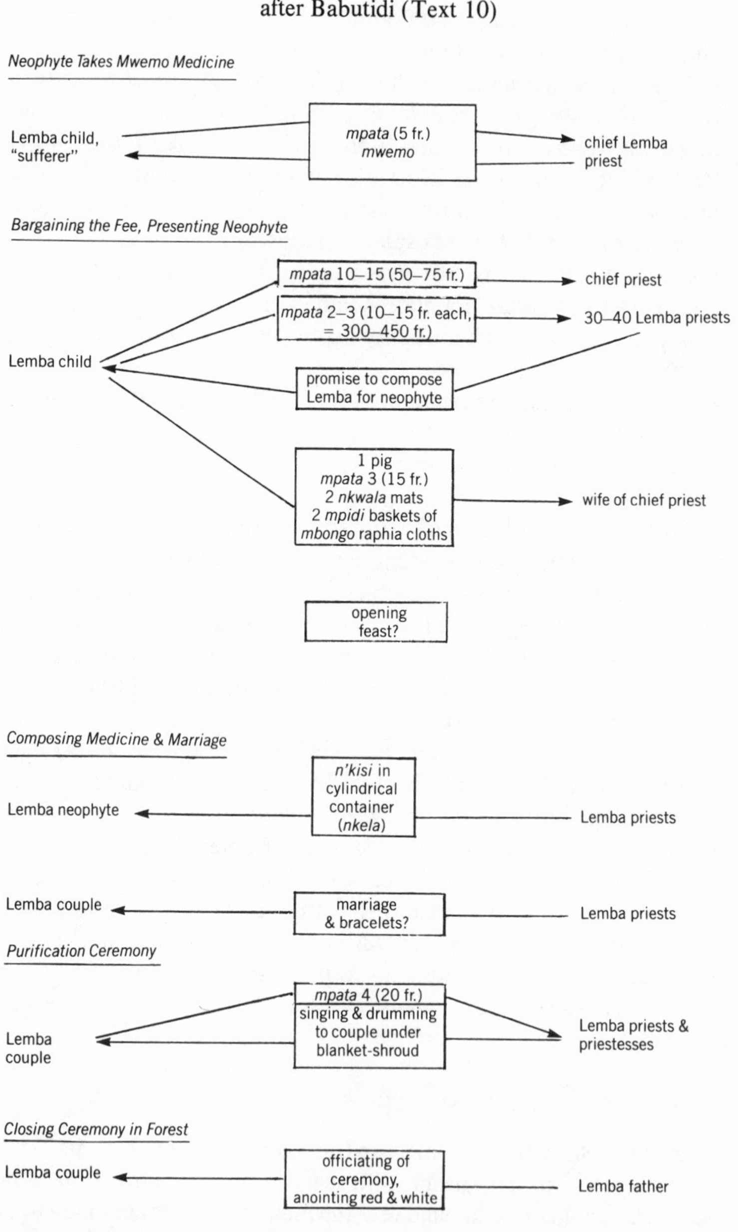

ments to the chief priest's wife are in the traditional currency of mats, *mbongo* raphia cloth, and pigs.

Following the Free State's introduction of brass wires in the eighties to compete with indigenous copper wire, the *mpata* (=five Belgian francs, ten United States cents) was introduced in 1910 by the Belgian Congo concurrently with the imposition of the head tax in this currency. With the creation of railroads on the south bank of the Congo River and in the Mayombe forests, European commercial interests were more effectively able to reach the sizeable Lower-Congo, north-bank productive resources. The old ability to mount caravans was revived briefly as individuals, lineages, and local chiefs portered palm nuts, ground nuts, beans, tobacco, even sheep and pigs, to these commercial outposts in exchange for colonial money and manufactured goods. Direct equivalences are not easy to establish between pigs, francs, raphia, and *Lemba*, as Chapter 2 has already suggested. It may be noted, however, that Babutidi's account compiles about 580 francs, one pig, and two baskets of raphia cloth as hard items of cost. In terms of trade figures of ca. 1928, this would have required bringing something like fifty to seventy man-loads of palm nuts to the nearest purchasing station, at thirty kilograms per person. Or, in terms of workers' incomes in the towns in 1925–30, about forty months of rations for one person (at ten to twenty francs per month), and two years salary (forty to sixty francs per month).[8] In other words, only someone who possessed the patronage of his lineage or who was a merchant of means could afford *Lemba*'s initiation. It is surprising that anyone could still afford this type of ceremonial expenditure in an era of the head tax, *corvée* labor, and the emergence of wage labor and the exchange of wages for manufactured goods.

The level of expenditure, and the involvement of thirty or forty *Lemba* priests in the initiation, plus their wives, suggest something of the commitment to the institution in the 1910–15 era in eastern Mayombe, and the extent of *Lemba*'s authority even this late in the colonial era.

VERBAL CATEGORIES, RITUAL ACTION, AND *LEMBA* NAMES

There is something eternal about Kongo ritual. It is continually extracting from the events of daily life and human society the salient features which pertain to lasting perspectives, values, and categories of Kongo culture. This process is far more enduring than a particular individual, chiefdom, lineage, kingdom, drum of affliction or religious movement. But these latter are situated in terms of the enduring. In the western coastal region there are schemas in the historical record which relate the various kingdoms and ritual associations, and individuals within them. Thus, in the Loango of 1875, according to Bastian, someone suggested that Loango, Kakongo, and Ngoyo were like husband (*n'nuni*), wife (*n'kazi*), and priestly mediator (*itomwa*=one who is sent) to each other: a complementarity of roles. Ngoyo was the home territory of the prestigious Bunzi shrine, not only the ritual basis of the Ngoyo kingdom but also that of Kakongo and Loango as well. In actual practice this meant little more than that the northern kingdoms sent emissaries to Bunzi during important decisions and transitions, to consult Bunzi's oracle.[9] Throughout the region another principle of spiritual "rooting" existed in the notion of the *xina* or *zina* "name" that flowed from a person's father to himself or herself, and back again to the father's lineage in the next generation. In noble marriages this principle was very important, and a person's status depended on his having a "father" and a "name" (*zina*). Names and role terms, therefore, reflected a classificatory scheme deriving either from the values of kinship, class, or polity. *Lemba* was no exception, and its relationship to other social processes and schemes is the subject of this section.

Konda and Babutidi, like Kwamba in his description of the northern variant, offer very clearly labeled categories of ritual action in *Lemba*, and the names received during the inaugurals by *Lemba* priests reflect these categories closely. The ritual process is described in terms of a few central concepts, beginning with the term *koma*, "to strike, augment, obligate, assemble, or constrain." The term has achieved some notoriety in Kongo studies from its use in connection with nail or wedge charms and the driving in of the wedges (*koma nsonso, koma m'funyia*). Konda uses it in a broader sense to refer to the awakening of a force which may be either negative and injurious, or positive and redemptive. *Lemba* is "aroused" (*komwa*) through dreaming of a *Lemba* ancestor, having a nightmare that one is suffocating (being bewitched), or being possessed by a spirit (9.7). A person may also have his "speech blocked" (9.20). All are symptoms whose etiology may lead to the recommendation that the afflicted should take the *Lemba* medicine and be considered for initiation. Both Konda and Babutidi speak of the priest in *Lemba* experiencing further negative ritual action in his defilement (*sumuna Lemba*, 9.27; *sumuna mina dia Lemba*, 10.28).

Positive ritual action to overcome these negative states includes the expected prescriptions to drink the *Lemba* medicine (*nwa mwemo a*

Lemba, 10.21), consecrate *Lemba* (10.7), and initiate to the *n'kisi* (*vanda*, 10.19, 23, 32). There are also idiomatic terms of positive ritual action such as "cracking the *lutete* seed," done by the presiding priest as a sign to the "afflicted" that he may now loosen his words and tell all he has seen in his dream or nightmare, in particular the identity of the person or spirit afflicting him. The basic term of ritual action, *koma*, is used with the verb *loka*, to speak or cast a spell; thus *koma nloko*. Whereas many *Lemba* priests and couples use their *nkonko* drum to create a spell, some do this by rubbing or spitting palm wine on their copper *Lemba* bracelets (Konda, text 9.9–12).

Possibly the most indicative phrase in the western variant depicting *Lemba*'s ritual action is this: "*Lemba* is capable of exchanging wealth of the ancestors with that of the living so it may be at the latters' disposal . . . so they exchange in the entrances whence wealth comes, and those who are involved with Lemba with their problems receive *Lemba*'s wealth" (*Yandi Lemba lenda heha mbongo zena kwa bakulu ye zena kwa bamoyo mu diambu dialenda kiandi kiena kwandi mu twadisa mbongo . . . buna bahehanga mu mafula makwizila mbongo mpasi bantu bakaka mambu Lemba basinduka mo mana bakamana mbongo za Lemba*, 9.17). The key terms here are *heha* and *fula*. The first, also *veva* or *veeva*, means to blow, clean, softly vibrate in the breeze, flutter, as well as to be bewitched or have a spell cast over one. In its substantive form the term becomes *mpeve*, which Bible translators took to express spirit, whence *mpeve a nlongo*, Holy Spirit. The second term, *fula*, denotes to blow, spit, or channel a substance, or a path, route, and the wind following these paths. One may *fudila n'kisi*, arouse an *n'kisi* by spitting on it, or *fula nzonza*, arouse a quarrel (*zonza*, rhetoric, speaking). *Mafula* are entrances to villages, markets, cemeteries. The verb *fula* is used in the eastern variant, as well as in other accounts of *Lemba* in the Mayombe, to refer to the ritual resurrection of the neophyte. The adept, having "died" (*fwa* ngambu) and seen spirits, is awakened (*fulukidi*) and given to drink from the *tsasa* pot by the *Lemba* priestess. In the east, the priests sing the song "Resurrect the Child" (*kimfula, fudila mwana*) as an invocation to Nga Malamu while one of the priests blows into the neophyte's ear. Related to the same cognate is *mbondo fula*, the broom of justice and oratory, depicted on some *Lemba* bracelets (plate 12). The text (9.17) suggests that *Lemba* is able to arouse the ancestors in a type of sacrificial trade so as to enhance the wealth of the living. This process occurs most auspiciously in the "entrances" (*mafula*) which is, indeed, where much of the actual exchanging is done in markets (see plate 3). It is this term *fula*, to raise, blow, bring into being, to "spiritize," which becomes the key word in Konda's concept of "spirit of mercantilism" or "capitalism" (*heha mbongo*, arouse the spirit of wealth; or *hehanga mu mafula makwizila mbongo*, arouse the spirit in the entrances whence comes wealth).

The names of *Lemba* priests reflect preoccupations with the range of ritual actions already suggested: oratorical skill, grasping or seeing mystical power, enjoying full ritual purity, and increasing offspring as well as wealth. The names are chosen to characterize the new person, resurrected to *Lemba* and its prevailing values. But they also uncannily portray persons grappling with personal problems. Bittremieux cites the following.[10] Mvuza, "jabberer," is the name of one whose words now flow freely, recalling the affliction of the *Lemba* sufferer with "blocked words" (9.20). Makunduku, "he masters powers," suggests a preoccupation with the problem of power. The full name is drawn from the phrase *makunduku va mbata vwa*, "on our death God alone is almighty," recognizing human mortality. Ngambula (cf. Chapter 3) means "washer-off", from *menga ma tsusu*, *simba*: *kwambula*, "the blood of chickens; hold it: release it," that is, one who is not afraid to penetrate to the core of a serious social issue, and deal with it, but who then is able to extract himself from it. Nyambivana, "God-gives," is used for someone who has accumulated the requisite wealth to enter *Lemba* while still a youth.

Thus far these names reflect serene spiritual *Lemba* values. Others reflect economic values of acquisitiveness. Mvu, "year," is the name of a priest who says "a whole year I have slaved to be able to afford *Lemba*'s inauguration." Yindindi, "thinking," refers to one who was always thinking how he might make his fortunes cover *Lemba*'s costs. Valata, "scraping and scrounging," referred to one who considered himself having to scrape, scrounge, and struggle to afford a *Lemba* marriage. Phila-mose, "same-as," is the name of one who says to himself, "Now I stand on the same footing as the old men who had to collect the necessary sum over many years." Mueba is the name of the chief priest, after the *mueba* tree (*Irvingia Barteri*), referring to the notion that "everyone gets his just desserts—that is, fruits." Sabu, "crossing-over," refers to one who *tsabukidi Lemba*, crossed over into *Lemba*, one who "had his money working." Or Vandu-vandu, "charm-activator," from *Dilemba diedi kuiza vandulu zimbongo*, "my *Lemba*, when it's turned on will enrich me (in the funds and children)." These names bring out the variety of values emphasized in *Lemba*, and their rooting in broader categories of ritual action.

It remains, however, to explain the link between this spirit of acquisitiveness and mercantilism so prevalent in the foregoing names and ritual acts, and the symptomatology and etiology of the *Lemba* affliction. Konda suggests that the affliction is brought on by something the sufferer may have seen in a dream, a nightmare, or possession by a spirit (9.20–22). Babutidi speaks of it as something that may affect abdomen, heart, head, and side (10.20). Further consideration of this issue will be deferred till Chapters 9 and 10. It is clear, however, that this *Lemba* "spirit of mercantilism" provoked considerable antagonism in a society in which the ethic of redistribution is deeply engrained.

MEDICINE AND ART

In previous sections on *Lemba* medicine the contents of the *n'kobe* have been examined in terms of their function. Here an interpretation will be undertaken of all material objects created specifically under the rubric of *Lemba* medicine: the *n'kobe* (or western equivalents), the fixed shrine, the bracelet, the drum, the rattle or bell, pipes, and statues. In each of these mediums, individual objects—wood, plants, metal—are shaped, named, and brought together in associative categories. They are thus given a signification. Sometimes these objects may contain bodily elements of persons involved—the neophyte's semen, hair, nails—and thus have an added, iconic signification. In other cases they may bring together statements of symbolism known in the world of conventional meaning, such as the relationship of men to women with their characteristics. A complex ritual system such as *Lemba*, however, takes these iconic and symbolic statements and reshapes or reassociates them for its own purposes. This process, which has been shown to use and construct metaphor, can be analyzed to gain special understanding of the institution's major concepts and values. The metaphoric process uses parallel series of expressions to make a composite statement about society and the universe, about the relationship of resources to power, and about the living to the ancestors from whom all power flows. Because *Lemba* expressiveness reaches out to make statements of these social, natural, cosmic wholes, aesthetic criteria are implied. That is, elements are abstracted from the whole in order to represent it. For example, the western *Lemba* bracelets depict a man and a woman joined by a flower-petal motif or a cowrie shell (plates 8–12). Miniature drums worn on necklaces or sculpted on pottery lids depict the drums of *Lemba*. In many cases these miniatures are worn as jewelry and used as charms (see plates 15, 16, 18). Mythic heroes, represented in the *n'kobe* as shakers or rattles, are often hung from the priests' belts during dances dedicated to the deity or hero.

The most common statement of signification in the *Lemba n'kobe*

Figure 20
Tukobe of the Western *Lemba* region:
Loango and Ngoyo (Cabinda)

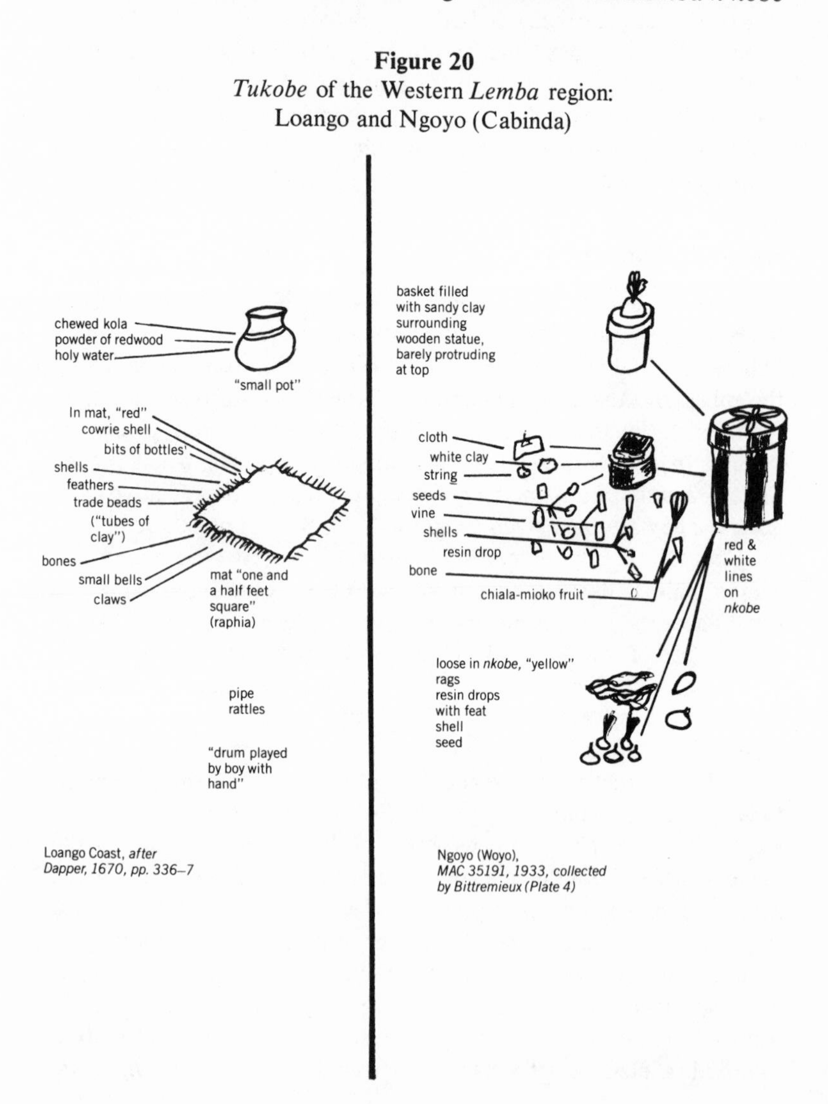

and shrine is the relationship between male and female. This relationship refers not only to the reproductive process in which children are born, but also it takes the male-female union as a model for all complementarity between social groups, for example, neighboring lineages. In the Yombe variants of the *Lemba n'kobe* (figure 21), male and female complementarity is couched in a number of metaphoric contrasts summed up in the names *Tsasa-Lemba* and *Pfemba-Lemba* respectively.

Figure 21
Tukobe of the Western *Lemba* region:
Mayombe

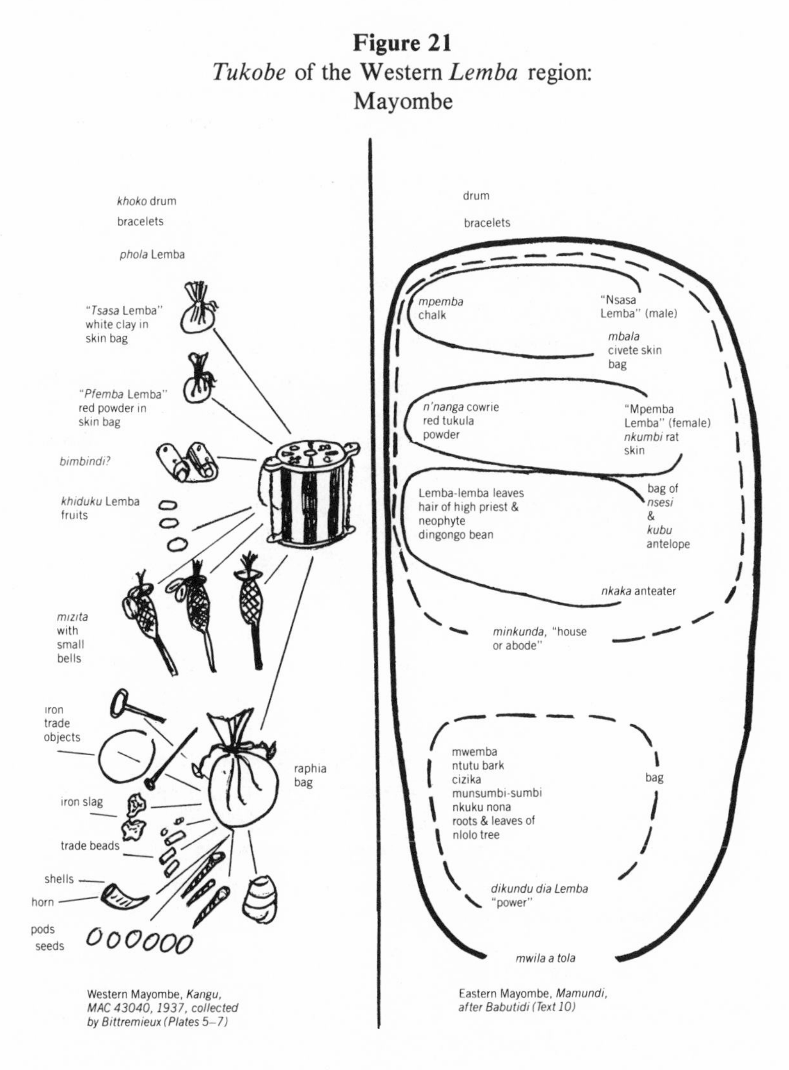

The iconography of *Tsasa* and *Pfemba* is rather complex and needs further clarification. Firstly, *Pfemba* is not the same as *mpemba* (chalk, whiteness, clarity), despite Babutidi's use of the term (10.6; 10.42; 10.48) and scholarly attempts to explain the apparent contradiction of "red" symbolism being named "white."[11] *Pfemba*, the "female" satchel, is indeed "red," as Bittremieux's research into the Mayombe *nkobe* he collected (figure 21) indicates.[12] The *Pfemba* packet in *Lemba* is closely associated with the well-known *Pfemba* (also *Phemba*) maternity figures of the Mayombe and the coast, figures which reveal often a reddish hue of *tukula* anointment. These figures, which attracted collectors' attention in the last century and are therefore widespread in European museums, are in turn related to an *n'kisi* cult which had to do with women's problems in general and midwifery in particular. Bastian and Pechuel-Loesch, who visited a *Pfemba* center in the 1870's, recorded a legend about the well-known midwife who founded the movement.[13]

Ethnographic research by Lehuard has identified the pose of these children in arms and laps of *Pfemba* maternity figures as dead children being mourned by their mothers.[14] One possible interpretation of this puzzling posture, one which I propose, is that these children are immaculate-conception, spirit children akin to *simbi* children "taken" by the spirits. In this way they reconcile, or mediate at an abstract level, the domestic role of childbearing with the notion of female rulership. In Chapter 2, I suggested that one could find many variations on the theme of fertility—augmenting local kin groups—and leadership transcending kinship to create an overarching political order. Ancient Loango and Sonyo noble marriages served a purely political purpose, as was seen in Chapter 2, and were commonly not even consummated. In *Lemba*, where fertility of the local clan section was combined with political alliances, *Pfemba* "redness" in the "female" section of the *n'kobe* offered a unique alternative resolution of this problem of fertility and leadership, of the exclusivity of local kinship and the need to create broader alliances.

This male-female relationship as articulated in whiteness and redness, respectively, is extended further by the relationship of the tree-climbing *mbala* civet cat to the burrowing rodent *nkumbi*, in whose skins *Tsasa-Lemba* and *Pfemba-Lemba* are kept. This metaphor is nearly identical to that of the eastern variant (Chapter 5) except that there the *nkumbi* skin contained the male "white" ingredients, and the *musimba*, another tree-climbing cat, contained the female element. However, eastern sources are not reliable enough to make anything of this symbolic inversion.

The third satchel in Babutidi's depiction of the *n'kobe* (figure 21) extends several domains of the above metaphor—social roles and small animals—to the patrifilial line of *Lemba*. Hair from the heads of the *Lemba* chief priest, from the presiding *Lemba* father, and the neophyte, along with leaves of *lemba-lemba* and *dingongo* beans, are placed in a container of the skins of *nsesi* and *kubu* antelopes and *nkaka*, the pangolin. The correlation of these skins to the three roles is not given; however, their stereotypes are suggestive. *Nsesi* is slight and clever, swift and evasive, and is depicted in fables as able to outwit larger animals. *Kubu* is a marsh antelope. Pangolin is recognized not only for its anomalous character, its scales and its mammalian features such as suckling its young, but also for its long tongue which can penetrate any cavity in a termite mound. Indications are that the metaphor linking *Tsasa* and *Pfemba* to *mbala* and *nkumbi* skins also relates the three figures of patrifilial continuity—from mystical purity to profanity—to the three animals whose characteristics extend from water to land, from inner to outer qualities. Combined, the three satchels in animal skin situate the key social roles of *Lemba* through marriage and patrifiliality in terms of natural attributes, animal and cosmological, as shown in figure 22. The cosmological "coordinates" appear to be plotted on two axes: one vertical, linking trees to underground burrows, the other linking the water, sign of mystical communion, with land and the outside with the inside of an anthill or termite mound.

The column of plants links the above-mentioned three satchels, known as the "domestic abode of *Lemba*," to the fourth satchel in the *n'kobe*, known as the "power of *Lemba*." Whereas "abode" is contained in wild animals' skins, "power" is contained in a domestic plant, raphia. Whereas "abode's" plants are semidomesticated, wild plants growing in the village, "power's" plants, many in number, grow wild. Subtle contrastive principles of inversion appear to be at work here. Whereas the cosmological spacing and character traits of the animals explained their use in defining social roles in *Lemba*, the use of raphia, and the contents of the satchel called "power," define another attribute in *Lemba*, its adherent's skill or ability in capturing the extensive, outside, wild, and public forces. The plants listed in Babutidi's "power" satchel are like those collected in Kwamba's northern variant during the priests' final trek onto the savanna and to the cemetery. In Fukiau's account raphia is included because it stands for the *Lemba* priest's ability to journey far without being interrupted. The cognate satchel in another Mayombe *n'kobe* (see figure 21, collected by Bittremieux) contains many trade goods, including iron slag,

Figure 22
Dominant metaphor of correspondences,
Western variant of *Lemba*

author's analytic category	name	sexual roles and social identities	substance and color	animal order	cosmologic space	plants
domestic abode	"Tsasa"	male	white "clear" *mpemba*	*mbala* cat	aboveground, tree-level	
	"Pfemba"	female	red *tukula*	*n'kumbi* rat	burrows underground	
		high priest		*kubu* antelope	water	lemba-lemba
		Lemba Father		*n'kaka* pangolin	termite mound	di-ngongo bean
		Lemba child		*nsesi* antelope	forest	
public power					savanna	raphia palm

a nail, a key, a ring, trade beads, and shells. Dapper's account of *Lemba* from seventeenth-century Loango has European goods (trade beads, a bottle, a bell) and shells bespeaking the coast laid upon a "mat," surely a raphia mat. Running throughout the contents of the *tukobe* is this theme, then, of the power that comes from knowing and controlling the outside, the realm beyond the domestic.

In most *tukobe* this concept "beyond the domestic" is linked to the ancestors, either in the form of a cultic hero's effigy in the *nkobe* in the form of a small "*nzita*" figure used on a dance rattle, or as an *mbinda* figure hung on the belt, or as a piece of *ntobe* tomb earth. The inclusion of savanna or forest plants in this concept's representation, as in the satchel "power of *Lemba*" above, would be consonant with a broader, cosmological statement linking ancestral and natural powers.

The Lemba drums, bracelets, rattles, and statues are the instruments with which this power is captured and used. Numerous texts speak of the ancestors or mythic heroes being "in" the drums, or of them "speaking" through the drums, or of *Lemba* being "drummed up" by the *Lemba* father or chief priest. The drum of *Lemba*—whether *nkonzi*, *nkonko*, or *ngoma*—was frequently copied in miniature, the cavity being filled with plant substance (the "powers" above) to retain or conjure a spell (*ndokolo*). Such a process of representing a representation, or metaphorizing a metaphor, may permissibly be termed fetishization. The miniature drums of *Lemba* were either hung on statues, or carried about on one's body as a charm (see plates 13–16). On Woyo pot-lids illustrating proverbs, *Lemba* was represented by the drum motif.[15]

Bracelets, like drums, contained the power of *Lemba*. The *Lemba* bracelets were sometimes wrapped in raphia fronds to capture the palm fiber's connotation of movement beyond the domestic realm.[16] Elsewhere the bracelets were regarded as substitutes for the drums, for, as Konda suggests (9.9–11), the wearer could spit palm wine on the bracelet, rub it, or simply wear it in public to demonstrate his real social status and power. Motifs appearing on *Lemba* bracelets indicate specific applications of power. In the western variant, male and female images representing the *Lemba* household are very common. The male figure, usually seated, is accompanied by one, two, or three female figures. The male figure is holding a staff, whereas the female figures occasionally have in their hands what appears to be a pestle or pipe. Between the figures, and on bracelets without human figures, other motifs make their appearance.

One of the most common of these decorative motifs on the bracelets is the cowrie shell. It may also appear atop the *n'kobe*, or atop one of the interior containers of the *n'kobe*, or within a satchel. Its general meaning is that of cherished continuity in the populace, that is the precious quality of children, and the importance of fertility. It thus defines, on the bracelets, the relationship of the male to female figures also represented there.

In a cognate position to the cowrie, many bracelets display a flower or "spider-web" motif, with four, six, eight, or ten "threads." The exact meaning of this motif remains unclear. It resembles Cameroon spider masks which have the same motif atop the human head. The spider occurs as mystical mediator in Kongo legends, including the trickster *Lemba* origin myth to be examined shortly. The motif may also represent the *diyowa* of *Lemba*, the place of purification and clarity in the face of the powers of the beyond. On one bracelet the motif is presented as a four-petaled flower or wheel and as a cross. Other bracelets juxtapose the flower/wheel "cosmogram" with a motif resembling a bow tie, but which is the rhetorician's charm *mbondo fula*, worn or held during intensive palaver sessions by the professional advocate (*nzonzi*) (plate 12). *Mbondo fula* appears on pot-lid proverbs along with the *Lemba* drum and other musical instruments, to acclaim the virtues of authority in the household and of persuasiveness in public life.[17] In light of the importance of rhe-

Plate 5. Lemba medicine chest lid from Mayombe, with evidence of pointed *zinga* shells, cowrie shell stand (center), and smith's bellow motif. Collected by L. Bittremieux prior to 1937. (MRAC 43040.) Contents depicted in Figure 21.

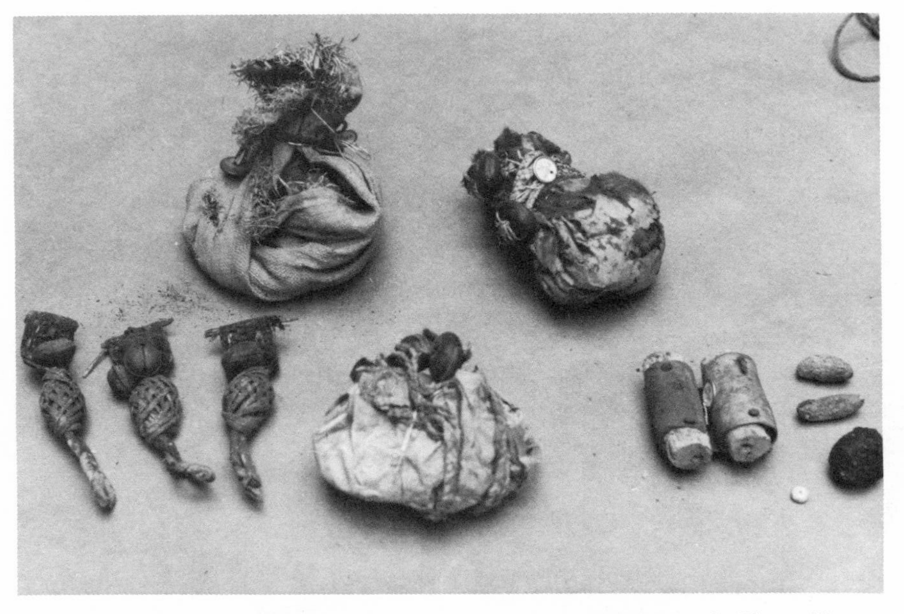

Plate 6. Contents of Lemba chest (in Plate 5), identified further in Figure 21.

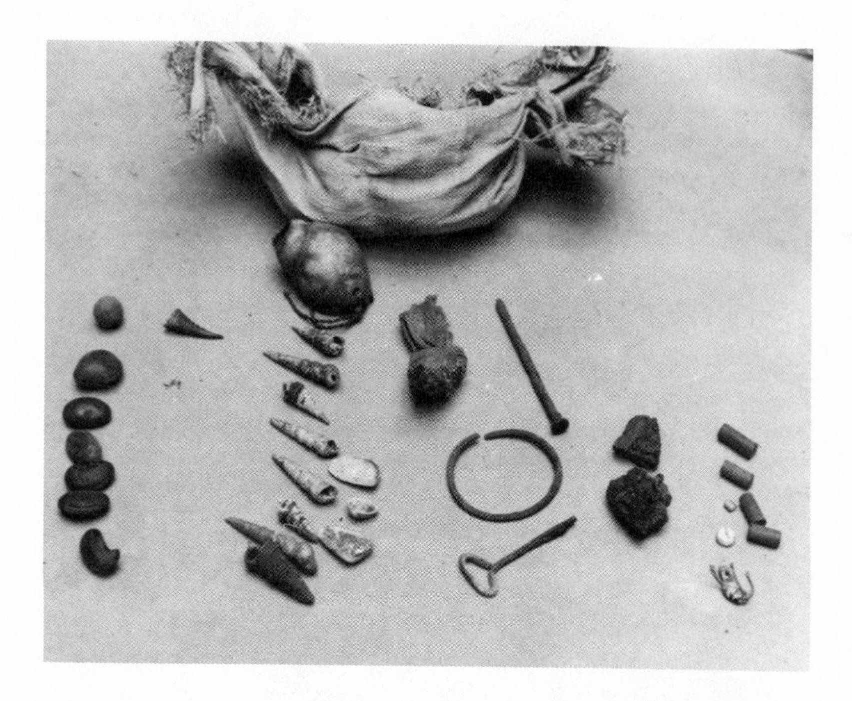

Plate 7. "Powers of Lemba" raphia bag contents from Lemba chest (Plates 5 and 6), including ironworking articles, locally manufactured and traded; trade beads, shells, horns, and seed pods. (MRAC 43040.) See Figure 21.

Plate 8. Detail of cast copper *Lemba* bracelet from Loango coast, collected by Adolph Bastian, ca. 1870. Museum für Völkerkunde, Berlin-Dahlem III C 347. Drawing of full bracelet with three figures and multi-petal motif from A. Bastian, *Deutsche Expedition an der Loango Küste*, Jena, 1874. Inside cover plate.

Plate 9. Brass bracelet with cowrie motif, often denoting fertility, possibly in this case in connection with *Lemba*, Kunya. (Museum für Völkerkunde, Berlin-Dahlem, III C 6524. Donated by Robert Visser, 1896.)

Plate 10. Wooden model for *Lemba* bracelet imprint in casting sand or clay, with multi-petal motif over human figure; Vili. (Museum für Völkerkunde, Berlin-Dahlem, III C 8136. Donated by Robert Visser, n.d. [1890's].)

Plate 11. Cowrie motif on opposite side of wooden bracelet model pictured in Plate 10. (Museum für Völkerkunde, Berlin-Dahlem, III C 8136. Donated by Robert Visser.)

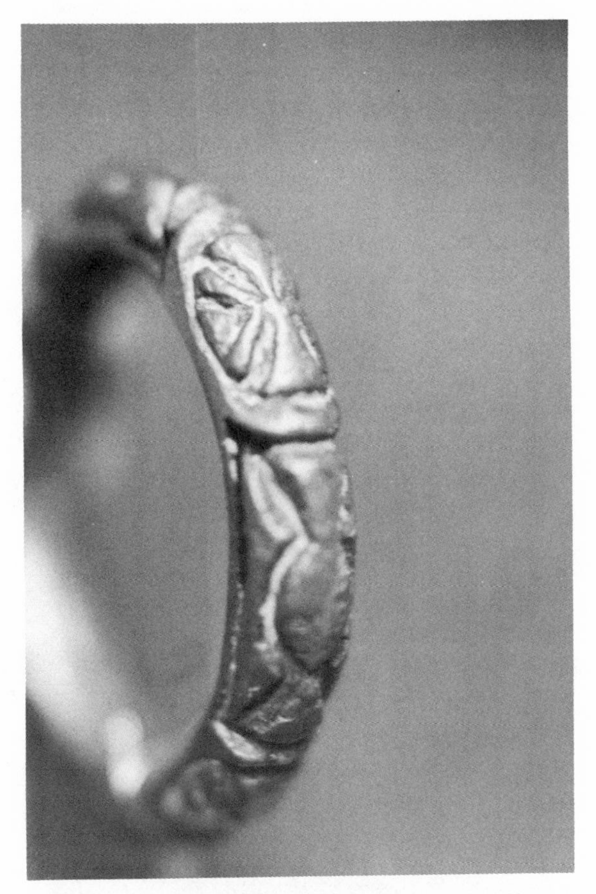

Plate 12. Copper Lemba bracelet with floral motif (top) and orator's charm *mbondo-fula* (bottom). (MRAC 24985, collected by J. Renkin, 1909.)

Plate 13. Brass Lemba bracelet with four human figures. (MRAC 54.60.2, collector unknown.)

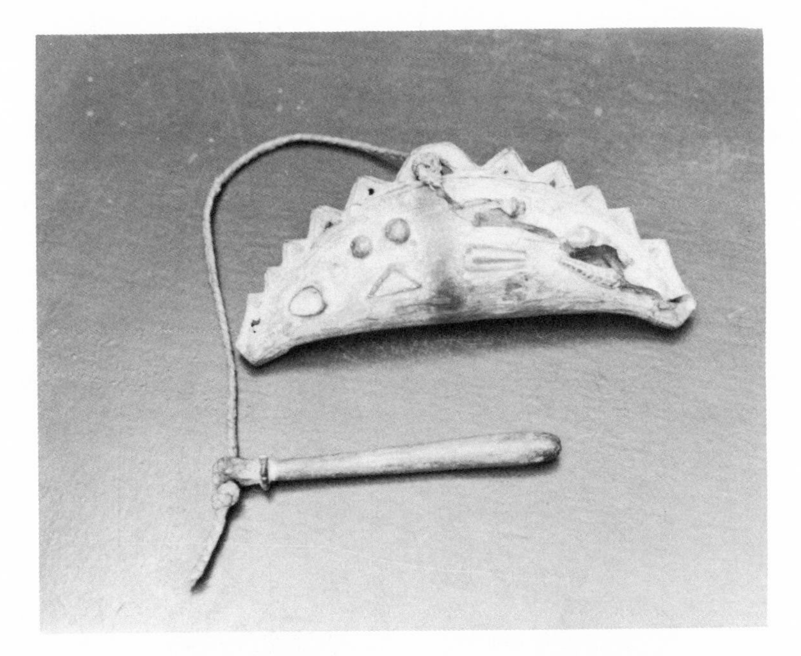

Plate 14. *Ngoma-Lemba* drum, Mayombe. (MRAC 34778, donated by L. Bittremieux, n.d.)

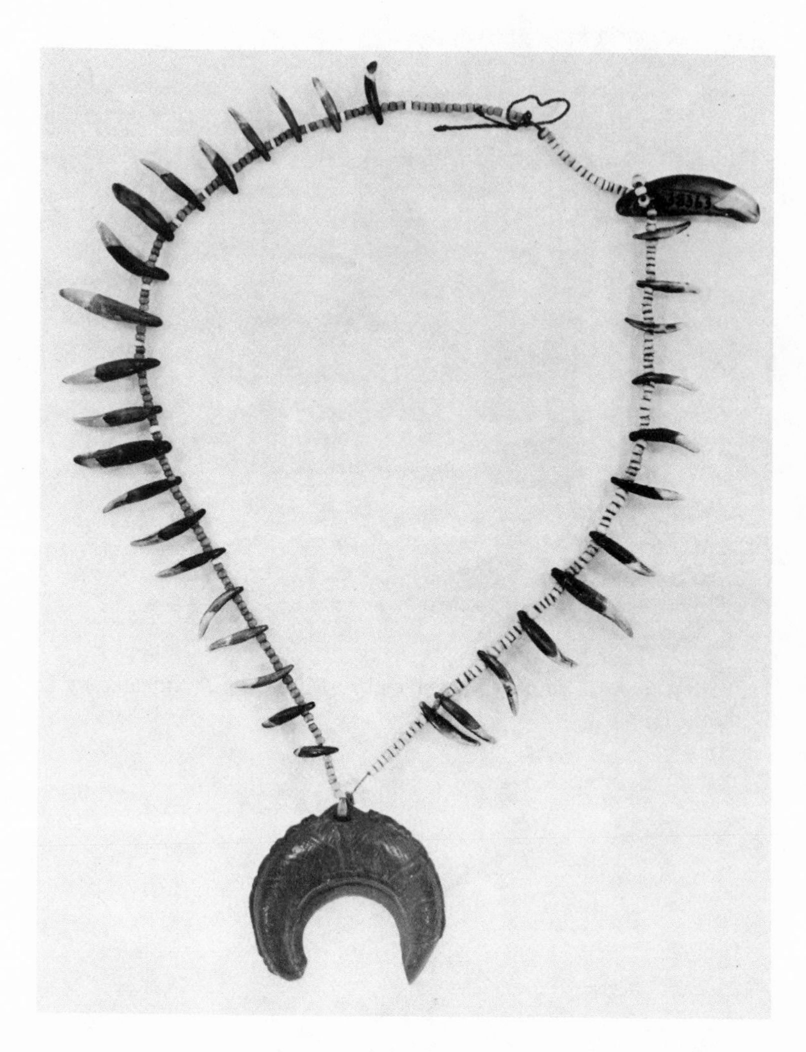

Plate 15. Miniature charm *Lemba* drum necklace, probably Loango coast. (Linden Museum, Stuttgart, 38363, donated by Robert Visser, 1905.)

Plate 16. Miniature Lemba drum charm pendants; left to right, in wood (MRAC 35342), bone (MRAC 43695), wood (MRAC 69, 59, 498 from Mayumba, collected by M.J. Seha), metal (MRAC 53.74.1323 from Kangu Lufu, Mayombe, collected 1953 by A. Maesen).

Plate 17. *Mukonzi a Lemba* drum, Mayombe. (Statens Etnografiska Museum, Stockholm, 1919.1.437, donated by Karl Laman.)

Plate 18. Couple seated on trunk (in wood, 14 cm.), Landana, Cabinda. (Afrika Museum Berg en Dal, 177, n.d.) That this is a depiction of a *Lemba* couple is suggested by the figures' matching bracelets, female figure's miniature drum necklace pendant, the posture of closeness, and the caps with characteristic "multi-petal" motif on male's cap (see Plate 19).

Plate 19. Couple seated on trunk, Landana, Cabinda (rear view). (Afrika Museum Berg en Dal, 177, n.d.) Multi-petal motif on top of cap of male figure contains spiral recalling similar motifs on bracelets—above heads—and on *Lemba* chest lids. Although obscure, this design is thought by some to denote idea of "navel of head," i.e., the fontanelle, or "fount of wisdom" from beyond. This would explain why many *Lemba* figures, like contemporary Kongo prophets, wear caps, or protect hair.

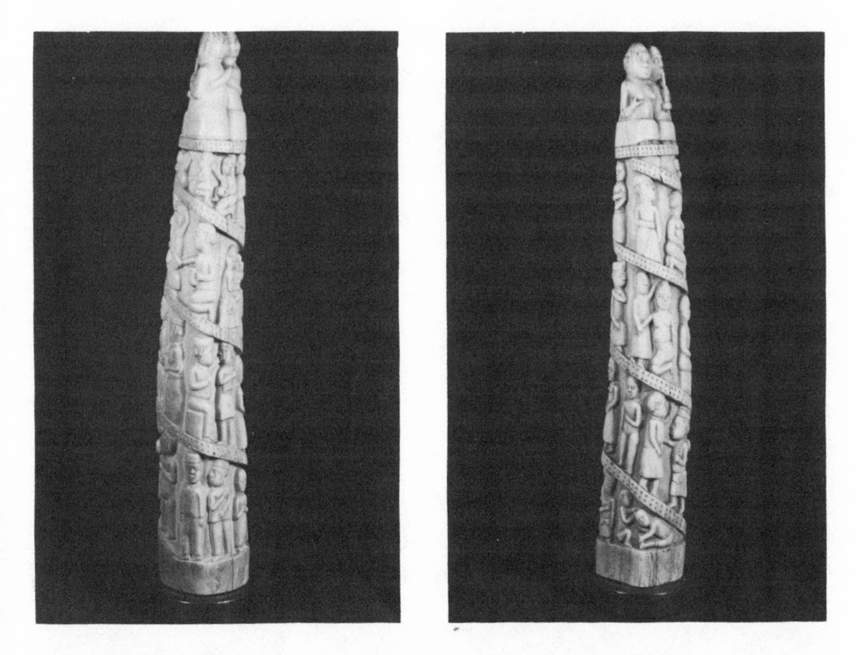

Plate 20. This undated (40 cm.) Loango ivory ((**A**) front view, (**B**) rear view) from the Julian and Grace Rymar collection depicts a series of couples and polygynous household groups in poses and costumes characteristic of a nineteenth-century Loango gathering, possibly including *Lemba* séances. As shown in the detailed view on the next 2 pages, the top couple, arms embracing, suggests the closeness of a *Lemba* couple. He is smoking a pipe, recalling references to *Lemba* pipes (B-D III C 13873 and B-D Katalog No. 372, Appendix) and to smoking in the *Lemba* ceremony (see Brazil *Lemba* song, Chapter 8, opening). She is holding her breast in a Kongo gesture of benediction. The tops of their caps bear spiral designs similar to those of the couple depicted in Plates 19 and 20. Other figures and scenes in the panels of the ivory are less clear, but depict possible ceremonial meaning as well. The top scene, which suggests defloration, childbirth, and an emphasis on fertility, stands in interesting inverse relationship to the bottom scene, in which the accent is the top of the head. Presumably the top figure is female, the bottom male. The two depictions match the iconic duality in *Lemba* symbolism on the integral complementarity of fertility, symbolized often by the cowrie shell on bracelets and the medicine chest, and on power or clairvoyance, symbolized by the multi-petal motif on bracelets, the medicine chest, and atop caps. However, a fuller interpretation of this rich piece awaits the systematic study of several centuries of Loango ivory carving and related art.

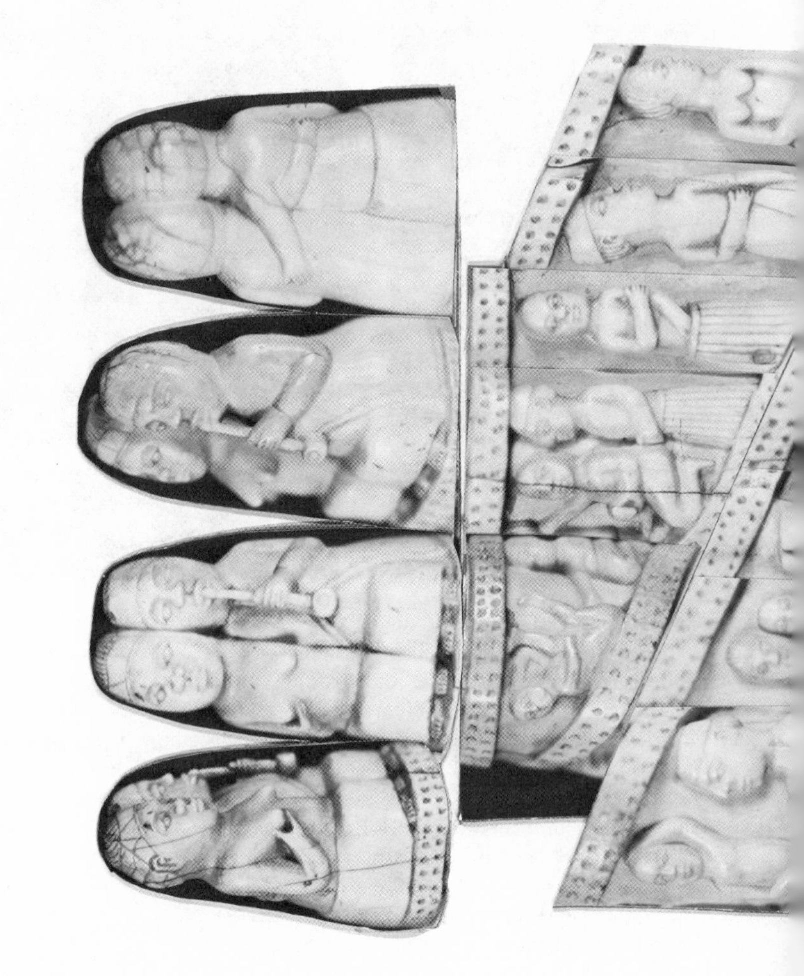

torical skill in public elsewhere in *Lemba*'s self-image and of the equal importance of a flourishing household represented in the cowrie, it is likely that the flower/spider/wheel motif, which in one or two cases is a "cross" of four spokes, is a unique *Lemba* cosmogram embodying the complex values of *Lemba* at a more abstract level than is given in any of the texts at my disposal. In the Ngoyo region it appears in red on the lid of the *n'kobe* (see plate 4). Another *Lemba n'kobe* lid (figure 21, plate 5) restates comparable values with the arrangement of four-pointed, long *zinga* shells surrounded a center, interspersed with blacksmith's bellows and some other round object. Again, these are the objects of the "powers of *Lemba*" in Babutidi's account, which link the *Lemba* adherent with the forces of nature, the beyond, trade, and public politics.

THE LYRICAL: MONI-MAMBU TRICKSTER AND THE ORIGINS OF *LEMBA*

Trickster, represented across Kongo society, is variously called "Seer of troubles" (Moni-Mambu, Tsimona-Mambu), "Troublemaker" (Mumboni-a-Mpasi), quarreller, or some other term describing his problem-making nature in most secular tales. He is also called visionary and healer where legends of him are related to a cultic context, as in the *Lemba* etiology myth to follow, where he is cast as the culture hero who goes to God the father to seek a solution to his wives' troubles, encounters many difficulties and trials, but eventually receives his father's recognition, and brings back *Lemba*.

If Mahungu's principal characteristic was the inherent dualistic nature of a social role, Moni-Mambu's is the lack of a sense of what is right at the right time in social discourse. In most legendary settings, his character is in the process of developing. Usually his civil, moral, and even physical sensibilities are incomplete. In episode after episode he is caught up in social intricacies and ambiguities he does not understand, confused by semantic nuances too subtle for his experience. It is as if he has learned the phonemes of human interaction but has not heard of syntax. He is like Mahungu in one sense. In some narratives Moni-Mambu develops into a figure of mediation and wisdom, yet in other narratives he is parodied as unsuccessful mediator, indeed, as a tragic figure who gets caught on the dilemmas of his own tricks. Whereas both tendencies are developed in a single Mahungu narrative, they are separate in the trickster narratives. In the first of the following texts, trickster brings *Lemba*.

Text 11

(1) There once was a man with two wives, each with a food prohibition: one could eat no lizard, the other no partridge. Their husband brought home the prohibited meat and, after discussing whether they should eat it, they gave in to temptation and prepared the food, not knowing what would be their due. They ate and suffered swollen stomachs and cramps.

(2) To find a cure for his wives the man went to Fly. He told Fly of his wives' food prohibitions, and asked him to "smell out" the cause of the swelling. Fly "smelled" and danced about, but could not divine the cause. The man, dissatisfied, got his money back. Then he went to another *nganga* diviner, Night-Swallow, who researched the cause and told him he would need to go see God the Father with his problem.

THE JOURNEY

(3) Taking his *nkutu* travel sack, the man set out to see God the Father. Just outside his village he stubbed his toe on a small stump which spoke out at him, "Go on, Tsimona-Mambu, pay attention, this is a mysterious *n'kisi* affair."

(4) Tsimona-Mambu walked on until he came to an abandoned village with only one house left in it. As he approached, the keyhole in the door spoke out at him, "Go on but pay attention, for this is a mysterious *n'kisi* affair."

(5) He met a woman working her groundnut patch. She inquired where he was going, and he replied, "To God the Father, with the blessing of the *nganga*." She invited him to eat a snack, offering him potatoes with her child, who was resting under a shelter. Meanwhile she returned to her work. After a time she called to ask how he liked the potatoes—and where was her child? He had eaten it, he retorted, as she had told him to do. "Tsimona-Mambu has eaten my child! The murderer! Come and seize and bind him," she called out to the menfolk. Tsimona-Mambu was taken before the judge, but because he had not been aware of what he was doing, he was freed.

(6) Again free, Tsimona-Mambu walked on until he came to a stream, surprised to see the water flowing upstream. Disbelieving, he exclaimed, "That can't be! You will run dry!" The

stream answered, "Don't worry, and go on. This is a mysterious *n'kisi* affair."

(7) Tsimona-Mambu next saw a young man tapping palm. To his amazement, the man had left his bones on the ground and was climbing the tree flesh only. When Tsimona-Mambu asked him the meaning of all this, he retorted, "Go on, it's a mysterious *n'kisi* affair."

(8) He walked on again and encountered a man with a gun across his shoulder. "Where are you going?" the man greeted him. Tsimona-Mambu explained about his wives and the doctor's blessing. The man interrupted him, "Can you shoot?" Tsimona-Mambu replied that he could. "Take my gun then and go hunt monkeys." Tsimona-Mambu returned to the palm, where the youth told him to "stay hidden, for the monkeys will soon come for nuts." As soon as there was a rustle Tsimona-Mambu shot out, dropping the game to the ground. He made a net of palm fronds, and dragged his catch to the nearest village. Curious people gathered. Alas, it was their headman. In anger the people seized Tsimona-Mambu and brought him to the judge. But because he had not known better, and because he had used the hunter's gun, Tsimona-Mambu was freed.

ASSEMBLING THE SATCHEL CONTENTS

(9) Tsimona-Mambu encountered a wood-borer working on a log. He called out, "Tsimona-Mambu, where are you going?" He told him "To see God the Father." The beetle requested to be taken along, so Tsimona-Mambu put him in his *nkutu* bag.

(10) They came to another village with only an old cripple at home. "Where are you going?" this latter asked. "To God the Father" was the reply. The cripple asked to be taken along, but Tsimona-Mambu refused because of his many sores, and left. Before long the path thinned and became a wild animal track. Returning, he asked the cripple where the road could be found. The old man ribbed him, saying "Aren't you sorry you didn't take me along?" So Tsimona-Mambu packed him into his bag, and was off, the cripple directing.

(11) They walked a while until they came to a giant spider spinning her house. "Good-day, Tsimona-Mambu" she spoke out. "Where are you going?" He told of his two wives and how he was going to see God the Father. "Can I come along?" the

spider requested. Reluctantly, because of her big crooked legs, he put her in his bag and continued.

(12) A big wasp flew down to meet them. "Where are you going?" it inquired. "Can I come along?" He told her where he was going, but refused at first to let her come along because he felt she would make an angry nuisance of herself. But she insisted, so he put her in his bag and moved on.

(13) Shortly they came upon the summer wind, which blows in the hottest month of the year. "Yeka, yeka, yeka" it was singing. "Tsimona-Mambu, where are you going? I can reward you for letting me come along by drying up everything." Tsimona-Mambu replied, "You who scorches the whole earth, how can I take you?" "In your bag, of course." So he packed up the hot wind and moved on.

(14) As soon as he had gone from there he was met by another gust of wind. "Brrrrr, Tsimona-Mambu," it blustered, "where are you going?" "The wives are sick and I am going to God the Father," answered Tsimona-Mambu. The wind wanted along. "What? A storm in a satchel?" But in the end Tsimona-Mambu packed it too in his bag and went on.

(15) Soon he came across a big *kumbi* bush rat who greeted him with "Where to Tsimona-Mambu?" "Why to God the Father." "Can I come along?" Tsimona-Mambu agreed, put the *kumbi* rat in his satchel, and walked on.

(16) Eventually he came to a village and encountered the headman in the square. "Ho, Tsimona-Mambu, what's new?" And Tsimona-Mambu again told his story about the two wives, how they were sick, and that he was going to God the Father. "Can you shoot well?" interrupted the headman. "Of course," said Tsimona-Mambu. So the headman gave Tsimona-Mambu his gun and told him to go stand guard at the banana grove overnight and shoot the first creature which would come along to steal bananas. Early the next day along came the headman's wife to get her supply of bananas. Tsimona-Mambu, believing her to be a beast out to steal bananas, shot her. Making a quick holder of banana leaves, he laid his prey in it and came to the headman proudly showing it off. People gathered. Shocked, the headman exclaimed, "Why, you've killed my first wife, my beloved MaMbanda!" He called the young men to bind Tsimona-Mambu hand and foot, but to leave his mouth free.

Then he took him to the judge. When he had told his story, how the headman had given him the gun, he was declared innocent and released.

(17) Then Tsimona-Mambu came to the edge of the Loango River, and hesitated. How would he get from the river bank to God? An idea came to him. *Tsik'utuk'utu*, he said to his satchel, "Are you still there?" "Yes," it answered. "Say, is the spider still along?" "Certainly." "Well then, bring her out." And in one-two-three she had spun a thread across the river, a bridge from earth to heaven.

(18) Tsimona-Mambu mounted the bridge, higher and ever higher, until he walked right into heaven. As soon as they had arrived there, the small cripple gave him these instructions. "When we come to the middle of a village, you will see a big man sitting on a stool. Don't greet him. But you'll see another, sitting on a mat on the ground. That is God the Father, whom you will greet." Tsimona-Mambu did just as told, and passed the big man and came before God the Father. With three hand-claps—*mue-mue-mue*—he greeted God and began to tell Him his problems.

THE TRIALS OF FATHER'S RECOGNITION

(19) "O Father God! I have two wives. One is not supposed to eat lizard, the other no partridge. Both have eaten what is forbidden, and have swollen stomachs. I went to the doctors for advice, and was told to come to You. That's why I've come."

(20) God spoke no word. Tsimona-Mambu implored him, "O God Father, hear my problem, for I am your son." But God denied this, saying "I shall believe that you are my son if green banana stems carry ripe bananas, and if black palm nuts turn red. Only then shall I know that I bore you."

(21) Fortunately Tsimona-Mambu's bag knew what to do, and suggested in a whisper to him that everyone should first sleep. The bananas and palm nuts would be ripe by morning. God agreed. During the night Wasp went out to sting up the banana stems so that the bananas ripened hurriedly, and the palm nuts similarly so they would color.

(22) Then next morning Tsimona-Mambu told God's overseer to go and inspect the bananas and palms. To his amazement they

were ripe. He notified God and asked, "Do you believe now that Tsimona-Mambu is your son?" God did not yet believe it, demanding that before he would recognize him, Tsimona-Mambu would need to gather a large package of the strongest forest vines in one night. Again Tsimona-Mambu consulted his bag, and through it, advised all to first sleep. When morning came the bag called the gust of wind which blew the vines together. The overseer saw this and implored God to recognize his son, but God refused to recognize Tsimona-Mambu.

(23) To recognize him as His son, Tsimona-Mambu would have to burn down the moist wood in the just-cleared field. Only then would God acknowledge that he had engendered him. Once again the satchel advised that all should sleep before the test. In the morning God's overseer took Tsimona-Mambu out to the field and invited him to prove himself by setting fire to and burning the decaying vegetation. Tsimona-Mambu called into his satchel for the hot summer wind; it came, blasted and withered the clearing—*yaya, yaya, yeka, yeka, yeka*—and all dried up so Tsimona-Mambu could easily burn it down to the ground.

(24) The overseer implored God to consider TsimonaMambu's problem so that he might return home, but the great Lord insisted, "I engendered him not!" Tsimona-Mambu must first drink a calabash of palm wine while hanging from the palm tree on the back slope. So with God's overseer Tsimona-Mambu found the tree. He climbed it, found the calabash, and began to drink. As he drank the wine—*na kiu, klukkluk*—the overseer addressed the tree, "fly up—*kuna tsala kayeka*—into the highest heights so that Tsimona-Mambu dies from it." And the palm tree jerked itself loose and sprouted higher and higher into the sky with Tsimona-Mambu hanging on his life belt from the tree's crown. High up in the air Tsimona-Mambu asked his bag what he should do, certain he would die. The bag said, "pronounce the spell that the overseer sinks into the ground so far that he too dies." So as Tsimona-Mambu spoke the overseer began to sink into the ground, deeper and deeper to his neck. "Help, Father God!" he cried. And to Tsimona-Mambu he said, "Surely you are God's son." As he spoke the palm tree settled down to where it had been before. And Tsimona-Mambu permitted the overseer to crawl up out of the ground,

saying to him, "Let's go together because we are equal in supernatural strength."

(25) Again they were before God the Father. Again the overseer implored God to consider Tsimona-Mambu's affair and acknowledge him as His son. But still God refused, stating he would only recognize Tsimona-Mambu if he would first show himself capable of felling the *mfuma* cottonwood tree growing on the back slope with one blow of the axe. Only then would he recognize Tsimona-Mambu as his son.

(26) Tsimona-Mambu asked the bag what to do now, and received the word that everyone must first sleep. This they did, including God. Then Tsimona-Mambu called the wood-borer out of the bag and told him to go to the mfuma tree and hollow out the inside so that only a thin ring remained. When morning dawned Tsimona-Mambu asked the overseer to show him the tree. The wood-borer had left a mark on the tree to show him where to let the axe fall. Tsimona-Mambu took the axe and with one blow brought the tree crashing down.

(27) The overseer once more implored God to "Take up the affair of Tsimona-Mambu so he can return home. Admit that you are his Father." And God finally showed his pity, saying "Go set him something to eat in the house; he has worked hard." Tsimona-Mambu entered, sat down on the bed, and ate what had been put before him. But after he was in the house God told his overseer to lock the door so that Tsimona-Mambu could not leave, and would surely die inside.

(28) When Tsimona-Mambu realized that the door had been locked, he consulted his bag. He was told to have the *kumbi* rat dig a tunnel under the wall of the house. Several days passed and Tsimona-Mambu became hungry. He instructed the rat to bring him food by dragging it under the wall through the tunnel. In this way he got a fat she-goat, a wild beast, and another goat.

(29) After a long time God ordered the overseer to open the house and remove Tsimona-Mambu's body. When the overseer opened the door, and Tsimona-Mambu jumped out alive, the overseer ran back to God saying that Tsimona-Mambu was alive. He implored God, "Can't you see that he's your son? Take up his affair now." And thus Tsimona-Mambu at last won his audience before God the Father.

THE *LEMBA* MEDICINE REVEALED AND TAKEN HOME

(30) God spoke to Tsimona-Mambu: "Bring me a small pot covered with a palm *kete-kete* leaf. Also bring the two copper rings that are in the house. The one ring you are to put on your wife's arm, the other on your own. These are the arm-rings of *DiLemba*.

(31) Tsimona-Mambu brought all the things God had instructed and then God questioned him: "Do you have the fruit of the eggplant and the *dilemba-lemba* plant in the region where you live?" Tsimona-Mambu said he did. "Then," said God, "take all these things and use them to heal your wives. At the outskirts of the village, pick some egg-plant fruit and *dilemba-lemba*. Crush them in your hand into a pulp. Take the leaves from the pot, and squeeze the juice of the two plants into it and give the juice to both wives to drink. Their bellies will surely go down and they will be cured and will be able to recount what they have seen with their own eyes. With the two bracelets, you shall do as I said: Put one on the arm of your wife, and the other on your own arm. Go in Peace, and do as I have told you."

(32) As soon as Tsimona-Mambu came to the edge of God's village he instructed the giant spider to crawl out of the satchel and spin a web down to earth. On his way back he set off all the creatures he had brought along. When all had been let off, he came near to his village and went immediately to see his wives. Their stomachs were still swollen—*dio yukuku! dio yila yila!*—up to their necks. He went to the village outskirts and picked the *lemba-lemba* leaves and the egg-plant fruit, and prepared the medicine in the small pot as God had instructed. When the wives had drunk it, both stood up and were healed.

(33) To one of his wives he gave the copper bracelet and placed it on her arm, calling her his *Nankazi Lemba*. The other ring he put on his own arm. Then he told his wives everything he had heard from God the Father. They were amazed, saying that this is indeed an important enough cure that people the whole world over ought to be inaugurated to it, for it came directly from God the Father.

(34) Since then, people in this land are initiated to *Lemba*.[18]

The manner in which an array of objects, personalities, and situations confronts the hero on his journey suggests that if he is careful order will emerge from the confusion of mundane life, as the divination suggested. He encounters warnings, traps, and offers of assistance. The dichotomy of fly, the unsuccessful daytime seer, and night-swallow, the successful nighttime seer, indicates the type of cosmological order that will emerge if he follows the right path. This initial divination scene (11.2) picks up the same imagery as songs elsewhere in *Lemba*'s initiation of the "sight" of the night-jar and the bat (1.76–7).

The warnings about dabbling with mystical powers come from auspicious objects and characters. Keyholes are passages, and abandoned villages are cemeteries inhabited by transitory ancestor-type figures. Streams, especially those that run the wrong way, are mystical paths, and palm wine is the embodiment of communion with invisible agents, and palmwine tappers their mediators. These warnings are a prelude to the true mediation that will follow; they, therefore, suggest the first "true speech" the hero can trust.

The traps come in the form of encounters with conventional human beings making perfectly reasonable requests of the hero. However, in each case the hero takes the instruction wrongly—in fact, literally—thereby ignoring the more important moral order. So, Moni-Mambu, asked to "eat groundnuts with the child," eats groundnuts and the child (11.5). Asked to shoot the monkey robbing palmnuts, he shoots the headman instead (11.8). Asked to guard the banana tree in the village, he shoots the chief's favorite wife (11.16). In each case he has heard only the shallow meaning of the instruction, and in carrying out the instruction literally he has violated basic moral precepts which also happen to be *Lemba*-related precepts: the respect for offspring, strong moral authority that controls collection of palm tree products (recall the palm symbolism in the powers of the outside), and order within the village under the tutelage of a first (*Lemba*) wife.

The offers of assistance increase as he moves along, and in due course he has assembled in his satchel a host of helpers, the *bilongo* ingredients, for his *n'kisi* bag. These helpers are, of course, those symbols of mediation that assist him in gaining recognition of God the father. The woodborer, the first to be placed in the satchel and next to the last to be used, relates the vertical, untouched tree to the fallen, horizontal tree, used in domestic arts and crafts. The cripple, found in an abandoned village, shows Moni-Mambu the "path" to God his father, just as later, when he is drawn from the satchel, he shows the hero his true father. The spider's web from "this shore to that," from earth to heaven, links the visible and invisible worlds. A common symbol of mediation, the spider or the spider's web may be represented in the "flower/wheel" motif discussed above (see figure 20; plates 4, 8, 10, 12). Wasp's sting mediates raw (black) palmnuts and ripe (red) palmnuts. Hot wind of the dry season allows the fields and savannas to be burned, preparing the way for the fertile growth of crops to follow. The whirlwind brings a bundle of forest vines out and makes them accessible for human cultural order. Finally, *kumbi* rat, predictably, opens up the closed and choked, permitting the flow of food, patrifilial recognition, and life itself.

The ingredients of the satchel thus mediate a series of oppositions or rhythms ranging from the seasons, to the processes of human culture, to the intricacies of human interaction, especially patrifiliality and husband/wife alliance. It is also apparent that the processes of differentiation and mediation are being worked out. In society one must learn to differentiate between people and animals, between major and secondary wives, and so on. As well, there must be effective mediation of differences, as the satchel's contents point out. In the case of Moni-Mambu the ambiguity of social life—its traps—is overcome by learning to differentiate and then to mediate. In the next text, failure to learn life's underlying true categories is illustrated by the same trickster. Although Moni-Mambu discovers the rules of life and interaction, he uses them to destroy instead of to construct.

Text 12

(1) Eleven women went fishing and paired off two by two, leaving one out. She was joined by a stranger (a *ntebo* spirit), with whom she fished ten pools. When they had finished, they began dividing the fish under a palm tree, atop of which was a man. Every time the fish were counted, they had a different number. The stranger called fellow spirits to witness the count, and eventually many spirits had congregated. These spirits became very hostile to the woman, and would have killed her, but the palmwine tapper atop the tree dropped his calabash on the chief spirit's head and frightened them away. He descended, married the woman, and one of their many children was Moni-Mambu.

(2) On his way home from market one day Moni-Mambu came through a village of two brothers, sons of the same mother, who had never quarrelled. Moni-Mambu bathed in the river nearby and saw the nets of younger brother, a fisherman. At night he

exchanged the nets with the calabashes of the older brother on a palm tree. In the morning each blamed the other, cursing, "your mother!" Moni-Mambu mocked them and left.

(3) Moni-Mambu was offered "some peanuts with the children" by a woman harvesting a field. He made a fire, and roasted her children until their heads burst. Accused before the court, he was vindicated because the woman had told him to "eat peanuts with the children."

(4) Moni-Mambu arrived in a new village, saw no one, but heard pestles pounding mortars. The women at the outskirts of the village called him over to "pound them their mortars." He accepted, went and struck two dead with the pestle. A third escaped, seeking help. Moni-Mambu, bound and brought before the court, was accused but vindicated because he obeyed the women's instructions.

(5) A chief decided to hunt a savanna using fire. After clearing the air of witchcraft and activating his medicines, the men slept. Next morning arms and powder were distributed. Moni-Mambu was given a gun and told to shoot "anything that moves." When the hunt began he followed his instructions, killing snakes, lizards, one small girl, four hunting dogs, fifteen hunters, and the chief's wife. The chief threatened to kill him on the spot, but Moni-Mambu begged to be drowned in a river, not killed in a village. On route to the river he escaped.

(6) During a rainstorm Moni-Mambu found shelter in a cavity of a large tree, and discovered it was a leopard's den. The leopard arrived with a goat for her young to eat, whereupon Moni-Mambu attached a wooden hunting bell to the animal's tail. Believing herself hunted, the leopard fled and died of fright. Moni-Mambu killed her cub and took the goat for himself.

(7) The chief arranged for Moni-Mambu, who had little motivation, to be married. After having been married a while, his wife complained that she needed more than just manioc to feed him and sent him hunting. He shot an antelope which, as he grabbed it, fled leaving its skin in his hands. He pursued it to a river, but it escaped upstream while he went downstream. After a time he reached the village of his parents-in-law, who gave him to eat. His nose was dripping into the food, so he took it off and laid it down on a leaf, assuring it that he would pick it up later. A dog came along and stole it. He threw a firebrand at the dog, which

hit his in-laws' house, burning it to the ground. Going to the riverside to cut logs with which to build a new house, Moni-Mambu lost the axe in the water on the second tree. Diving into the water to fetch the axe, he was seized by a crocodile. Hawk (Na Yimbi), curious as to the identity of Crocodile's victim, asked to see it. Thrice Crocodile opened its mouth so the bird could see Moni-Mambu's face, and the third time the bird seized Moni-Mambu thus rescuing him.

(8) After Moni-Mambu left the village of his parents-in-law, he met a young girl bathing in a side channel of a river, repeatedly dipping her head into the water. She told Moni-Mambu that bathing like this caused her no shame, even if he were her father-in-law. Hearing this, he cut off her head and put it in his bag. Presently he encountered a second girl eating some viands with pepper. He asked her to share them, but she retorted that she had none left. So he asked her to go fetch more. While she was away he ate the meat in the bowl and put in its stead the head of the first girl. When the second girl returned and saw the head in her bowl, she screamed in horror. Men came running with their weapons, Moni-Mambu told them how the ancients had eaten human heads. They believed him, and killed the girl.

(9) Moni-Mambu, walking through an abandoned village, saw a human head drying on a pole and asked it how it had died. Its reply: "sickness and what not all else." When he came home and related the men in the men's hut this, they called him a liar. He challenged them to examine the head for themselves. If his story were false, they could kill him. They went, but when they asked the head the cause of its death, it remained silent. Returning, they threatened to kill Moni-Mambu immediately. The chief calmed them and convened a court. Moni-Mambu was charged as guilty and condemned to death. When he asked for water "to calm his heart" the chief refused, saying he had no heart; he was ordered speared to death. The dogs licked his blood and his corpse was thrown out on the savanna where witches are thrown. The people rejoiced the death of Moni-Mambu.[19]

The present text differs quite remarkably from the foregoing one in the character of the mediations enacted. Tsimona-Mambu bringer of *Lemba* medicine initially committed a number of errors, but then went on to become an effective mediator in not only cosmological but also human oppositions such as his relation to his father, his relation to his wives, and theirs to each other. In the present text, Moni-Mambu, the cynical farceur, commits errors, is initially forgiven, but ultimately judged guilty of having willfully designed situations of misunderstanding, conflict, and violence, and he is condemned to the death of a witch.

In both texts generous use is made of the incongruous, the ambiguous, and the outright contradictory to stage episodes in which the hero may be cast as either an effective or ineffective mediator. In both texts episodes are related of the trickster's misunderstanding of an instruction: he understands a phrase literally without understanding its underlying intention. He is invited to "eat groundnuts [alternately potatoes, 11.5] with the children" (12.3), and he eats the children too. He is invited to join women working with mortars and pestles, to "strike them their mortars" (12.4), and he kills two women. He is invited to watch for a monkey in a palm tree, and he shoots the chief (11.8). He is invited to stand guard of a banana tree, and he shoots the chief's wife (11.16). He is invited to join a hunt and to "shoot everything that moves" (12.5), whereupon he shoots dogs, hunters, children, and so on. These passages of "rhetorical ambiguity" obviously make for excellent and anticipated storytelling devices to bring an audience into a responsive mood. They belong to the genre of the African dilemma tale represented across the entire continent.[20] Their incorporation in the trickster tale has the effect, however, of probing under the fabric of harmonious daily life to the difficulties of social discourse.

At the level of actions, as differentiated from words, the trickster figure commits deeds that are in sharp violation of the moral code of the society. He kills esteemed figures such as chiefs, first wives, headmen. But he also hunts the hunters, kills innocent children, confuses species when it comes to eating meats, approaches girls and women while they are bathing, and so on. Moni-Mambu thus not only ignores the moral codes of society, he exposes their vulnerable points. Every imaginable kind of scandal erupts in connection with the trickster of Text 12: brothers who had never quarreled are led to curse each other; his parents-in-law's house is burned down; he falsely induces a charge of cannibalism upon a poor girl, causing her death; in another episode not related in Text 12 (but see note 19), he causes an intervillage feud, in which an entire village is burned to the ground.

Resolution of rhetorical and structural ambiguity in these texts may follow one of several paths. The dilemma may be left to follow its own course, with wildly unpredictable consequences—for example, the hunter being hunted, seized by an animal (12.7). This is good for laughs, and a talented storyteller can go on and on with this type of narrative. At a more serious level, ambiguity and contradiction may be resolved in a number of ways. Structural interpretations may be offered of solutions to the difficulty. Thus, the ambiguity of status-equal brothers or wives will be resolved by establishing a priority of one over the other; failure to meet one's father will be resolved by reconciliation with the father; and, as in some Mahungu texts, "endogenous" social structures that are conducive to incest, matrilineage isolation, and warfare are transformed into "exogenous" structures through appropriate alliances, emphases on trade, and brotherhoods such as *Lemba*. As is clear, these conjunctive myths are favorites for use in cult-related circumstances. Disjunctive or "tragic" myths such as Mavungu with python-woman-in-tree (Text 8) and Moni-Mambu trickster-turned-witch (Text 12) suggest a third type of resolution, already mentioned in the conclusion of the previous chapter.

Such disjunctive myths hinge on the hero's conscious decision, at some point midway through the narrative, to embark on a particular course of action regardless of the consequences. In Mavungu and the python-woman-in-tree the hero follows the woman and riches knowing that this will negatively condition his future relations with his father. In Moni-Mambu trickster-turned-witch the hero is held responsible for having consciously plotted to kill, deceive, and destroy. In other words, these narratives are studies of the implications and consequences of consciously-made decisions in the context of alternative choices. They focus on those decisions which lead to the hero's tragic death, and by implication the alternative choices which might lead to life.

Studies of trickster cycles have depicted their heroes as moving in the development of the cycle from a primordial or aboriginal phase, lacking conscience, morality, and intelligence, to a stage of full conscience, morality, intelligence, and civility. Radin's Winnebago trickster very clearly portrays these developmental features, and much of the hero's activity is cast midway between these poles. He can assemble or disassemble culture, integrate and disintegrate, transcend or particularize, depending on the intent of the narrator.[21] Makarius' writing on the relationship of mythological trickster figures to clowns emphasizes the characteristic of "inverseness" as especially germane to tricksters. Even more evident than their representation of nonconscious, primordial, puppet-like movement in society's conventions is their contrariness, their violation of rules and prohibitions. The purpose of this, she argues, is to call attention to the importance of the very rules being violated. The trickster is usually alone in his behavior, he is an outcast. By committing the forbidden—incest, cannibalism, wrong speech—he is taking on an expiatory role. "It is necessary that he should be conceived as 'the other,' in opposition to the group, even though he acts on their behalf."[22]

Certainly Kongo mythic heroes accessible to *Lemba* practitioners utilized both traits of the trickster Moni-Mambu: his development toward consciousness and effective mediation with which they identified themselves, and the negativeness of wrong choices in the anti-trickster who meets death. Other characteristics that have elsewhere been given the trickster, such as the embodiment of opposites (male-female, elder-junior, father-son) are in north-Kongo myths given to Mahungu, who, like the trickster, expresses both conjunctive as well as disjunctive narrative possibilities. The implications of these two modes of resolution will be explored in Part III of the book after examining *Lemba* in the New World.

Chapter 8

Lemba in the New World

"It is undeniable that the survivals outnumber the variations." —R. Bastide, *African Religions of Brazil* (1978)

"The term *petro* is not used in the north and northwest of Haiti where these spirits go under the name *Lemba*."—A. Métraux, *Voodoo in Haiti* (1959)

Introduction

It has been abundantly established that the massive Atlantic slave trade over several centuries transplanted many features of north-bank Kongo society into Brazil, Haiti, Jamaica, Cuba, the United States, and elsewhere in the New World. Priorities given to the study of *Lemba* in its African setting permit only a cursory review of the general historical and cultural framework of this cultural migration. This chapter's chief aim is to present and evaluate evidence at hand on *Lemba* and related ritual features in the New World.

Scholarly awareness of *Lemba*'s presence in the New World has been scanty. A few examples suffice to show the sketchy or marginal status attributed to it and to related Kongo or Bantu elements. Brazilian historian Arthur Ramos published in 1934[1] a number of songs to Bantu deities, including this:

Lemba, O Lemba.
Lembá de canaburà
Zambiapongo no coporolá
Lembá Lembá de lei ô salei
Sinhô Lembá enganga
Já furamo sé sé
Lembá enganga já fumo
Carolé.

Lemba of the law, law
Senõr *Lemba* priest
Already we have dug the hole
Lemba's priest has already smoked.

The song's meaning is enigmatic without any contextual explanation. In any event, Ramos used it to illustrate the presence of Zambi-a-Pongo, the Bantu high God, rather than *Lemba*. Drawn from a Candomblé in Bahia, Brazil, this song and others including those to Zambi, Kalunga, Kalundu, and other Bantu cult or deity names illustrated the persistence of elements, however poorly understood, of Bantu religion.[2]

Herskovits, who worked in West Africa and in the New World, spoke of the dearth of understanding of Congo, or Bantu, influence in the New World.

> Despite the multitude of designations for the great numbers of gods that must have been worshiped by the various tribes from which came the slave population, few deities except those from the central region have present-day devotees on this side of the Atlantic. *Zambi, Simbi, Bumba, Lemba*, who are worshiped in the Congo, are exceptions to this rule . . . yet we know enough about the gods of peoples outside this "core" to be struck by the paucity of correspondences to them found in the New World, especially when this is compared to the wealth of carry-overs of Ashanti, Dahomean, and Yoruban supernatural beings.[3]

Herskovits acknowledged that further research might reveal survivals or connections between elements hitherto unrecognized in a Bantu, or Congo, complex comparable to those from West Africa. Individual features of this Congo complex in New-World African religion are at times so little recognized, however, that they are lumped in with West-African materials. Thus Bastide, in his otherwise remarkable work, places *Lemba*, in passing, in the Dahomean pantheon,[4] not recognizing it as the same entity listed, misspelled, in another reference to work by Brazilian colleague Carniero on Bantu influences in Brazilian religion.[5].

Despite these occasional errors, Bantu and Congo influence is widely acknowledged in the New-World African religion and culture, as a category comparable to influences from Yoruba (Nagô), Dahomey (Gêgê), and Ashanti. In Brazilian scholarship Yoruban and Dahomean influences are commonly distinguished from Congo and Angola influences. In Haiti, Dahomean and Congo (or Guinea) are recognized as distinct influences. Commonly West-African influences are seen by scholars as dominant—Yoruba in Brazil, Dahomey in Haiti—whereas the Congo or Bantu influence is seen as having adapted to, or subordinated itself within, the West-African system of ritual symbols and deities. However there is reason to suspect the finality of such scholarly judgment, since Congo and Bantu influences have not until recently been the subject of thorough scholarly inquiry to match the extensive fieldwork of a Herskovits in the Old and the New World on Dahomey,[6] or the in-depth reconstruction of a single tradition in the New World comparable to Bastide's work on Yoruba (Nagô) in Brazil.[7] Thompson's current work comparing art and dance styles in Kongo with those of the Kongo-influenced portions of the New World,[8] replicating similar work on the Yoruba,[9] is an important step toward understanding the Atlantic continuity of Kongo artistic culture, including *Lemba*.

In Brazil scholars such as Carniero and Bastide have, however, identified correspondences between Bantu and West-African ritual systems in order to establish the path by which a dominant symbolic system might absorb, or supplant, a subordinate one. If, as Bastide suggests, the Nagô (Yoruba) rites exercised a sort of hegemony over those from other African "nationalities," and the Catholic deities and saints over all African ritual symbols, then it is possible to identify distinctive Bantu and Congo elements in their appropriate places. In other words, assimilation has not been haphazard, but has followed rules of correspondence (figure 23). These correspondences between Congo (Kongo) and Angola *inkisses*, Dahomean (Gêgê) *voduns*, Yoruba (Nagô) *orixás*, and Catholic saints and deities, are drawn largely from court registers of African cults in Brazilian cities of Recife, Pernambuco, and Bahia. They suggest that, as Bastide says, Bantu deities retain their existence in ecstatic "language" songs in which they are named *Zambi*, *Bumba*, *Lemba*, and so on, while the rites are basically the same across the nationalities. Even so, there has been a tendency for *inkisses* and *voduns* to be submerged in *orixás*, and these in Catholic deities and saints. Cultic movements such as *Candomblé*, *Macumba*, and most recently *Umbanda* which cut across these nationalities have a tendency to rearrange and submerge autonomous elements even further.

The list of Congo deities or *inkisses* in figure 23 bears a certain resemblance to comparable inventories of *inkisses* from the seventeenth- and eighteenth-century Congo, in particular that given by Dapper (see Chapter 2), for the Loango coast. *Zambi* is not mentioned by Dapper but is widespread in other early references. However, correspondences between *Pongo* and *Zambiapongo*, *Malemba* or *Lemba* and *Lomba* (sp?), *Bomba* or *Bombo* and *Bombongira*, *Kossi* and *Incôssi*, *Makongo* and *Quincongo*, and

Figure 23

Correspondences of African and Catholic deities and saints in Brazil, based on Bastide, pp. 195, 264–7, in cities of Bahia and Recife

Congo *inkisses*	Angola *inkisses*	Gêgê [Dahomey] *voduns*	Nagô [Yoruba] *orisha*	Catholic *deities & saints*
Zambiapongo	Zambi	———	Olorun	———
Lomba [Lemba]	Lombarengenga, Cassunbenca	Olissassá	Oxalá	St. Anne; N.S. of Bomfim; Christ Child; Holy Spirit; Eternal Father; Trinity
Bombongira	Aluvais	Elegba, Legba	Exú	The Devil; St. Bartholomew; St. Gabriel; The Rebel Angel
Incôssi Mucumbé	Roche Mucumbé	Gun	Ogun	St. Anthony; St. Jerome; St. George; St. Paul; St. John
Mutacalombo	Mutalombo	Odé, Agué	Oxóssi	St. George; Archangel Michael; St. Expedit; St. Anthony
Gongonbira				
Quincongo	Cajanja	Ayoani, Sakpata	Omolú	St. Benedict; St. Roch; St. Lazarus; St. Sebastian
Kambaranguanje	Zaze, Kibuco, Kiessubangango	Sobo (Sogbo), Bade	Shangó	St. Barbara, St. Jerome, St. Peter; St. John as a Child; St. John Baptist, St. Anthony
Nunvurucomabuva	Matamba	Oia	Yansan	St. Barbara
Pandá	Dandalunda Kaiala		Yemanjá	Virgin Mary; O.L. of Rosary; O.L. of Compassion; O.L. of Immaculate Conception of Beach; O.L. of Lourdes & Candlemas; O.L. of Sorrows
Angoroméa	Angoro	Obéssem	Oxun-mare	St. Bartholomew
Agué, Catende		Loko	Ossain [Iroko-Loko]	St. Francis; St. Sebastian; St. Lawrence; St. Gaetano; O.L. of Navigators; St. John
		Aziri	Oxun	Mary Magdalene; O.L. of Pleasures; O.L. of Carmel; O.L. of the Immaculate Conception

possibly *Pansa* and *Panda* suggest on the basis of name similarity alone an important source of continuity from early Congo and later Brazilian ritual culture.[10] As important as these similarities are, the names of spirits or medicines (*min'kisi*) in the Dapper list include several which do not appear in Brazil, nor anywhere else in the New World. Of these we know that *Thirico*, *Kikokoo*, *Injami*, and *Bunzi* were local or regional earth shrines, and as a set they do not appear to have been reconstituted in the New World. Further evidence may be noted of the continuity of a Congo system. *Zambi* and Olorun, the Nagô high god, do not become transformed into a particular Catholic deity or saint, and generally *Zambi* is not made the object of a particular cult, nor does it become a possessing deity (true in Haiti as well). This suggests a transfer of the Bantu idea of a distant or ungraspable ultimate power. The Christian God the Father is rather equated with Oxala, Olissassá, and *Lemba*, and He appears in the context of a dyadic relationship with his son Jesus, or in the Trinity, or in the Holy Family of Joseph, the Virgin Mary, and the Christ child. This equation of *Lemba* with Oxala [Orisanlá] the Nagô (Yoruba) god of the sky and deity of procreation and creativity, and with the cluster of Christian features of the Trinity, the Holy Family, and the God (Father)-Christ (Son) relationship—all features characteristic of *Lemba* in preceding Kongo variants—indicates another important conceptual carry-over to New-World Bantu religion.

In Haiti the African cultural and religious influences were, as already noted, similarly divided into West-African and Bantu cycles of worship. Both in ritual observance and in scholarship the dominant West-African influence is acknowledged to be that of Dahomey, as witnessed by the cultic vocabulary of spirits (*loa*), cult complexes (*voudou*), cult leadership (*houngan*, *mambo*), cult locations (*hounsi*), and so on, although even here there is the possibility of Kongo influence (for example, *mambo* from Moni-Mambu, or *mambuk*, healer). Dahomean deities are collectively known as Rada (from the slaving port town Arada, itself named after Allada), whereas those of Congo and Bantu origins have recently been identified as strongly reappearing in the Pétro cycle of deities.[11] This dichotomy needs to be seen, in Haiti, against the backdrop of Haitian history.

Haitian history is a running record of impulses for independence on the part of black immigrants to the island, who by 1600 had inherited an agricultural economy from the by then extinct Taino Indians.[12] Spain gradually ceded its dominance of the island to the French, who by the eighteenth century had developed a plantation economy around sugar, which required massive regular injections of slave labor. During this century 15,000 slaves a year were being shipped from the ports of Cabinda, Malemba, and Loango. Slaving ships would run a triangular route: to Africa for slaves, then to Santo Domingo where these were traded for sugar which was shipped to Bordeaux and Nantes. In the late eighteenth century this society based upon slaves, sugar and slave-owners was hit with undercurrents of the French Revolution, which did not leave the blacks untouched. The oppression of the slave plantations combined with exclusion from any participation in the emancipation offered by revolutionary ideas touched off a massive slave revolt in 1791 that turned into a decade-long war of liberation. Legendary history recounts how one Boukman, a giant of a man and a religious priest, led the partisans in the taking of an oath near Mourne Rouge, and how an old Negress sacrificed a black pig, catching the blood in a gourd and passing it around for each to drink as they swore loyalty to Boukman. The plantations were set to the torch and the oppressors killed.[13] Warfare continued until all Europeans had been driven out, and in 1804 Haiti was pronounced an independent republic. Toussaint L'Ouverture became its founder, and Dessalines, Christophe, and Pétion, his lieutenants in the revolt, became his ministers, and his successors.

Although Haiti was now independent, its early governments were hardly less repressive than had been the colonial predecessor. Dessalines created a type of serfdom and was assassinated. Christophe followed with similar laws to the effect that cultivators had to stay rooted to the soil—the plantations—where they worked, while a titled aristocracy was allowed to emerge. Pétion, however, instituted some liberalization, such as individual peasant holdings. He is also known for the construction of the Citadel, a fortress of Old-World castle proportions, as a beleaguered free black state's last defense from its potential enemies. It was never used. These founding fathers remain legendary heroes in Haitian public and religious rituals, including as will be seen *Lemba-Pétro*.

This link of early Haitian history to *Lemba* is tenuous, but what historical details are known are very suggestive, principally put in perspective through Jean Price-Mars' reading of the work of Moreau de Saint-Méry, a late eighteenth-century French writer.[14] Saint-Méry collected his observations in the late colonial era and published in 1797, before Haitian independence. Already then, at the beginning of the rebellion, the distinction was apparent between Voodoo and *Pétro* (or Pédro) complexes in African-Haitian dance. The orgin of the "Don Pedro" dance, according to Saint-Méry, went back to 1768 when a Spanish black from Petit-Goâve, by the name of Don Pedro, introduced a dance analogous to the Voodoo rites but of a far greater rapidity and level of excitation. To reach even greater levels of excitement and pitch, devotees of "Don Pedro" spiked their rum with gunpowder. The effect, in Price-Mars' summary of Saint-Méry's observations, was "electrifying," producing a "convulsive drunkenness" which, heightened by the singing and the rhythm of the drums, evoked a collective crisis.[15] Writing again in 1803, explicitly about Haitian dance, Saint-Méry reiterated the stylistic contrast of "Don Pedro" to "Voodoo," noting that the former frequently touched off public disorder. This and the banning of the dance by authorities, however ineffective in their efforts, suggest that the Don Pedro dance may have had an important role in sustaining resistance to French authority.[16]

The grounds for equating this historic Don Pedro dance with today's *Pétro* complex of rites, and by inference the Congo influence in Haitian religion and culture, are several, according to Price-Mars. First, there is its contrast to Voodoo in Saint-Méry's eighteenth- and nineteenth-century account, and there is the linguistic transformation from the Spanish Don Pedro to the Haitian-French Creole "Jean Pétro." Second, Price-Mars notes the concentration of the *Pétro* complex of dances in the west and south of Haiti, corresponding to Saint-Méry's reference to the Don Pedro dance in the west of Saint Dominique. And a third indication of this dance's continuity is the recurrent harassment it has received from government, both colonial and independent. Indeed, Dessalines, when he was Toussaint L'Ouverture's Inspector of Culture, is known to have had fifty worshippers of a religious dance bayonetted in the Plain of Cul-de-Sac, the general region where Don Pedro was concentrated.[17]

The *Pétro* complex of deities (*loa*) in Haitian religion, acknowledged to be a reflection of the Congo-Guinea influence, is held apart from the unique *Lemba-Pétro* rite witnessed by Price-Mars in the Cul-de-Sac valley in the 1930's. Of all Haitian rites *Lemba-Pétro* is the only one, in Price-Mars' words, which is celebrated secretly, deep in the forest, rather than in the village or town near the *hounfor* Voodoo temple. Price-Mars goes so far as to state that *Pétro* and *Lemba* are synonymous, and that the ancient Don Pedro was probably some version of the African rite of *Lemba*.[18] However, this is not very illuminating, since his only source on *Lemba* in Africa is Chatelain's brief reference to a household fertility medicine in

Angola.[19] Métraux, who calls *Lemba* an African "tribe," suggests that it takes the place of *Pétro* in the north and northwest of Haiti as a category of divinities and rites equal to and identical with the *Pétro* complex.[20] Thompson is the first to identify *Lemba*'s rightful source in connection with Haitian religion as the north-Kongo healing cult by that same name.[21]

Before describing the autonomous *Lemba-Pétro* rite of Haiti, it is appropriate to describe the more commonly known *Pétro* segment of *loa* gods and services in well-known Voodoo settings.

The Pétro *Complex of Deities in a* Voodoo Lao *Service*

In the valley adjoining the Cul-de-Sac where the *Lemba-Pétro* rite was reported, near the town of Mirebalais, Herskovits in the 1930's carefully documented a *loa* service he belived to be typical for the region.[22] This section will identify features in this rite that are important in the comparison of Voodoo with Congo, especially *Lemba*, ritual structure and intent.

Resemblance of the *loa* service to *Lemba*, in strictly choreographic—spatial and temporal—ordering, is striking. The Haitian rite is constructed around two major phases, separated by an interval. The first such day/night/day phase is devoted to the *Pétro* rite, the second to the Rada rite and its deities (see figure 24).

The family putting on the service had experienced numerous deaths and illnesses and, as customary, it had to celebrate once in a decade or so a major ceremony for the *loa* spirits. The first phase was observed around three altars: the first, a table called the "*trône*," which is covered with white cloth and a canopy, holds a variety of plant offerings, crucifixes, holy water, candles, oil, and other food offerings, as well as chromolithographic *images* of saints; the second, a table devoted to the *loa* named *Simbi*, bears various cooked and uncooked foods; the third, and most important, is a table devoted to the *loa* Bosu, bearing food and drink, nearby which are tied offerings of sacrificial animals including a large black boar, two small black pigs, a black goat, a black turkey, a guinea hen, two white pigeons, and several chickens.

In the early evening the family putting on the service, and the officiants, held the "*action de grâce*," a Catholic-like ritual led by the *pret savanne*. Holding a candle in his hand, the leader directed the family in "desultory" singing from time to time pouring water from a

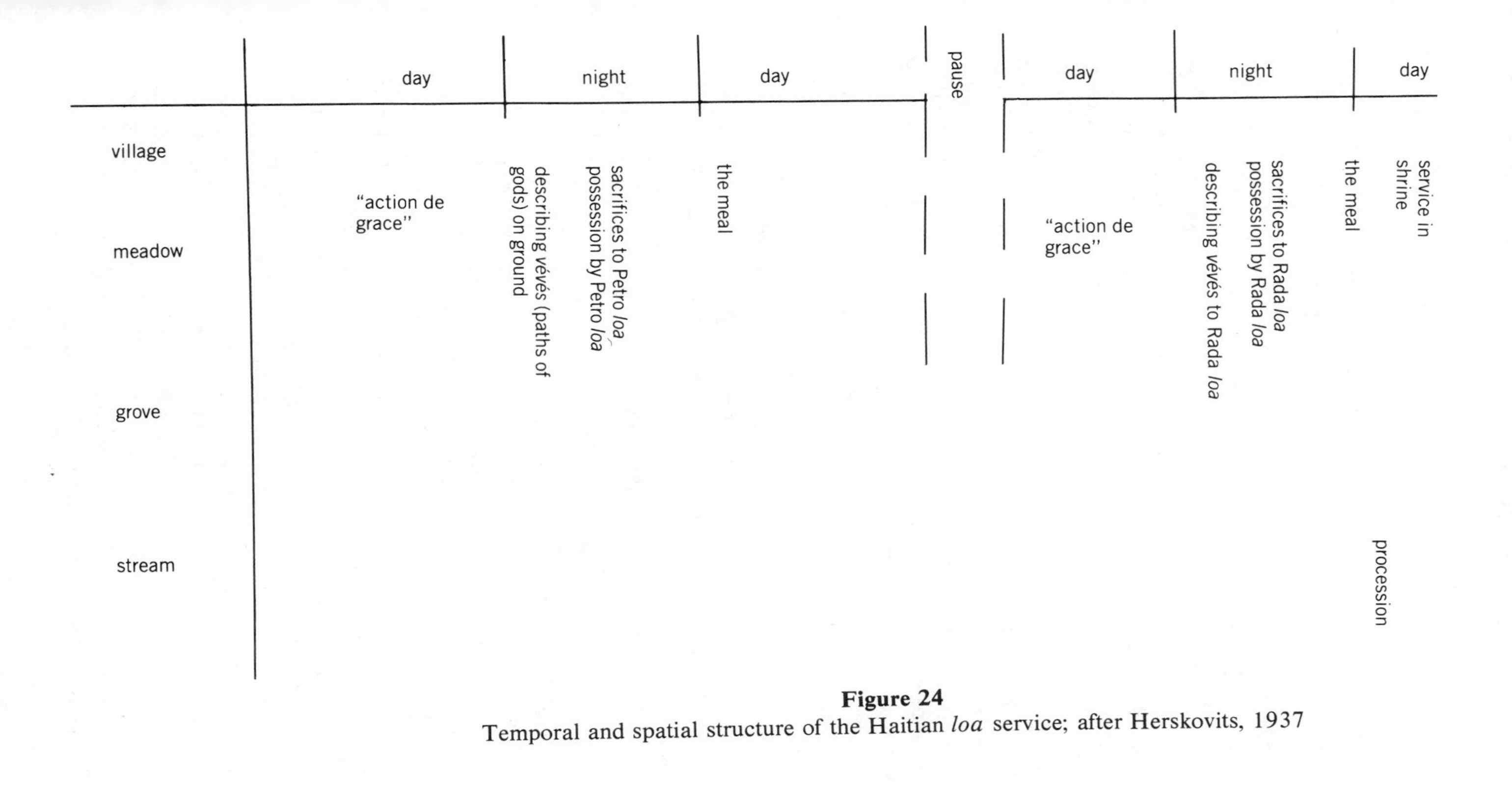

Figure 24
Temporal and spatial structure of the Haitian *loa* service; after Herskovits, 1937

container on the *trône* into a small depression directly before the altar. All knelt for the Pater Noster, the Credo, the Ave Maria, and for a long adoration and benediction.

The European music of the *action de grâce* gave way then to African rhythm and drumming, at which time the *hungan* took over the officiating from the *pret' savanne*. The *hungan* ordered each family member to tell the *loa* spirits which troubles had befallen them and what favors were desired. His assistant then took six candles and proceeded, in a counterclockwise direction, to trace in the meadow near the village a large circle, fixing four candles at cardinal points representing the four corners of the earth. In addition, one was for the *Mait' 'Bitation* (Master of the Habitation) and another for *Mait' Source* (Master of the Stream). The family members, holding candles, placed their individual candles near those already emplanted in the meadow, forming several clusters in the overall shape of a cosmogram, dotting the hillside in the deepening dusk.

After all had returned to the altar, the *hungan* began to "trace *ververs*" on the ground. (*Ververs*—usually called *vévés*—are lines or paths for the spirits to follow, often in the Port-au-Prince area drawn in highly decorative patterns with flour or other powders.) Initially he traced a white line in corn meal from the first table for Bosu to the second table and tree for Simbi, on to the *trône* where subsidiary motifs were added in gray and black. The *vévé* paths anticipated the coming of the gods up to the human world where they would be recognized, fed, placated, and then "restrained" or put away" for another decade.

At this point in the ritual, sacrificial animals and birds were brought to their respective altars for washing and presenting to the gods. The *hungan* became possessed by *Simbi*, announced his "fee" for performing the rite, and began a long invocation to the various *Pétro loa*, while the participants waited for the animals to "recognize," that is begin eating, their appropriate food. Thus, the red and black cock was offered grains for Legba, the black fowl grain for Gede, the red fowl grains for Ogun, the white pigeon grains for Damballa, the fowl with ruffled plumage grains for Congo Zandor, the small pigs grains for 'Ti Kita Démembré, the boar grain for Bosu, the goat leaves from the sacred tree for Erzilie Gé Rouge, and so on. The animals, later to be sacrificed to their appropriate *loa*, were to take to their food in the same way as the *loa* were to possess members of the family and receive their sacrificial meals. members of the family were "crossed" with animals by the *hungan* to encourage the gods to come to them. This action was repeated before the Bosu altar.

As the singing became louder and more rhythmical, with the drums leading the pace, the deities finally responded to the calls, "mounting," possessing, the family members one by one, each enacting the characteristic ecstatic behaviors, for example, jumping into the fire for Legba. Herskovits notes that the devotees moved back and forth between the three altars—the Catholic *trône*, the altar to Bosu, and that to Simbi—as the *loa* possessed family members before each appropriate altar, thus pattern and structure were evident despite the appearance of utter chaos in the outcries and diverse agitated behaviors of possession. One of the several songs sung during the possession service lists and to some extent characterized the deities who appeared during this *Pétro* phase.

Bosu found something on the ground,
Do not pick it up.
Bosu goes about,
He found something on the ground,
Do not pick it up.
You will come to harm.
If you pick it up,
You will anger Bosu.
Simbi en Deux Eaux,
I do for you,
Do for me;
Help, O Congo,
Congo Zandor.
Simbi Kita Kita, work for us,
Today for us,
Tomorrow for others.
Erzilie, O Lemba,
I ask, where is Erzilie,
The food is ready.
Gedenibo, behind the cross, Gede.
Before Baron, Gede,
Behind the cross, Gede,
Today I am troubled,
Gedebi, call Gede, this Gede,
Today I am troubled.
Cease to sweep, sprinkle, hoe.
I am troubled, Baron Samedi.[23]

At about midnight, when all the animals to be offered had been washed and prepared, and all possession had ceased, the time had come for the sacrifices. The *hungan*, with knife in hand, decapitated or punctured the jugular vein of the appropriate animal for each *loa*, while an assistant collected some of the blood in a small calabash. Thus killed, the offerings were taken elsewhere for dressing and cooking. The *loa* which had been troubling the family were then "sent away," that is, buried symbolically with an offering of meat. Thus handled were Erzilie Gé Rouge (Red Eyes), Bosu Trois Cornes (Three Horns), Ti Kita Démembré, and 'Ti Jean Pié Sèche. Those "restrained" were *Lemba* and Simbi djo (*de l'eau*, of the water), *Lemba* under the mango tree where the altar to Bosu had been, Simbi djo where the *trône* had stood. Each was buried with its offering and an iron cross or other object to "preoccupy it" for a period from seven to seventeen years. The *loa* sent away were told to go back to Guinea or Africa and not bother the family. Those restrained were dealt with more favorably, the family needing their help. The idea was clearly conveyed that these *Pétro* deities were responsible for the family's misfortunes, and that they should stay away now that they had been placated. The feast was intended for them, at least rhetorically, although the human community finished that which the gods had left. Gods' leftovers are human sustenance. This meal persisted into daylight, with final ceremonies.

The Rada phase was held a few days later, and approximated the same structure, opening with the *action de grâce*, and continuing with the tracing of *vévés*, possession by Rada *loa* such as Damballah Wedo, Legba, Ogun, Ashade, and so on, the sacrifice at midnight, and the meal.

The issue of to what extent Haitian *loa* services reflect African continuities may be discussed in terms of similarities of structure which reveal underlying patterns or motifs, and similarities of content which reveal direct terminological or semantic continuities. Although the dominant Dahomean influence is evident in the vocabulary of Haitian Voodoo, the role names of officiants, and many liturgical symbols, the resemblance of the temporal structure with Old-World *Lemba* variants suggests that Congo-Bantu continuities must be given serious consideration. In addition, the tracing of ritual spaces in the *Pétro* phase of the Mirebalais *loa* service offers some striking resemblances to several *Lemba* variants and other Kongo rituals (for example, the *diyowa* in N'khimba, Munkukusa). In the staking out of the cardinal points with candles, the *hungan* used a common, perhaps world-wide, motif. However, in circling this space in a counterclockwise direction and then dividing it into two, one half representing the domestic realm (governed by "lord of the house," Mait' 'Habitation), the other half the realm of the wilds, the deep, of water (governed by "lord of the deep," Mait' Source), he was tracing a cosmogram the way it is done in many Kongo contexts. The opposition of the human realm and that of the beyond (whether the world of spirits, wild nature, or trade routes) serves as the paradigm for ritual action wherever one must come to terms with the interaction of the visible and experiential with the invisible and intangible. The cyclic movement turns this opposition into a statement about time in the life of man and society, denoting rhythmic cycles such as life and death, coming and going, and perhaps, as in this *loa* service, the awakening of the gods and the return of the same to their appropriate resting places.

Going beyond the general to particular continuities of the Kongo-Haiti axis is more difficult; however, some interpretations seem warranted. The two altars erected to "*Pétro*" deities, Bosu and Simbi, suggest this opposition of the domestic and the beyond so common in *Lemba* and other Kongo ritual settings. Simbi spirits are well known in Kongo to indwell water courses, pools, springs, rocks, forests, ravines, and other passages to the nether world of mystical power, a characteristic which makes them suited for the elaboration of public authority symbols. Kita, also present in the *Pétro* cluster of *loa* spirits, is a type of Kongo simbi. Bosu represents a problem in interpretation, not the least of which is because of his well-known origin in the Fongbe (Dahomean) pantheon as a three-horned, hunch-backed monster. Despite this clear origin, corroborated both by historical research and in Haitian folk thought, Bosu is "put" into the *Pétro*, that is *Lemba* and Kongo, class of *loa*, to represent forces at work in the domestic, human society, realm.[24]

The two deities who are "restrained," namely *Lemba* and Simbi djo, appear to replicate this complementarity between the realm of the wilds and that of the community. Both oppositions span the tensions inherent in the life of Haitian peasants, on the one hand uniting and yet on the other dividing the human world and the supernatural, the New World and ancestral Africa, as well as the older span between the trade routes, markets, and home. These fundamental tensions, ritually integrated into one system of rhythms and contrasts, regenerate the community.

Lemba-Pétro *in the Cul-de-Sac Valley, Haiti*

The *Pétro* complex, in general, has much in common with Kongo religion, and its structure is shared with *Lemba*. To find specific elements and meanings which correspond to *Lemba*, however, it is necessary to look at *Lemba-Pétro*, the secretive rite which Price-Mars witnessed, in part, in the Cul-de-Sac Valley in the 1930's.[25] He strayed onto the service one afternoon while on a hunting expedition, and because he was recognized by the celebrants as their physician he was invited to stay. The service was already under way, deep in the protective forests.

At the foot of a tree Price-Mars noted two altars. The first was a table upon which had been erected a bamboo elevation with a niche in it. In this niche there were painted figures representing the Sacred Heart of Jesus, the Infant Jesus, the Holy Virgin, St. Joseph, and images of other Catholic saints. This partial list suggests correspondences to *Lemba* similar to those in Brazil. On the table were placed a bell, a castor oil lamp, a jug, a bottle of kola, and several plates of candy and cake. Under the table, extended on the ground, was a white towel, on which had been placed four forged iron crosses, plates of grilled corn, bread, small cakes, almond sugar, and two bottles of kola.

The second altar was a table covered with red and blue cloth. Before it had been dug a large, deep hole, in which had been placed two carved pieces of mahogany wood about a meter long, each wrapped in the middle with a band of Thai silk, and that wrapped with crimson cloth.

The officiating *hungan* took one piece of wood, looked at it for a time, turned it and held it in his hands, then chanted these words:

Bordé, bordé
coci, manga
va atiloca sorci
macorni, au, vati.

Then he took a hammer and nails and drove the nails into the two pieces of wood in rhythmic alternation to the points of this chant sung by the participants:

Ko! M'tendé ko!
M'apé cloué bois!
Ko! M'tendé Ko!
M'apé cloué bois!

Then the *hungan* took a ball of strong cord and measured out five meters, twice. Each piece of string was taken by a robust man at each end and held taut with the two crossing each other. Then, with the help of assistants, the *hungan* tied the pieces of mahogany wood, clothed in crimson, with nails in them, onto the cross-like form of cord. As each knot was tied with great force, he intoned this refrain:[26]

Assuré! Assuré!
N'ap'assuré point lá!
Hi! Hi!
Nou pralé maré loa Pétro!
Hi! Hi!
Jean Pétro! Chainne qui chainne
Li cassé li
Qui dirait corde!
Hi! Hi!
N'ap maré n'ap maré
Loa Pétro
Hi! Hi!

We are going to tie down the *petro loa*, Hi! Hi!
Jean-Petro, chain which is a chain; he has broken it as if it were a rope.
Hi! Hi!

This continued until the cords were entirely knotted around the pieces of wood. This package together with another carved mahogany cross and two crosses forged of iron were placed at the bottom of the hole, at the foot of the altar. They were then buried with a deep layer of earth. (This ceremony probably represented the restraining of the *loa* Jean Pétro, within the *Lemba* framework.[27] Price-Mars remains silent as to its meaning.)

Meanwhile darkness had fallen. The *hungan* sounded his bell and the congregation formed two rows and walked a distance westward along a path until they came to another site where another deep pit had been dug. The *hungan* asked for complete silence. Raising his index finger over the pit, he spoke this prayer:

Earth, holy earth,
We are a few of your children
among the best in these parts
gathered to ask forgiveness
for offenses to you, which
we may have involuntarily committed.

Especially in the name of
all the members of the family,
present or absent,
I implore their absolution
from all errors committed toward you.

In their name
I offer you drink and food.

Deign to accept these humble offerings.
We wanted to bring you
lavish presents; however,
our means are less and less adequate.
We are but poor folk
who beg your mercy.

O Earth, our mother and patron!

Jean Pétro, Toussaint-L'Ouverture,
Rigaud, Dessalines, Christophe, Pétion,
You know that we are not of this land.
Our ancestors, to all of us come from Africa,
Be favorable to our requests to you.

Jean Pétro, we have done all to please you.
Save us from the calamities which beset us.
Save us from fever, smallpox, leprosy,
Tuberculosis, automobile accidents.

Accept these libations which we make
In your name. Amen.

And the participants replied, "amen." Then the *hungan* took five female animals, a goat, a chicken, a guinea fowl, a turkey hen, and a dove, which he decapitated one after another and held over the pit so their blood flowed copiously into it, after which he threw their bodies into the pit as well. Then, with the help of an assistant, he poured water into a basin and from that into the pit, asking each member of the family to repeat this gesture after him. From another container he also took liquid, and did the same, again asking the family to repeat it after him. The same action followed with a bowl of diverse grains which were thrown into the large pit in honor of the earth and the ancestors.

As the *hungan* pronounced final incantations—inaudible to Price-Mars—and prepared to return to the initial ritual site, a man in the congregation suddenly let out a loud cry and began gesticulating about with such petulance that the assistants cleared the area around.

Possessed by a *Pétro* god—Price-Mars does not say which—he cried:

Brisé!	Broken!
Je suis brisé!	I am broken!
C'est moi brisé!	It is I, broken!

This flood of words, the agitation, rage and convulsiveness, according to Price-Mars, indicated the *Pétro* god's recognition, in possessing a member of the family, of their penitence over violation of its ordinances. The *hungan* failed to calm the man by speaking to him and finally tied his hands with a cord, whereupon he quieted down some but continued to tremble and plaintively mutter *"Je suis brisé"* as the congregation, again in two rows, filed back to the initial ritual site following the *hungan* who was murmuring pronouncements of forgiveness.

Having returned to the site of the two altars, the *hungan* untied the man who had been possessed, and proceeded with the next phase of the rite, the final sacrifice. A sow, the last animal at the site, was brought to the foot of the altar, and held fast by the assistants. The *hungan*, while phrasing a mostly unintelligible (to Price-Mars) incantation to "criminal *Pétro*" deftly stuck his knife into the sow's jugular vein, catching the blood as it throbbed out in a white vase. The vase of blood was placed on the altar and mixed with another beverage. Then, continuing to chant, the *hungan* gathered the family group of men, women, and children, now dressed in white and wearing red bracelets, around the altar in a half-circle. Taking the vase, he dipped two fingers of his right hand into the blood and spread it onto the lips of each person around him, continuing the chant about "*Pétro* criminal." Price-Mars observes that during this "blood communion" numerous participants shivered, momentarily losing their composure in brief attacks of ecstasy or deep sighs of emotion, witness of their "collective agony."

With this, the main part of the rite was over, and Price-Mars left the scene. It was now after midnight. The devotees would continue with a nocturnal meal.

It is apparent that Price-Mars has not witnessed the entire *Lemba-Pétro* ritual. For example, no action is described before the altar bearing Catholic images. What occurred there may have been comparable to the *action de grâce* in the *loa* service recounted earlier; it may, however, relate more directly to a *Lemba* perception of familial roles as seen in correspondences of Bantu divinities to Catholic saints and gods. The symbolism of food for the gods relates it, as well as all of Haitian Voodoo, to African ritual. The theme is highly developed in *Lemba*, for example in the eastern variant, where the priests receive food offerings from the neophyte, in exchange for medicines. As the rite progresses, the return medicine gift contains increasing doses of food. By the close, *Lemba* is issuing banquets to the general public, and the neophyte priestly couple, with senior priests, are receiving and eating banquets of symbols and sacred "dirt." It is as if the gods, whose food is medicine, and those who mediate the relationship between gods and men, participate in negotiation: offering tokens to the gods who ultimately return generosity and well-being to the human community. To be sure, this feature is not unique to *Lemba*, but the imagery of "priming the pump" of well-being, of the earth's fertility and the ancestors' beneficence, is prominent in *Lemba*, both in the Old and the New World. It is perhaps more prominent in the Haitian *Lemba-Pétro* rite, subordinated in the African variants by the commercial motif.

A further theme that is prominent in Kongo religion, which was noted in the *loa* service and present in *Lemba-Pétro* as well, is the complementarity of powers. The wrapped mahogany sticks and the cords which are used in "binding" *Pétro* recall not only the tracing of the cosmogram of Kongo ritual, but also a specific feature of *Lemba* in which similar sticks are brought together to represent the creative complementarity of male and female. In the south-central variant, as the neophyte stands before the cruciform *diyowa* trench preparatory to the oath-taking, each priest (*vua*) and priestess (*mizita*) is represented in such a stick. These are held together by the neophyte as he swears his oath of loyalty to his *Lemba* father and to *Lemba*. Later the sticks are bound in "couples," as in the Haitian séance, and placed in the *n'kobe*. Male and female together represent Mahungu, the androgynous demigod of complementarity. It is as if the *diyowa* cruciform trench of Kongo ritual combines the idea of a hole in the ground with the cross-form represented momentarily by the cord and the sticks. The oath that is sworn, in the south-central variant, by the neophyte who submerges his face in the ancestral mud of the trench while holding the sticks is, in the Haitian variant, projected into the binding up of the two sticks of mahogany.

The language of the Haitian rite, the resounding "*ko!*" of the nails being driven into hard wood, makes it clearly Kongo in origin. This "strike word" is, of course, an abbreviation of *koma*, a term which denotes the act of driving nails or wedges into a ritual object, or of spitting on a bracelet. It also is used to describe the abstract idea of awakening in a person the mystical force of the spirits. Konda, for example, uses it to speak of the effect on the *Lemba* neophyte of a dream of ancestors, or a nightmare (Text 8.7). The burial of *Pétro*, thus "bound," before the altar, may be a unique Haitian procedure, picked up from Voodoo rites. However, it may, in the *Lemba-Pétro* context, indicate the survival of a form of activating and "recharging" a mystical force that is older than *Lemba*'s adoption of the moveable shrine-*n'kobe*, most certainly related to long-distance commerce.

Lemba's continuity is perfectly clear in the final ritual episode recounted by Price-Mars, in which the sow is sacrificed and the bracelet-bearing congregants gather around in a half-circle for the final "communion." It is a greatly simplified rendering of the elaborate rite of the northern (Kamba) variant in which the *Lemba* priest receives many pigs for the instruction of the neophyte's profanation (1.35–59). The pigs' blood is collected in an *nsaba* pot and taken behind the house to the ceremonial "kitchen," where the *Lemba* neophyte couple is given its code of behavior and blessed by the *Lemba* father as the bracelets are issued. The blood is spread on the doorposts of their house.

How can one speak of continuity, though, when there is, in the Haitian rite, no village with courtyard and hearth, no house with doorposts? *Lemba-Pétro* has totally adapted the ritual rhythm of the African rite—the movement from courtyard to hearth, from the village to the beyond—to the hidden forest setting, befitting its status since the eighteenth century as a persecuted sect. Amazingly, however, the rhythm of spatial movement has been retained; thus, the site of the two altars is the village, by analogy. The two altars may serve the courtyard/hearth opposition, although details are missing. The sacrifice of birds before the large earth pit, the site of possession by *Pétro*, replicates the esoteric phase of the African variants. What is important is that the significance of the ritual rhythm has survived, over several centuries in two traditions diverging from a common point, in mutually intelligible ritual gestures.

Retentions and continuity alone do not assure vitality. Perhaps the opposite. Thus some variations are as indicative of *Lemba*'s survival as are the continuities. In the African variations *Lemba* adherents invoked a variety of gods, appropriate according to regional mythological systems and structures of authority. In the east, a Teke-related chief spirit, Nga Malamu, was addressed; elsewhere it was Kuba, Mahungu, or Moni-Mambu; on the coast and some inland regions it was earth god Bunzi. What could be more fitting, in Haiti, than to address Jean Pétro, the "criminal" of the dominant system, and to build on that beginning with Haiti's founding heroes Toussaint L'Ouverture, Rigaud, Desslaines, Christophe, and Pétion.

Part III

Structure and Movement in *Lemba* Therapeutics

"Myth shields us from music while at the same time giving music its maximum freedom. In exchange, music endows the tragic myth with a convincing metaphysical significance, which the unsupported word and image could never achieve, and, moreover, assures the spectator of a supreme delight—though the way passes through annihilation and negation, so that he is made to feel that the very womb of things speaks audibly to him."—Friedrich Nietzsche, *The Birth of Tragedy*

Introduction

Lemba sources studied so far reveal a strong preoccupation with conscious thought and deliberative action. The *Lemba* adherent is admonished to keep secrets, be vigilant, argue effectively, prevail in public debate, trade skillfully, and maintain a strong household and a peaceful community. Legendary figures and ritual symbols reflect these virtues; antiheroes define them negatively by demonstrating the sad consequences of erroneous choices.

The general content of these ideas of *Lemba* well-being and *Lemba* illness may now be spelled out more fully. We have analyzed the expressive domains to understand the *Lemba* ritual setting, and we have clarified the codes of these domains to determine the logic of the expressions. Now we can attempt the difficult task of examining *Lemba*'s self-perception. In other words, is it possible to identify the perspectives of *Lemba* priests and priestesses themselves?

It would seem possible to reconstruct such a *Lemba* consciousness, given the emphasis on clarity of thought and skillful rhetoric. However, there is a problem. Paradoxically, *Lemba*'s origin and ritual is often elaborated in terms of apparently mystifying creations such as rodents, earth colors, plants, and mythic heroes. Yet these seem to be interwoven with allusions to the familiar ground of daily experiences such as family life, collecting food, and relations between clans. There is thus an obvious tendency to align mundane experience with more abstract principles from myth, cosmology, and social structure. The manner in which the two levels of reality are combined reveals a selectivity of choice of alternatives, a conspicuous manipulation of bits and pieces from the received lore of myth and cosmology to reinforce a particular set of alternatives. The moment this occurs in an institution's or society's culture, it has created an ideology for itself. Why this occurs, the context in which it occurs, and why such an ideology must take recourse to a multitude of images from the natural world will be examined in this section.

Chapter 9 identifies the mechanisms of thought which lie behind the construction of *Lemba*'s unique world view, the process by which it anchors social forms with specific ideals, selecting particular types of authority, defining moral order through specific heroes and antiheroes. And it goes on to explain how *Lemba* elaborates conjunctive and disjunctive modes of mediation within relationships and situations, and shifts disjunctive mediation from the verbal realm of discourse to the nonverbal, a process which is the key to understanding *Lemba*'s "illness" and "therapy."

Chapter 10 brings this structural preference of choices—*Lemba*'s ideology—together into a theory of order and meaningful existence in a segmentary society caught up in the great trade of coastal Africa from the seventeenth century to the twentieth.

Chapter 9

Modes of *Lemba* Thought

Anchoring in Myth, and the Problem of History

Each *Lemba* variant has reflected a concern for relating its main concepts, medicines, and ritual symbols to a legitimate source, be it culture hero Moni-Mambu, ancestors, first priest and "founder" Nga-Malamu, or someone's *Lemba* Father. Kerenyi and Jung call this feature an etiological myth's "anchorage."[1]

Kongo *min'kisi* reflect an anchoring structure in their charters. The *n'kisi* is revealed to an individual or community, and through its priest it is handed on, extended (*vandisa*), or received (*tumiswa*). An *n'kisi* "apostle" is, therefore, a sent one (*n'tumwa*). Chiefly commissions function in like manner, except that they are exclusive corporations whose officeholders succeed one another, and modern Kongo prophets tend to be consecrated by a comparable structure. All consecrated roles and functions in the society, of whatever generality or specificity, share a common anchoring structure.[2]

The structure of a mythic charter, whether of an *n'kisi*, a ruling dynasty, a prophetic or clan genealogy, has three stages of reference, reflecting a temporal, spatial, social, and cosmological sequence: first, the original "anchoring" figure; second, the mediator; last, the human here-and-now. An attempt is made to relate the fragmentary, multiple, dispersed, or confused state of present human society to the unitary, idealized, and orderly condition "in the beginning." The charter myth's sequence of names, priests, officeholders, or places inhabited, and conditions met and dealt with, thus refer to the structure of society and the universe, or to recollected human events and individuals.[3] Frequently Kongo etiology myths have been confused with history, or with pure legend, because of the parallel (metonymic) series of persons, roles, legendary figures, animals, colors, or cosmological categories which inhabit them. An effort to resolve this problem of history in myth is pertinent to understanding *Lemba*, whose lyrics contain, as the last section shows, a combined view of human and nonhuman structures.

The historical school of ethnology has a clear answer to this problem, one which numerous analysts of Kongo and Lower-Zaire culture have adopted. Frobenius' theory of "spiritization" (*Vergeisterung*) of ancestors holds that masks, cult deities, mythic heroes such as Nga Malamu, perhaps even Mavungu, were manistic creations standing for the long-deceased in the time-dimmed memories of the living.[4] According to this theory, the ancestors' individual identities became blended with sun, plant, and animal identities in the process of working out cultural conflicts, whence the frequency of masks with two, three, and four faces throughout the secret-society region of West and Equatorial Africa. This view of African ritual symbols and art was very common at an earlier period in European ethnology. Laman adopted it in regard to Kongo *min'kisi*, arguing that one could justifiably abandon the *min'kisi* without doing damage to a postulated fundamental Kongo religion of which they were merely a manistic degradation.[5] Bittremieux used the theory to suggest that *Lemba* was a more recent institution than earth-shrine Bunzi.[6] Recently Thiel has analyzed regional Zaire and Kasai-basin religion in terms of the gradual spiritization of human figures into middle-range deities who are situated in a religious cosmology alongside or beneath true "high God" figures.[7]

The problem with this approach is the partiality introduced by the historical bias. Some of the figures of *Lemba* charters may very well have been historic persons of prominence, such as an eponymous Teke chief Nga Malamu, or Haitian national heroes Jean Pétro, Toussaint L'Ouverture, Rigaud, Dessalines, Christophe, and Pétion in the New-World *Lemba* variant. Yet at the other end of the continuum there are those charters whose figures are typological male/female, androgynous beings, or some other characterization of a social role or relationship. One variant of *Lemba* called *Lemba-Nsongi* states outrightly its goal as assuring the continuity of the patrifilial blessing over three generations, from fathers to children and grandchildren, thereby closing the circuit of exchanges so important to social harmony.[8] In this latter example a rather abstracted function is attributed to the *n'kisi*, one of succession as well as relationship, of diachronic continuity as well as synchronic coherence.

A view of human thought which clarifies this problem in myth analysis allows models of society and human experience to be devised by either (1) personalizing the individual who has an experience or (2) emphasizing the relational situation in which he may be involved. History is enhanced by personalizing, individualizing, an experience, but at the risk of exposing the individual to social threats and conflicts. Even so, *Lemba* initiation, like other initiations, gave an intiate a new personal name, often one expressing his accomplishments and anxieties. Emphasis on the relational, by contrast, enhances the social and religious categories that lend meaning to an experience. In *Lemba* thought, which is characteristic of Central-African throught, the relational emphasis in ritual invokes the various domains of the natural and cosmological world, often it would seem simply for the purpose of connecting the individual experience to all the rest of the universe, to give it a totalizing framework. Another important reason for naturalizing a ritual situation is to deal more readily with those uncomfortable, ugly human emotions associated with anger, witchcraft, envy, competition, and power, which cannot well be diagnosed by isolating individual, named persons.

The next several sections will show how, and at which moments, these possibilities of metaphoric transference and movement are invoked. Figure 25 illustrates some of the features of the Kongo ritual metaphor vocabulary.

Successional and Relational Modes of Authority

The successional and relational aspects of Kongo ritual charters may be manipulated to express authority modes ranging from hierarchic to egalitarian, as well as ranging from the autonomy of a person or corporate unit to its complementary involvement with other units. Clan genealogies that express extensive complementarity of local and regional lineages frequently show three houses descending from a common source. Exclusive genealogies tend to show a direct lineal descent from an original founder. A similar structural transformation is possible in *n'kisi* charters, including *Lemba*. Often charters of individualistic medicines and commissions are inserted in a more inclusive charter of a collective nature. The individualistic charters are fragments of the larger ones. It is in the major *min'kisi* and related commissions of chiefship, kingship, and prophet movements that transformations from centralized and hierarchic to decentralized and complementary may be found. For example, in a set of texts by Laman's catechists derived from the Kamba region around Mboko Nsongo, the same set of deities and mediators—Funza, Mpulu-Bunzi, Mahambu-Lukabu, and so on—are ranged in one instance as a successional hierarchy through which all power passes until in

Mpulu-Bunzi it is dispersed to "all other *min'kisi*."[9] But in the other variant, this dispersal is made from Funza, the god of twins, to three mediator gods, Mahambu-Lukabu, Mpulu-Bunzi, and Mabiala ma Ndembe, from whom power is distributed to all other *min'kisi* (figure 26, a and b).[10]

Figure 25
Categories of ritual transformation in Kongo

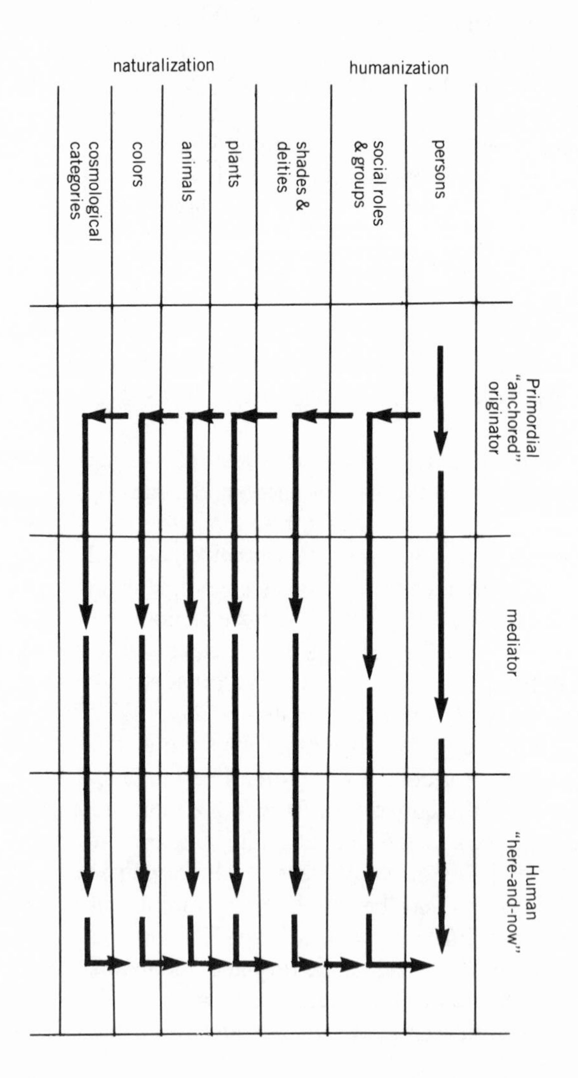

Figure 26
Charter myths of several *Lemba* variants
and other *min'kisi* and kingdoms

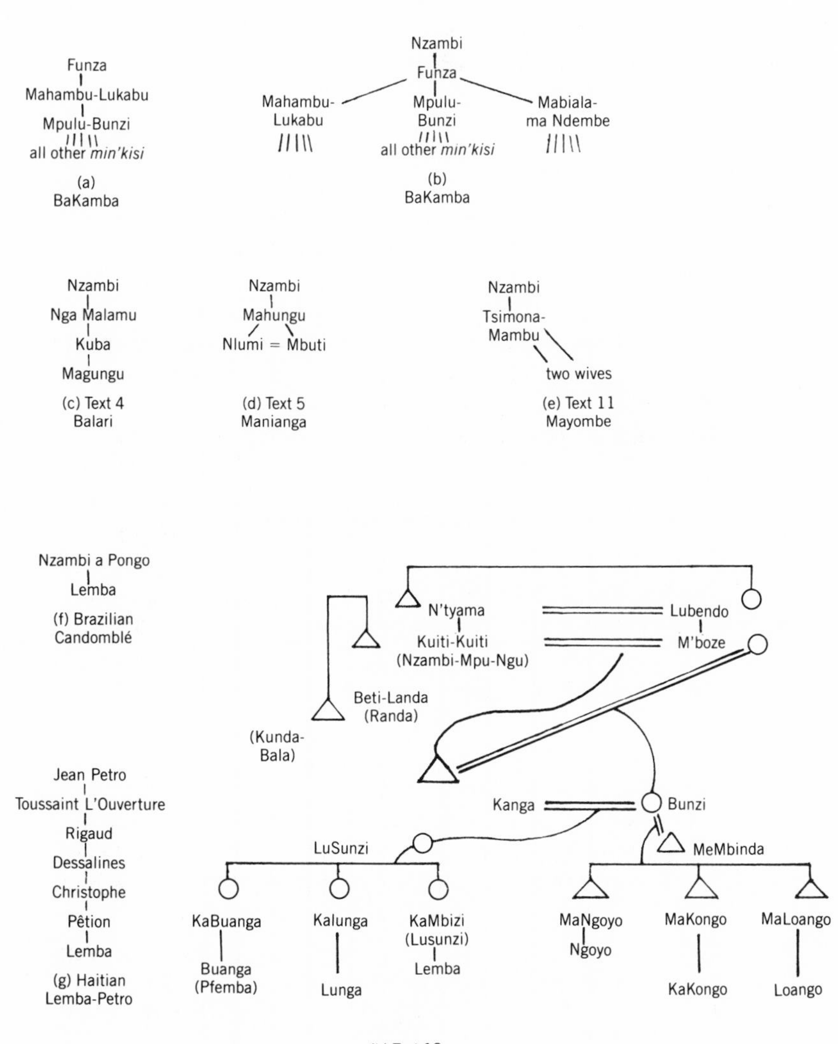

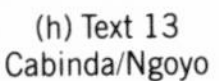
(h) Text 13
Cabinda/Ngoyo

The relational mode of authority is in *Lemba* and other charters often expressed as a marriage, out of which flow further qualities or heroic figures, emphasizing the complementarity of social and cosmic units. A series of original incestuous sibling/couples inhabits these myths, as is characteristic of many Bantu etiology myths. The most inclusive of these myths that includes *Lemba* comes from Cabinda, as told by the last court historian of Ngoyo.

Text 13

(1) The earth, sky, ocean and Nzadi river have always existed, and all that moves, moves in this framework. At the beginning of life, in Yalala Songo, a lake at the foot of the second cataract upstream on the Nzadi, there appeared the heads of the three god: Kuiti-Kuiti, most powerful of all, creator of all, master of the world, also named Nzambi Mpu Ngu, and Kisi-a-Nsi, earth god; at his right side appeared Bati Randa, also called Kunda Bala, ruler of animals with tails and their creator, who is in charge of rain and water; the third deity was M'boze, chieftess of prayer. At first they were one, but as they grew up they separated. The three gods take any form, preferably orphidic. Kuiti-Kuiti and his sister/wife take the shape of huge male and female serpents named N'Tyama and LuBendo. N'Tyama is the "stallion" of Kuiti-Kuiti, LuBendo the "mare" of M'Boze. Kuiti-Kuiti and M'Boze never separate, nor N'Tyama and LuBendo, their masters, twins who form whirlpools in the Nzadi.

(2) Kuiti-Kuiti went out with Bati Landa leaving behind M'Boze his wife with her son Kanga. When he returned he saw to his consternation that M'Boze was pregnant. He accused his son, who said his mother had enticed him. Kuiti-Kuiti killed them both in rage. While she was being murdered a deep fog settled over the world, and she bore a girl named Bunzi. Later Kuiti-Kuiti regretted his act of murder, and resurrected his sister/wife and son. Then he gave the new goddess Bunzi in marriage to Kanga, telling him to go away with her and never return. Kanga went to live at Nto on the right bank of the Nzadi; Bunzi upstream at Ne M'lao, Tchi-Sinda, near Banana.

(3) At Nto, Kanga had a large temple, six meters long and three wide, surrounded with fromagière trees. On a throne there was a cane of *m'bota* wood (which also could be found in the temple of

Lusunzi), ornamented with a buffalo tail and an ivory figure of Kanga. Kanga is invoked when rain fails to come because of sexual violations in the land.

(4) Kanga and Bunzi are the main gods of Ngoyo, their devotees giving pre-eminence to one or the other. They preside with their daughter, the mermaid LuSunzi, at the crowning of the MaNgoyo, king of Ngoyo. Bunzi, not wanting to be dependent on her father and mother, M'Boze and Kuiti-Kuiti, went out to Ne M'Binda, first man, and father of the triplet kings MaLoango, MaKongo, and MaNgoyo, receiving from him white chalk with which to consecrate the kings.

(5) Among the BaVili, Bunzi, tranquil, retiring, and moderately interested in affairs of the soil, is called mother of mermaid Tchi Kambizi, who is extremely violent like a soldier with arms, ready to fight to protect the authorities. She favors her friends, offering them money; she destroys her enemies. At Loango the tempests are attributed to her. At Ngoyo she is called LuSunzi (N'sunzi), who lives in a river of her name, the Tchi Buanga, matron of education.

(6) LuSunzi is a female with two faces, one white, the other black. Her body is similarly colored. From a distance, she is the color of fire. Nzambi Mpungu sent her to be married to Ma N'kakala. She is the legislator of men, who gives the laws of LuSunzi. At midnight she protests excesses of those who have her laws, telling her priests in each village to condemn or absolve them. She appears in dreams, revealing the reasons for her actions. She permits *kisi-ba-si* to represent themselves as living or dead; those *bakisi* who are her lieutenants, the *njimbe,* each take on the name of their genie, such as Bunzi, Tchi Sinda, Kanga. (Thus, the MaNgoyo became Njimbi Kanga a Nto.)

(7) LuSunzi created the cults: *Bingo (Buanga)* to distinguish and classify families; *Lemba,* to protect households; *Kalunga,* to confess sins between married spouses and to absolve them. She also instituted medicine doctors, diviners, talismen, funerary statues, to cure illness and reveal the hidden, and to protect against witches.

(8) Progeny are asked from *min'kisi Lemba, Kalunga,* and *Bingo (Mua Bua Nga). Lemba* is the spirit of peace, as its name indicates. In *Lemba*, Nzambi is asked, "Nzambi *Lemba*, give us fecundity." He guards us, and must be respected and obeyed.[11]

A number of modes of relationship are used to build this cosmological picture of complementary kingdoms and cults derived from Bunzi. Patron founder of the kingdoms is the first human MeMbinda, and of the cults, mermaid Lusunzi. Male and female are used here, as at every stage of the myth, to bridge contrasts. At first, in the myth's progression, these pairs are endogenous, incestuous, whereas in the later stages of the myth the differentiation grows, and exogenous pairs, even triads, are recognized. Other contrasting pairs of figures are noteworthy. Peace and violence appear to be brought together in related terms. Bunzi, who is calm, gives birth to LuSunzi, the violent one. Bunzi is an earth shrine of very general application. LuSunzi possesses men and provides laws with which to rule, and to maintain peace, whence the name *Lemba,* "calm," "peaceful." The myth also combines the successional mode of authority in the sequential pairs of sibling/couples and male/female dyads, while at the same time establishing sets of triple public structures in an intricate relational pattern of authority (for example, the cults to each other, the kingdoms to each other, the cults to the kingdoms). The Cabinda origin myth also addresses the problem of history as it was formulated earlier in this chapter. Human history, as distinct from the history of the gods and autochtonous creatures, begins with MeMbinda, father of the kingdoms. As in most Kongo origin myths, this one clearly differentiates series of beings: humans, ancestors, nonhuman creatures, plants, cosmological domains, and the like, and relates them according to several modes of association and succession. Whatever order emerges is not erroneous history, or the history of humans forgotten, but the resolution of human and cosmic dilemmas through analogy and metaphor, by transference to parallel domains. This chapter builds up the hypothesis that humanization and naturalization in myth and ritual are directly related to the perception of these dilemmas. What needs to be determined yet is under what conditions, and in what situations, humanization or naturalization of the discourse occurs.

Conjunctive and Disjunctive Mediation

An important feature of the lyrical in *Lemba* is the manner in which songs and origin myths diagnose characteristic human dilemmas and then offer the "*Lemba* solution." In foregoing chapters it has been suggested that heroes such as Mahungu and Tsimona-Mambu become, in these *Lemba*-related narrations (for example, Texts 5, 11), the masters of conjunctive mediation. Outside of *Lemba*, these heroes and others become involved in disjunctive or failed mediation. These concepts, loosely borrowed from structural analysis, need to be more sharply defined for purposes of the present study.[12]

The lyrics introduced above are replete with common problems of historical and present life in north-Kongo society. Some of these have to do with attitudes, rhetorical or surface problems, and confusions. There is the concern for barrenness (Text 1.46), for harassing spirits (1.21–5), pain (1.94), dreams, nightmares, and possession (9.8), for failure to return a borrowed tool that has been lost (7.5ff.), and other problems of daily life. Some of the trickster tales focus on another type of problem of daily life, that of misunderstandings, the consequences of which can be disastrous. Yet other facets of these same lyrical passages should be called structural analyses of deeper societal dilemmas, such as the consequences of wrong or inadequate political alliances in society (Texts 7–8, 11), the importance of following the counsel of ancestors and spirits, and being at peace with the supernatural (Texts 5, 11), and the great desirability of open relations between fathers and children (Texts 5, 8, 11).

A considerable degree of attention is given to formulating the negative side of these dilemmas, to narrating the confusing words and leading the character of the story through wrong action; or of developing at great length the antihero who embodies the negative values and traits. Some of this negativity, as the dilemmas which are embodied in the hero, is simply an inversion of the commonly understood social and cultural norm. Frequently the trickster Moni-Mambu is put into this role. Mahungu's characteristics differ from this, in that here he (it) is often cast as a dichotomized character type, whose two parts develop the polar implications of a dilemma, or the two roles in a relationship. Sometimes both parts will be "false" solutions (for example, Text 8, life with the python woman excludes life with father, and vice versa). At other times one will be victorious and the other defeated (for example, Text 7, one brother a slave, the other a master). There are here then a number of ways of formulating the negative, implying related ways of reaching solutions.

Some of the exaggerated negativity, particularly that having to do with misunderstood verbal instructions, has to do with a play on "comic" possibilities, ludicrous developments of horrors and errors setting the hero off from real life but reminding listeners of the dangers of ambiguous situations. The early Moni-Mambu, supposedly unaware of social syntax, is typically cast in these situations.

As soon as the trickster, or some other lyrical figure, becomes conscious of the syntax—the structure—and begins to manipulate it or be manipulated by it, the dilemmas are more serious and take on the aura of deeply heroic, religious, and tragic motifs. The conclusion of the myths, their denouement, may take several turns, conjunctive or disjunctive: bringing together the odds, resolving the dilemma, overcoming the contradiction; or being destroyed by the dilemmas, contradictions, and odds.

The figure who is cast as antihero, inverse of norms, may be reincorporated into society, redeemed so to speak. Mahungu as ogre-of-the-forest (Text 6) meets this kind of end when he is arrested and brought into civil society. Moni-Manbu as bringer of *Lemba* medicine is brought back into normal healthy life by his effective maneuvering of the satchel—and *n'kisi*—and his recognition by his father, God (Text 11). The conjunctive resolution of the dichotomous hero, such as Mahungu, may be seen in the reintegration of the two parts into one complementary whole (for example, male and female in marriage, Text 4, or perhaps the two brothers working out a complementarity as hunter and cultivator, superior and inferior mediator, in Text 7).

The disjunctive conclusion of these lyrical accounts makes the antihero, the inverse of the norm, into a victim who is killed by the forces of authority in society. Moni-Mambu in Text 12 picks up all the sins imaginable in Kongo society, from innocently misunderstanding instructions to consciously flaunting rules and conventions such as relating wrongly with his in-laws, to confusing codes of food, and to causing death and destruction around him. Perhaps he could be called a scapegoat figure,[13] but he is more the hero of tragedy in that his fate and character change when he becomes conscious of the contradictions in society.[14] In this he is different from the Greek tragic hero who is destroyed despite his ignorance of cosmic and social laws. The Kongo tragic hero is vindicated for his errors until he becomes aware of the laws, then he is punished for continuing mistakes that destroy others.

The disjunctive conclusion is somewhat different in the case of the dichotomous hero who embodies alternative possibilities in a dilemma. This type of hero, personified by Mahungu in the present study and in *Lemba*, seems always drawn beyond singular characterization to the dramatization of a relationship. His failure to develop such a relationship within his complementary facets (male/female, elder/junior), results in his destruction and death because of the paralysis arising from incompletion, as was true of Mavungu in Text 8 who went with the python woman and rejected his father. The hero of these types of disjunctive conclusion myths is closer to the Greek tragic hero. Mavungu of Text 8 is portrayed as if irrevocably bound to his decision, made at a time when he was a youth bored by life under his father's tutelage, unaware of the significance of adult exchange with his father. The tragic hero here may be characterized by his entanglement in circumstances and structures that lead him to a confrontation with disparate and irreconcilable alternatives and thereby to his own destruction.

It would be wrong and oversimplified to conclude here that *Lemba*'s therapeutic concept was, then, the fabrication of an image of society and personalities in which all dilemmas are somehow overcome through "the *Lemba* way" of doing things. It has been suggested that rising self-confidence characteristic of a bourgeoisie engenders a positive self-image, without an element of the tragic.[15] The elite status of *Lemba* might account for the absence of tragedy in the origin myths. But to stop here would be to ignore the significance of *Lemba*'s medicines and their ritual function, the subject to which I turn next.

Humanization and Naturalization of the Discourse

Bernard Dadié, the well-known African novelist, has stated openly what many observers of African cosmology and thought have suspected, namely that African fables about human-like animals are indeed commentaries about the human scene.[16] The material of the present study suggests that this process of substituting animals, or other dramatis personae, for real living human beings is a rather old practice. It is not just a literary convention for the purpose of amusing an audience but an integral necessity of life in a society where it is dangerous to speak openly of anger, conflict, power, and the other dilemmas of social structure. My explanation of *Lemba* medicines and their ritual function, deferred until here because of the complexity of the issue, is related to the naturalization of expression in those situations and at those moments when it is impossible to handle the discourse of human interaction by direct, verbal means. Moreover, I shall hypothesize that naturalization of the discourse between persons permits feelings and phenomena intrinsically muddled, contradictory, and many-sided to gain a more coherent understanding within a community. *Lemba*'s various modes of expressiveness, the domains studied in parallel, reflect a tendency to move the conscious, verbal narratives toward a positive, conjunctive resolution of characteristic dilemmas of social life—for example, patrilateral ties reinforced, marriage alliances strengthened, market trade encouraged, and so on—all the while the naturalized rituals of medicine "draw off" the dirty, contradictory, polluted, and evil aspects of the neophyte's illness.

Both the songs and the origin myths of *Lemba* demonstrate a certain tendency toward naturalization of imagery in those settings where negative ritual statuses are considered. The antelope's growth from fawn to adult is invoked as an appropriate analogy for the transition of the *Lemba* neophyte from harassed candidate to full and secure member (Text 1.21–5). Barrenness is spoken of in terms of a "field's barrenness," which will be made fertile (1.46). The transition from ritual death to resurrection in *Lemba* is described by referring to the movement of the sun (1.92–6). The incompetent orator is compared to the *nsibizi* rodent, whereas the effective orator, the *Lemba* advocate, is likened to *nkumbi* rat (Text 3). The palm of God is the natural object at the center of the separation of Mahungu male and female (Text 5), necessitating their efforts at thought and mediation. And, of course, the satchel of helpers is assembled by Tsimona-Mambu during his quest for relief for his wives and is unpacked and used during the various tests set up by a father reluctant to give his recognition (Text 11). In *Lemba*, however, the lyrical domain usually retains as its point of reference the humans who are in *Lemba*—father, son, wives, priests, priestesses—and their virtues. Passages of naturalization in the lyrical scores are fairly specific analogical metaphors to amplify the character traits of a specific affliction or adverse condition. This is possible, as suggested, because the full content of adverse emotions and perceptions is diverted to the medicinal ingredients, the nonverbal domains of expression.

In non-*Lemba* myths the naturalization of disjunctive passages is more pronounced. Semihuman characters such as the python-woman (mermaid?) make their appearance, or individuals become changed to animals or birds midway through the story. In the tale of Mavungu-son's marriage that will exclude exchanging with his father, the clue that this will be an impossible and tragic marriage is the woman's half-god or god-disguised identity. Mavungu-father's attempted mediation is signalled by stray pigs wandering from Mavungu-son's village, pursued by hunters, signifying an unconscious effort to accomplish the forbidden (Text 8).

The transformation of the hunted elephant with a spear in its side into a human sufferer (Text 7) represents a confirmation of the principle by negative example: humanization of the discourse. The successful mediator, Mavungu-spear-loser (elder), attempts to reconcile contrasting domains and follows his mystical guide obediently, thereby bringing the interaction of the two main characters to a human level. Mavungu-unsuccessful-mediator, his brother, again demonstrates the case of naturalization, in that his dilemma of the lost banana tree is not resolved but is transformed into a "bad trip" of hemp smoking, further transposing the discourse away from the open human level in the face of an impasse. The hunting scene with Moni-Mambu, tragic trickster, (12.7) illustrates the potential of naturalization in the face of disjunctive mediation. Attempting marriage but finding his wife hungry for meat, Moni-Mambu misses his game, destroys his in-laws' house, drops the axe into a river, and gets eaten by crocodile. The scene shifts to a drama between crocodile and hawk, the original hunter having become "hunted" game.

Much of this material deals with patrifilial and alliance relations because of such an emphasis in *Lemba*. However myths may be found in Kongo oral literature to reflect the matrilineage viewpoint. There, even more than in the present texts, naturalization of discourse imagery is used to mediate dilemmas. The Kuba-Ntu cycle, for example, describes the fate of a woman and her daughters and son when they discover that their oft-absent merchant father is really a witch wishing to sell them.[17] Kuba-Ntu the son by mistake breaks his father's powder box and is hidden in a tree by the mother. To avoid being trapped by the father, now disguised as a hunter (or in league with a hunter), the son transforms himself into a brightly-spotted guinea fowl which, on the day the father is selling the daughters at the market, drops feathers or bright beads to distract everyone and snatches his sisters away to safety. Another variant depicts the father, turned crocodile, seizing the daughters while they are fishing and keeping them in a cavern nearby where they are finally discovered by their bird-brother. In all variants the son succeeds in taking his mother and sisters to the safety of their maternal uncles' home, from where they initiate a legal suit against the father. In some variants he is accused of witchcraft and killed.

Of course, symbolic naturalization of dilemma situations is widespread in Central-African thought and verbal act, as well as ritual. If the foregoing examples represent attempts to discuss varieties of human experience, then it is true, as Dadié says, that fable-like transformations are made up in many instances of human relationships too volatile to discuss openly yet which require commentary. Also, belief in animals as witch's familiars, as in the father-crocodile example above, may prompt the choice of a particular animal. The transformation of discourse from explicitly human to veiled animal, like Bateson's understanding of redundancy in a noisy or clogged communications channel, permits discourse to continue even though troubled by conflict, anxiety, fear, jealousy, or other negative emotions.[18]

Naturalization of the discourse may also result from the ritual operator's or storyteller's desire to describe a human situation more cogently by invoking an image drawn from the world around him and known to everyone. For example, to contrast the fumbling *nsibizi* with the clever *nkumbi* and to identify *Lemba*'s rejoicing with the twitch of *nkumbi*'s whiskers charges the expression with nuances more vivid and lively than is possible in abstractions. The art of speaking in Kongo requires this sort of metaphor building. Moreover, ritual is based on the amplification of nonverbal metaphor. In *Lemba*, the music of chiming bracelets and throbbing drums as backdrop for the lyrics, as well as the totalizing statement of the medicines drawn from natural and human domains, together construct a universe of meaning that can readily objectify inchoate feelings of anxiety or ill. As Nietzsche noted in "The Birth of Tragedy," music—the nonverbal—could express the objectivity of the will itself "and therefore represent the metaphysical of everything physical in the world," far better than "unsupported word or image." Music created the tragic myth because it alone could penetrate to the real depths of a person's experience, "through annihilation and negation, so that he is made to feel that the very womb of things speaks audibly to him."[19]

Structure, Choice, and Medicine

Given, then, that naturalization of the discourse occurs in dilemmas of human experience and is used by metaphor-makers to focus or amplify their messages, is it possible to identify precisely the situations in which this naturalization occurs? Lévi-Strauss's early understanding of the logic of mythic discourse suggested that it provided a manner of resolving a cultural contradiction through metaphoric "templates" each slightly different from the previous one.[20] This characteristic of myth would explain the transfer of the father-son conflict over control of the daughters (sisters) in the Kuba-Ntu cycle to the plane of the bird-crocodile drama within natural cosmological parameters. Lévi-Strauss did not at first find the context of such metaphoric mediations within social life; rather, he found it in the oppositions created by the "savage"—human—mind. He was criticized for this apparent confusion of "structural oppositions" and "contradictions." Burridge, for example, has defined a contradiction as alternative, goal-oriented activities or processes which effectively and simultaneously negate each other.[21] "Life" and "death" are alternatives, meaning either to be alive or to be dead. Later Lévi-Strauss revised the notion of mythic mediation to include the "symbolic," the "imaginary," and the "real,"[22] suggesting that some oppositions might stem from structures of classification such as earth/sky, birds/reptiles, and the like, but that others might be based upon contradictions within the structures of society and cultural values. For Burridge, true contradictions could only occur in dramatic situations in recognizable historic events. That is, they must be based upon alternatives between which an actor must choose. Thus Burridge injects into the analysis of myth structure the concrete terms of given historic moments as well as the structure of ideology.

Such moments of choice in the face of alternatives constitute in Kongo society the context of metaphorization of the discourse. Judicial palaver (*nsamu*) may well be the prototypical context for this. When antagonists become uncomfortably alienated from one another, a third party or two spokesmen take up their causes. In the negotiations that ensue, they invoke songs, proverbs, and other rhetorical devices. Up to a point these techniques examine evidence and probe possibilities for conciliation. The texts examined in this work show moments like this, as for example when the trickster (in Texts 11 and 12) is judged for having killed. A chief or judge decides the matter, and the decision of guilt or innocence is final. However, it is in the portrayal of irreconcilable alternatives such as that which the python-woman presents Mavungu (Text 8) that we find naturalized metaphors.

Examination of *Lemba* lyrics suggests that recourse to naturalized metaphors may also have to do with the psychological process of drawing a sufferer/neophyte out of an intractable personal dilemma. A framework for analysis of this process is lent by Lacan's interpretation of psychoanalytic processes as applied to language.[23] The frequency in *Lemba*-related lyrics of dreams, visions, nightmares, and possession (see Texts 1.18, 1.45, 1.115, 7.13–16, 8.4–6, 9.5–7) indicates the presence of a mode of image association Lacan would call "the sliding of the signified under the signifier," in which a hidden message is postulated because of the mystification of the subject.[24] In Kwamba's report (Text 1) on the *Lemba* initiation, repeated reference is made to a hidden referent or signified force such as that which is "given and taken away" by *Lemba*, that which "falls in the water when the payments are made," or that which "dies and laughs with the dogs." These lyrics, like many types of divination, float an image which will "catch" the subject's perception of his condition.

Another psychodynamic process may be identified in the *Lemba* attempt to construct a metaphor of parallel expressive domains once an appropriate image is discovered for the affliction or its cause. Often one domain or point of reference in the metaphor is the hidden force or referent in the life of the neophyte, and the second point, to which the first is associated, is drawn from nature, resulting in such constructs as, "What *Lemba* given, *Lemba* takes away; what the sun given, the sun takes away." Signifiers which stand in a relationship of near similarity are "piled up" until their common point of reference, the hidden referent, is made clear. This symbolic process is sometimes called condensation.[25] Its role in the psychodynamics of *Lemba* healing appears to be that of attaching the presumed affliction to a set of symbolic anchors so that it may be more effectively "moved" in the subject's life.

A third type of process in the psychological effect of the metaphor seen in *Lemba* is the "displacement" of signifier to signified, which Lacan speaks of as the "veering off of meaning" from one object or person to another, comparable to the action in grammar of the transitive verb in getting the noun to influence the object.[26] *Lemba* lyrics such as "that which was the fawn, is today the grown antelope" (1.21), or "that which was barren . . . has become fertile" (1.46), or "that which was a 'stitch' of pain, has become the path to the priesthood" (1.94), take one quality or entity and transform it into a related, different member of the same class. The series of naturalizing allusions to spirits, plants, animals, and cosmological spaces serve to bring movement into the neophyte's or the neophyte couple's status. Evidence from other drums of affliction suggests that this is the way they too use ritual metaphor.

In transferring the image of conflict, contradiction, and evil "down" to natural metaphors, *Lemba* was able to emphasize a lyrical, verbal consciousness of positive mediation. The conscious image of positive mediation was clothed through the ideal roles of the *Lemba* Father, the culture-hero trickster, or the androgynous hero who invented marriage. Simultaneously the natural metaphors were made to draw away from the neophyte couple all the dirt, evil, pollution, and contradiction. This activity was absorbed by *Lemba*, and apotheosized through identification with a mythic hero or ritual object like the *n'kobe*. Personal and social contradictions once contained in this manner became "powers" (*makundu*) in the rule of *Lemba* and its image of an ideal society.

It should by now be apparent how *Lemba* healed, and why it was heuristically advantageous to adopt a model of analysis which identified distinctive expressive domains, each with its own codes and characteristics of discourse. This image of an ideal society and a therapeutic ideology may be spelled out even more explicitly, drawing from pronouncements by *Lemba* adherents, early ethnographers, and recent interpreters of this major drum of the Congo region.

Chapter 10

The Ideology of *Lemba* Therapeutics

In this chapter I shall consider the evidence for an explicit *Lemba* theory of therapeutics. In the previous chapter it becomes clear how *Lemba* ritual and thought manipulated symbolic frameworks to put forward a coherent lyrical or verbal picture of human society—the *Lemba* model—transferring downward into nonverbal symbols the negative and contradictory where it became sacralized and powerful "medicine." The task of this chapter is to engage in a somewhat hypothetical conversation with *Lemba* priests and priestesses over the conscious mission they had. Texts presented in this work and other sources give localized and historically specific versions of this *Lemba* consciousness. Interpretations since *Lemba*'s demise by scholars, both African and non-African, are almost as localized and time-specific. It is the role of the historian and the ethnologist to take all such evidence and extrapolate from it a synthesized consciousness, theory, or ideology from which to make sense of the institution.

The Affliction and its Etiology

Probably all *Lemba* adherents would agree that *Lemba* was a "drum of affliction." It was spoken of as an *n'kisi* whose rituals were drummed up with its unique hand-held instrument (*ngoma* or *nkonko*). In earlier chapters, the indigenous theory of drums of affliction was spelled out in terms of public, corporate, sacred medicines. In one region of the Lower Congo/Zaire, such drums were devoted to clan leadership, chiefship, water spirits, judicial affairs, and order in markets and public sites (the case of *Lemba*).[1]

A more difficult to understand aspect of *Lemba* therapeutics has been the conception of the affliction it was intended to treat. Particular symptoms designated as the "*Lemba* illness" vary greatly. Thus one finds a host of physical symptoms mentioned such as "evening fever" (Text 3.2), "chest cough, stitch, or breathing with difficulty," or other respiratory ailments (1.1), sterility of self or spouse,[2] "swollen stomach" (10.22), and the like. Other accounts offer psychosocial afflictions such as "spouse's infidelity" (10.31–4;1.105ff.), dreams or nightmares of *Lemba* ancestors or authorities (1.18;9.7), hallucinations and outright possession by "*Lemba* spirits" (9.7,9.20). Several writers attribute to *Lemba* panacean claims of universal healing. The European version of this notion attributes to *Lemba* even the ability to heal the "incurably ill"![3] The African version of this is that *Lemba* deals with all afflictions of the abdomen, head, heart, and sides, that is to say, the whole person as defined by Kongo thought (10.10). Specific afflictions such as these no doubt originate in personal accounts of individuals having been treated by *Lemba*, but they convey far too particularistic and individualistic a view of *Lemba*'s orientation. They originate in second- and third-hand accounts quite removed from *Lemba*'s therapeutic consciousness and distantly removed from any sense of *Lemba*'s ideology of healing.

Closer to *Lemba*, and even among *Lemba* adherents, one still finds particularistic notions of a "*Lemba* illness," such as one priest's view that *Lemba* dealt with persons who had experienced a miraculous cure from an incurable disease[4] and was a type of votive offering by the neophyte to the power that had cured him.

Kongo authors of the past twenty years who have sought to clarify this aspect of the *Lemba* affliction have tended to argue that there was no single, specific *Lemba* illness. Ngoma, for example, in his dissertation on Kongo initiation, suggests that a variety of illnesses, indeed any illness, could precipitate the curative stages entailed in a *Lemba* initiation.[5] The duration of the cure would be determined by the wealth of the candidate. Malonga and Mampuya agree with Ngoma that there was no specific *Lemba* affliction. However they shift the perspective of the question around to make the entire therapeutic symbolism of the initiation an artifact of *Lemba*'s explicit approach to social control. In Malonga's view the manifestation of one or another affliction was a shrewd feigning of illness proposed by the *Lemba* Father. With the help of a diviner treatment or pretreatment might induce a skin rash or other symptoms which the full therapy then pretended to relieve. *Lemba* afflictions were thus "iatrogenic" elements in the maintenance of *Lemba*'s public posture.[6] Mampuya is harshly critical of *Lemba*, suggesting that this sickness induced in the neophyte, whether through psychical manipulation or through outright mystical threat, served only the "antisocial" ends of coercion and exploitation. Malonga, however, respectfully calls this aspect a feature of the major "social institution"—the government—of the region, echoing Munzele's view that *Lemba* integrated "markets, villages, and people,"[7] or echoing that of a *Lemba* wife that *Lemba* was "a medicine of government," or that of a clan head that it was the "government of multiplication and reproduction."

Although the scholarly views of Ngoma, Malonga, and Mampuya thus reflect an understanding of *Lemba*'s function which corresponds to the views of others close to *Lemba*, they still fall short of comprehension of the nature of *Lemba*'s ideology of affliction and therapy. All three scholars, as well as Fukiau whose work on *Lemba* has been reviewed extensively in Chapter 6, portray *Lemba* as it was in the early colonial era: an institution losing its control of resources and influence. Only the primary texts in the catechists' accounts, written early in the twentieth century, offer a glimpse of what must have been an earlier, more characteristic picture of *Lemba* therapeutics.

Konda, in Text 8 (Chapter 7), offers a remarkable picture of the *Lemba* affliction. *Lemba* may be "aroused" (*komwa*) through dreams of *Lemba* ancestors, nightmares of suffocation, or outright possession. These modes of affliction are sometimes accompanied, he notes, by blockage of speech requiring therapeutic "loosening," or "opening." Bittremieux's depiction of *Lemba* priests as reflected in their names suggests that they were persons driven, even obsessed, with success in trade, influence, and public prestige.[8] Konda, of all writers, comes closest to relating the affliction to this reputation of *Lemba* adherents and aspirants for seeking wealth and influence. He suggests that the force emanating from the ancestors to make one wealthy and influential will also make one sick unless one is somehow protected. The therapy for this affliction is appropriately first a confession by the sufferer of blocked speech revealing what he has seen in dreams and nightmares, followed by the prescribed rituals of marriage and massive redistribution of goods to his patrifilial children and other bystanders.

This view of *Lemba*'s affliction corresponds to what is known of the historic surroundings of *Lemba* adherents. They were wealthy (or wealth acquiring) and influential merchants, judges, healers, diviners, and chiefs. Frequently they were at the head of slave segments of clans. Their alliances to other clans, consecrated in *Lemba*, constituted a network of sociopolitical relationships across a vast region, in particular where the inland routes of the international trade required some form of social control. Such wealth and influence as this brought introduced strong currents of envy and jealousy into the small-scale clan communities, touching off in the minds of these wealthy and influential persons such symptoms as dreams, nightmares, fears of sorcery attack, sterility, death, and a host of other specific symptoms. It is thus not wrong to identify specific symptoms such as cough, respiratory troubles, headaches, and other psychic afflictions as "*Lemba* afflictions," if they are seen as deriving from the vulnerable condition of the influential in a society with a strong egalitarian ethic. The *Lemba* affliction is seen then as a psychic or physical symptom of vulnerability and marginality among the influential in a society with a normative ideology emphasizing egalitarian authority and redistributive economics.

The Therapy

Lemba's therapy followed from such a conceptualization of the *Lemba* affliction. The *Lemba* sufferer, having perceived either his "calling" to gain wealth or his marginality and vulnerability before his kinsmen or the loss of his productive base in his natural clan community and household, wanted to gain adherence to the corporate body which could protect him. A variety of tests were administered to such a candidate. Was he really a capable, influential person? Then let him pay huge fees or find the patronage to do it for him. Did he have strategic alliances with other clans? Then let him identify the wife or wives who with their clans would undergo the *Lemba* marriage sanctifying this alliance. Was he torn apart by fear of sorcery directed against him and his offspring? Then he must take medicine of purification to find a new integration above and beyond the divisive forces that threatened to destroy him. Let him dedicate his household(s) to *Lemba* so that they could continue to have children and survive into the next generation. Was the candidate indulging in antipublic, prima-donna rhetoric with his speaking skills and his talents for curing or trading? Then he must by all means be "drafted" or even harassed into *Lemba* circles so his influence would not tear asunder the regional social fabric.

Lemba initiatory therapy moved the influential but vulnerable sufferer into a course of greater self-awareness and social responsibility. The symbolism of the *Lemba* initiation came to grips with massive contradictions, working them out in the aura of *Lemba*'s greater coherence as expressed in the etiology myths. For example, the envy, greed, and destruction seen to accompany irresponsibly held wealth was neutralized in the *Lemba* medicine, while the generosity of the feast served notice that the neophyte was after all concerned with his dependents' welfare. In several local variants, as has been shown, the neutralizing, purifying power of white chalk (*luvemba*) was combined with food and excrements and sometimes the body parts—hair, nails—of the *Lemba* members. As the neophyte moved into the protective sancity of *Lemba* and was made to distribute massive amounts of his wealth so that others might feast, his own food consisted mainly of chalk, excrements, and token bits of real food.

At the same time as such social contradictions were transferred to nonverbal ritual objects in food, medicine, and the permanent mementos of the *n'kobe* shrine, mythic heroes in the etiological narratives—trickster, androgynous demigod, earth deity, ancestor—were made to iron out all these dilemmas and contradictions, thereby constructing a conscious, positive ideological unity. As with most public ideologies, this perfected version of the institution stands at odds with the actual lives of individuals.

At *Lemba*'s end in the colonial era, with a strong lingering memory of wealth and influence but with few remaining goods to distribute, *Lemba*'s "lies and exploitation" as Mampuya calls them[9] may have well been very far from the institution's earlier self-image. W.H. Bentley, a pioneer British missionary, wrote that in "the 1860's *elembe* was a word that filled people with fear. The cry '*elembe edio*' (this is *Lemba*) would stop a caravan in its path and make it submit to capture, robbery, and death without a struggle. . . . It is difficult to understand why the word had such an effect, but many who knew the '*elembe* period' as it was called have told the same story. It was shockingly abused and made the means of much violence and robbery."[10] But here too there is evidence of second- and third-hand anecdotal information about *Lemba* in its latter phases, succumbing to the disintegrative influences of the late, coastal slave trade.

The Virtuous Society

It is important to press the inquiry of a conscious therapeutic ideology of *Lemba* further, to the point of asking what may have been the *Lemba* ideology of health? That is, what was *Lemba*'s "theory" of social order, of the good life, and of the ideal person? A major institution which prevailed over so vast a region for three centuries leaves its mark on public consciousness. It must have a notion of the virtuous society. This notion is made up of a specific model of society—a conscious set of alternatives—in this case arising from an acephalous, segmentary society in which problems of trade and authority needed to be dealt with.

It must have been an item of *Lemba* theory to identify the natural base of power in the society—the talented orator, the skilled merchant, the able healer, and so on—and to bring such persons together into *Lemba*'s ranks. Many informants tell of *Lemba*'s character criteria of clarity, gracefulness, integrity, and the like. Malonga notes that *Lemba* arrogated to itself all knowledge in Lari society through techniques of spying and information sharing.[11] On this basis it was able to maintain order in a society lacking centralized institutions of law, police, and taxation. Its governmental methods were derived from this need to keep abreast of the real basis of legitimacy. For this reason there is recurring mention of the membership of slaves in *Lemba*. In contrast, a hereditary aristocracy would have had to maintain control by means of institutional centralization.

Because of the integral role of trade in the regional economy, *Lemba*'s self-concept included an elaborate code of market and trade-route behavior. The marketplaces became the nodes of economic interaction, as well as the sites for the execution of criminals. *Lemba* priests, as trade and market police, were said to enjoy immunity from tariffs and seizure of the entire region. Economic life and public order were thus conceptually joined.

Emphasis on trade and regional social order merged in another feature of *Lemba*, the initiation marriage. The importance of alliances between prominent clans has been frequently mentioned. It may be noted here that marriage and the protection of the *Lemba* household were central in the ritual symbolism and in explicit prohibitions binding priest and priestess. The importance of strong alliances was grounded in symbols of purity in the *Lemba* marriage. This is so striking that observers of the highly moral tone of *Lemba* marriages have suggested influence from eighteenth-century Christian missionaries. However, similar marital conservatism among coastal nobility and royalty in the sixteenth and seventeenth centuries makes it altogether probable that this emphasis was internal and indigenous, growing out of the keystone role of marriages to the social order. In some places in the Nsundi and Bwende regions (the Manianga), the emphasis on alliances bears a very specific ideological label, the "reciprocal blood" marriage. Usually embodied in a patrilateral, cross-cousin marriage, this reciprocation in an alliance requires a male to return, in his marriage, the descent substance received from his father's lineage. An alliance of the reciprocating type combines the emphasis on marriage with that on patrifilial continuity. This special understanding of social order, often found in communities of the *Lemba* region, thus possessed not only a territorial component but also a long-term, temporal component.

This temporal continuity contained in the diachronic structure of reciprocal marriages between exogamous clans is also the model of the religious hierophany. Just as the father-child dyad embodies the *Lemba* master-neophyte relationship of continuing spiritual power (*kundu* or *kitswa*), so it serves as the model of relationships between major spiritual beings and lesser, and between these and medicines via the human priests who convey their power to human society. Patrifiliality in *Lemba* was the relational metaphor of all ascending and descending pairs in the religious hierophany.

There is no doubt, therefore, that the *Lemba* therapeutic ideology was a model for a fully-formed social state. That it was realized to a great degree in the form of a drum of affliction surprises only those who have failed to take Central-African society on its own terms.

Chapter 11

Conclusion: What Were the Questions?

The immediate aim of this work has been to elucidate the emergence, duration, and decline—the life cycle—of a major drum of affliction in the hope of better understanding this important genre of African therapeutic institution. Because the drum (*ngoma*) combines features often kept discrete in Western institutional perception—healing, politics, commerce, marriage—it has been necessary to show how these features articulated in an original manner. Once this was done, a second aim could be addressed: whether the drum of affliction in general, and *Lemba* in particular, is a reflection of the socioeconomic order or whether, in striving to resolve certain dilemmas and contradictions in that order, it actually shapes society in a unique way. In other words, is the drum of affliction an independent or a dependent variable of social change?

The first part of the work consisted in a reconstruction of the economic, political, and social history of the Malebo Pool-Cabinda-Loango triangle. This exercise, a regional history which needed to be written, showed the interdependent character of the well-known states of the area—Loango, Kakongo, Ngoyo, Nsundi, Kongo, Tio—as well as the less-well-known cults and shrines. In analytic language this history of the *Lemba* region demonstrated the interlinked corporate structures of local landed estates, the large-scale polities, and the movable corporate estates. The same interdependence characterized the relationship of the local economic base to the international trade. In other words, local, regional, and international economies were definitely found to intersect one with the other, just as was true of the "economy" of power symbols and medicines. In all of this *Lemba*, the major transcending institution of the region from the seventeenth century to the twentieth century, apparently played the key role of creating a ceremonial context for the economy of trade to mesh with the economy of agricultural production, and a context in which to generate medicinal symbolism to assuage the lives of those at the intersection of the two economies.

The second part of the work was devoted more pointedly to *Lemba* rituals and to the study of their variations along the lines of differential corporate structures of the region. Going beyond a good measure of free variation in *Lemba*'s ritual style, there was evidence of a correspondence between the rites of *Lemba* as a portable medicine shrine and the long-distance overland trade, on the one hand, and between *Lemba*'s fixed shrines on the Loango coast and the endpoint of the trade, on the other hand, where the brokerage role of a sedentary commercial elite in touch with European traders was a determinant.

At another level the *Lemba* rituals of therapy functioned to address a concern for the protection of *Lemba* members and their households from the envy of others and for relief from symptoms of such envy and the social precariousness accompanying it, for example, dreams, nightmares, possessions, and a range of physical symptoms such as "stitch in the side." *Lemba*'s therapeutic functions went beyond the individual and the household to the society at large where an effort was made at restructuring social relations. Ceremonial goods were distributed to the neophyte priest's dependents; stable alliances were created and legitimated; a new reality was forged through hero narratives which resolved some otherwise implacable dilemmas of the prevailing culture. These narratives deserve closer attention here.

The significance of the resolution narratives of *Lemba* lies not so much, however, in particular outcomes as in the way the mode of narrative used in *Lemba* therapy contrasts with other types of problem-resolution efforts, particularly those offered by the creation, or attempted creation, of new polities, especially centralized state-like regimes. There is widespread evidence of experimentation in the creation of institutions, especially coastal institutions, in the centuries surrounding *Lemba*, institutions that vary from centralized mini-states to alliance networks and ritual movements. In other words it is apparent that *Lemba* might have been displaced or replaced by the creation of another kind of institution. Thus it is significant that inhabitants of the region made a selective choice for the kind of public order that emerged, that, instead of imposing a new order to deal with the coastal trade which resembled a state, they developed a solution to the challenge of trade which emphasized the redefinition of reality in therapeutic terms. There are important implications in this for the writing of intellectual history, very much a concern among Africanists.[1]

It is important to explore beyond historical "solutions" offered by institutions and their ideologies to discover the problems or dilemmas they were intended to resolve, and to discern the way a society imagined alternatives open to itself and the consequences of such alternatives if taken. A brief allusion to a comparative setting will emphasize the approach I have tried to follow. In a recent work on the origin of the "political" in ancient Greece, Christian Meier suggests that the recognition of alternative courses of action in the Athenian polity was greatly enhanced by the public arena of the theaters, especially the tragic theaters. Public funds were expended on playwrights who were invited annually to produce new dramas. They often took story material from Greek mythology and legends which they then reshaped into commentary on contemporary (fifth century B.C.) life in Athens and the surrounding region. Thus arose a keen appreciation for tragedy, which spelled out the consequences of courses of action around the family, the polity, and the individual in relationship to the gods and the forces of fate.[2]

The task of the third part of this present work has been to identify comparable settings or idioms in which alternatives, contradictions, and ambivalences were raised and dealt with, an analytic course which is imperative if one wants to explain the emergence of a distinctive institution such as a major drum of affliction, or for that matter of a state or any other institution that alters the texture of society. The questions raised by Part III suggest that one can identify traces, vestiges, of the perceived purpose of *Lemba*. Text 8, for example, shows Mavungu moving through the alternatives open to any individual coming to terms with the coastal trade, a situation which certainly provoked debate and questioning. Mavungu is lured to the "city at the coast" (8.16) where there are "whites" and "great wealth" in the "ships." However the same text goes on to show how Mavungu believed he needed to exchange his newly-earned wealth with his father and other kin. The dilemma of accumulation versus exchange is however couched in terms of conventional alliance versus identity, thus pitting marriage and affluence against patrifilial relations. This "tragic" exclusion of one of two idealized goals is accounted for in terms of the seductive lure of the "Mammy-Water" like female embodied in the serpent, but the conscious formulation of alternatives and consequences in connection with the trade is clear. Other narratives (Text 7, for example) speak of social cleavages in society or the dangers of ambiguous language (Texts 9–10). The point at issue here is that we can best compare attempted resolutions of these dilemmas, contradictions, and alternative courses of action in terms of the backdrop of implicit and explicit formulations of their extreme, that is tragic, consequences. It is safe to assume that without a cultural awareness of such alternatives no solution of any kind would be attempted.

The therapeutic rites and associated etiological narratives record in much greater detail the attempted solutions of various dilemmas, contradictions, and alternative courses of action. I have shown that with the help of separate "expressive domains" an ideology of health is promoted at the level of verbal narrative. This is, as I have shown, more than a denial or sublimation of the contradictory. As close study of the "medicinal" code shows, a great deal of symbolic tension is present between the dilemma-negating narrative and the other levels where an all-out program is involved in harnessing, capturing, or containing the power of the "illness." Through a paradigmatic shift from the "human" to the "natural" the power of the illness is transformed into the power of the priesthood, recalling recent biofeedback experiments designed to give a patient a visual concept of his affliction so as to gain mental, emotional, and, one hopes, physiological control over it.

Whether a given drum of affliction in the Central-African setting is then a dependent or an independent variable of social change and all its forces of contradiction can only be answered once the questions which become the grounds for attempted solutions are elucidated, including a variety of rituals that pour answers into the questions as well as a variety of efforts to impose new orders of institutions such as the centralized state. In Greek antiquity such questions had to do with the freedom of the individual in the face of impersonal fate. In Kongo during at least part of the era of the great trade such questions had to do with the accumulation of wealth and influence in a society of egalitarian expectations, the protection of the individual engaged in commerce, his relationship to his kin, and the creation of a regional institution alongside local clans and dependents. Greek society thought out its alternatives and their consequences in the tragic theater and acted on them through a form of participatory democracy. Kongo society thought out its alternatives in legends, dreams, and in affliction etiologies and acted on them in a therapeutic-alliance-trading association. There is no doubt that *Lemba* shaped the public order, although by no means all medicines did so or may be expected to.

Notes, Sources, Index

Notes

Chapter 1

1. De Jonghe wrote widely on African religion and ethnology, and his views on "secret societies" and ethnological theory are found condensed in the following works: *Les sociétés secrètes au Bas-Congo* (Bruxelles, 1907); "Les sociétés secrètes en Afrique," *Semaine d'Ethnologie Religieuse* Ser. 3 (1923); "Formations récents de sociétés secrètes au Congo Belge," *Africa* 9, no. 1 (1936): 56–63. Unless otherwise indicated, the review of works is drawn from De Jonghe's 1923 article.

2. H. Schurtz, *Altersklassen und Männerbünde* (Berlin, 1902).

3. S. Freud, *Totem and Taboo* (New York, 1950). See especially the introduction for explicit mention of this influence.

4. W. Wundt, *Völkerpsychologie*, 10 vols. (Leipzig, 1910–20).

5. A. Kuper, *Anthropologists and Anthropology: The British School 1922–72* (New York, 1973), p. 24.

6. J. Frazer, *The Golden Bough*, 2 vols. (London, 1890); *Totemism and Exogamy*, 4 vols. (London, 1910).

7. A. Van Gennep, *Les rites de passage* (Paris, 1909).

8. L. Frobenius, *Die Masken und Geheimbünde* (Halle, 1898).

9. K. Laman, *The Kongo, III* (Uppsala, 1962), p. 67.

10. F. Gräbener, "Kulturkreise und Kulturschichten in Ozeanien," *Zeitschrift für Ethnologie* 37 (1905): 84–90.

11. De Jonghe, *Les sociétés secrètes au Bas-Congo*.

12. De Jonghe, "Les sociétés secrètes en Afrique."

13. De Jonghe, "Formations récents de sociétés secrètes."

14. J. Van Wing, *Etudes BaKongo* (Bruxelles, 1959), pp. 426–508.

15. L. Bittremieux, *La société secrète des Bakhimba au Mayombe* (Bruxelles, 1936).

16. V. Turner, *Drums of Affliction* (Oxford, 1968), p. 15.

17. Certainly E.E. Evans-Pritchard's classic *Witchcraft, Oracles, and Magic among the Azande* (Oxford, 1937) set the tone for recognition of a system of explanation of misfortune and the means of dealing with it. Recent regional studies in Bantu-speaking Africa that illuminate the general lines of this system include the following: from Tanzania, M.L. Swantz, *Ritual and Symbol in Transitional Zaramo Society* (Uppsala, 1970); from Uganda, J. Orley, "African Medical Taxonomy," *Journal of the Anthropological Society of Oxford* 1, no. 3 (1970): 137–150; from Zimbabwe, G.L. Chavunduka, *Interaction of Folk and Scientific Beliefs in Shona Medical Practices* (London, 1972); from South Africa, H. Ngubane, *Body and Mind in Zulu Medicine* (London, 1977); from Western Zambia, G. Prins, "Disease at the

Crossroads: Towards a History of Therapeutics in BuLozi since 1876," *Social Science and Medicine* 13B (1979): 285–315, and W.M.J. Van Binsbergen, "Regional and Non-Regional Cults of Affliction in Western Zambia," in R.P. Werbner, ed., *Regional Cults* (London, 1977), pp. 141–175; from Western Congo (Zaire), J.M. Janzen, *The Quest for Therapy in Lower Zaire* (Berkeley, 1978), and Janzen, "Ideologies and Institutions in the Precolonial History of Equatorial African Therapeutic Systems," *Social Science and Medicine* 13B (1979): 317–326. For an essay that seeks to describe the historical subcontinental system, see W. DeCraemer, J. Vansina, and R. Fox, "Religious Movements in Central Africa," *Comparative Studies of Society and History* 18 (1976): 458–475.

18. I am drawing these phrases from my own work, but they appear in most of the above-mentioned publications, frequently using the very same cognates from region to region.

19. The phrase is drawn from Y. Kusikila, *Lufwa evo Kimongi e?* (Kumba, 1966), published in English translation in J.M. Janzen and W. MacGaffey, eds., *Anthology of Kongo Religion* (Lawrence, 1974), pp. 48–55, although the idea is widespread in Bantu Africa.

20. These terms are drawn from Kongo, although the verbal stem of *n'ganga* appears across the entire Bantu-speaking region, as do other terms associated with the therapeutic system under consideration. M. Guthrie's *Comparative Bantu*, 4 vols. (Hants, 1967) is an important reference for tracing the distribution of verbal concepts connected with this system.

21. Janzen, *The Quest for Therapy*, 1978.

22. Prins, "Disease at the Crossroads," has demonstrated the effectiveness of this approach in reconstructing intellectual history. Long-term surviving values and categories, amidst changes, indicate for him the "core" of a culture. He has used therapeutics as such a barometer of Lozi culture in the long term in his historical study *Hidden Hippopotamus* (Cambridge, 1980).

23. Nsemi, "Min'kisi: Sacred Medicines" in Janzen and MacGaffey, *Anthology of Kongo Religion,* pp. 34–38.

24. This is especially true of the work in Werbner, *Regional Cults*, and is exemplified in Werbner's introduction, pp. ix–xxxviii.

25. Ibid. Werbner bases his analytical perspective on regional cults in large measure on V. Turner, "Pilgrimages as Social Process," Chapter 5 in his *Dramas, Fields, and Metaphors* (Ithaca, 1974), p. 185.

26. Turner, "Pilgrimage as Social Process," pp. 185ff.

27. Werbner, *Regional Cults*, p. ix.

28. Van Binsbergen, "Regional and Non-Regional Cults," pp. 141–175.

29. J.M. Schoffeleers, "Cult Idioms and the Dialectics of a Region" in Werbner, *Regional Cults*, pp. 219–239.

30. J. Vansina, *The Tio Kingdom of the Middle Congo, 1880–1892* (Oxford, 1973), pp. 221–243.

31. K. Garbett's "Disparate Regional Cults and a Unitary Ritual Field in Zimbabwe" in Werbner, *Regional Cults*, pp. 55–92, is an exception to

this. Garbett, in his analysis of the Mutota cult of Zimbabwe, develops a clear picture of several cults interpenetrating in a single region. Alongside the centralized, hierarchic ancestor cults he finds other nonhierarchic and territorially undefined cults (p. 58).

32. Werbner, *Regional Cults*, pp. xvii–xxii.

33. Van Binsbergen, "Regional and Non-Regional Cults," p. 144.

34. B.T. Van Velzen, "Bush Negro Regional Cults: A Materialist Explanation," in Werbner, *Regional Cults*, pp. 93–116.

35. Ibid., p. 94.

36. K. Burridge, *New Heaven, New Earth* (Toronto, 1969), says that millenarian activities provide a test case in social analysis for the joining of statements valid for both participants and investigator. "Beyond their intrinsic human interest . . . millenarian activities constitute an acute theoretical challenge. They invite a statement through which particular actions and rationalizations may be given a more general validity" (p. 2).

37. C. Geertz, in "Religion as a Cultural System," in M. Banton, ed., *Anthropological Approaches to the Study of Religion* (New York, 1966), cites Santayana to the effect that "any attempt to speak without speaking any particular language is not more hopeless than the attempt to have a religion that shall be no religion in particular. . . . Thus every living and healthy religion has a marked idiosyncracy" (p. 1).

38. T.O. Ranger, "Healing and Society in Colonial Southern Africa." Unpublished MS, 1978.

39. J. Vansina has developed models of state formation specific to the Tio and Kuba kingdoms in his *The Tio Kingdom*, and in *The Children of Woot: A History of the Kuba Peoples* (Madison, 1978).

40. J. Goody, in his *Technology, Tradition, and the State in Africa* (London, 1971), develops an analysis of state formation for Africa. He acknowledges the importance of Southall's concept of the "segmentary state" in which central and local powers have equal weight, a condition that has often arisen as larger empires or states disintegrate (pp. 9–10). For reasons of technological small scale in food production (the use of the hoe rather than horse- or ox-drawn plow), Goody rejects a "feudal stage" in state formation for most of West and Central Africa, arguing instead for a variety of historical types: the hereditary structuring of ritual powers; the ability to attract and keep a following (privileged descent groups); conquest; diffusion of the institution and idea of a state; the emergence of a central state from a nucleus in lineages, age sets, cult associations, and other institutions in acephalous society; in opposition to slave raids; or the need to move trade goods across long distances occupied by peoples lacking chiefs (pp. 12–18). Goody would then concur, perhaps, that it is difficult, even unnecessary, to make a sharp distinction between "state" and "cult," and that either can fulfill the functions of centralized or regional institutions.

41. J. Miller, in his *Kings and Kinsmen: Early Mbundu States in Angola* (Oxford, 1976), has reviewed models of state formation in Central

Africa, arguing that generally "state" institutions are created in response to the need and desirability of contact between unrelated lineages. Relationships created are by definition political. They may come about in one or several of the following ways: to control scarce but valuable resources such as salt, iron and copper ore, or trade advantages; military or strategic advantage; as innovations capable of attracting manpower, for example, the Mbundu and Imbangala *kilombo* war camp, a converted initiation camp used to overcome particularistic loyalties of descent groups; ideological innovation relating to large-scale institutional integration; the assistance of outside allies; the control of commercial monopolies such as those taken over by so-called "broker states" like Angola, between Kasanji and Portugal and Brazil; agricultural surpluses, a necessary but not sufficient factor in state formation; technological superiority; and individual genius. Most of these factors could be cited as elements in the emergence of *Lemba*, suggesting the pitfalls of reading into a combination of them any teleological tendency to political consolidation.

42. L. de Heusch, in "Structures de réciprocité et structures de subordination," in his *Pourquoi l'épouser?* (Paris, 1971), has studied the Nyimi (kingship) institution among Bushong peoples—Kuba, Lele—and has suggested that centralized "statehood" is but a variation of several possibilities found throughout the cluster of Bushong peoples. This leads him, in the explanation of state formation, to emphasize a rather willful historical event such as the murder of a kinsman, the act of royal incest, or similar break with the past, to destroy the "structure of reciprocity" having existed in a society and to establish in its place a "structure of subordination." This sheds much light on transformations of authority symbolism in the *Lemba* region and related centralized systems. Extensive experimentation occurred to reach appropriate combinations of "subordination" and "reciprocity."

43. H. Maine, *Ancient Law* (London, 1917).

44. M.G. Smith, *Corporations and Society* (London, 1974).

45. W. MacGaffey, "The Religious Commissions of the BaKongo," *Man*, n.s. 5, no. 1 (1970): 27–38; "Corporation Theory and Political Change," in S. Newman, ed., *Small States and Segmented Societies* (New York, 1976), pp. 121–138; "Economic and Social Dimensions of Kongo Slavery," in S. Meirs and I. Kopytoff, eds., *Slavery in Africa: An Historical and Anthropological Perspective* (Madison, 1977), pp. 235–257.

Chapter 2

1. H. Koch, *Magie et chasse au Cameroun* (Paris, 1968).

2. C. Droux and H. Kelly, "Récherches préhistoriques dans la région de Boko-Songho et à Pointe-Noire (Moyen-Congo)," *Journal de la société des Africanistes* 9 (1939): 71–87.

3. P. Martin, *The External Trade of the Loango Coast, 1576–1870* (Oxford, 1972), p. 57.

4. *Globus* (1876), p. 307. Ambriz alone exported 185 tons of ivory in 1874, at 150 pounds per tusk, which represented 1295 elephants that year.

5. E. Dupont, *Lettres sur le Congo* (Paris, 1889), p. 340.
6. Ibid., p. 345.
7. H.M. Stanley, *Through the Dark Continent* (London, 1877), p. 182.
8. Kwamba, *Text 1* (Chapter 4, below), line 68.
9. Dupont, *Lettres sur le Congo*, pp. 338–339.
10. J. Vansina, *The Tio Kingdom of the Middle Congo, 1880–1892* (London, 1973), p. 326.
11. Martin, *The External Trade*, p. 57.
12. Ibid., p. 59.
13. Vansina, *The Tio Kingdom*, p. 282.
14. Ibid., p. 326.
15. Ibid., p. 287.
16. Martin, *The External Trade*, p. 106.
17. Ibid., p. 94.
18. Ibid., p. 86.
19. Ibid., pp. 113, 107.
20. Ibid., p. 107.
21. Vansina, *The Tio Kingdom*, p. 448.
22. Martin, *The External Trade*, pp. 113–114, 132. See also W. Randles, *L'ancien royaume du Congo* (Paris, 1968), p. 203, for similar figures.
23. Vansina, *The Tio Kingdom*, p. 304; P. Bohannan, "The Impact of Money on an African Subsistence Economy," *Journal of Economic History* 19, no. 4 (1959): 491–503.
24. Vansina, *The Tio Kingdom*, pp. 288–292.
25. M. Soret, *Les Kongo Nord-Occidentaux* (Paris, 1959); G.P. Murdock, *Africa, Its People and their Culture History* (New York, 1959); J. Maes and O. Boone, *Les peuplades du Congo belge* (Bruxelles, 1935).
26. Stanley, *Through the Dark Continent*, p. 183.
27. Martin, *The External Trade*, p. 123.
28. Dupont, *Lettres sur le Congo*, pp. 330–340.
29. The intellectual source of this simplistic notion of homogeneous ethnicity is the "culture-area" (*Kulturkreis*) school inspired by Gräbener, Wissler, Frobenius, and perhaps Murdock. Lacking in understanding of the dynamics of social organization, the adherents of this approach map out cultural units on the basis of features such as language, dialect, or material culture affixing them to a given territory. By definition, a culture area defined by its most "characteristic" elements or complex of elements is therefore "pure." An improvement in the Africanist literature is the work of Baumann and Westermann of the so-called "historical" school. In their maps and ethnographies, one can note the superimposition of one identity over another, the accretion within a population of successive historical trends and polities. See H. Baumann and D. Westermann, *Les peuples et civilisations de l'Afrique* (Paris, 1967).

30. H. Deleval, "Les tribus Kavati du Mayombe," *La Revue Congolaise* 3 (1912): 34.

31. E. de Cleene, "Les chefs indigènes au Mayombe," *Africa* 8, no. 1 (1935): 63–75; Deleval, "Les tribus Kavati," p. 33; L. Bittremieux, "Un vieux chef," *Missions en Chine, au Congo, et aux Philippines* 6 (1909): 121–123.

32. Vansina, *The Tio Kingdom*, on the Tio *ndzo*.

33. P.-P. Rey, "L'esclavage lignager chez les tsangui, les punu et les kuni du Congo-Brazzaville," in C. Meillassoux, ed., *L'esclavage en Afrique précoloniale* (Paris, 1975), pp. 509–528. Rey's approach to defining the levels of Kunyi organization concentrates on the large territorial estate (*mukuna*) comparable to the *nsi*. However, because he is interested mainly in the visible unit of production, the lineage (*diku*), ignoring other levels of categorial classification, he is led to make the statement that the clan (*ifumba*) may span ethnic boundaries of such peoples as the Kunyi, Tsangui, and Punu which are therefore presumably territorial and discrete. This approach stops short of solving problems inherent in the view of one ethnic unit seen as territorially discrete.

34. W. MacGaffey, "Economic and Social Dimensions of Kongo Slavery," in S. Meirs and I. Kopytoff, eds., *Slavery in Africa: An Historical and Anthropological Perspective* (Madison, 1977), p. 243.

35. M. Gluckman, *The Ideas in Barotse Jurisprudence* (New Haven, 1965), pp. 88–90.

36. Foremost is C. Lévi-Strauss's classic, *Les structures élémentaires de la parentée* (Paris, 1949).

37. De Cleene, "Les chefs indigènes," pp. 63–75; Deleval, "Les tribus Kavati," pp. 34–36.

38. See for example Martin, *The External Trade*, pp. 3–5, who reviews the sources.

39. A. Battel, "The Strange Adventures of Andrew Battel," in J. Pinkerton, ed., *A General Collection of the Best and Most Interesting Voyages and Travels in all Parts of the World* (London, 1814), p. 331.

40. J. Cuvelier, "Traditions Congolaises," *Congo* 10, no. 1 (1931): 203.

41. Ibid.

42. Battel, quoted in Martin, *The External Trade*, p. 19.

43. A. Bastian, *Die Deutsche Expedition an der Loango-Küste*, 2 vols. (Jena, 1874), p. 238.

44. C. Tastevin, "Idées religieuses des indigènes de l'enclave de Cabinda," *Etudes missionaires* (1935), pp. 105–111, 191–197, 257–273.

45. Martin, *The External Trade*, pp. 24–25, 162.

46. Bastian, *Die Deutsche Expedition*, p. 327.

47. F. Hagenbucher-Sacripanti, *Les fondaments spirituels du pouvoir au royaume de Loango* (Paris, 1973), p. 21.

48. Martin, *The External Trade*, p. 121.

49. R. Visser, "Der Kaufmann unter Wilden (Entwicklung des Handels am Kongo)," *Jahresbericht des Naturwissenschaftlichen Vereins zu Krefeld* (1907–8), pp. 59–60.

50. Deleval, "Les tribus Kavati," p. 33.

51. De Cleene, "Les chefs indigènes."

52. L. Bittremieux, *Mayombish Idioticon* (Gent, 1923), map.

53. De Cleene, "Les chefs indigènes"; A. Doutreloux, *L'ombre des fétiches* (Louvain, 1967), pp. 176–208.

54. Bittremieux, "Un vieux chef."

55. Martin, *The External Trade*, p. 168.

56. A. Proyart, "Histoire de Loango, Kakongo, et autres royaumes d'Afrique," in Pinkerton, *A General Collection of... Voyages*, p. 579.

57. Hyacinthe de Bologne, *La pratique missionaire des PP. Capucins Italiens dans les royaumes de Congo, Angola et contrées adjacents* (Louvain, 1931), pp. 102–103.

58. Ibid., pp. 109–110.

59. Ibid., p. 118.

60. Suggested by L. Bittremieux in his *Société secrète des Bakhimba* (Bruxelles, 1936), p. 187.

61. Deleval, "Les tribus Kavati," p. 147.

62. O. Dapper, *Umständliche und Eigenliche Beschreibung von Afrika* (Amsterdam, 1670), p. 536.

63. Ibid., pp. 534–535.

64. Ibid., pp. 535–537.

65. In addition to Bastian, *Die Deutsche Expedition*, the Loango expedition was published in P. Güssfeldt, J. Falkenstein, and E. Pechuel-Loesche, *Die Loango Expedition 1873–6* (Leipzig, 1879), and in E. Pechuel-Loesche, *Volkskunde von Loango* (Stuttgart, 1907).

66. Pechuel-Loesche, *Volkskunde von Loango*, p. 380.

67. Ibid., pp. 383–384.

68. Ibid., p. 382.

69. Bastian, *Die Deutsche Expedition*, pp. 162–163.

70. Ibid., p. 163; Pechuel-Loesche, *Volkskunde von Loango*, p. 381.

71. Pechuel-Loesche, *Volkskunde von Loango*, p. 385.

72. R. Lehuard, *Les phemba du Mayombe* (Paris, 1977).

73. Bastian, *Die Deutsche Expedition*, p. 164.

74. Pechuel-Loesche, *Volkskunde von Loango*, p. 374.

75. Ibid., p. 377.

76. Güssfeldt, et al., *Die Loango Expedition*, p. 71.

77. Bastian, *Die Deutsche Expedition*, pp. 170–173.

78. Vansina, *The Tio Kingdom*, pp. 439–443.

79. Ibid., pp. 323–324.

80. Ibid., p. 330.

81. Ibid., p. 331.

82. Ibid., p. 332.

83. Ibid., p. 396.
84. Ibid., p. 384.
85. Ibid., p. 456.
86. Ibid.
87. Ibid., p. 324.
88. Ibid., p. 326.
89. J. Van Wing, *Etudes Bakongo* (Bruxelles, 1959), Map I.
90. Ibid.; J. Vansina, *Kingdoms of the Savanna* (Madison, 1965), p. 236; J. Cuvelier, *L'ancien royaume de Congo* (Bruxelles, 1946), Map I.
91. Vansina, *Kingdoms of the Savanna*, Chapter 3.
92. Montesarchio, in Cuvelier, *L'ancien royaume de Congo*, pp. 298–299.
93. Ibid., Map I, and Montesarchio's list, p. 301.
94. K. Laman, *The Kongo II* (Uppsala, 1957), pp. 140–142.
95. Ibid.
96. W. MacGaffey, *Custom and Government in the Lower Congo* (Berkeley, 1970).
97. Cuvelier, *L'ancien royaume de Congo*, p. 304.
98. Vercraeye, Dossier No. 129, Luozi Territorial Archives, 31 Aug. 1932.
99. Bittremieux, *Mayombish Idioticon*; K. Laman, *The Kongo I* (Uppsala, 1953), Chapter 1; Maillet, Luozi Territorial Archives, n.d.
100. Maillet, Luozi Territorial Archives.
101. Ibid.
102. Ibid.
103. Ibid.
104. *Rapport annuel Affaires Indigènes et Main d'Oeuvre*, "Etat d'esprit de la population," Luozi, 1938.
105. J. Munzele, *Bakulu Beto ye Diela Diau* (Kumba, 1965), p. 12.
106. Pierre Nzuzi of the Kimbanga clan of Kisiasia, Luozi Territory, narrated this to me in 1969.
107. Munzele, *Bakulu Beto*, p. 19.

Chapter 3

1. E. Dupont, *Lettres sur le Congo* (Paris, 1889), pp. 330–340.
2. C. Coquery-Vidrovitch, *Le Congo au temps des grandes compagnies concessionnaires, 1898–1930* (Paris, 1972), p. 187.
3. O. Stenström, "The Lemba Cult," *Ethnos* (1969), pp. 1–4.
4. *Reports*, Luozi Territorial Archives, 1930.
5. L. Bittremieux, *Van Een Ouden Blinden Hoofdman* (Antwerpen, 1925).
6. J. Ndibu, Notebook 345, Laman Collection, Svenska Missionsforbundet, Lidingö, n.d.

7. For example the introduction to J.M. Janzen and W. MacGaffey, *Anthology of Kongo Religion* (Lawrence, 1974); and Janzen, "Deep Thought: Structure and Intention in Kongo Prophetism, 1910–21," *Social Research* 46, no. 1 (1979): 106–139.

Introduction to Part II

1. V.W. Turner, "Colour Classification in Ndembu Ritual," in M. Banton, ed., *Anthropological Approaches to the Study of Religion* (New York, 1966), pp. 47–84; A. Jacobson-Widding, *Red-White-Black as a Mode of Thought* (Uppsala, 1979).

2. For present purposes, V.W. Turner's *Drums of Affliction* (Oxford, 1968) is the leading example of this approach in the area of African therapeutics. More generally, C. Geertz's work on religion as a symbol system characterizes it, as for example in his "Religion as a Cultural System" in Banton, *Anthropological Approaches to . . . Religion*, pp. 1–46. This approach is given historical depth and critical justification in J.L. Dolgin, D.S. Kemnitzer, and D.M. Schneider, eds., *Symbolic Anthropology* (New York, 1977).

3. C. Geertz, "Deep Play: Notes on the Balinese Cockfight," *Daedalus* 101, no. 1 (1972): 1–38.

4. C. Geertz, *The Social History of an Indonesian Town* (Cambridge, 1965), pp. 153–202.

5. V.W. Turner, *Revelation and Divination in Ndembu Ritual* (Ithaca, 1975).

6. V.W. Turner, *Dramas, Fields, and Metaphors: Symbolic Action in Human Society* (Ithaca, 1974).

7. See Turner, *Drums of Affliction*, and accounts of the Isoma and Wubwang'u rituals among the Ndembu in Turner, *The Ritual Process* (Chicago, 1969).

8. Turner, "Symbols in African Ritual," in Dolgin, et al., *Symbolic Anthropology*, pp. 183–194.

9. Exemplified in R.P. Armstrong, *The Affecting Presence* (Urbana, 1971); but see also J. Fernandez, "Persuasions and Performances: Of the Beast in Every Body . . . and the Metaphors of Everyman," *Daedalus* 101, no. 1 (1972): 39–60.

10. I am thinking primarily of the work of C. Lévi-Strauss, *La pensée sauvage* (Paris, 1962); *Mythologiques, I–IV* (Paris, 1964–71); and that of P. Maranda and E. Köngäs-Maranda, eds., *Structural Analysis of Oral Tradition* (Philadelphia, 1971).

11. D. Sperber, *Rethinking Symbolism* (Cambridge, 1974); also Fernandez, "Persuasions and Performances."

12. Primarily I have in mind the semiotics of R. Barthes as formulated in *Système de la mode* (Paris, 1967), or his literary essays such as *S/Z*

(Paris, 1970), with its emphasis on levels or codes, and the relationship between these codes, although I am aware of the theoretical sophistication of C.S. Peirce's much earlier work.

13. G. Bateson, *Steps to an Ecology of Mind* (New York, 1972), and E. Leach, *Culture and Communication: The Logic by which Symbols are Connected* (Cambridge, 1976), are two examples of the kind of work I have in mind.

14. An issue raised by most of the above writers and resolved or formulated in a great diversity of ways too involved for further discussion in this study.

Chapter 4

1. Text 1 by E. Kwamba is taken from Notebooks 142 and 143, dated about 1910, of the Catechists' Cahiers section of Karl Laman's collection in the Svenska Missionsforbundet Archives (SMF), Lidingö, Sweden. Parts of the full text presented here have appeared in English in Laman, *The Kongo III* (Uppsala, 1962), pp. 113–116, and in J.M. Janzen and W. MacGaffey, *An Anthology of Kongo Religion* (Lawrence, 1974), pp. 97–102.

2. Text 2 by M. Lunungu is drawn from Notebook 181 of the Laman Collection, SMF, Lidingö, and may be dated at about 1915.

3. I have elsewhere discussed the origin and fate of this extensive KiKongo corpus: see my "Laman's Kongo Ethnography: Observations on Sources, Methodology, and Theory," *Africa* 42, no. 4 (1972): 316–328. When Laman returned to Sweden in 1919 with the notebooks, they provided him with the basis in idioms and vocabulary to produce his masterful *Dictionnaire KiKongo-Francais* (Bruxelles, 1936). He also translated (into Swedish) passages on Kongo custom using categories of his original questionnaire, selecting from the notebooks what he regarded as most representative and best written. Posthumously, Laman's Swedish text was translated into English, under the direction of S. Lagerkrantz, and published in the Studia Ethnographica Uppsaliensia series as *The Kongo I–IV* (Uppsala, 1953, 1957, 1962, 1968). Fortunately scholars of Kongo and Central-African studies have had access to these English sources although they have been difficult to work with because of the lack of reference in them to place, context, and authorship. Also, some of the materials having gone through double translation have lost their original meaning or have become very elliptical. The reader may wish to compare Kwamba's original text on *Lemba* given here with the version offered in Laman, *The Kongo III*, pp. 113–116.
Lunungu's description of *Lemba* (Text 2) has not been published anywhere to my knowledge.

4. R. Rappaport, *Pigs for the Ancestors* (New Haven, 1968).

5. For such a rewriting, used as partial model in this work, see A. Dundes, E. Leach, P. Maranda, and D. Maybury-Lewis, "An Experiment: Suggestions and Queries from the Desk, with a Reply from the Ethnogra-

pher," in P. Maranda and E. Köngäs-Maranda, eds., *Structural Analysis of Oral Tradition* (Philadelphia, 1971), pp. 292–324.

Chapter 5

1. Kimbembe, Notebook 80, Laman Collection, Svenska Missionsforbundet (SMF), Lidingö, ca. 1915.
2. O. Stenström, "The Lemba Cult," *Ethnos* (1969), pp. 37–57.
3. E. Andersson, *Contribution à l'ethnographie des Kuta I* (Uppsala, 1953), pp. 247–249.
4. J. Malonga, "La sorcellerie et l'ordre du Lemba chez les Lari," *Liaison* 62 (1958): 45–49; 63 (1958): 51–61.
5. Ibid., p. 53.
6. Ibid.
7. Ibid., p. 59.
8. Ibid., p. 60.
9. Ibid., p. 54.
10. J.M. Janzen, *The Quest for Therapy in Lower Zaire* (Berkeley, 1978), pp. 196–203.
11. Malonga, "La sorcellerie et l'ordre," p. 61.
12. M. Douglas, *Purity and Danger* (New York, 1966).
13. Stenström, "The Lemba Cult," p. 38.
14. Ibid., p. 41.
15. Malonga, "La sorcellerie et l'ordre," pp. 54, 61; also, V. Turner, "Colour Classification in Ndembu Ritual," in M. Banton, ed., *Anthropological Approaches to the Study of Religion* (New York, 1966), pp. 47–84; Fukiau, *N'kongo ye Nza/Cosmogonie-Kongo* (Kinshasa, 1969), pp. 35–39.
16. Stenström, "The Lemba Cult," p. 41.
17. Malonga, "La sorcellerie et l'ordre," p. 61.
18. Ibid., p. 55.
19. Ibid., p. 56.
20. Stenström, "The Lemba Cult," p. 44.
21. Malonga, "La sorcellerie et l'ordre," pp. 59–60.
22. Andersson, *Contribution*, pp. 247–248, based on notes taken 1930–31 at Madzia from Milonga Jean and Muyakidi, at Musana from Masamba Philippe and Ngusa Ruben, a Lali. It is noteworthy that this origin account traces *Lemba* to a founder with the "Nga" title, similar to most of the Teke *nkobi* holders.
23. Stenström, "The Lemba Cult."
24. Ibid.
25. Ibid.

Chapter 6

1. Fukiau, *N'kongo ye Nza/Cosmogonie-Kongo* (Kinshasa, 1969).
2. Batsikama ba Mampuya, "A propos de 'la cosmogonie Kongo,'" *Cultures au Zaire et en Afrique* 4 (1974): 239–264.

3. Solomo Nitu, noted storyteller and catechist of Cabinda, narrated these Mavungu texts (5, 6, 7) to Charles Harvey in 1961 at the age of 75 years. I am indebted to Harvey for recording Nitu's narrative treasure as well as for the generosity of allowing me to use them here. Nitu lived in the village of Masala, near the Portuguese administrative post of Luadi, also near the mission of M'boku, on the banks of the Mbika River, in the so-called Zala area, in tall forest country.

4. Fukiau, *N'kongo ye Nza*, pp. 41–56.

5. Ibid., p. 47, my translation.

6. Ibid., p. 46.

7. Ibid., p. 50.

8. Ibid., p. 43.

9. Ibid.

10. Ibid.

11. Ibid., pp. 43, 49.

12. K. Laman, *Dictionnaire KiKongo-Francais* (Bruxelles, 1936).

13. Fukiau, *Nkongo ye Nza*, pp. 18–21.

14. Batsikama, "A propos . . . Kongo," pp. 250–252.

15. Fukiau, *N'kongo ye Nza*, pp. 19–21.

16. Nitu, Text XXIIIa, MS.

17. Nitu, Text XXXIX, MS.

18. Nitu, Text XLIV, MS.

19. J. Malonga, *La légènde de M'pfoumou ma Mazono* (Paris, 1954).

20. C. Lévi-Strauss, "The Structural Study of Myth," *Journal of American Folklore* 67 (1955): 428–444.

Chapter 7

1. J. Konda, Notebook 119, Laman Collection, Svenska Missionsforbundet (SMF), Lidingö, ca. 1915.

2. T. Babutidi, Notebook 16, Laman Collection, SMF, Lidingö, ca. 1915. This account of a *Lemba* initiation is identified as having occurred at Mamundi, "westward of Kinkenge." I have been unable to locate this site exactly, but Kinkenge is at the boundary of the Yombe area, therefore I have identified it as Eastern Mayombe. Parts of this text have been published in K. Laman, *The Kongo III* (Uppsala, 1962), p. 116.

3. L. Bittremieux, *Mayombsche Namen* (Leuwen, 1934), pp. 41–42.

4. Ibid., p. 41.

5. Paul Güssfeldt, Julius Falkenstein, and Eduard Pechuel-Loesche, *Die Loango Expedition, 1873–6* (Leipzig, 1879), p. 71.

6. A. Bastian, *Die Deutsche Expedition an der Loango-Küste*, 2 vols. (Jena, 1874), pp. 167, 169.

7. L. Bittremieux, *Van Een Ouden Blinden Hoofdman* (Antwerpen, 1925), pp. 31–34.

8. Based on Belgian Colonial Ministry economic reports on the Bas-

Congo, in *Congo* (1925), II, pp. 651–676; (1928), p. 691; (1929), II, pp. 714–726; (1932), II, pp. 293–313.

9. Bastian, *Die Deutschen Expedition*, vol. I, p. 258.

10. Bittremieux, *Mayombsche Namen*, pp. 42–44.

11. A. Jacobson-Widding, in her *Red-White-Black as a Mode of Thought* (Uppsala, 1979), pp. 250–251, makes much of the discrepancy between the "white" name Mpemba *Lemba* and the "red" *tukula* ingredients in Babutidi's report, from which she is working in Laman's Kongo ethnography, possibly without realizing it. She relates this to her theory of the need to reconcile what she speaks of as the "inner" with the "outer" man, and with the "matrilineal principle of inheritance of male characteristics." Unfortunately, this elaborate theory is based on the perpetuation of a simple phonetic error by Babutidi who, not being a *Lemba* initiate, confused *pfemba* or *phemba* for *mpemba*. The same mistake was made by Lehuard, and before him by Maes, and before him by Bastian and Pechuel-Loesche. Bittremieux's research (see note 12 below) and circumstantial evidence in Lehuard's monograph and in Pechuel-Loesche's account of *n'kisi Phemba* permit a correct interpretation.

12. Bittremieux's original research on the distinction of *pfemba* (or *phemba*) and *mpemba* is reported in unpublished letters written in 1939 to the then director of the Musée d'Afrique Central, at Tervuren, J. Maes, from Kangu where he had collected two *nkobe Lemba*, including the one sketched in figure 21 and pictured in plates 5–7.

13. E. Pechuel-Loesch, *Volkskunde von Loango* (Stuttgart, 1907), p. 385.

14. R. Lehuard, *Les phemba du mayombe* (Paris, 1977), is an excellent presentation of this sculptural genre, except for the confusion of *mpemba* with *phemba*, which I have discussed at greater length in my review of this monograph in *African Arts* 11, no. 2 (1978): 88–89.

15. J.M. Vaz, *Filosofia Tradicional dos Cabindas* (Lisboa, 1969). Figures 30, 103, 140, 142, 143, 160, 187–A, 199, 216, 230, and 242 show *Lemba* as a drum in the company of other *min'kisi*, including *Mbondo-Fula*, *Mbonzo*, *Mikono*, *N'kobe-Ibingu*, *Nkwangi*, *Koko*.

16. Lehuard, *Les phemba du mayombe*, p. 87.

17. Vaz, *Filosofia Tradicional*, fig. 187. See also L. Bittremieux, *Symbolisme in de Negerkunst* (Brussel, 1937), Object 112, for a discussion on *Mbondo-Fula*.

18. W. Dionga, narrator of "Tsimona-Mambu, de Wonderziener of de Oorsprong van het huwelijk bij Dilemba, naar een Mayombsche legende," in L. Bittremieux, *Congo* 2 (1926): 398–404; 551–6. English translation of this tale appears in J.M. Janzen and W. MacGaffey, *An Anthology of Kongo Religion* (Lawrence, 1974), pp. 102–106.

19. This summary is based on J. Van Wing and C. Schöller, "Les aventures merveilleuses de Moni-Mambu le querelleur," in their *Légendes des BaKongo orientaux* (Louvain, 1940), pp. 11–44, which is a heavily

edited Kongo narrative for school children based on an earlier text published in KiKongo, circulated in ca. 1935, itself transcribed from an unknown narrator. I have not been able to find the KiKongo original, but it was retold by A.-R. Bolamba as "La légende de Moni-Mambu chez les BaKongo," in *Arts et metiers indigènes* 9 (1938): 17–19. I have added Bolamba's episode 8 to the Van Wing and Schöller version since it was apparently in the original KiKongo. Other accounts, much shorter, were given by Jules Benga and Pierre Ndakivangi, as "Mumboni-a-Mpasi, celui qui avait beaucoup de palabres," *Arts et metier indigènes* 9(1938): 20–21.

20. For a general analysis of the genre and an anthology of examples, see W. Bascom, ed., *African Dilemma Tales* (The Hague, 1975). Locally, in North Kongo, they are called *ngana zakindembikisa*, a collection of which is available in J. Bahelele, *Kinzonzi ye ntekolo'andi Makundu* (Matadi, 1961), pp. 36–38.

21. P. Radin, *The Trickster: A Study in American Indian Mythology* (New York, 1956).

22. L. Makarius, "Ritual Clowns and Symbolic Behavior," *Diogenes* 69 (1970): 67; also, R.D. Pelton, *The Trickster in West Africa* (Berkeley, 1980), offers a similar but more extensive analysis of the trickster in four West-African traditions.

Chapter 8

1. A. Ramos, *O Negro Brasileiro* (Rio de Janeiro, 1934), p. 106, partial translation by Roberto Fiorillo. The reference to the priest's smoking recalls *Lemba* pipes from Loango and reference to smoking in the Mavungu legends (Texts 7–8).

2. Ibid., Chapter 4, "Os cultos de procedencia Bantu," pp. 99–135.

3. M. Herskovits, *The Myth of the Negro Past* (Boston, 1958), p. 84.

4. R. Bastide, *African Religions of Brazil* (Baltimore, 1978), p. 196.

5. E. Carneiro, *Negros Bantús* (Rio de Janeiro, 1937).

6. In addition to Herskovits, *Myth of the Negro Past*, see his *Dahomey: An Ancient West African Kingdom* (New York, 1938); and *Life in a Haitian Village* (New York, 1937).

7. R. Bastide, *Le candomblé de Bahia (rite Nagô)* (The Hague, 1958); and Bastide, *African Religions of Brazil.*

8. R.F. Thompson, "Transatlantic African Art Traditions," MSS 1975, 1977; and Thompson, "The Flash of the Spirit: Haiti's Africanizing Vodun Art," in Ute Stebich, ed., *Haitian Art* (Brooklyn, 1978), pp. 26–37.

9. R.F. Thompson, *Black Gods and Kings* (Los Angeles, 1971).

10. Bastide, *African Religions of Brazil*, p. 195; O. Dapper, *Umständliche und Eigenliche Beschreibung von Afrika* (Amsterdam, 1670), pp. 534–537.

11. Thompson, "The Flash of Spirit," p. 26.

12. A. Métraux, *Black Peasants and Voodoo* (New York, 1960).

13. Ibid., p. 14.

14. J. Price-Mars, "Lemba-Pétro, un cult sécrèt," *Revue de la société haitienne d'histoire, de géographie, et de geologie* 9, no. 28 (1938): 12–31.

15. Ibid., pp. 18–19.

16. Ibid., p. 19.

17. Ibid., pp. 19–20.

18. Ibid.

19. H. Chatelein, *Folk-tales of Angola* (Boston and New York, 1894), p. 11.

20. A. Métraux, *Voodoo in Haiti* (New York, 1959), p. 86.

21. Thompson, "The Flash of Spirit," pp. 26–27.

22. Herskovits, *Life in a Haitian Village*, pp. 154–176.

23. Ibid., pp. 164–165.

24. It would be tempting, both on grounds of terminological similarity and of functional resemblance, to suggest an association between Bosu of the Haitian rite and Boessi-Batta of the Loango coast and Cabinda cosmologies and rites (see Chapter 2). The latter included components of the domestic realm and the wild or the beyond, as represented in the trade. There is also in Boessi-Bata's ritual, as reported in Dapper, *Beschreibung von Afrika*, pp. 534–537, a divinatory process which identifies the subject's needs through the ecstasy of the officiating priest. This same dualism of the domestic realm and of the beyond is present in nineteenth-century Cabinda figures M'boze, female domestic personage, and Beti-Randa, male, keeper of the wilds, the two being mediated by Kuiti-Kuiti (also known as Nzambi-Mpungu), as recorded by C. Tastevin, "Idées religieuses des indigènes de l'enclave de Cabinda," *Etudes missionaires* 3 (1935), no. 1, 105–111; no. 2, 191–197. However, if Bosu is to be identified with Boessi-Bata or M'boze it would mean either some resemblance between the Fongbe (Dahomean) and Kongo deities, or a conjuncture in Haitian thought of the two. What is striking is Bosu's presence in the *Pétro* (or Congo) set of deities in the Haitian rite.

25. Price-Mars, "Lemba-Pétro," pp. 12–31.

26. This translation of Price-Mars's 1938 text is published in Métraux, *Voodoo in Haiti*, p. 307.

27. An interpretation given by Métraux, *Voodoo in Haiti*, p. 307.

Chapter 9

1. C. Kerenyi, "Prolegomena," in C. Jung and C. Kerenyi, eds., *Essays on a Science of Mythology* (Princeton, 1969), pp. 1–24.

2. W. MacGaffey, "The Religious Commissions of the BaKongo," *Man* n.s. 5, no. 1 (1970): 27–38.

3. A more extended discussion of this process in Kongo culture structure is found in J.M. Janzen and W. MacGaffey, *Anthology of Kongo Religion* (Lawrence, 1974), pp. 87–89.

4. L. Frobenius, *Die Masken und Geheimbünden* (Halle, 1898), Part II.

5. K. Laman, *The Kongo III* (Uppsala, 1962), p. 67.

6. L. Bittremieux, *La société sécrète des Bakhimba* (Bruxelles, 1936), p. 67.

7. J.-F. Thiel, *Ahnen, Geister, Höchste Wesen* (St. Augustin, 1977).

8. E. Lutete, Notebook 229, Laman Collection, Svenska Missionsforbundet (SMF), Lidingö, ca. 1915.

9. Ibid.

10. Ibid.

11. C. Tastevin, "Idées religieuses des indigènes de l'enclave de Cabinda," *Etudes missionaires* 3 (1935), no. 1, 105–111; no. 2, 191–197; no. 3, 257–273. For a shortened version of the Woyo origin myth see J. Knappert, "The Water Spirits," in his *Myths and Legends of the Congo* (Nairobi and London, 1971), pp. 138–139.

12. Especially the distinction between "opposition" and "contradiction" as indicated by K. Burridge, "Lévi-Strauss and Myth," in E. Leach, ed., *The Structural Study of Myth* (London, 1967), pp. 91–118.

13. In the sense understood by R. Girard, *La violence et le sacré* (Paris, 1972).

14. G. Boas, "The Evolution of the Tragic Hero," in R.W. Corrigan, ed., *Tragedy: Vision and Form* (San Francisco, 1965), pp. 117–131.

15. Corrigan, *Tragedy*, p. ix.

16. B. Dadié, personal communications, 1971.

17. "L'histoire de Kuba-Ntu" in J. Van Wing and C. Schöller, eds., *Légendes des BaKongo orientaux* (Louvain, 1940), pp. 53–60.

18. G. Bateson, *Steps to an Ecology of Mind* (New York, 1972).

19. F. Nietzsche, "The Birth of Tragedy," in Corrigan, *Tragedy*, p. 448.

20. C. Lévi-Strauss, "The Structural Study of Myth," *Journal of American Folklore* 68 (1955): 428–444.

21. Burridge, "Lévi-Strauss and Myth."

22. C. Lévi-Strauss, "Finale," in his *L'Homme Nu* (Paris, 1971), pp. 559–621.

23. J. Lacan, "The Insistence of the Letter in the Unconscious," in R. and F. DeGeorge, eds., *The Structuralists: From Marx to Lévi-Strauss* (Garden City, 1972), pp. 287–323.

24. Lacan's point of reference here is Freud's notion of *Einstellung* from the "Interpretation of Dreams," a term which has also been translated as "distortion" or "misrepresentation."

25. Freud's *Verdichtung*, a bringing together of several signifiers.

26. Freud's *Verschiebung*.

Chapter 10

1. I. Nsemi, "Min'kisi: Sacred Medicines," in J.M. Janzen and W. MacGaffey, eds., *Anthology of Kongo Religion* (Lawrence, 1974), pp. 34–38.

2. E. Andersson, *L'Ethnographie des Kuta* (Uppsala, 1953), pp. 247–249; A. Bastian, *Die Deutsche Expedition an der Loango-Küste* (Jena, 1874); H. Chatelain, *Folktales of Angola* (Boston and New York, 1894), p. 11.

3. O. Stenström, "The Lemba Cult," *Ethnos* (1969), p. 37.

4. Zablon Makunza, Kinganga village, in De la Kenge, Luozi Territory.

5. F. Ngoma, *L'initiation BaKongo et sa signification* (Lubumbashi, 1963), p. 120.

6. J. Malonga, "La sorcellerie et l'ordre du 'Lemba' chez les Lari," *Liaison* 63 (1958): 53–54; Batsikama ba Mampuya, "A propos de 'La cosmogonie Kongo,' " *Cultures au Zaire et en Afrique* 4 (1974): 257.

7. J. Munzele, *Bakulu beto ye Diela diau* (Kumba, 1965), p. 19.

8. L. Bittremieux, *Mayombsche Namen* (Leuwen, 1934), pp. 42–44.

9. Batsikama ba Mampuya, "A propos . . . Kongo," p. 257.

10. W.H. Bentley, *Pioneering on the Congo* (London, 1900), p. 290.

11. Malonga, "La sorcellerie et l'ordre," p. 53.

Chapter 11

1. J. Vansina, in his *Children of Woot: A History of the Kuba Peoples* (Madison, 1978), p. 209, offers a negative assessment of the possibility of retrieving an intellectual history for much of precolonial Africa. For a more optimistic appraisal of the situation and an attempt at an intellectual history of a precolonial setting through the use of therapeutic central values in Lozi history, see G. Prins, *Hidden Hippopotamus* (Cambridge, 1980), pp. 150–157.

2. C. Meier, *Die Entstehung des Politischen bei den Griechen* (Frankfurt, 1980), pp. 154–158.

Sources

The Reconstruction of Lemba

During fieldwork campaigns in the Manianga (Territory of Luozi) in 1964–1966 and 1969 I began to perceive *Lemba*'s historic importance to the region. I pursued some inquiries into the context of its political activities and the role of its priests and priestesses in marketing, conflict resolution, and other judicial and economic activities. Those *Lemba* priests and priestesses initiated before 1920 who were willing to speak to me and whose memories were lucid were of inestimable help in reconstructing the local nature of *Lemba* in the Kivunda district. Of these, special mention must be made of Katula Davidi of Nseke Mbanza. Nzuzi Pierre of Kisiasia and Munzele Yacobi of Kumbi although too young to have been initiated were both very helpful in explaining *Lemba*'s role in their communities. Fukiau was a valuable guide in technical KiKongo discussions with these people.

Published and unpublished accounts from various specialized sources have been used to reconstruct Lower-Congo society and *Lemba*'s role within it. I have combed many historical chronicles and ethnographies for explicit or circumstantial details on *Lemba*. Mention of the term "*lemba*" does not always mean *Lemba* the drum of affliction, since the name is used in a number of towns and villages. As far as I can determine, there is no historic connection between *Lemba* the drum of affliction and the use of *lemba* as the title for a chiefly order in Bandundu and Kasai societies, although *lemba* does appear as a Western Bantu cognate in Guthrie's *Proto-Bantu* word list. Fortunately, *Lemba* is not a clan name in Lower-Congo societies. First mention of *Lemba* as *n'kisi* appears in print in Dapper's 1668 *Beschreibung* of Loango. Thereafter allusions appear in reports by traders, missionaries, and other travellers and eventually in writings by Kongo authors. These have been consulted in numerous specialized libraries and archives. Such writings as those by the missionaries Hyacinthe de Bolonge and Montesarchio and other sources published by the Catholic church I have located mainly in the Jesuit Institute of Bonn and in the Anthropos Institute of St. Augustine. The German Loango coast expedition of the 1870's organized and carried out by Adolph Bastian offers the first professional ethnographies of Congo-Basin societies, including some perceptive passages on *Lemba*. These are all in published works, but unfortunately I was not able to locate any unpublished documents of the Loango expedition, except for some pertaining to material culture collections in the Berlin-Dahlem Museum of Ethnography, which will be detailed below. Neither the Catholic missionaries nor the Loango expedition personnel link *Lemba* to trade. Personal correspondence of the merchant Robert Visser in the Linden Museum, Stuttgart, offers some light on this trade, although *Lemba* is not mentioned explicitly by him. On other aspects of *Lemba*, missionaries, both Catholic and Protestant, of the turn of the century and a bit later offer exceptional material on *Lemba* and its setting. Tastevin's work in Cabinda I located in the Jesuit Institute of Bonn, and much of Bittremieux's unpublished work from the Kangu district in Mayombe is available in the Musée d'Afrique Central at Tervuren. Swedish missionaries' work and correspondence were consulted either in the Svenska Missionsforbundet in Lidingö, in the Stockholm Ethnographic Museum, or in the Göteburg Ethnographic Museum. These include Laman, Hammar, Westlind, Börrison, Andersson and Stenström, all of whom worked in Nsundi, Kamba, and Lali regions, and who offer excellent although often anecdotal information on *Lemba*.

A source of comparable importance in the reconstruction of the setting of *Lemba* is the local colonial archival network, particularly those documents resulting from detailed inquiries made in the early decades of this century by colonial agents seeking to understand the region's history and basis of legitimacy so as to achieve fuller penetration of the colonial administration into African society. Although the Luozi Territorial Archives and offices were burned to the ground by partisans during the interval from Free State rule to Belgian colonial rule in 1907–1910, later surveys made by territorial agents and administrators such as Maillet, Vercraeye, and Deleval are available and were consulted in Luozi, giving accounts, based on interviews, of inaugurations of precolonial chiefs, clan migrations, and village compositions. Little mention is given *Lemba* in these archives. What they convey is a contempt for "northern" anarchy in which there are no big chiefs. Repeated efforts were made to identify or create such chiefs, in the process of which the segmentary social system and its horizontal mechanisms of integration were generally overlooked and misunderstood. One exception to this is the work of Deleval, whose writings both published and in the archives reflect remarkable insight. Known locally as *mundele si-si-si*, "Whiteman Yes-yes-yes," after the petulant manner in which he answered questions, Deleval's materials go well beyond the standards of administrative requirements for information and constitute very helpful scientific accounts.

The most exciting unpublished written sources on *Lemba* are accounts of initiation séances and exegetical remarks prepared by Kongo catechists for Swedish missionary Karl Laman from ca. 1905–1919, before *Lemba*'s demise. Local accounts culled from the 430 notebooks, used by Laman to prepare his KiKongo-French dictionary and the four volumes of Kongo ethnography, provide much of the primary material for the regional variants of *Lemba* in Chapters 4–8. These notebooks by largely unheralded Kongo writers are in the Laman Collection in the Svenska Missionsforbundet archives in Lidingö, and have been microfilmed for easier access.

The tradition of Kongo writing begun with the catechists continues, offering further accounts of *Lemba* by modern writers such as Malonga Jean, Brazzaville novelist and essayist, Ngoma Ferdinand, Zairian sociologist, and Mampuya and Fukiau, both active writers. All four have been seriously concerned with *Lemba*, the major institution of their recent culture history. We may add to this list Haiti's well-known ethnologist-physician, Jean Price-Mars, who has written the only in-depth account, however brief, of *Lemba* in the New World. These efforts by indigenous writers to describe and interpret *Lemba*'s significance provide the base for my own résumé of a conscious *Lemba* ideology of therapeutics in the *ngoma*, drum-of-affliction tradition in the final part of the book.

A final, and very important, source on *Lemba* is artifactual. Many of the aforementioned missionaries, traders, travellers, and colonial officials gathered cultural objects and deposited them in African and European museums. Rarely have *Lemba* objects been labelled and displayed for what they are. However in several research trips to Central-European museums I discovered extensive holdings of *Lemba* objects, revealing a mute record of *Lemba*'s historic existence, its geographic distribution, and its integral role in Congo-Basin social and cultural history. Particular museums consulted are listed in the inventory of museum objects below.

In sum, I have used all possible sources for the reconstruction of *Lemba* and its context. Figure 1 records the geographical distribution of those which are identified with a specific location. The following lists of sources identify other nonlocalized objects and documents.

Scholarly References

Andersson, Effraim. *Contribution à l'ethnographie des Kuta I.* Uppsala: Studia Ethnographica Upsalensia, VI, 1953

Armstrong, Robert P. *The Affecting Presence.* Urbana, Chicago, and London: University of Illinois Press, 1971.

Bahelele, Jacques. *Kinzonzi ye ntekolo andi Makundu.* Matadi: Imprimèrie de l'Eglise Evangelique du Manianga et Matadi, 1961.

Banton, Michael, ed. *Anthropological Approaches to the Study of Religion.* New York: Praeger, 1966.

Barthes, Roland. "Eléments de sémiologie." *Communications* 4 (1964): 91–135.

———. *Système de la mode.* Paris: Editions du Seuil, 1967.

———. *S/Z.* Paris: Editions du Seuil, 1970.

Bascom, William, ed. *African Dilemma Tales.* The Hague: Mouton, 1975.

Bastian, Adolph. *Die Deutsche Expedition an der Loango Küste.* 2 vols. Jena: Costenoble, 1874.

Bastide, Roger. *Le candomblé de Bahia (rite Nagô).* The Hague: Mouton, 1958.

———. *African Religions of Brazil.* Baltimore: The Johns Hopkins University Press, 1978.

Bateson, Gregory. *Steps to an Ecology of Mind.* New York: Ballantine, 1972.

Batsikama ba Mampuya. "A propos de 'la cosmogonie Kongo.' " *Cultures au Zaire et en Afrique* 4 (1974): 239–264.

Battel, Andrew. "The Strange Adventures of Andrew Battel." In *A General Collection of the Best and Most Interesting Voyages and Travels in all Parts of the World*, edited by John Pinkerton. London: Kimber and Conrad, 1814.

Baumann, Hermann, and Westermann, Dietrich. *Les peuples et civilisations de l'Afrique*. Paris: Payot, 1967.

Benga, Jules, and NdaKivangi, Pierre. "Mumboni-a-Mpasi, celui qui avait beaucoup de palabres," *Arts et métiers indigènes* 9 (1938): 20–21.

Bentley, William H. *Pioneering on the Congo*. 2 vols. London: Religious Tract Society, 1900.

Bittremieux, Leon. "Un vieux chef." *Missions en Chine, au Congo, et aux Philippines* 6 (1909): 121–123.

———. *Van Een Ouden Blinden Hoofdman*. Antwerpen: Oude Beurs, 1925.

———. "Tsimona-Mambu, le visionaire; ou l'origine du mariage chez dilemba." *Congo* 2 (1926): 398–404; 551–561.

———. *Mayombsch Idioticon*. 3 vols. Vols. 1, 2, Gent: Erasmus, 1923; Vol. 3, Brussel: Essorial, 1927.

———. *Mayombsch Namen*. Leuven: H.H. Harten, 1934.

———. *La société sécrète des Bakhimba*. Bruxelles: Institut Royal Colonial Belge, 1936.

———. *Symbolisme in de Negerkunst*. Brussel: Vromant, 1937.

Boas, George. "The Evolution of the Tragic Hero." In *Tragedy: Vision and Form*, edited by Robert W. Corrigan, pp. 117–131. San Francisco: Chandler, 1965.

Bohannan, Paul. "The Impact of Money on an African Subsistence Economy." *Journal of Economic History* 19, no. 4 (1959): 491–503.

Bolamba, André Roger. "La légende de Moni-Mambu chez les BaKongo." *Arts et métiers indigènes* 9 (1938): 17–19.

Burridge, Kenelm O. "Lévi-Strauss and Myth." In *The Structural Study of Myth and Totemism*, edited by Edmund Leach, pp. 91–118. London: Tavistock Publications, 1967.

———. *New Heaven, New Earth: A Study of Millenarian Activities*. Toronto: Copp Clark, 1969.

Carneiro, Edison. *Negros Bantus*. Rio de Janeiro: Civilização Brasileira, 1937.

Chatelein, Heli. *Folk-tales of Angola*. Boston and New York: G.E. Stechert and Co., 1894.

Chavunduka, G.L. "Interaction of Folk and Scientific Beliefs in Shona Medical Practices." Ph.D. dissertation, University of London, 1972.

Congo. Belgian Colonial Ministry Economic Reports on Bas-Congo: (1925), pp. 651–676; (1928), p. 691; (1929), pp. 714–726; (1932), pp. 293–313.

Coquery-Vidrovitch, Cathrine. *Le Congo au temps des grandes compagnies concessionnaires 1898–1930*. Paris: Mouton, 1972.

Corrigan, Robert W., ed. *Tragedy: Vision and Form*. San Francisco: Chandler, 1965.

Cuvelier, J. "Traditions congolaises." *Congo* no. 2 (1930): 469–487; no. 1 (1931): 193–208.

———. *L'ancien Royaume de Congo*. Bruxelles: Desclée de Brouwer, 1946.

Dadié, Bernard. *Le pagne noir*. Paris: Présence africaine, 1955.

Dapper, Olfert. *Umständliche und Eigenliche Beschreibung von Afrika*. Amsterdam: Jacob von Meurs, 1670.

De Cleene, N. "Les chefs indigènes au Mayombe." *Africa* 8, no. 1 (1935): 63–75.

DeCraemer, Willy; Vansina, Jan; and Fox, René. "Religious Movements in Central Africa." *Comparative Studies of Society and History* 18 (1976): 458+.

DeGeorge, Richard and Fernande, eds. *The Structuralists: From Marx to Lévi-Strauss*. Garden City: Anchor Books, 1972.

De Heusch, Luc. *Pourquoi l'épouser?* Paris: Gallimard, 1971.

DeJonghe, Edouard. "Les sociétés secrètes au Bas-Congo." In *Revue des questionnes scientifiques*. Bruxelles: Joseph Polleums, 1907.

———. "Les sociétés secrètes en Afrique." *Semaine d'ethnologie religieuse* (1923), Ser. 3.

———. "Formations recentes de sociétés secrètes au Congo Belge." *Africa* 9 (1935): 56–63.

Deleval, Henri. "Les tribus Kavati du Mayombe." *La Revue Congolaise* 3 (1912): 32–40, 103–113, 170–186, 253–264.

Dionga, William. "Tsimona-Mambu, de Wonderziener of de Oorsprong van het huwelijk bij Dilemba, naar een Mayombsche legende." *Congo* 2 (1926): 398–404, 551–556. (See also Leon Bittremieux, "Tsimona-Mambu, le visionaire," above.)

Dolgin, Janet L.; Kemnitzer, David S.; and Schneider, David M., eds. *Symbolic Anthropology: A Reader in the Study of Symbols and Meanings*. New York: Columbia University Press, 1977.

Douglas, Mary. *Purity and Danger*. New York: Praeger, 1966.

Doutreloux, Albert. *L'ombre des fétiches: société et culture yombe*. Louvain: Nauwelaerts, 1967.

Droux, C., and Kelly, H. "Recherches préhistoriques dans la région de Boko-Songho et à Pointe-Noire (Moyen-Congo)." *Journal de la société des Africanistes* 9 (1939): 71–87.

Dundes, Alan; Leach, Edmund; Maranda, Pierre; and Maybury-Lewis, David. "An Experiment: Suggestions and Queries from the Desk, with a Reply from the Ethnographer." In *Structural Analysis of Oral Tradition*, edited by Pierre Maranda and Elie Köngäs-Maranda. Philadelphia: University of Pennsylvania Press, 1971.

Dupont, Edouard. *Lettres sur le Congo*. Paris: C. Reinwald, 1889.

Evans-Pritchard, Edward E. *Witchcraft, Oracles, and Magic among the Azande*. Oxford: Oxford University Press, 1937.

Fernandez, James. "Persuasions and Performances: Of the Beast in Every Body . . . and the Metaphors of Everyman," *Daedalus* 101 (1972): 39–60.

Frazer, James. *The Golden Bough*. 2 vols. London: Macmillan, 1890.

———. *Totemism and Exogamy*. 4 vols. London: Macmillan, 1910–37.

Freud, Sigmund. *Totem and Taboo*. New York: W.W. Norton, 1950 (1913).

Frobenius, Leo. *Die Masken und Geheimbünde*. Nova Acta Abhandlung der Kaiserliche Leopold-Carolinische Deutschen Akademie der Naturforscher, vol. 74, no. 1. Halle: 1898.

Fukiau kia Bunseki-Lumanisa. *N'kongo ye Nza / Cosmogonie-Kongo*. Kinshasa: Office National de la Recherche et de Dévelopement, 1969.

Garbett, Kingsley. "Disparate Regional Cults and a Unitary Ritual Field in Zimbabwe." In *Regional Cults*, edited by Richard Werbner, pp. 141–173. New York and London: Academic Press, 1977.

Geertz, Clifford. *The Social History of an Indonesian Town*. Cambridge, Mass.: M.I.T. Press, 1965.

———. "Religion as a Cultural System." In *Anthropological Approaches to the Study of Religion*, edited by Michael Banton. New York: Praeger, 1966.

———. "Deep Play: Notes on the Balinese Cockfight." *Daedalus* 101 (1972): 1–38.

Girard, René. *La violence et le sacré*. Paris: Grasset, 1972.

Globus (1876), p. 307.

Gluckman, Max. *Ideas in Barotse Jurisprudence*. New Haven: Yale University Press, 1965.

Goody, Jack. *Technology, Tradition, and the State in Africa*. London, Ibadan and Oxford: Oxford University Press, 1971.

Gräbner, Fritz. "Kulturkreise und Kulturschichten in Ozeanien." *Zeitschrift für Ethnologie* 37 (1905): 84–90.

Güssfeldt, Paul; Falkenstein, Julius; and Pechuel-Loesche, Eduard. *Die Loango-Expedition: 1873–6*. Leipzig: Verlag v. Paul Frohberg, 1879.

Guthrie, Malcolm. *Comparative Bantu*. 4 vols. Hants: Gregg Press, 1967.

Hagenbucher-Sacripanti, F. *Les fondaments spirituels du pouvoir au royaume de Loango*. L'office de la recherche scientifiques et technique outremer, no. 67. Paris: 1973.

Herskovits, Melville. *Life in a Haitian Village*. New York: Knopf, 1937.

———. *Dahomey: An Ancient West African Kingdom*. 2 vols. New York: Augustin, 1938.

———. *The Myth of the Negro Past*. Boston: Beacon Press, 1958 (1941).

Hyacinthe de Bologne. *La pratique missionaire des PP. Capucins Italiens dans les royaumes de Congo, Angola et contrées adjacents*. Louvain: Editions de l'Aucam, 1931 (1747).

Jacobson-Widding, Anita. *Red-White-Black as a Mode of Thought: A Study of Triadic Classification by Colours in the Ritual Symbolism and Cognitive Thought of the Peoples of the Lower Congo.* Acta Universitatis Upsaliensis (Uppsala Studies in Cultural Anthropology, no. 1). Uppsala: 1979.

Janzen, John M. "Laman's Kongo Ethnography: Observations on Sources, Methodology and Theory." *Africa* 42 (1972): 316–328.

———. *The Quest for Therapy in Lower Zaire*. Berkeley and London: University of California Press, 1978.

———. Review of *Les phemba du Mayombe* by Raoul Lehuard. *African Arts* 11, no. 2 (1978): 88–89.

———. "Ideologies and Institutions in the Precolonial History of Equatorial African Therapeutic Systems." *Social Science and Medicine* 13B, no. 4 (1979): 317–326.

———. "Deep Thought: Structure and Intention in Kongo Prophetism, 1910–1921." *Social Research* 46, no. 1 (1979): 106–139.

———, and MacGaffey, Wyatt. *An Anthology of Kongo Religion: Primary Sources from Lower Zaire*. University of Kansas Publications in Anthropology, no. 5. Lawrence: 1974.

Jung, Carl, and Kerenyi, Carl. *Essays on a Science of Mythology*. Bollingen Series 22. Princeton: Princeton University Press, 1969.

Kerenyi, Carl. "Prolegomena." In *Essays on a Science of Mythology*, by Carl Jung and Carl Kerenyi, pp. 1–24. Princeton: Princeton University Press, 1969.

Knappert, Jan. *Myths and Legends of the Congo*. Nairobi and London: Heinemann Educational Books, 1971.

Koch, Henri. *Magie et chasse au Cameroun*. Paris: Editions Berger-Levrault, 1968.

Kuper, Adam. *Anthropologists and Anthropology: The British School 1922–72*. New York: Pica Press, 1972.

Kusikila, Yoswe. *Lufwa evo Kimongi e?* Kumba: Académie Congolaise, 1966.

Kwamba, Elie. "A Lemba Initiation." In *An Anthology of Kongo Religion*, edited by John M. Janzen and Wyatt MacGaffey, pp. 97–102. University of Kansas Publications in Anthropology, no. 5. Lawrence: 1974.

Lacan, Jacques. "The Insistence of the Letter in the Unconscious." In *The Structuralists*, edited by Richard and Fernande DeGeorge, pp. 287–323. Garden City: Anchor, 1972.

Laman, Karl E. *Dictionnaire Kikongo-Français*. Bruxelles: Institut Royale Coloniale Belge, 1936.

———. *The Kongo I*. Studia Ethnographica Upsaliensia, no. 4. Uppsala: 1953.
———. *The Kongo II*. Studia Ethnographica Upsaliensia, no. 8. Uppsala: 1957.
———. *The Kongo III*. Studia Ethnographica Upsaliensia, no. 13. Uppsala: 1962.
———. *The Kongo IV*. Studia Ethnographica Upsaliensia, no. 16. Uppsala: 1968.
Leach, Edmund. *Culture and Communication: The Logic by which Symbols are Connected*. Cambridge: Cambridge University Press, 1976.
Lehuard, Raoul. *Les phemba du mayombe*. Paris: Collection Arts d'Afrique Noire, 1977.
Lévi-Strauss, Claude. *Les structures élémentaires de la parentée*. Paris: Presses Universitaires de France, 1949.
———. "The Structural Study of Myth." *Journal of American Folklore* 67 (1955): 428–444.
———. *La pensée sauvage*. Paris: Plon, 1962.
———. *Le cru et le cuit: Mythologiques I*. Paris: Plon, 1964.
———. *Du miel aux cendres: Mythologiques II*. Paris: Plon, 1966.
———. *L'origine des manières de table: Mythologiques III*. Paris: Plon, 1968.
———. *L'homme nu: Mythologiques IV*. Paris: Plon, 1971.
MacGaffey, Wyatt. *Custom and Government in the Lower Congo*. Berkeley, Los Angeles, and London: University of California Press, 1970.
———. "The Religious Commissions of the BaKongo." *Man* n.s. 5 (1970): 27–38.
———. "Corporation Theory and Political Change." In *Small States and Segmented Societies*, edited by Stephanie Newman. New York: Praeger, 1976.
———. "Economic and Social Dimensions of Kongo Slavery." In *Slavery in Africa*, edited by Suzanne Meirs and Igor Kopytoff. Madison: University of Wisconsin Press, 1977.
Maes, Joseph, and Boone, Olga. *Les peuplades du Congo belge*. Bruxelles: Imprimèrie Veuve Monnom, 1935.
Maine, Henry. *Ancient Law*. London: Dent, 1960.
Makarius, Laura. "Ritual Clowns and Symbolic Behavior." *Diogenes* 69 (1970); 44–73.
Malonga, Jean. *La légènde de M'pfoumou ma Mazono*. Paris: Editions Africaines, 1954.
———. "La sorcellerie et l'ordre du 'Lemba' chez les Lari." *Liaison* 62 (1958): 45–49, 51–61.
Maranda, Pierre, and Köngäs-Maranda, Elie, eds. *Structural Analysis of Oral Tradition*. Philadelphia: University of Pennsylvania Press, 1971.
Martin, Phyllis. *The External Trade of the Loango Coast 1576–1870*. Oxford: Oxford University Press, 1972.

Meier, Christian. *Die Entstehung des Politischen bei den Griechen*. Frankfurt am Main: Suhrkamp Verlag, 1980.

Meillassoux, Claude, ed. *L'esclavage en Afrique précoloniale*. Paris: Maspero, 1975.

Meirs, Suzanne, and Kopytoff, Igor, eds. *Slavery in Africa: An Historical and Anthropological Perspective*. Madison: University of Wisconsin Press, 1977.

Métraux, Alfred. *Voodoo in Haiti*. New York: Oxford University Press, 1959.

———. *Black Peasants and Voodoo*. New York: Universe Books, 1960.

Miller, Joseph. *Kings and Kinsmen: Early Mbundu States in Angola*. Oxford: Oxford University Press, 1976.

Munzele, Jacques. *Bakulu beto ye Diela diau*. Kumba: Académie Congolaise, 1965.

Murdock, George P. *Africa, Its People and their Culture History*. New York: McGraw-Hill, 1959.

Newman, Stephanie, ed. *Small States and Segmented Societies*. New York: Praeger, 1976.

Ngoma, Ferdinand. *L'initiation bakongo et sa signification*. Lubumbashi: Centre d'Etude des Problèmes Sociaux Indigènes, 1963.

Ngubane, Harriet. *Body and Mind in Zulu Medicine*. New York and London: Academic Press, 1977.

Nietzsche, Friedrich. "The Birth of Tragedy." In *Tragedy: Vision and Form*, edited by Robert W. Corrigan. San Francisco: Chandler, 1965.

Nsemi, Isaac. "Min'kisi: Sacred Medicines." In *An Anthology of Kongo Religion*, edited by John M. Janzen and Wyatt MacGaffey, pp. 34–38. University of Kansas Publications in Anthropology, no. 5. Lawrence: 1974.

Orley, John. "African Medical Taxonomy." *Journal of the Anthropological Society of Oxford* 1, no. 3 (1970): 137–150.

Pechuel-Loesche, Eduard. *Volkskunde von Loango*. Stuttgart: Strecker and Schroeder, 1907.

Pelton, Robert D. *The Trickster in West Africa: A Study of Mythic Irony and Sacred Delight*. Berkeley, Los Angeles, and London: University of California Press, 1980.

Pinkerton, John, ed. *A General Collection of the Best and Most Interesting Voyages and Travels in All Parts of the World*. London: Kimber and Conrad, 1814.

Price-Mars, Jean. "Lemba-Pétro, un culte sécrèt." *Revue de la société d'histoire et de géographie d'Haiti* 9, no. 28 (1938): 12–31.

Prins, Gwyn. "Disease at the Crossroads: Towards a History of Therapeutics in Bulozi since 1876." *Social Science and Medicine* 13B (1979): 285–316.

———. *The Hidden Hippopotamus: Reappraisal in African History, the Early Colonial Experience in Western Zambia*. Cambridge: Cambridge University Press, 1980.

Proyart, A. "Histoire de Loango, Kakongo et autres royaumes d'Afrique." In *A General Collection of the Best and Most Interesting Voyages*, edited by John Pinkerton. London: Kimber and Conrad, 1814.

Radin, Paul. *The Trickster: A Study in American Indian Mythology*. New York: Bell Publishing Co., 1961.

Ramos, Arthur. *O Negro Brasileiro*. Rio de Janeiro: Civilização Brasileria, 1934.

Ranger, Terence O. *Dance and Society in Eastern Africa: The Beni Ngoma*. London: Heinemann, 1975.

———. "Healing and Society in Colonial Southern Africa." Unpublished MS, 1978.

Rappaport, Roy A. *Pigs for the Ancestors: Ritual in the Ecology of a New Guinea People*. New Haven and London: Yale University Press, 1968.

Rey, Pierre-Philippe. "L'esclavage lignager chez les tsangui, les punu et les kuni du Congo-Brazzaville." In *L'esclavage en Afrique précoloniale*, edited by Claude Meillassoux, pp. 509–528. Paris: Maspero, 1975.

Schoffeleers, Matthew. "Cult Idioms and the Dialectics of a Region." In *Regional Cults*, edited by Richard Werbner, pp. 219–239. New York and London: Academic Press, 1977.

Schurtz, Heinrich. *Altersklassen und Männerbünde*. Berlin: G. Reimer, 1902.

Smith, Michael G. *Corporations and Society*. London: Duckworth, 1974.

Soret, Marcel. *Les Kongo Nord-Occidentaux*. Paris: Presses Universitaires de France, 1959,

Sperber, Dan. *Rethinking Symbolism*. Cambridge: Cambridge University Press, 1975.

Stanley, Henry M. *Through the Dark Continent*. 2 vols. New York: Harper, 1879.

Stebich, Ute, ed. *Haitian Art*. Brooklyn: The Brooklyn Museum, 1978.

Stenström, Oscar. "The Lemba Cult." *Ethnos* (1969), pp. 37–57.

Swantz, Marja-Liisa. *Ritual and Symbol in Transitional Zaramo Society*. Uppsala: Gleerup, 1970.

Tastevin, C. "Idées religieuses des indigènes de l'enclave de Cabinda." *Etudes missionnaires* 3 (1935): 105–111, 191–197, 257–273.

Thiel, Josef Franz. *Ahnen, Geister, Höchste Wesen*. Studia Instituti Anthropos, no. 26. St. Augustine: 1977.

Thompson, Robert Farris. *Black Gods and Kings*. Los Angeles: University of California Press, 1971.

———. "Transatlantic African Art Traditions." Unpublished MSS, 1975, 1977.

———. "The Flash of the Spirit: Haiti's Africanizing Vodun Art." In *Haitian Art*, edited by Ute Stebich, pp. 26–37. Brooklyn: The Brooklyn Museum, 1978.

Turner, Victor W. "Colour Classification in Ndembu Ritual." In *Anthropological Approaches to the Study of Religion*, edited by Michael Banton, pp. 47–84. New York: Praeger, 1966.

———. *Drums of Affliction: A Study of Religious Processes among the Ndembu of Zambia*. Oxford: Clarendon Press, 1968.

———. *The Ritual Process*. Chicago: Aldine, 1969.

———. *Dramas, Fields and Metaphors: Symbolic Action in Human Society*. Ithaca: Cornell University Press, 1974.

———. *Revelation and Divination in Ndembu Ritual*. Ithaca: Cornell University Press, 1975.

———. "Symbols in African Ritual." In *Symbolic Anthropology*, edited by Janet L. Dolgin, et al. New York: Columbia University Press, 1977.

Van Binsbergen, Wim. "Regional and Non-Regional Cults of Affliction in Western Zambia." In *Regional Cults*, edited by Richard Werbner, pp. 141–173. New York and London: Academic Press, 1977.

Van Gennep, Arnold. *Les rites de passage*. Paris: Emile Nourry, 1909.

Vansina, Jan. *Kingdoms of the Savanna*. Madison: University of Wisconsin Press, 1965.

———. *The Tio Kingdom of the Middle Congo, 1880–1892*. Oxford: Oxford University Press, 1973.

———. *The Children of Woot: Essays in Kuba History*. Madison: University of Wisconsin Press, 1978.

Van Velzen, Bonno Thoden. "Bush Negro Regional Cults: A Materialist Explanation." In *Regional Cults*, edited by Richard Werbner, pp. 93–116. New York and London: Academic Press, 1977.

Van Wing, Joseph. *Etudes BaKongo*. Bruxelles: Desclée de Brouwer, 1959.

———, and Schöller, Claude. *Légendes des BaKongo orientaux*. Louvain: Aucam, 1940.

Vaz, José Martins. *Filosofia Tradicional dos Cabindas*. Lisboa: Agencia-Geral do Ultramer, 1969.

Visser, Robert. "Der Kaufmann unter Wilden (Entwicklung des Handels am Kongo)." *Jahresbericht des Naturwissenschaftlichen Vereins zu Krefeld* (1907–8), pp. 59–60.

Werbner, Richard, ed. *Regional Cults*. New York and London: Academic Press, 1977.

Wundt, Wilhelm. *Völkerpsychologie*. 10 vols. Leipzig, 1911–20. Vols. 1–2 published by W. Engelmann; vols. 3–10 published by Alfred Kröner.

Archival Sources

AIMO. "Etat d'esprit de la population." *Rapport annuel affaires indigènes et main d'oeuvre.* Luozi Territorial Archives, 1936.

Babutidi, Timotio. Notebook 16. Laman Collection, Svenska Missionsforbundet (SMF), Lidingö, ca. 1914.

Bittremieux, Leon. Correspondence with Musée d'Afrique Central (Tervuren) from Kangu Mission, Mayombe. 2 August 1939.

Congo belge. *Reports.* Luozi Territorial Archives, 1930.
Kimbembe. Notebook 80. Laman Collection, SMF, Lidingö, n.d.
Konda, Jean. Notebook 119. Laman Collection, SMF, Lidingö, n.d.
Kwamba, Elie. Notebooks 142–3. Laman Collection, SMF, Lidingö, 1915.
Lunungu, Moise. Notebook 181. Laman Collection, SMF, Lidingö, 1917.
Lutete, Esaie. Notebook 229. Laman Collection, SMF, Lidingö, 1915.
Maillet, Robert. *Report.* Luozi Territorial Archives, n.d.
Ndibu, Joseph. Notebook 345. Laman Collection, SMF, Lidingö, n.d.
Nitu, Solomo. Cabinda Legends Transcriptions. Recorded by Charles Harvey, 1961.
Vercraeye, J. *Dossier No. 129.* Luozi Territorial Archives, 31 August 1932.
Visser, Robert. Correspondence. Linden Museum, Stuttgart.

Museum Collections

ABBREVIATIONS OF MUSEUMS

AMBG	Afrika Museum, Berg en Dal, The Netherlands
B–D	Berlin–Dahlem Museum für Völkerkunde
GEM	Göteborg Ethnographic Museum, Sweden
KM	Kimpese Museum, Lower Zaire
LMS	Linden Museum, Stuttgart, West Germany
LRM	Leiden Rijks Museum, The Netherlands
MAC	Musée d'Afrique Central, Tervuren, Belgium
SEM	Stockholm Ethnographic Museum, Sweden

LEMBA DRUMS

SEM	1907.8.34	"Konko Lemba" from Kimbunu. don. J. Lindström, 1907.
SEM	1907.8.38	"Nkonko a Lemba" from Mbamba, Lower Congo, don. J. Lindström, 1907.
SEM	1919.1.437	"Mukonzi a Lemba" from Mayombe, don. K. Laman 1919 (No. 40, fig. 1).
SEM	1919.1.445	"Nkonko a Lemba" from Sundi in Ludima, don. Laman, 1919 (No. 39, fig. 1).
GEM	68.11.230	"Nkonko Lemba".
GEM	68.11.241	"Nkonko Lemba" from Nganda, Kingoyi, don. J. Hammar, 1910 (No. 9, fig. 1).
B–D	III C 18921	"coco Lemba", from Bavili, don. R. Visser, 1904 (No. 29, fig. 1).
MAC	34778	"Ngoma Lemba".
MAC	34774–34782	"Zingoma za Dilemba", don. L. Bittremieux.
MAC	35342	miniature bone Lemba drum amulet.
MAC	43695	miniature wood Lemba drum amulet.

MAC	69.59.498	miniature wood Lemba drum amulet from Mayumba, don. M.J. Seha, 1946.
MAC	53.74.1323	miniature metal Lemba drum amulet.
MAC	35052	Lemba miniature drum, don. Bittremieux.
LMS	38363	Necklace strung with teeth, miniature Lemba drum as main ornament, don. R. Visser, 1905.

LEMBA BRACELETS

B–D	III C 347	Copper Lemba bracelet, Tschicambo, Loango, don. Loango Expedition, 1875.
B–D	III C 710b	Brass Woman's Lemba bracelet, 8 cm., don. Loango Expedition, 1875.
B–D	III C 6524	Brass bracelet "Bilunge Chilenge," BaKunya, don. R. Visser, 1896.
B–D	III C 8136 C	Wood bracelet form for casting, don. Visser.
B–D	III C 13810a–f	Clay forms for casting Lemba bracelet, don. R. Visser, 1901 (no longer existent).
LRM	1032/136 (I.C.E. Inv. No.)	Casting mould of clay for a bracelet, Boma (No. 31, fig. 1).
LRM	1032/60 (I.C.E. Inv. No.)	Red copper engraved bracelet, Banana (No. 32, fig. 1).
LRM	1032/59 (I.C.E. Inv. No.)	Yellow copper (brass) engraved bracelet, Banana.
LRM	1034/53 (I.C.E. Inv. No.)	Red copper engraved bracelet, Banana.
GEM	66.15.3	Bronze "Nsongo a Lemba," Kitoma, Atlantic coast, don. J. Lagergren, 1966. 5 cm. (No. 34, fig. 1).
GEM	1938.31.12	"Mulunga Lemba," Indo Bayaka, Bakuta, 7 cm. don. Andersson (No. 37, fig. 1).
GEM	1938.31.11	"Mulunga Lemba," Ntele, Bayaka, Bakuta, 10 cm.
MAC	35021	Lemba bracelet, don. Bittremieux.
MAC	21372	Red copper bracelet, don. S.G. Arnold, 1917. 9 mm.
MAC	54.2.10	Lead bracelet, purch. Walschot, 1954.
MAC	43587	Red copper, traces of ngula (*sic*), Lemba bracelet, Mayombe, don. M. Seha, 1946.

MAC	43578	Copper Lemba bracelet, Mayombe, don. Seha, 1946, 9 cm.
MAC	43584	Yellow copper Lemba bracelet, don. Seha, 1946, 8 cm.
MAC	24985	Copper bracelet, don. Renkin, 1909, 8 cm.
MAC	23275	Copper bracelet, don. Michel, 1919, 9 cm.
MAC	75.51.21	Lemba bracelet, lead or brass.
MAC	(recent acquisition)	Lemba bracelet, don. J. Walschot.
MAC	54.60.2	Lemba bracelet, brass, 10 cm.
MAC	53.74.1312	Copper bracelet "Lunga milemba," Tshela, Sundi tribe, Zubu, don. A. Maesen, 1954.
MAC	53.74.1339	Copper "lunga Lemba," Tshela, Mayumbe, Kai ku Tsanga, don. A. Maesen, 1954.
MAC	53.74.1313	"Lunga miLemba," Tshela, Sundi/Fubu, made in Mama Tsanga village, sector Tsanga Nord, don. Maesen, 1954.
MAC	53.74.1324	Copper bracelet for Lemba wife, right arm, Tshela, Sundi tribe, Kangu-Lufu, don. A. Maesen, 6 cm.
MAC	53.74.1333	Copper bracelet, "Lunga Lemba," Tshela, Mayumbe, Kai ku Tsanga, don. Maesen, 9 cm.
MAC	53.74.1332	Copper "lunga Lemba," Mayumbe, Kai ku Tsanga, clan Makaba, don. A. Maesen, 9 cm.
MAC	54.74.1335	Copper "lunga Lemba," Mayumbe, Kai ku Tsanga, don. Maesen, 8 cm.
AMBG	417.50	bracelet.
AMBG	415 I 536 (inv. no. 29-536)	Three copper bracelets, one unworked, of Vili manufacture, two with incised snakes, ordered from Europe.
B–D	III C 423	Bracelet, Loango Expedition 1875, Bastian.
B–D	III C 6535	Copper Lemba bracelet, don. Visser, 1896 (missing since WWII from collection).

LEMBA MEDICINE CONTAINERS

B–D	III C 13871	Rafia Lemba charm sack ("Sackfetisch Lembe"), Caio, Loango Coast, don. R. Visser, 1900 (no longer in collection since WWII).
B–D	III C 13743	"Lembe Sackfetisch", Caio, Loango Coast, don. Visser, 1901 (no longer in collection).
B–D	III C 13744	"Lembe Sackfetisch", Caio, Loango Coast, don. Visser, 1901 (no longer in collection).
MAC	43040	"N'kobe Lemba," Kangu, Mayombe, don. Bittremieux.
MAC	37972	"Khobe Lemba," don. Bittremieux, 1937.
MAC	35191	"Khobe Lemba," Woyo, don. Bittremieux, 1933.
MAC	35192	"Khobe Lemba," Woyo, don. Bittremieux, 1933.
SEM	1919.1.583	"Nkisi Lemba," Nsundi, Mukimbungu, don. Laman, 1919.
KM	(no identif. number)	Lemba n'kobe (no documentation).

MISCELLANEOUS LEMBA OBJECTS

MAC	34766	Smoking pipe head.
B–D	III C 13873	Lemba pipe ("N'timbeliambe"), don. Visser, 1900.
B–D	Katalog 372	Lemba opium pipe ("Hanfrauche Lemba"), don. Bastian, 1874 (missing from collection).
AMBG	177	Probably Lemba couple, statue, Landana, Cabinda.
MAC	35176	Lemba anthropomorphic statue ("Ndubi Lemba"), with left arm raised and croissant-drum hanging from same elbow.
GEM	68.11.208	Lemba dance rattles, Basundi, Nganda, don. J. Hammar, 1906.

Index